MESSAGES OF MURDER

MESSAGES OF MURDER

A Study of the Reports
of the Einsatzgruppen of the Security
Police and the Security Service,
1941–1943

Ronald Headland

Rutherford • Madison • Teaneck
Fairleigh Dickinson University Press
London and Toronto: Associated University Presses

Associated University Presses
440 Forsgate Drive
Cranbury, NJ 08512

Associated University Presses
25 Sicilian Avenue
London WC1A 2QH, England

Associated University Presses
P.O. Box 39, Clarkson Pstl. Stn.
Mississauga, Ontario,
L5J 3X9 Canada

The paper used in this publication meets the requirements
of the American National Standard for Permanence of Paper
for Printed Library Materials Z39.48-1984.

Library of Congress Cataloging-in-Publication Data

Headland, Ronald, 1946–
    Messages of murder: a study of the reports of the Einsatzgruppen of the Security Police and the Security Service, 1941–1943 / Ronald Headland.
       p.   cm.
    Includes bibliographical references and index.
    ISBN 0-8386-3418-4 (alk. paper)
    1. Jews—Soviet Union—Persecutions—History—Sources.
2. Holocaust, Jewish (1939–1945)—Soviet Union—Sources.
3. Nationalsozialistische Deutsche Arbeiterpartei. Schutzstaffel. Sicherheitsdienst—History—Sources.   4. Nationalsozialistische Deutsche Arbeiterpartei. Schutzstaffel. Sicherheitspolizei—History—Sources.   5. World War, 1939–1945—Secret service—Germany—Sources. 6. Soviet Union—Ethnic relations—Sources.
    I. Title. II. Title: Einsatzgruppen.
DS135.R92H4   1992   90-56046
323.1'1924'047—dc20   CIP

PRINTED IN THE UNITED STATES OF AMERICA

Contents

Acknowledgments

I wish to acknowledge my gratitude to several people who, in ways too numerous to describe here, were helpful to me during the preparation of this book. Included among these people are Gisela Steinle, Peter Martyn, Maria Fröhlich, Jenny Collier, and Odile Dobler.

For their clarification of the Einsatzgruppen related material in the holdings of the National Archives, Washington, I am indebted to the late John Mendelsohn and to Robert Wolfe. I am also thankful to Daniel Horn, whose thoughtful suggestions for expanding the manuscript were instrumental in realizing the final draft.

I must express my profound gratitude to the late Helmut Krausnick and to Hans-Heinrich Wilhelm. Their interest in my work and their willingness to deal with some of the perplexing questions confronting me were a source of great encouragement. Both took the time to carefully read an earlier draft of the manuscript and offered detailed and authoritative criticism that was invaluable in subsequent revision of the manuscript. That Helmut Krausnick extended help in spite of failing health is something for which I am especially thankful. I am indebted to Dr. Krausnick and Dr. Wilhelm both for their insightful and substantive advice and their generosity of spirit.

While appreciative of the assistance provided by all those mentioned above, I realize that the responsibility for any shortcomings or errors in this study lies with me.

RONALD HEADLAND

MESSAGES OF MURDER

Introduction

When the German armed forces invaded the Soviet Union on 22 June 1941, they were accompanied by special task forces called Einsatzgruppen.[1] The Einsatzgruppen consisted of four mobile units, designated A, B, C, and D. Each Einsatzgruppe operated in the rear areas of the army groups on the eastern front that eventually ranged from Estonia in the north to the Crimea and the Caucasus in the south. Each Einsatzgruppe was subdivided into functioning units called Einsatzkommandos and Sonderkommandos, which, in turn and if required, were subdivided into smaller units called Teilkommandos. Altogether the four Einsatzgruppen numbered approximately three thousand men. During the previous month, these men had assembled to receive training and political instruction in the town of Pretzsch and the nearby villages of Düben and Schmiedeberg in Germany. The leaders and members of the Einsatzgruppen were drawn from the ranks of the Security Police, the Security Service (SD), the Gestapo, the Criminal Police (Kripo), the regular uniformed police or Order Police (Ordnungspolizei), the Waffen SS, as well as emergency conscripts who were unfit for front-line duty.[2] A series of agreements between army and SS representatives had been reached that delineated the jurisdiction of authority that was to exist between the Einsatzgruppen and the army commands within whose area the Einsatzgruppen were to operate.

The Einsatzgruppen were responsible to Heinrich Himmler. The stated task of the Einsatzgruppen was the security of the occupied eastern territories and the gathering of political, cultural, economic, and other forms of intelligence.[3] In reality the primary task of the Einsatzgruppen was the deliberate annihilation of Jews, Gypsies, communist officials, and others who were considered enemies of the Nazi regime. The operations of the Einsatzgruppen marked the beginning of the systematic liquidation of the Jews in Estonia, Latvia, Lithuania, Eastern Poland, and the former Russian territories occupied by the Germans. This process of destruction was to widen in 1942 to include the Jews of western Europe.[4]

As the German army overran the Russian territories, towns and villages fell swiftly into German hands. The mobile Kommandos of the Einsatzgruppen, following in the wake of the German troops, immediately secured the territory, capturing the civilian population within their grasp. For the

Jews, it was the unfolding of a tragedy unparalleled in the long history of their persecution.

The merciless destruction carried out by the Einsatzgruppen was chronicled in great detail by a series of reports issued during the period from June 1941 to May 1943. These reports, documents that in a number of respects are unique in the history of crime, are the subject of this study. They are divided into the following categories: Ereignismeldungen UdSSR, hereafter Operational Situation Reports;[5] Tätigkeits- und Lageberichte der Einsatzgruppen der Sicherheitspolizei und des SD in der UdSSR, hereafter, Activity and Situation Reports; Meldungen aus den besetzten Ostgebieten, hereafter Reports from the Occupied Eastern Territories; and three important reports, the two reports known as the Stahlecker reports,[6] and the Jäger report.[7]

These reports are not the only reports issued dealing with the eastern territories, nor are they our only documentary source on the history of German occupation policy and practice during this period.[8] They are, in spite of certain qualifications that we will be examining later, the most important source from the German point of view. The mind-boggling statistics of mass murder contained in these reports at first seem utterly beyond belief. One cannot grasp how such atrocities were performed on such a scale, day after day, let alone recounted with such cold precision. Yet as one wades deeper and deeper through these reports, as one adjusts slowly to a world permeated by an ideology contemptuous of normal human decency, one begins to realize that this *did* happen and that the events described are real. One is then left with the uniquely Nazi phenomenon of actions of such barbarity as to require absolute secrecy on the one hand, and the strange desire to record the events on the other.

A document is a link with the past. A document tells us, to varying degrees, two things about that past: it tells us directly about events and opinions that may be described in the document; and it may also tell us, often indirectly and inadvertently, something about the author of the document, quite apart from whatever may be discerned in the document's actual objective content. In other words, a document may be significant for what it says and for what it does not say. On both these levels we shall see the Einsatzgruppen reports are an important source. The Einsatzgruppen had their own interests to consider, and quite apart from a factual accounting of events, these interests were reflected in the reports. The reports, therefore, tell us much, but they do not tell us everything. Naturally, in these official reports we see only through German eyes, and because of this we hear no cries of the victims. No dissenting voices shout to challenge what was done and so faithfully recorded. We learn very little directly of the terror and agony that accompanied the measures described. The clipped, impersonal style of the reports sheds no light on Jewish suffering, or that of other victims. Such suffering can only be imagined by the reader.

It should be mentioned immediately that the central focus of this study of the reports will be the massacre of Jews and other civilians in the occupied Soviet territories. It should also be stated that it will be the Operational Situation Reports that will provide the major source of our attention. There are several reasons for this emphasis on these particular reports. The Operational Situation Reports are the most numerous of the reports we are to consider (195 were issued between June 1941 and April 1942 and all but one [Report 158] have survived). They recount their story on an almost day-to-day basis, while the events were unfolding. Therefore, there is a telling sense of immediacy in the Operational Situation Reports not present to the same extent in the other reports, which were issued less frequently. Also, the Operational Situation Reports deal in greater detail with the killing of Jews and other civilians than the subsequent Reports from the Occupied Eastern Territories. The latter reports contain little reference to killings other than those connected with antipartisan warfare.

The Activity and Situation Reports, issued concurrently with the Operational Situation Reports, and the Stahlecker and Jäger reports, were summary reports dealing with longer time periods. They covered basically the same ground as the Operational Situation Reports. As a result there was much repetition and overlapping. The Activity and Situation Reports, in particular, summarized much of the material already found in the Operational Situation Reports. For these reasons the latter reports are our major source and will be scrutinized in greater detail.

The Operational Situation Reports and most of the Reports from the Occupied Eastern Territories were not used as evidence at the Trial of the Major War Criminals held in Nuremberg in 1945–46.[9] Their existence was not known at the time. When interrogated as a prosecution witness at this trial, Otto Ohlendorf, the head of Einsatzgruppe D, was specifically asked about reports by General Nikitchenko, the Soviet member of the Tribunal. Ohlendorf stated that reports describing the killings were sent from the Einsatzgruppen to the Reichssicherheitshauptamt in Berlin, but Ohlendorf was not pressed further concerning these reports during his interrogation either by Nikitchenko or by any of the defense counsel.[10]

Where and when were the Einsatzgruppen reports discovered? From the available evidence it would appear that one set of these reports (the only known surviving set) was found in the Gestapo building in Berlin on 3 September 1945. A receipt register started on 29 August 1945, found in the files of the Berlin Document Center, states that the reports were part of a collection of documents weighing approximately two tons that were collected by the 6889th BDC, the forerunner of the present Berlin Document Center. More precisely, this receipt register states as follows:

(The Collecting) Agency was the 6889th BDC team; Description of Documents: approximately two tons, Gestapo files; Source of Document: Gestapo Headquarters, Berlin; Remarks: Documents were evacuated from the fourth floor of Gestapo Headquarters, Berlin, on 3 September 1945. According to other documents furnished by the Berlin Document Center, the two tons of documents evacuated from the Gestapo building included 578 folders of documents from files of the Gestapo and Reichssicherheitshauptamt (RSHA) or Reich Main Security Office. These files included an enormous variety of documents covering a wide range of areas. The Operational Situation Reports and the Reports from the Occupied Eastern Territories were later given folder numbers E316 and E325 to E335 by American investigating agencies.[11]

It would seem that the terrible content of these reports was not discovered for some time after their arrival in the Berlin Document Center on 3 September 1945.[12] This was understandable, considering the vast amount of documents that had been captured in many locations in Germany. By late 1945 as many as one thousand six hundred tons of documents were housed, awaiting processing in various document centers throughout the country.[13] Not until over a year later did the reports become known. This happened as a result of the search for documentary evidence by staff researchers of the Office of Chief of Counsel for War Crimes (OCCWC). According to Benjamin Ferencz, who was then chief of the Berlin Branch of this office, the reports came to his attention sometime in late 1946 or early 1947. A researcher of his team showed him several Leitz Ordners (loose-leaf folders) containing the original reports (which were mimeographed copies). The staggering content of the reports was immediately apparent to Ferencz, who then showed them to Brigadier General Telford Taylor, who was the chief prosecutor in the subsequent trials at Nuremberg. Taylor then appointed Ferencz as the chief prosecutor for the trial of the captured Einsatzgruppen leaders.[14] During the months that preceded this trial, the members of the OCCWC staff were engaged in analyzing and summarizing the reports (as well as other documents) in preparation for their use as evidence by the prosecution. In this way the reports came to light, and photostatic copies were immediately shipped to Nuremberg.[15]

Since their discovery and use in Nuremberg, the Einsatzgruppen reports have largely been accepted at face value by historians. They have been consulted to tell the story of the Holocaust in the Russian territories as well as the occupation policies enacted there by the various German agencies. Mentioned earlier was the fact that this book will concern itself primarily with the Einsatzgruppen killing operations and their presentation in the reports. To this end, the central chapters will deal with this subject from several perspectives. Included among these will be a description of the main structural features of the reports, examples and methodology of presentation of the killings, and a comparison of reporting procedures and totals of victims of each of the four Einsatzgruppen. In addition to these various methods of analysis of the reports themselves, this study will attempt to place the Einsatzgruppen and their reports within the larger context of the National Socialist State. In order to do this a brief historical overview of the SS and its related agencies will be presented, as well as a general discussion of the reporting practices of these agencies. Also to be examined will be certain important aspects of the reports concerning questions of their use as both historical source material and as legal evidence. In concentrating on the killing operations, our study cannot claim to be an exhaustive examination of these reports. The sheer bulk of the reports (in their entirety the Operational Situation Reports alone number over two thousand nine hundred pages) confronts us with a cumbersome body of material. We will center our attention on the unfolding of mass murder, clearly the most significant part of the reports. The reports did not deal only with the shootings, but also included reports on a wide range of social, economic, and political matters. These reports, which were prepared by those members of the Security Service (SD) who were attached to the Einsatzgruppen, will be touched upon in a general way only, mainly insofar as they relate to the areas of inquiry cited above.[16]

It is hoped that by dealing selectively with the minutiae of information in the reports, and by examining the framework in which they were created, that this will deepen our understanding not only of what happened, but also of the people who caused these things to happen.

1

SS Power and the RSHA

The Einsatzgruppen were under the operational control of the Reichs-sicherheitshauptamt or Reich Main Security Office (RSHA) in Berlin. Created in 1939, the RSHA was, in turn, an integral part of the SS and police empire that, by 1939, had acquired virtually unrivalled power in Germany. It was from the RSHA that the Operational Situation Reports, the Activity and Situation Reports, and the Reports from the Occupied Eastern Territories emanated. In order to better understand the reports and the context in which they were created, it is necessary to examine briefly not only the RSHA and the circumstances of its formation but also the development of the SS and its major component agencies, only one of which was the RSHA.

Broadly speaking, the history of the SS is the history of the gradual accumulation, centralization, and separation of police power in Germany. This power eventually rested in the hands of Heinrich Himmler and Reinhard Heydrich, key figures in the destruction of the Jews. The roots of the SS may be traced back almost to the beginning of Adolf Hitler's political career. Aware of the need to maintain his control of the party leadership and, in particular, suspicious of the independent function that Ernst Röhm sought to give to the SA (Sturm-Abteilung), the strong arm forces of the National Socialist Party, Hitler in 1923 formed for his own protection a Personal Headquarters Guard (Stabswache) consisting of twelve dependable men. This unit was soon after expanded into a fifty-man squad known as the Hitler Assault Squad (Strosstrupps Hitler). In the spring of 1925 these units formed the model for the teams of ten men established in various cities throughout the country. By the late summer of 1925 they became known as Guard Detachments (Schutzstaffeln) or SS.[1] These forces were thus small in number. Their initial purpose was to protect Hitler, other party leaders, and party meetings. The members of the SS were to consist of only the most reliable party members and were to be used for "any political, technical or strong-arm purpose."[2] They wore black caps with a skull and black-bordered swastika armbands.[3]

During the period from 1926 to 1928 the SS went through changes of leadership and made relatively little progress in expanding its membership.

It remained subordinate to the SA, and it was not until Heinrich Himmler was appointed Reichsführer SS on 6 January 1929 that the SS began to grow in importance in relation to other institutions in Germany.[4] In January 1929 the SS had 280 members.[5] Four years later, by the spring of 1933, the SS membership was over fifty thousand.[6]

From this point on the story of the SS was the story of Himmler's personal rise to prominence, a feat all the more incredible given the apparent ordinariness of the man himself. Considering the power that he later acquired and the destruction that he enacted, Himmler's personality almost eludes our understanding, so filled as it was with contradictions. There is little evidence from Himmler's youth that indicates what he was to become.[7] By many comtemporary accounts Himmler was considered mediocre.[8] He lacked security and independence; he entertained mystical, eccentric ideas that he later incorporated into the life-style of the SS membership. Himmler was born on 7 October 1900 in Munich,[9] the son of a teacher. It was likely that Himmler acquired the pedantic quality that was to characterize his later years from his father.[10] As a young man Himmler was unable to decide on one particular occupation. First he wanted to join the navy,[11] and failing that, he joined the Eleventh Bavarian Infantry Regiment in 1917, but he never got to fight at the front. In 1919, after a period in the Free Corps, Himmler began to study agriculture at the Institute of Technology and the University of Munich.[12] Ironically, it was as the result of meeting Ernst Röhm—the man he was later to kill in 1934—that Himmler came to join the National Socialist Party and thus began his political career.[13] It was not long before Himmler became a fanatic follower of Hitler. Himmler's loyalty and devoted work for the movement led to his appointment as Reichsführer SS.[14]

Almost immediately upon his appointment Himmler began to expand the size of the SS by attempting to recruit men from the SA. At the same time he began to impose his own restrictive standards for membership in the SS, thus imbuing the SS with the idea that it was a racially elite force.[15] As a result of these developments the rivalry with the SA intensified as the latter continued to regard itself as a force independent of the party. Late in 1930 the SS was made independent of the SA, receiving its own distinctive black uniform, with black cap, tie and pants, and swastika with black border.[16]

In 1931 another event occurred that was to have ramifications for SS power in Germany. This was the beginning of the intelligence service, later known as the Sicherheitsdienst (Security Service) or SD. As was true of the SS, the SD emerged from humble origins. During the summer of 1931, Himmler appointed Reinhard Heydrich, a former naval communications officer, to run the IC-Abteilung or intelligence section he had created within the SS.[17] Heydrich, who was born on 7 March 1904 in Halle,[18] had been forced to resign from the navy because of a dishonorable affair with a young woman.[19] He was tall, blond, and possessed a calculating intelligence combined with a cold contempt for human beings.[20] He excelled at everything he undertook, whether it was athletics, fencing, or playing the violin. If Heydrich was in fact the "true architect" of the future SS police state, it was largely due to the unblinded realism of his conception of power.[21] Beginning with a small staff in Munich, Heydrich plunged into his new assignment with great skill and energy. He was very soon rewarded for his effort by a series of promotions.[22] The slow expansion of his intelligence organization involved recruiting ruthless, reliable agents[23] to gather information on enemies within and without the party. The initial aims of the SD investigations were to uncover informants within the movement in order to protect Hitler's grip on the leadership, and to keep close watch on other parties and groups. This function later expanded, however, to include more general reports on the attitudes of the German population with regard to the Nazi leadership.[24]

During 1932 the SD grew to the point that by 30 January 1933 between twenty and thirty agents were being paid for their services. These professional recruits are to be distinguished from the unpaid volunteers that at this time numbered about two hundred.[25]

A notable feature of the SD, throughout its development, was its membership, which tended to be drawn from educated professional circles—lawyers, academics, government and business people—often at the beginning of their careers, and many of whom worked for the SD for some time before joining the SS.[26] This recruitment of educated personnel gave a sense of superiority to the SD in relation to other organs of the party and state, especially the SA.[27]

The efficiency with which the SD members carried out their work was soon acknowledged by the decree of 9 June 1934 that stated that the SD was to be the exclusive intelligence agency of the National Socialist Party.[28] On 4 July 1934 Himmler went further, naming the SD as the sole political counterespionage service for the Gestapo.[29] This rise in the standing of the SD was accompanied by an increase in the allocation of the party funds.[30] The unique status of the SD in relation to the party was later confirmed in a decree issued on 14 December 1938 although, theoretically at least, the SD was not allowed to investigate party members or party matters.[31]

By January 1935 the SD had expanded so that the transference of the SD headquarters from Munich to Berlin took place. The new offices were located at Wilhelmstrasse 102 on the corner of Prinz-Albrecht-Strasse, across from the Gestapo Headquarters.[32]

The not insignificant part played by the SD in the Röhm purge in June 1934[33] emphasized its usefulness as a partner with the SS and the Reichswehr against the mutual enemy, the SA. The killing of Röhm and other SA officials was the first mass murder operation of the Hitler regime[34] and demonstrated how the SD and the Political Police could work together. This cooperation foreshadowed the more terrible consequences of the partnership that was to take place in the east during the war. At any rate, after June 1934, the SA, despite its numerical strength, ceased to be a factor in the political power structure of the Third Reich.[35] The military leadership, now rewarded for its "hands off" attitude toward the National Socialists,[36] was grateful for the SS role in destroying its chief rival for military power. The military hierarchy could now look forward to the long-awaited political stabilization and economic growth wherein its own power could be affirmed and expanded.

Parallel to the growth during the years of both the SD and the General SS or Allgemeine SS,[37] as the main body of the SS came to be called, was the creation of special armed SS formations. These were the Verfügung-struppe (Special Duty Troops) and the Totenkopfverbände (Death's Head Battalions). The Verfügungstruppe, as it was known after December 1934[38] and that included the Leibstandarte SS "Adolf Hitler"[39] and the Totenkopfverbände had grown out of earlier auxiliary formations.[40] These units gradually increased in strength and formed the basis for the fighting units of the SS, or Waffen SS, as they were called officially in 1940.[41] A Hitler decree issued on 17 August 1938 dealt with the relationship of these armed SS units with the Wehrmacht. In peacetime these units were under Himmler's control and were responsible for internal "political tasks." In the event of war they were to be mobilized under army control although they were to remain "politically" a unit of the National Socialist Party.[42] These pronouncements were similar to arrangements drawn up later dealing with jurisdictional questions between the army and Einsatzgruppen and other SS formations operating in the occupied territories. Indeed, these additional groups were to play a significant part in the killings in the east, alongside, and in concert with, the operations of the Einsatzgruppen.[43]

Important as this expansion of the SS was, however, it was the step-by-step assumption of control over the Political Police and its separation from normal state authority that marked the real source of SS domination. During the Weimar Republic, police activity of a political nature had been carried out surreptitiously by the Abteilung IA of the Berlin Police Headquarters.[44] It was this department that formed the origins of the Secret State Police or Gestapo. The Ordinance for the Protection of People and State, issued on 28 February 1933, allowed Hitler to bypass the normal existing structures of law, and gave the Gestapo the "legal" basis for its security activities.[45] On 30 January 1933 Hermann Göring was appointed leader of the Prussian Ministry of the Interior, naming Rudolf Diels[46] as head of Abteilung IA. A further series of laws gradually freed the Political Police in practice from the authority of the ministry and of existing law.[47] On 9 March 1933 Himmler became acting police president of Munich, and

Heydrich took over the political desk in Abteilung VI of the Munich Criminal Police. The appointments stressed the purely political nature of these assignments, as well as loyalty to Hitler—as opposed to the mere maintenance of security and public order.[48]

The takeover of Political Police control continued rapidly. Both Himmler and Heydrich soon extended their power base with further appointments, the former becoming political advisor to the Bavarian Ministry of the Interior as well as commander of the Bavarian Political Police, while the latter became his executive deputy.[49] During the winter months of 1933–34 Himmler gained control of the Political Police in all the Länder, or territorial government divisions of Germany.[50] The most critical takeover in this series occurred on 20 April 1934 when Himmler became deputy chief and inspector of the Prussian Secret State Police. Two days later Heydrich became chief of the Prussian Gestapo Office.[51] Underlying all of these developments was the fact that they represented a real *separation from* the state administration—the Reich Ministry of the Interior—by the Political Police. This gave Himmler, essentially as leader of a party organization, virtual independence from the ineffectual government apparatus to which he was nominally subordinate.[52] Coupled with the infusion of key positions of the Political Police by SS personnel and the ever-increasing importance of the SD and its merging of activities with the Political Police, the SS machinery was quickly achieving its goal of control over the state bureaucracy and the German people.[53]

On 30 January 1935 the SS-Hauptamt (SS Main Office) was established, consolidating existing SS institutions and establishing a complex bureaucratic structure to oversee its various departments.[54] The following year, 1936, was a crucial year for the SS. On February 10 the Prussian Gestapo Law was issued concerning the Gestapo and the civil administration. While on paper this law appeared to subordinate the lower ranks of the Gestapo to the civil authorities, in reality this was not the case at all. In effect the Gestapo, as did the SS, operated on the authority of Hitler himself, and was not tied down to the norms of legal procedure.[55] Of even greater importance that year was the naming on June 17 of Himmler as Reichsführer SS *and* chief of the German Police,[56] the crowning act in the earlier police takeovers in the Länder. This merging of the roles of SS leader (a party office) with that of the leadership of the police (a government office) permitted Himmler to transform the police into an organization that was now connected to the SS.[57] Again, as in 1934, implied in this was the practical separation of the police from the state administration as such. Himmler's power to execute Hitler's will was now unhampered by any restrictions.[58] The Political Police now ceased its "defensive" role and assumed an "offensive" role subservient to the inclinations of the Führer.[59]

Shortly after becoming chief of the German Police, Himmler, on 26 June 1936, created the Hauptamt Sicherheitspolizei (SIPO) and the Hauptamt Ordnungspolizei (ORPO). SIPO, which was under Heydrich's direction, combined the Gestapo and the Kriminalpolizei (Criminal Police) or KRIPO. The ORPO, under Kurt Daluege, consisted of the uniformed urban, rural, and municipal police.[60] Daluege was long a rival of Himmler, but had been outmanoeuvred by Himmler in the bid for power within the Ministry of the Interior.[61] As head of the Hauptamt ORPO, Daluege still retained control of an extremely large police organization within Germany. The next several years witnessed the steady infiltration by the SS and the SD of the various regular police ranks throughout the Reich. By 1938 many of these units were permitted to wear SS runes on their uniform and top-ranking members of the Ordnungspolizei entered the SS with the equivalent SS rank.[62] Furthermore, the creation of the post of inspectors of the Ordnungspolizei and Sicherheitspolizei in 1936 also provided an avenue for SS penetration of the police.[63]

While not integrated into the RSHA, the Ordnungspolizei, along with the Waffen SS formations, provided recruits for a significant portion of the rank and file of the Einsatzgruppen. Therefore, while SS penetration of the police was generally relatively limited in terms of numbers,[64] the fact that many policemen were later drafted into the Einsatzkommandos was sufficient opportunity for their participation in atrocities.[65]

The union of police, state, and party described in the foregoing brief outline, took place over a period of several years. This process may be said to have reached its culmination on 27 September 1939, with the creation of the Reichssicherheitshauptamt, or RSHA. This agency had been under discussion for some time,[66] and came into being as the result of the outbreak of war in September 1939, mainly in response to the need for a coordinating agency for the SS and police operations in Poland.[67] The RSHA, which became operational on 1 October 1939, joined the offices of the Security Police and the SD. Heydrich became its head and assumed the title of Chef der Sicherheitspolizei und des SD. All offices of the RSHA were to employ this heading on any correspondence or reports dealing with other authorities.[68] We shall see that this was the practice in the Einsatzgruppen reports. In a directive also issued on September 27, Heydrich ordered that all correspondence was to be signed by the office chiefs: "I.V." (in Vertetung, or acting for). [69]

In spite of this amalgamation of the state agency, the Security Police, and the party agency, the SD, Himmler's establishment of the RSHA did not alter either the existing relationship of the various RSHA offices with the party and the civil administration, or the previous financial arrangements of this relationship,[70] nor was it ever made clear whether the RSHA was a state agency or not.[71] Heydrich and his subordinates took advantage of this ambiguity, and as they had earlier, went about their business under the guise that existing "legal" institutions were still in place.[72] Yet, in the formation of the RSHA, Himmler and Heydrich had now created a central mechanism that was to direct the monstrous killing of millions of helpless human beings.

The main headquarters of the new institution was located in the Gestapo Headquarters at Prinz-Albrecht-Strasse 8 in Berlin. In merging the Hauptamt Sicherheitspolizei and that of the Sicherheitsdienst, the RSHA simply realigned various sections of these previous departments into six new Offices.[73] Each Office (AMT) had Groups (Gruppen) designated by Roman numerals, each of which, in turn, had subsections (Referate) designated by Arabic numbers. These subsections were concerned with one aspect of the parent Office's activities. The initial plan of the RSHA may be summarized as follows:

Office I, directed by Werner Best, consisted of personnel from the SD and Gestapo.

Office II, directed by Franz Six, consisted of personnel from the SD.

Office III, directed by Otto Ohlendorf, consisted of SD personnel. (Domestic Intelligence)

Office IV, directed by Heinrich Müller, consisted of personnel from the Gestapo.

Office V, directed by Arthur Nebe, consisted of personnel from the Criminal Police.

Office VI, directed by Heinz Jost, consisted of SD personnel. (Foreign Intelligence)

As time passed this basic setup underwent modifications in structure and personnel.[74] Personnel changes were a frequent occurrence, due to transfers, demotions, and organizational restructuring. It was not uncommon for a subsection to be without a director for a period of time while awaiting the selection of a replacement.[75] As explained above, each Office consisted of a number of Groups. Each Group had both a chief and a deputy chief, as well as subsections within each Group. Office IV, for example, headed by Heinrich Müller, administered the Gestapo. It dealt with investigation and the combatting of enemies. By 1 January 1941, in addition to an administrative Office, Office IV included Groups A, B, C, D, and E. Groups A to D had subsections numbered 1 to 4. Group A, for instance, was organized in the following way:

IV A 1: Dealt with communism, Marxism, and similar organizations, wartime crimes, and hostile propaganda. Section leader: Joseph Vogt.

IV A 2: Dealt with the combatting of sabotage, political police counter-intelligence (Abwehr) commissioners, and political forgeries. Section leader: Kopkow.

IV A 3: Dealt with reaction, opposition, legitimism, liberalism, emigrant affairs, and treachery. Section leader: Litzenberg.

IV A 4: Dealt with protective service, reports of attempted assassinations, guarding, special missions, pursuit troops. Section leader: Franz Schulz.[76]

At this time Group IV E was divided into six subsections.[77] A similar complexity was to be found in the other RSHA Offices. The example of Office IV A indicates the degree to which the tasks of the police and SD were broken down and distributed among the staff according to specific areas of expertise. In some cases the size of the Office is further indication of the scope of the RSHA organization. For example, Office VI, which was concerned with foreign intelligence, was located in the southwest central section of Berlin on the corner of Berkaerstrasse and Hohenzollerndam. The headquarters was a curvilinear, four-story building, which had formerly been a Jewish old folks' home. The RSHA took over the building in 1941, and during the war an estimated four hundred to five hundred people worked there—reading, evaluating and annotating reports, as well as carrying out other administrative work of the department. An additional total of about five hundred persons worked as agents in foreign countries. Thus in all, approximately one thousand people were in the employ of Office VI alone at the height of its operations during the war.[78]

With regard to the RSHA and the Einsatzgruppen personnel two points should be made. First, it is important to recognize that in the areas occupied by the German forces, the Security Police and SD Offices constituted departments that corresponded to the Offices within the RSHA. We have already taken note of the fact that the members of the Einsatzgruppen were drawn from the Gestapo, Criminal Police (KRIPO), and SD as well as the Ordnungspolizei and the Waffen SS. For our purposes it is also important to observe that, in addition to the similar rank and file membership of the Einsatzgruppen and the RSHA, the operational structure of the staff of each Einsatzgruppe corresponded closely to that of the RSHA. This similarity of organization was crucial with regard to the reports sent by the Einsatzgruppen. As a result, SD personnel in the Einsatzgruppen gathered intelligence material on various aspects of life, the local situation, and so on, while Gestapo representatives filed reports on their areas of activity—"executive" matters, and actions carried out against Jews, communists, and other enemies. Criminal police matters and administrative questions were each handled by the appropriate members of these Offices.[79]

The second point involves the Einsatzgruppen leaders. Not only were the rank and file members of the Einsatzgruppen to a great extent taken from those agencies that also fed the RSHA, but many of the leaders of the Einsatzgruppen and the Einsatzkommandos before the attack on the Soviet Union had themselves actually been leaders of Offices or Groups within the RSHA. They went to the east directly from their posts in the RSHA. Some returned to the RSHA after their service in the Einsatzgruppen. Among others, the leaders in these categories included Otto Ohlendorf, Arthur Nebe, Heinz Jost, Martin Sandberger, Willy Seibert, Erwin Weinmann, Alfred Filbert, Erwin Schulz, Albert Rapp, Karl Tschierschky, Friedrich Panzinger, Franz Six, Eugen Steimle, Werner Braune, Emil Haussman, Erich Müller, Heinz Schubert, Walter Haensch, and Erich Ehrlinger.[80] While these men had been or were later associated directly with the RSHA, the other leaders within the Einsatzgruppen had also begun their careers in some capacity either within the SS, the Gestapo, the Criminal Police, or the SD.

Finally, one must keep in mind that from the very beginning the SS had always primarily been concerned with security. At first it was the security of one man, Hitler, and his immediate entourage, then of the party and its struggle for power, then of a totalitarian government and its hammerlock grasp of the nation. After September 1939 it became security against captive populations in occupied territories. Throughout this evolution the strength of the SS rested in both its ever-increasing number of fanatic recruits, who were unqualifyingly loyal exclusively to Hitler himself, and the steady infusion of SS personnel and ideology into other organs of power. Furthermore, the concept of security itself soon became all-embracing. It rapidly came to include as being essential the gathering of all kinds of bits and pieces of information on all manner of subjects. Virtually everyone and everything were subject to the probings of the investigators. One could never feel safe, for one could never really be sure what information the authorities had obtained.[81] In this way the SD and other intelligence reporting organizations played a major part in the transformation of police activity in Germany. As we noted earlier, the virtual separation of the state police from normal governmental restraints in *law* led to the reversal of defensive and offensive roles within the police. Police power no longer existed to provide the citizens with the protection of law and order, but had become the instrument of Hitler's control for his own purposes.

We have also seen that the Einsatzgruppen leaders were men with experience in police work and intelligence gathering. On paper their assignment was ostensibly the establishment of security in the conquered eastern territories. Yet just as the meaning of security had undergone transfiguration in Germany before the war, so had the war and Hitler's ideological demands further radicalized the context of security in the east. The horrific atrocities carried out by the SS against Poles and Jews during the Polish campaign,[82] reprehensible as they were, were still essentially random and limited acts. They were not the last stage in this radicalization. It was not until the Soviet campaign that the final stage was reached. Then, under the mantle of alleged security measures, the Einsatzgruppen unleashed a program of genocide.

2

Reporting in the Third Reich

It is certainly correct to say, as one historian has pointed out, that reporting, as practiced by the Einsatzgruppen, was nothing new.[1] The distribution of police and intelligence tasks, as constituted in the RSHA, had had a considerable history in Germany before 1939 as had the writing of reports. The writing of reports is a natural part of the administration of bureaucratic structures everywhere, and the bureaucracy-laden fabric of Hitler's Reich was no exception. In Germany, both before and after 1933, the writing of reports was actually an indispensable activity performed by a variety of organizations in addition to the police and the SD. It was an essential part of the day-to-day work of the various departments of the regime, both during the so-called years of struggle, when spying on opposition groups was necessary in the battle for power, and in the years following Hitler's assumption of power, when the maintenance of an ever-deepening control over people and state required the constant monitoring of the German people. The range of such monitoring was wide. Consequently, throughout the Reich there existed a multiplicity of information gathering services that filed reports on a broad range of subjects.

It has been said that one of the commonplaces of totalitarian systems of rule is that such systems claim to understand what might be called the "intention of world history."[2] Such an idea marked the thinking of Hitler and his followers, who believed that in National Socialism and the New Order there lay the fulfillment of a great historical mission. A further characteristic of totalitarian rule is the belief that what the state imposes on its people is really an expression of that people's will.[3] This idea, too, informed Hitler's thinking. The sweeping nature of such grandiose claims to political knowledge was a far cry from the reality confronting the Nazi leadership, however. Theirs was the job of obtaining knowledge of a more mundane kind. Though faced with no real overt opposition to their policies and allowing no means whereby such opposition could be actively voiced, the leaders still felt the need to discover what the German people were actually thinking, their morale, how they were responding to political events, party policy, measures undertaken by government leaders, and so on.[4] If the National Socialists were carrying out the will of the people as

27

they purported, they certainly were expending a lot of energy trying to discover just what that will was.

Therefore, in order to both protect and police its own institutions, and to receive information that could help shape policy and at the same time provide ways of better mobilizing the masses,[5] the regime sent its reporters about their business. Almost every National Socialist agency to some degree, at some time, or in specific areas, reported on the internal political situation.[6] So comprehensive and flexible were the subjects for inquiry that almost from the start there was overlapping in the areas of investigation. With time certain major themes emerged that came to be included in the reports from different organizations. In particular, the fundamental task of reporting on the activities of those sections of society who were viewed as dangerous opponents of the regime (Jews, Freemasons, communists, and others) was taken up by almost every reporting agency. This duplication was perhaps inevitable, given the need for each group to protect its own interests. No doubt it also reflected the lack of careful planning and coordination that seemed endemic to the early days of information gathering.[7]

One of the principal reporting agencies within Germany was the National Socialist Party itself. Within each region at every level of its organization "Political Situation Reports" (Lageberichte) were written dealing with many topics, but concentrating mainly on public opinion. By the end of 1938 a complex system of classification allowed for as many as thirty headings and eighty-two subheadings for the material to be discussed in the reports. This elaborate reporting scheme had to be modified with the onset of the war.[8] Generally, the regional party reports were drawn up on a monthly basis, although reports of particular interest could be sent out in special "midweek reports." Regional party groups also sent weekly reports to the party Chancellery. These reports included material from district level reports as well as from branches of the regional offices and other government sources.[9] Directives issued to the party organizations constantly stressed the importance of exhaustive, truthful, and regular reporting.[10] As in the reports of other agencies, the party reports dealt with a wide range of topics. Emphasized in particular in the reports were the errors and malpractices of government departments, propaganda, justice, commerce and crafts, general morale, church activities, and the actions of "hostile elements."[11]

In the party reports (as in others) the general opinion of the population was embodied in the concepts of mood (Stimmung) and attitude (Haltung). Explanation of these dual concepts was given in an instructional report of the NSDAP Reich Organization Directorate. "Mood," according to this report, implied feeling, an emotional response to events freed of rationalization. "Attitude," on the other hand, went further, and rested upon a spirit of "trust in the Führer."[12] As the fortunes of the war deteriorated for the Germans and Allied bombing of German cities increased, Goebbels was to order that he did not wish "Mood" to be discussed any more. He now wanted to hear only of "good attitudes" in the reports.[13]

Other reports from the party were those of the party "indoctrination officers" (Schulungsleiter) who sent reports on the general reaction to official ideology to Alfred Rosenberg. Rosenberg, who later was to become head of the civilian administration in the Soviet territories, was in charge of the overall spiritual and ideological education of the party leadership.[14]

In the Third Reich there was a reciprocal relationship between reporting on the general opinion and morale of the people and the manipulation of that opinion and morale by means of carefully orchestrated propaganda. Joseph Goebbels, and Reich Press Chief Otto Dietrich, continuously instructed the media on just what and how to report to the German people.[15] Goebbels had his own opinion-defining agency, based on the activity reports of the Reich Propaganda offices, whose task was supposed to be limited to the public mood as it affected the activity of the Propaganda Ministry. As a matter of course the mandate of Goebbels' Ministry came into conflict with that of the SD in its reporting on the general mood.[16] This did not prevent Goebbels, at least at first, from making use of the rival SD reports in shaping his propaganda.[17]

Reports from other sources existed as well. The large German Labor Front under Robert Ley received periodic reports from its factory representatives on the general morale of the workers.[18] Appeals court presidents and public prosecutors also sent situation reports dealing with justice and civil service as well as the general mood of the population to the Reich Justice Ministry.[19] The close connection between propaganda and the assessment of its effect was also reflected in the military sphere as far back as 1938. The propaganda department of the Wehrmacht, partly in connection with other organizations, attempted to instill within its ranks a fighting spirit based on ideological indoctrination.[20]

A different but important area of reporting was that carried out by the Publikationsstelle, which was set up in late 1933. This agency formed the center for Ostforschung, or research done on the east by scholars who, under the framework of alleged academic research, wrote reports on a full range of subjects related to the east that were somewhat similar to the lengthier reports of the SD.[21] The academics recruited to undertake this work did so voluntarily and with enthusiasm. These men simply served the ideology of their leaders and produced reports that largely reflected that bias.[22] As of August 1943 the Publikationsstelle was subordinate to Office VI G of the RSHA under Wilfried Krallert, and thereby became one of several information sources on foreign countries. The Publikationsstelle furnished the SD with information,[23] and was itself the recipient of assistance from the SD.[24]

The reports discussed thus far had features that were to be shared with the reports of the Einsatzgruppen. It was, however, the SS/SD and Political Police reporting systems that were to form the most immediate and closest antecedents. With respect to the Secret State Police or Gestapo it will be remembered that its origins rested in the Abteilung IA of the Berlin Police during the Weimar Republic. Reporting had been even then an essential activity, as this department had constituted an important police intelligence center. The law of 26 April 1933 creating the Geheimes Staatspolizeiamt confirmed the assignment of the Gestapo as being concerned with political police tasks. Each Staatspolizeistelle, or regional office of the Gestapo, sent monthly Situation Reports to the headquarters in Berlin, as did the regional government administrator.[25] As did reports from other agencies, the Gestapo reports included several sections: a general overview of developments within the country; reports on antigovernment activities, which dealt with Marxism, communism, and other opposition groups and tendencies; reports on the churches and other religious movements;[26] reports on economic and agricultural policies; cultural reports, especially those concerning the press; reports related to the party and its various sections; reports on Jews and Freemasons; and reports on foreigners, espionage, and treason.

Other reports issued parallel to the Einsatzgruppen reports were the reports from Office IV on Important State Police Operations (Meldungen wichtiger staatspolizeilicher Ereignisse) issued from August 1941 to the end of 1944.[27] Special reports from various Staatspolizeistelle in the Reich were also actually included in the Operational Situation Reports on a regular basis, as were reports from various Security Police and SD leaders throughout the occupied European territories, as opposed to those areas occupied by the four Einsatzgruppen. These reports included in the Einsatzgruppen Reports were generally quite short, and appeared under the heading Political Overview (Politische Übersicht). The Security Police reports from the occupied territories also appeared under this heading, and along with the State Police reports, were generally concerned with matters that were relevant to. what was taking place in the east.[28]

The early years of the SS were also years when systematic reporting occurred. As far back as September 1925 it had been the practice of the SS to draw up reports on the private affairs of questionable members of the party. This was done to protect against breaches of conduct by party members. The SS also reported on anti-Hitler factions within the party as well as outside opposition groups.[29] A September 1927 order is typical of orders given concerning reporting, that is, SS officers were specifically required to obtain intelligence on important developments among opponents, prominent Freemasons and Jewish leaders, political and other important events, and secret orders of the opposition. They were also to send significant newspaper clippings to the Party Propaganda Department.[30] Subsequent directives issued in 1930 and 1931 further emphasized similar aims concerning the intelligence work of the SS.[31]

By June 1931 the need for a more structured SS intelligence service led to the formation in that month of intelligence units in the local SS formations. Their function was to report on major political developments within their area. This desire for a more efficient intelligence service led to the establishment of an IC-Abteilung within the SS directorate and constituted the beginning of the SD.[32] The SD was to slowly emerge as the most important intelligence reporting service in Germany. Indeed, the writing of reports was the very raison d'être of the SD. Soon going beyond the initial task of reporting on opponents within the party, the SD both expanded this security role via an extensive system of card files on opponents of all kinds and developed a broader type of reporting on the general political attitude of the population along the lines we have noted in other organizations.[33] The SD agents were given specific guidelines for their reports. The reports were to be impartial and truthful. Petty or spiteful informers were to be removed from their positions. This objectivity was seen by the SD officials as necessary in realizing their role as "counsellors" to the Reich leadership.[34] The SD not only became the sole political intelligence service of the party in 1934, but among all the German reporting agencies it produced the most comprehensive and most objective reports.[35] The lengthier SD reports just mentioned included the writing of Special Reports (Sonderberichte) on specific subjects of interest to the leadership.[36] As a result of the comprehensive nature of the investigations and reporting of the SD and the desire of the SD leaders to increase its importance within the power structure of the nation, the SD soon came into conflict with the Gestapo in its reporting activities.[37] Attempts to coordinate and differentiate the field of operations of these organizations were made by Heydrich in 1937.[38] The resulting delegation of purely ideological questions to the SD was to limit the SD domestically to reporting on the various German Spheres of Life (Deutsche Lebensgebiete).

Later, just after the formation of the RSHA, the new Office III began to file reports that were certainly among the most important documents to survive the war. The first group of reports appeared on 9 October 1939 and were called Reports on the Domestic Political Situation (Berichte zur innenpolitischen Lage). These reports continued until December 1939. They consisted of five sections: General Mood and Situation, Opponents, Cultural Areas, Law and Administration, and the Economy.[39] On 8 December 1939 the first of 387 reports known as Reports from the Reich (Meldungen aus dem Reich) appeared. These reports were issued until 31

May 1943. They appeared three times a week until mid-May 1940 and were thereafter issued twice weekly.[40] Consisting of double-spaced typed pages, the Reports from the Reich ranged in length from twelve and thirty-six pages, but with an average length of between eighteen and twenty pages. The reports often included supplemental sections devoted to special topics.[41] Unlike the Operational Situation Reports of the Einsatzgruppen the Reports from the Reich were not numbered nor did they include a distribution list. As a consequence it is not possible to state with precision who received them beyond Heydrich, Himmler, Goebbels, and Kalten- brunner, although copies were probably given to all government ministers and party Reichsleiter.[42]

The reports of the Einsatzgruppen were a continuation of the prevalent norms of reporting as practiced by party, government, police, SD, and other organizations within Germany. The reports described above had structural features as well as similarities of content that corresponded to the Einsatzgruppen reports. The latter reports shared the established custom of separating areas of investigation into several categories, each of which was to be dealt with by different agencies. This simple general format provided a convenient formula of presentation whereby the reporters and editors could easily present the material. As was the case in early reports, the concept of a situation report or a report on the general mood of the population remained an important ingredient in the reports. Also, as in earlier reports, in spite of the delegation of subject areas, the perimeters of a particular topic were frequently wide enough to allow for overlapping under the headings in the reports. For example, information relating to Church matters in the Reports on the Domestic Political Situation were generally discussed under the headings, General Mood or Situation, or Cultural Areas. In the Reports from the Reich church matters were often also included under Opponents, Administration and Law, and Folkdum and Public Health.[43] Finally, as we will discover in the next chapter, the Einsatzgruppen reports were prepared in roughly the same manner as those of the party and government offices already discussed. Reports evolved from drafts sent in by regional offices that, in turn, were assembled and edited by specialists in different areas. The method therefore involved sending reports upward through channels. Each level consisted of editing and consolidating the information sent in and then passing it on to the higher authority.[44]

These earlier and concurrent reports furnished models both as to subject and structure for the Einsatzgruppen reporters. The operations of the Einsatzgruppen, however, were something totally new and terrible. Even though similarities of format prevailed, the Operational Situation Reports, especially those sections in them written by the Security Police describing the actions against the Jews, were quite unlike previous reports.[45]

We have noted some of the directives concerning reporting that were given to the groups. Concerning reporting guidelines, in this case for Gestapo reports, two examples from 1934 may be cited here.[46] On 3 March 1934 a directive was issued to Gestapo offices, which stipulated that copies of the general situation reports sent in were to be easily legible and neat and written on one page per sheet. The reports were to be self-explanatory. No mention of previous reports was to be made, since these might not always be readily at hand for reference. This directive indicated that there was obviously frequent dissatisfaction with the reports sent in. The directive cautioned that the uniform format specified in earlier instructions had not been followed and that this format was important since the reports were to be passed on immediately to higher authorities. Further complaints centered on the fact that enclosures sent with the material were often incomplete and that an earlier directive of 23 December 1933 concerning additional copies of the reports had been ignored. This had led to delays in the exchange of information. When no reports were forthcoming, the local offices were to specify this fact, so that it would not be assumed that the reports had been simply lost. (This latter instruction was observed in the Einsatzgruppen reports. The reports always mentioned when a particular Einsatzgruppe had nothing to report.) A secret directive from Munich issued a few months later on 17 July 1934 gave further instructions concerning political reports and the structure they were to assume. The state governor and the head of the police in Munich were to submit monthly political situation reports to the Ministry of the Interior. The deadline for these reports was the tenth day of the month following the month covered in the report. The first such report was to appear on 10 August 1934. The reports were to be exhaustive, objective, and secret. Unnecessary details and subjective comments of the reporters were to be excluded. The reporting officer was to be held personally responsible for the accuracy and completeness of the reports that he sent in. The reports were to be submitted in five copies, on one side of each sheet only. This directive mentioned that the purpose of the standard headings was to facilitate evaluation of the reports. The use of these particular headings did not rule out including other subjects if necessary.

Instructions came from the RSHA to the Einsatzgruppen about reporting information specifically from the east. An early example of what was to be included in reports was found in a letter dated 21 September 1939 to the Einsatzgruppen leaders in the occupied territory (which at that time was western Poland). This letter laid the groundwork for the confinement of Jews in certain centers and signified the beginning of the larger process of the ghettoization of the Jews of Poland. In this letter Heydrich ordered the leaders to "report continuously (to Heydrich) on such matters as Jewish census, names of towns used as 'concentration' points, time limits set for migration, summary of branches of vital Jewish industries."[47]

In a series of orders drawn up in 1941, Heydrich also issued instructions concerning the handling of prisoners in the prisoner-of-war camps. Here the guidelines regarding reporting were even more detailed. The screening of the prisoners and the subsequent shooting of those categories of people considered undesirable was to be carried out by the Kommandos of the Security Police and SD from the Einsatzgruppen. A preliminary Directive to the Stalags, dated 28 June 1941, gave the following orders regarding the reporting of the prisoners who were to be shot:

> The Kommandos are to keep records of the fulfillment of special handlings; which must include:
>
> Serial number
> Family and Surname
> Date of birth and place
> Military rank
> Profession
> Last residence
> Reason for special handling
> Day and place of special handling.[48]

Further directives on reports dealing with prisoner-of-war camps were found in Operational Order no. 8 issued on 17 July 1941:

> The leader of the Einsatzkommando will give every week a short report by telephone or an express letter to the RSHA containing:
>
> 1. *Short* description of their activities in the past week.
>
> 2. Number of all definitely suspicious persons (report of number sufficient).
>
> 3. Individual names of all persons found to be functionaries of the Komintern, leading functionaries of the Party, Peoples-Commissars, leading personalities and Political Commissars.
>
> 4. Numbers of all persons found not to be suspicious informers, with a short description of their position:
>   A. Prisoners-of-War
>   B. Civilians
>
> On the basis of these activity reports the RSHA will issue immediately the further measures to be applied.[49]

The directives found in the just cited June 28 document were then repeated with regard to data to be tabulated concerning victims. The directive then continued.

In regard to executions to be carried out and to the possible removal of reliable civilians and the removal of informers for the Einsatzgruppe in the occupied territories, the leader of the Einsatzkommando must make an agreement with the nearest State Police office, as well as with the Commandant of the Security Police Unit and Security Service and beyond these with the Chief of the Einsatzgruppe concerned in the occupied territories.

Reports of that kind are to be transmitted for information to the RSHA IV A 1.[50]

In a Supplement to the July 17 directive, Heydrich reiterated his order to find "trustworthy" informers among the prisoners. In the weekly reports, "The war prisoners who are found to be trustworthy and who were formerly in leading positions in the Soviet Russian economic circles, are to be listed, if possible according to branch, their last employment, and by name."[51]

From these special regulations dealing with prisoners of war as well as from the all-encompassing nature of the reports of the organizations just outlined, some idea can be grasped as to what Heydrich expected in the reports from the Einsatzgruppen. If Heydrich's directives were followed there certainly must have been a considerable amount of material sent in. There was to be a careful attention to details. The reports sent to Berlin were to be a thorough and accurate account of intelligence information and executions. The Einsatzkommandos were not to be slapdash in their reporting. Similar instructions may have been given to the Einsatzgruppen and Einsatzkommando leaders directly during May and June 1941, and possibly by Heydrich and Himmler at the Berlin conference on 17 June 1941. We can only speculate on this as no evidence dealing with reports is available from this meeting. It seems plausible, however, that at this meeting, when the Einsatzkommando leaders received their final instructions, that guidelines for reporting could have been discussed. The experience of the personnel with writing reports and the very general uniformity of the reporting of all four Einsatzgruppen would suggest that by the time the war broke out the requirements of reporting were well understood. In any case, as time passed, the Kommando reporters no doubt soon learned via feedback from the RSHA just what was required in their reports.[52]

The kind of precision called for by Heydrich was not always followed in the reports sent to the RSHA, nor had it always characterized the reports of other organizations within Germany. We have taken note already of the complaints in the two Gestapo documents discussed above. Even during the early years of the SS, Himmler had reproached his men about unclear or incorrect reports, or reports filed carelessly on scraps of paper, and so on.[53] The reports of the party also often left much to be desired in the opinion of some officials. For example, in November 1942 the district party leader of Freiburg labeled the reports that reached him as "mostly vacuous, superficial, and wordy."[54] As leader of the SD, Heydrich had earlier complained about the quality of the SD foreign reports, saying that they were "nothing more than a poor conglomeration of newspaper clippings and broadcast reports." He warned that the reports had to be improved and ordered that he was to be given only reliable intelligence material.[55] When we examine the Einsatzgruppen reports, it will be seen that Heydrich's complaints about errors and omissions in the reports from the east were not without foundation. It is evident that the degree of detail that Heydrich wanted was not consistently provided in spite of his strong objections.[56] Errors and omissions were made, although on the surface it would appear that Heydrich's requirements were being met. Undoubtedly a massive amount of information was sent to Berlin, and in spite of many shortcomings much of it was still characterized by attention to detail. A question we will consider later is the extent to which the information sent to the RSHA did or did not find its way into the final reports.

3

How the Einsatzgruppen Reports
Were Compiled

The manner in which the Einsatzgruppen reports came into being involved several stages. These stages will now be examined.[1] To begin with, it is helpful to comment on the leaders and the organization of the Einsatzgruppen themselves. Generally speaking, the Einsatzgruppen and Kommando leaders were of similar background. Like many leaders of the Third Reich, such as Himmler, Heydrich, and Heinrich Müller, most of the Einsatzgruppen leaders were born between 1900 and 1910. They were in their thirties or early forties during the war. The Einsatzgruppen leadership, therefore, was notable for its extraordinary youth. Because of their age few of these men were "old fighters" of the party (unlike the Higher SS and Police Leaders[2]), and few had seen service in World War I.[3] At the same time they were too old to have been part of the Hitler Youth movement.[4] Most were well-educated; several had doctorates. Most had worked in various professions (law, architecture, medicine, theology, economics, education, business) before beginning their rise through the ranks of the SD and police. It was during the 1930s that the majority of these men had joined the party and the SS, and within the latter organization they had held positions of importance.[5]

In the occupied Soviet territories there were four Einsatzgruppen in all, designated A, B, C, and D. Einsatzgruppe A operated mainly in the Baltic region and parts of White Russia and was attached to Army Group North. It was subdivided into Sonderkommandos 1a and 1b and Einsatz-kommandos 2 and 3. Einsatzgruppe B operated in the area of White Russia and was connected with Army Group Center. It consisted of Sonderkommandos 7a and 7b, Einsatzkommandos 8 and 9 as well as a special Kommando, "Vorkommando Moskau." Einsatzgruppe C operated in the northern and middle areas of the Ukraine and was attached to Army Group South. It consisted of Sonderkommandos 4a and 4b and Einsatzkommandos 5 and 6. Einsatzgruppe D, which operated in the areas of Bessarabia, the southern Ukraine, the Crimea, and the Caucasus, was attached to the Eleventh Army. Einsatzgruppe D was made up of

Sonderkommandos 10a and 10b as well as Einsatzkommandos 11a, 11b, and 12.[6]

It is difficult to say with exactness the size of each of the four Einsatzgruppen, as this fluctuated as time passed. Generally an Einsatzgruppe ranged between approximately six hundred to one thousand men.[7] The subkommandos, too, differed in numerical strength. For instance, Einsatzkommando 2, as of 1 October 1941 had 170 members,[8] while Sonderkommando 7a consisted of about seventy to eighty men. The latter group was broken down as follows: approximately twenty drivers, fifteen Waffen SS, five administrative officials, about fifteen Gestapo and criminal policemen, about ten SD officials, and about five interpreters. Additional Waffen SS men were added as required.[9] Seen here at the Kommando level is the mixture of police, SD, and administrative and technical personnel that prevailed throughout the Einsatzgruppen. The fully motorized squads were very mobile[10] and were almost constantly broken up into smaller units (Teilkommandos) that worked in several locations at the same time. The territory where a Kommando operated could be quite extensive. The area of operations of Einsatzkommando 6, for example, covered approximately sixty thousand square kilometers.[11] Walter Blume, the leader of Sonderkommando 7a, stated that each of the subunits of his group had sufficient numbers of vehicles to transport the approximately fifteen members of each Teilkommando, along with their baggage and weapons. His Kommando, like others, included an officer who was in charge of the motor vehicles, as well as an administrative staff and a mobile kitchen.[12] The Kommandos were, therefore, ready to move quickly with the advancing army and were extremely flexible as to the formation of Teilkommandos, which could be established according to the demands of a particular situation.[13] In contrast to the continuous movement of the Kommandos, the headquarters and staff of each Einsatzgruppe remained relatively stationary, although this, too, changed as the battle lines advanced eastward.

Soon after an area had been captured by the German army, an Einsatzkommando, or Sonderkommando, or a detachment from one of these, would arrive and might then split up into Teilkommandos. Each Teilkommando would be assigned a task and would proceed to carry it out. Upon completion of this task, a report would usually be prepared by the leader of this smaller group, and the report would then be sent directly to the Teilkommando leader. His report would be summarized by the leader or an assistant and then sent to the Einsatzkommando or Sonderkommando leader.[14] The Kommando staff was generally small, consisting of the Kommando leader and his deputy, with several police and SD officers.[15] The various reports from the subunits sent to the Kommando staff dealt with all the little details of the operations carried out. The reports reached the Kommando leader by courier or by radio, depending upon whether the latter was available.[16] They were then discussed, collated, and drafted into more comprehensive reports by members of the Kommando staff, each of whom was concerned with a certain aspect of the activities.[17]

The reports that had been prepared by the Kommando leader and his staff were then passed on to the Einsatzgruppe headquarters. The staff of each Einsatzgruppe paralleled the membership and functions of the personnel at the Kommando level. In other words, they, too, had officials dealing with administrative, intelligence, and police assignments as designated by the representative RSHA Offices.[18] The reports reached the Einsatzgruppe staff fairly regularly. In Einsatzgruppe D, for instance, short radio reports were sent twice a month, on the first and the fifteenth. Executions were at first called "evacuations"; later they were simply called executions.[19] More extensive reports were written down and sent by messenger. At the Einsatzgruppe headquarters the reports received were analyzed by the officials assigned to deal with them and drafts were done. These were further arranged into a more complete state. In the headquarters of Einsatzgruppe D, Deputy Chief Willy Seibert was responsible for dealing with the incoming reports and for laying down his directives and those of his leader, Otto Ohlendorf, to the Kommando leaders as to what and how matters were to be treated in their reports. Seibert was particularly, although not exclusively, concerned with the various SD reports that came in about the attitude and morale of the local population. In the headquarters of Einsatzgruppe C the major official in charge of preparing the statistics concerning executions was Chief of Staff Walter Hoffmann. The SD leader in Einsatzgruppe C was Karl Hennicke, and the SD leader in Einsatzgruppe A was Karl Tschierschky. In Einsatzgruppe B this task was done mainly by both the leader of Einsatzgruppe B, Arthur Nebe, and the chief of Office IV on the staff, Ernst Ehlers. The Einsatzgruppen leaders themselves also worked on the reports, especially the more important drafts. The reports were signed by the Einsatzgruppe leader or his deputy and were then ready to be passed on to Berlin.[20]

Thus the reports to this point were the result of several steps in a series in which a number of people—the men carrying out the operations, their leaders, various officials in the Kommandos, and those on the staff of the Einsatzgruppen headquarters—all came to bear on the content of the reports. The Kommando leaders and ultimately the Einsatzgruppen leaders exercised control over the reports, either by writing, reading, editing, approving, or signing them before forwarding them to Berlin. Lacking many examples of reports at this stage, it is hard to determine how much editing of the reports took place. It is probable, considering their generally considerable length in the final reports, that many of the SD reports were not substantially altered. On the other hand, the reports on the operations of the Security Police may have undergone pruning down to essentials. As one Kommando leader testified, if everything concerning these actions had been retained, he would have been at a loss to "know what Berlin would have done with all these detailed reports."[21]

The reports were sent to Berlin in three ways: by radio, teletype, and courier.[22] Radio and teletype were used for short reports. It was far too lengthy and costly a process to send long reports by teletype. These shorter reports, therefore, contained either very important information that had to be sent quickly, or information on routine matters such as the changes of location and transfers.[23] At the staff headquarters of Einsatzgruppe D radio reports were sent weekly or biweekly and were kept strictly secret. Only the radio personnel were allowed into the radio station. Otto Ohlendorf or his deputy, Willy Seibert, dictated the messages directly to the head telegraphist, Willy Fritsch. After the report had been sent in this manner, Heinz Schubert, Ohlendorf's adjutant, received it for filing. The lengthier, more detailed written reports were sent to Berlin by courier approximately every month.[24] Again, in spite of a lack of substantial examples of reports from this stage, we do have some indication as to the kind of detail that Einsatzgruppe D included in its reports. According to Schubert, these reports gave information on the sites of executions, the course of the operations, losses, numbers of destroyed places, numbers killed, arrest of agents, and details of their interrogation, as well as reports on the civilian population. In sum, the very substance of the final reports.[25]

The Einsatzkommandos not only sent reports via their respective Einsatzgruppe staffs but also sent reports directly to the RSHA.[26] This was done to simplify the technical problems of signal communications that combined with the enormous distances between the front and Berlin, made it often easier to send the reports directly. According to one statement, another reason existed for this as well. In the Ostland, an area that embraced Estonia, Latvia, Lithuania, and part of White Russia, the heterogeneous mix of peoples living there resulted in quite different problems in each of these previously independent countries. The commandants of the Sipo and SD (BdS and KdS—see below) felt it impossible to attempt to work all the diverging information from these areas into one comprehensive report and to do this with a deadline in mind. As a consequence, many reports bypassed the usual channels and went straight to Berlin.[27]

The RSHA was not the only recipient of reports from the Einsatzgruppen and the Kommandos. The agreements reached with the army in April and May 1941 concerning the terms of the Einsatzgruppen operations in the eastern zone had allowed for a close cooperation between the Einsatzgruppen and the army.[28] The Kommandos were the only nonmilitary personnel allowed into the army's area of operations. The Kommandos had a liaison officer (Verbindungsführer) who transmitted and received reports and orders from the army commander in their area, especially via the IC section of the army. There was a continuous exchange of information between army and Einsatzgruppen units.[29] In fact, most of the very few surviving examples of earlier reports by Einsatzgruppen or Kommandos were reports sent to army units throughout the east.[30] In this way the army personnel within whose territory the Einsatzgruppen were operating were certainly kept informed as to the latter's activities. An exchange of reports also took place between liaison officers and the offices of the Higher SS and Police Leaders.[31] The Higher SS and Police Leaders were Himmler's personal representatives in the occupied areas, and technically they outranked the Einsatzgruppen leaders. Reports from the Higher SS and Police Leaders appeared occasionally in the final Operational Situation Reports and were usually connected with very large-scale massacres.

Having traced how the reports reached the RSHA in Berlin, it remains now to discover what happened to them at this point and to see how and by whom the final reports were prepared. The organization of the reports took place in Group IV A 1 of Office IV of the RSHA, which was the headquarters of the Gestapo.[32] The head of the Gestapo was Heinrich Müller. Born in Munich on 4 April 1900, Müller had been a detective in the Munich Police from 1919 on, and he had served as an aircraft pilot during World War I. Despite very serious criticism of his attitude in party circles, he was ambitious and ruthless enough to rise to become head of the Secret Police.[33] Müller was an expert on communism.[34] Müller played a leading role in the creation of the reports. At the beginning especially, Müller worked on the material from the Einsatzgruppen, and the early reports were either written by him, or were written "in accordance with his precise orders."[35]

The chief of Group IV A 1 in 1941 was the expert on communism, Joseph Vogt, and his deputy from October 1941 until mid-1942 was Kurt Lindow. Lindow's career was typical of many RSHA bureaucrats. He was born on 16 February 1903 in Berlin. After studying commercial science and law and then becoming a business apprentice from 1922 to 1928, Lindow joined the Criminal Police in April 1928. During the next ten years Lindow held various posts within the Criminal Police and in 1938 was transferred to the Secret State Police. Here he worked in the Protective Custody subdepartment from 1938 to 1940. He then worked in Group IV E 1 (counterintelligence) as head of this section. After serving as Vogt's deputy in Group IV A 1, in 1942 Lindow replaced Vogt as leader. Lindow held this position until the middle of 1944. He then worked in Office I of the RSHA.[36]

While in Group IV A 1 Lindow read the reports sent by the Einsatz-gruppen and passed them on to Dr. Günther Knobloch, the man who, with Rudolf Fumy, was responsible for consolidating the incoming reports. Knobloch, a Criminal Police inspector, worked in the RSHA from 2 August 1941 until the end of the war. Fumy, like Heinrich Müller, was born in 1900, and also like Müller, began his career in the Munich Police headquarters. At the beginning of the Russian campaign, Fumy found himself working in Group IV A 1. Along with Knobloch he worked on the reports until the end of 1944. Knobloch analyzed the reports and bracketed in red the "most interesting parts." The reports were structured according to certain topics and points of view that had been determined by Müller. Müller would be presented with the typed stencils of the reports by ten o'clock each morning. He would often make alterations, marking by hand on the stencils. In this way Müller exercised control over the content and format of the final reports. They were then corrected, and Lindow had them mimeographed and distributed to those persons and agencies who were supposed to receive copies. Knobloch also worked on the drawing up of the summary reports, the Activity and Situation Reports, which were derived from the daily Operational Situation Reports.[37]

The staff of Group IV A 1 consisted of fifty officials and employees, including about twenty female typists. This number had aparently decreased by the end of 1941 to about twenty-five to thirty employees. This decrease was due in part to the shortage of manpower in the eastern areas and necessitated the use of four or five volunteer workers who came out of retirement. This lack of sufficient numbers of staff workers led to problems in coping with the work of the department.[38]

The reception of the reports in Berlin during the first five months had included the services of the office of the Operational Signal Officer (Einsatznachrichtenführer), which was part of Group II D 2 in the RSHA. A top secret decree (II Hb No. II II/41) dated 3 July 1941 had established this practice.[39] In this earlier procedure a separate report of the day (Tagesbericht) had been issued concerning locations and lines of communications of the Kommandos. As of 26 October 1941 this method was dispensed with, and these duties were taken over by Group IV A 1 itself. The information about locations was now published in the Operational Situation Reports as a separate section.[40] The order respecting this October 26 change did so as follows:

> Beginning that day, the tasks hitherto performed by the Operational Signal Officer of the Reich Main Security Office will additionally be attended to by the Kommandostab existing at Office IV in the Main Office Building, Prinz-Albrecht-Strasse 8, room 320, telephone number: Postal 54, internal 318. Thus the Kommandostab will be responsible both for the technical and material evaluation

of the reports of the Einsatzgruppen and Einsatzkommandos employed in Operation Barbarossa.

Beginning that day all reports and communications from the Einsatzgruppe A to D, after having been registered and marked according to subject, are to be transmitted by the main office (special mail center) without delay to the Kommandostab via Office Chief IV; reports during the night to be submitted the next day at the beginning of office work.[41]

Therefore the Group IV A 1 under Lindow in October 1941 became known as the command staff or Kommandostab. It seems that Heydrich had originally wanted a general staff under his leadership to deal with the operations of the Einsatzgruppen. This did not come about because of opposition within the RSHA Office leaders. Consequently, the Kommandostab did not assume total organizational powers, but as one official described it, "merely had the task of rendering reports."[42]

The process of selection and analysis of the material in the RSHA was a continuation of the editing methods used earlier. In Berlin it became the turn of top RSHA officials to try and put some order into the incoming information. The process of compiling the reports described above lasted for the time covered by the Operational Situation Reports. In May 1942 the method of evaluating and assembling changed. The Kommandostab thereafter spread the sorting out and analysis of the reports among representatives from all the Offices of the RSHA.[43] This change did not prevent Office IV from retaining editorial supervision of the reports.[44] The following description by Friedrich Rang, chief of Group IV D, presents an insight into the workings of the Kommandostab:

> The representatives of the Offices brought with them partial reports of the Einsatzgruppen which were read and discussed in the conferences. Prior to the conference of the Kommandostab, these partial reports were condensed by the competent experts of the Offices concerned, certified by the Office Chiefs, and only then submitted to the Kommandostab. Alterations in the partial reports were made by the Kommandostab if necessary. The partial reports were then concentrated into a voluminous report, called "Situation Report" during the conference of the Kommandostab. In some Offices, (for example) Office IV, a partial report had to be returned to the Office Chief in the case that alterations had been made, and the Office Chief had to confirm the alterations. It was the task of the Kommandostab to obtain uniform leadership in the east by means of its reports.[45]

Along with this change of method came a change of name. The reports were now called Reports from the Occupied Eastern Territories. These new reports were issued by the Kommandostab from 1 May 1942 to 21 May 1943. It will be seen later that these reports differed in more than name from the Operational Situation Reports.

4

General Features of the Operational Situation Reports

The Operational Situation Reports are to be the major focus of this study. While it is perhaps incorrect to speak of a "typical" Operational Situation Report since some differences existed among the reports, in the majority of these 195 reports certain general features can be distinguished. It will be useful therefore to examine some of these general features.

Structurally the Operational Situation Reports had two basic formats, the first of which lasted roughly from the period of the second to the 124th report, and the second of which included all the reports from Report 125 until the end of the series. The overall sectional organization of the reports in each of these two periods consisted of the following headings:

Reports 2–126: 1. Political Overview (Politische Übersicht)
2. Reports of the Einsatzgruppen and Kommandos (Meldungen der Einsatzgruppen und Kommandos)
3. Military Operations (Militärische Ereignisse)
4. Distribution List (Verteiler)

Reports 125–195: 1. Locations and Lines of Communication (Standorte und Nachrichtenverbindungen)
2. Reports of the Einsatzgruppen and Kommandos
3. Reich and Occupied Territories (Reich und besetzte Gebiete)

Let us consider each of the sections in the above outline. First, it should be noted that the general format of the reports evolved quite soon after their inception. The first report was published on 23 June 1941 and was signed by Heinrich Müller.[1] The first page bore the title "Sammelmeldung UdSSR No. 1" (Collective Report USSR) and had as its top left hand corner heading, (Office) IV A 1. The second report used the thereafter permanent title of Operational Situation Report (Ereignismeldung UdSSR). The second and third reports also included "Reichssicherheitshauptamt" in the left side heading, a practice that was abandoned in Operational Situation Report 4, when Heydrich's official title, Der Chef de Sicherheitspolizei und des SD, appeared for the first time. This heading was found in every subsequent report.[2] That the heading "Reichssicherheitshauptamt" was employed in the second and third reports followed the practice in the RSHA of using this heading for internal correspondence.[3] It is probable that the status of the just started system of Einsatzgruppen reports was still uncertain and that a decision was taken by Heydrich to use the heading bearing his title, possibly anticipating the distribution of the reports beyond the RSHA. The next report, Operational Situation Report 5, was the first to include below Heydrich's title the complete Office and file number as follows: (Office) AMT IV-IV A 1-B NR. 1 B/41 gRs. Also appearing on the top right hand corner of each report was the place of origin of the report, Berlin, followed by the date. Then followed the number of copies made of the report and the number of the report within this overall set.[4] In the surviving set of reports found after the war every report except Operational Situation Reports 1, 4, and 37, was stamped Geheime Reichssache[5] on the first page. The title "Ereignismeldung UdSSR" followed, with the appropriate number. The title page of each report had a narrow border on all four sides.

As the outline presented above indicates, the section marked Political Overview was found at the beginning of the reports from Report 2 until Report 126.[6] It included three subheadings, divided geographically: A. Im Reich, referred to Germany or territories now incorporated into Germany; B. Im Generalgouvernement, referred to that area of Poland conquered in 1939 but not incorporated into the Reich; and Übrige besetzte Gebiete (Remaining Occupied Territories). The latter section included reports from France, Belgium, Lower Styria, Luxembourg, Carinthia, Bulgaria, Croatia, Czechoslovakia, Yugoslavia, Rumania, Greece, the Scandinavian countries, and other areas. The reports under these three subsections were either police reports from various State Police or Security Police and SD officials located throughout these areas. Occasionally reports came from Higher SS or Police Leaders. These reports also often included more general situation reports dealing with specific areas. In particular the reports from the Generalgouvernement were frequently of comparable length to the SD reports of the Einsatzgruppen. They were likely included in the Einsatzgruppen reports since they were concerned with regions, which early in the Russian campaign, had been traversed by the Einsatzgruppen. The police reports were of interest to the Einsatzgruppen as the reports often dealt with activities similar to those being undertaken by the Kommandos.[7]

The next section in the reports was headed Reports of the Einsatzgruppen and Kommandos. In the sixth and seventh reports a section, Reports of the Einsatzkommandos, anticipated the use of this heading, and in the eighth report the first full sectional heading appeared. It is this section, which was retained for the entire series of the remaining reports, that will be the prime focus of this study for it was in this part that the killings by each Einsatzgruppe were described in depth. Here the horror of the Einsatzgruppen atrocities was laid bare. The manner in which the killing operations were presented will be analyzed in detail in the following chapters.

While the mass killings remain the center of our attention, it must be recognized that this part of the reports also dealt with a wide range of descriptive and analytical information on many topics gathered by the Security Police and the SD. Included among them were general situation reports on economic matters, agriculture, education, the churches in the east, the attitude, mood, and political aspirations of the different ethnic groups throughout the conquered regions, cultural traditions, propaganda, and the fight against partisans. This material appeared under headings typical of SD reports. These matters in question were examined singly in depth or comprehensively with other subjects with reference to a specific city or region. As stated in the introduction, since the killings are the primary concern here, our examination of the various SD reports just cited will be limited mainly to what light they shed on the killings. (Appendix B provides a summary by subject of these reports and their location in the Operational Situation Reports.)

The third main section reported on the latest developments in the military situation. It was not until Operational Situation Report 8 that the heading Military Actions (Militärische Aktionen), under which military news had been filed to that point, was changed permanently to Military Operations. The military reports were much briefer than the other types of reports. They provided succinct information on the current operations in the various areas on the eastern front, including Finland, the Balkans, and Greece. The reports reflected the vicissitudes of the German advance—the progress of the army groups, what battles were taking place, what areas and cities had been reached, the directions in which the armies were headed, and other essentials. With a few exceptions[8] the Military Operations heading appeared in Reports 8 to 121. In a number of reports the heading appeared, but no reports were included.[9] In Report 121 a warning was included that forbade the use of the material from the military reports as a basis for drawing up maps. Whether or not military information continued to reach the RSHA as it had to this point, none of the subsequent reports included this military section.

The final section of the reports during the first period was the distribution list. This was a list of those RSHA offices and agencies of the party, the government, and the military that received copies of the reports. In the surviving set of reports only reports 1 to 49 and reports 51, 52, 53, and 128 have distribution lists included. The latter report is the last report containing such a list. Fifty-five copies were made. For subsequent reports in the series only the number of copies made indicates the extent of the distribution list. Since further lists are lacking, it is uncertain which additional groups or individuals were sent copies.

It is clear that the number of copies of the reports increased with time. The first report was only six pages long, and copies were sent to Himmler, Heydrich, and "all offices of the RSHA." Another early report, Operational Situation Report 9, had twenty-five copies, and in addition to the previously mentioned recipients, the list now included some subsections of Office IV, with reserve copies being kept at Office IV A 1.

During the month of July 1941 the number of copies increased steadily by an expansion of the number of subsections of the RSHA Groups who received the reports. By August, Operational Situation Report 40 had forty-five copies issued. The distribution list now included Himmler, Heydrich, the chief of the Order Police, Daluege, Oberstleutnant Tippelskirch (OKW Führungsstab), Einsatz Communication Officer Paeffgen, Polizei-Rat Pommerening, as well as all RSHA Office chiefs, plus subsections of Offices II, III, IV, and VI. Again extra copies were kept on file. The list for Operational Situation Report 128 included, in addition to the various RSHA offices and officials, the four Higher SS and Police Leaders in the occupied eastern territories, Inspectors Damzog, Biermann, and Canaris, Generalgouvernement Security Police and SD Commander Schöngarth, and Bormann in the party Chancellery. (See Appendix D.) If one skips ahead to the last report, Operational Situation Report 195, dated 24 April 1942, one sees that by this time the number of copies had increased to seventy-five.

There exists some evidence that indicates that copies of both the Operational Situation Reports and the Activity and Situation Reports were sent to more people than those included in the distribution lists. Although not specifically included in the lists, it would seem that all the Einsatzgruppen leaders received copies of the Operational Situation Reports. According to Günther Knobloch, who was uncertain whether or not copies were sent to the Einsatzkommandos, it was common practice for Heydrich to change the distribution list "as the mood took him." In particular the name of Wilhelm Canaris, head of the Abwehr, the military intelligence service, was often dropped and then included again.[10]

From the available evidence we can conclude that the surviving official distribution lists did not fully reflect the number of actual recipients of the reports or the people who became aware of them. One single copy of a report could be examined, analyzed, criticized, and summarized by a number of people, and as a result of the reports themselves, as opposed to other sources, the murderous nature of the Einsatzgruppen's activities was common knowledge among many people in army, government, and party circles.[11]

In the previous chapter we noted the change that took place concerning the way in which the locations of the Einsatzgruppen and Kommandos were reported. The first report to reflect this difference was Report 125. It was this report that initiated the new organization of the reports by replacing the Political Overview section with the heading, "Locations and Lines of Communication."[12] We may now examine more closely the evolution of this section and its essential features.

Soon after the invasion of Russia, Heydrich was angered when he discovered that RSHA officials were uncertain as to the whereabouts of the Einsatzgruppen and their Kommandos and that communication with them and the RSHA was very disorganized. A special information center within Office II D was set up to gather incoming reports and to pass them on to those officials responsible for their editing. This information center, which was placed under the leadership of Theodor Paeffgen, was also in charge of keeping track of the exact position of the Einsatzgruppen and their Kommandos. Paeffgen was known as the Einsatznachrichtenführer. The Einsatzgruppen radio reports were received at the information center, and it was part of the center's job to distribute copies of the compiled reports to the appropriate departments. Not long after the establishment of this information center, Paeffgen was informed that a similar service as was performed by his group existed already in Office IV. As a result, radio reports concerning locations and communications were sent to Paeffgen's office, while others concerning the activities of the Einsatzgruppen were forwarded to Office IV A 1.[13]

Paeffgen's department monitored closely the movements of the Einsatzgruppen and passed on this information. In the first 124 reports the locations of the Einsatzgruppen were incorporated into the reports of each Einsatzgruppe. As of 26 October 1941 Paeffgen's department was disbanded. Starting with Operational Situation Report 125, all of the remaining reports contained the separate Locations and Lines of Communications heading, which formed the first section of the reports. The next report (Operational Situation Report 126) contained the first complete list under this heading. The new section included each Einsatzgruppe, Einsatzkommando, and Sonderkommando, with the names of their leaders and their current locations. Much of the time the Sonderkommandos and Einsatzkommandos were split into smaller operating units, and the locations of these units were included with the name of each Kommando. Also mentioned, both before and after the use of the separate Locations and Lines of Communications heading, were the intended destinations of those units that were in transit at the time of a particular report. If there was no change in the locations of the Kommandos through several consecutive reports, the list was omitted, and it was simply stated that they had remained unchanged from the previous report where the list was included.[14]

The degree to which the reports kept track of the shifting positions of the Kommandos was underlined in a statement by Willy Litzenberg. Litzenberg was the head of subsection IV A 1b. While visiting Regierungskriminalrat Joseph Vogt, the head of RSHA Group IV A 1, Litzenberg noticed a map of Russia on which the German front-line was marked with little flags. Litzenberg was surprised that this front-line was traced more accurately than was the case by using information from regular military reports. Vogt informed him that it was on the basis of the reports from the Einsatzgruppen that the configuration of the front-line had been determined.[15]

The names and locations of the headquarters of the Higher SS and Police Leaders were also included in the list. The Higher SS and Police Leaders had been appointed by Himmler and were responsible to him directly and not to the RSHA. As Himmler's representatives it was their task to coordinate SS/Police integration and provide local political direction for them both. In practice the Higher SS and Police Leaders in the east were independent of both the civil administration and the Einsatzgruppen leaders. The names of the Higher SS and Police Leaders appeared above those of the Einsatzgruppen and Kommando leaders in the Location and Communication lists. They had the power to make use of any of the available police forces of the SS should the need arise. Their headquarters were located separately from those of Einsatzgruppen staff.[16]

Some reports listed as well the commanders of the Security Police and SD for certain districts with their locations. This list of commanders was limited to the areas of Einsatzgruppen A and C.[17] These commanders were appointed after the civil administration had been set up in a given area. This was done by turning the Kommando into a static territorial Security Police and SD organization. They were subordinate to the RSHA, but on certain occasions might be utilized by the Higher SS and Police Leaders, in which case orders were received from the latter, independently of the RSHA.[18]

The Locations and Communication lists provide us with a steady account of the movement of the Einsatzgruppen. Since the Einsatzkommandos followed closely behind the army, their movements tell us the range of operations of each Kommando during a specific time period, and in conjunction with the short military reports included in the reports, chronicle clearly the rise of the German offensive. Therefore one can easily trace the shifting of the main headquarters of each of the four Einsatzgruppen. Beginning, for example, with Operational Situation Report 19, which announced the final designation of each of the Einsatzgruppen, the main headquarters of the Einsatzgruppen were indicated as follows: Einsatzgruppe A: Riga, Nowoslje, Pesje, Kikerino, and Krasnogwardeisk;[19] Einsatzgruppe B: Minsk, Borisov, Orscha, and Smolensk;[20] Einsatzgruppe C: Rovno, Shitomir, Novo-Ukrainka, and Kiev;[21] Einsatzgruppe D: Piatra, Ananjew, Nikolajew, and Simferopol.[22]

The methods of communication used by the Einsatzgruppen and their Kommandos were also part of the locations list. The agreement between the Einsatzgruppen and the army stated that the Einsatzgruppen would share the communications network of the rear headquarters of the Field Army.[23] On the right side, opposite the Einsatzkommando number, the army field post office numbers and lines of radio and teletype communications of each Kommando appeared in the reports. Some Kommandos could be reached directly by radio or teletype while others could be reached only by courier or a combination of methods. It was usual for the Sonderkommandos and Einsatzkommandos to share the same army field post number in their area.

Following the Locations and Communication information, the already discussed section containing the reports of the Einsatzgruppen and Kommandos continued to form the central core of the reports. Starting in Operational Situation Report 149, the reports had as the final section the heading, "Reich and Occupied Territories." This was a carry-over from the earlier Political Overview section. Its appearance was sporadic throughout the remaining reports[24] and was limited to the kind of information found in the earlier section.

To conclude this discussion of the general features of the reports, a final observation about the distribution lists is of interest. In Operational Situation Report 18, the distribution list contained for the first time the name of Theodor Paeffgen,[25] the man responsible for keeping track of the movement of the Kommandos. When we compare the copy number for a particular report with the corresponding numerical listing of that copy in the distribution list of the report, it appears that many of the copies discovered after the war were those sent to Paeffgen himself. Thus it is to Paeffgen that we probably owe our knowledge of the reports. He, or his subordinates, obviously neglected to destroy the copies that were sent to him.[26]

5

The Killing Operations: Methods of Presentation

We now come to the actual killing operations of the Einsatzgruppen. The mass shooting of the Jews marked the first stage in the attempt to exterminate the Jews of Europe. This killing began immediately after the German attack on the Soviet Union. The Einsatzgruppen operations were supplemented by the gas chambers in the killing centers in Poland. The larger program of gassing European Jews was well underway in these centers by the middle of 1942.[1] The destruction of the Jews was grounded on a complex of Nazi racial ideological beliefs that, in turn, owed their origins to a variety of deeply rooted, anti-Semitic, philosophical, pseudo-scientific, and popular attitudes.[2] The physical destruction of the Jews inaugurated by the Einsatzgruppen represented a last radical step in the process of dealing with the so-called "Jewish Problem" that confronted Hitler upon his seizure of power in 1933. There is a great amount of controversy among historians as to precisely when a decision was made to kill the Jews.[3] What is more generally agreed upon is the importance of anti-Semitism to the National Socialist program and to Hitler's own thinking.[4] As one historian has stated, while the destruction of the Jews was inherent in the ideological theories underpinning Nazi thought, it was inherent "as a logical conclusion, not as a practical plan."[5] Consequently, even if, as a logical outgrowth of its ideology, the leaders of the Third Reich had wanted to destroy the Jews physically right from the beginning, in practical terms such a plan was impossible during the 1930s.

Most historians have come to see the persecution of the Jews as a process that developed slowly, with the Nazi leadership almost feeling its way along. The German Jews were subjected to laws that gradually deprived them of their property, their professions, their rights as citizens. The purpose of this legislation was to isolate the Jews and to force them to leave Germany. When the war broke out in September 1939, this concept had radicalized. Now the aim was to expel the Jews from German territory. The sites considered for such an expulsion included the Nisko region of Poland and Madagascar.[6] Although thousands of Jews were eventually deported to the

Nisko region, the continuation of the war prevented the Madagascar plan
from being realized. The essential thrust of German policy toward the Jews
until 1941 was thus one of *removal*—the expulsion of Jews from the
territory of the Reich proper. The decision to attack the Soviet Union
brought with it a fundamental shift in this attitude. With the acquisition of
the Soviet territories, the Germans realized they would now be faced with
having several million more Jews on their hands. Again, while one cannot
be absolutely certain, the available evidence seems to indicate that sometime
in the spring of 1941, in the context of preparations for the imminent
attack, the decision was taken to destroy the Jews in the Soviet territories.[7]

It was the Einsatzgruppen that began this horrific wholesale murder; their
Operational Situation Reports recorded their deeds. In a number of respects
these reports were, and remain to this day, unique documents. Within their
pages was presented an enormous amount of information concerning the
implementation of mass murder, a process without parallel in history. Mass
slaughter of civilian populations has, of course, been a frequent occurrence
throughout history, but no other set of documents has survived that
provides such a plentiful and meticulous description of mass killing while
it actually happened. Even later stages of the annihilation of the Jews, when
the process had become both more complex and systematic and when a
greater number of victims were involved, did not yield documents that
survived and that offer to a comparable degree the same relentless sense of
the day-to-day description of genocide. This ongoing account forms the
most important part of the Operational Situation Reports. While sections
dealing with other matters usually made up a proportionally greater part of
the text, there is no question that the Kommandos's listing of their killing
operations is the most historically significant and compelling feature of the
reports. In this chapter and the ones to follow, the manner in which the
killings were dealt with will be discussed.

The vast majority of the Operational Situation Reports contained
information about the killing operations. The section of the reports called
Reports of the Einsatzgruppen and Kommandos contained the details of
these operations. Within this section each Einsatzgruppe was listed in
alphabetical order, followed by the current location of its headquarters.
Not every report included reports from all four Einsatzgruppen. When an
Einsatzgruppe was not included, it was simply stated that no reports were
forthcoming.[8] The specifics of the shootings and related actions appeared
under a variety of separate headings such as Executions, Actions
(Aktionen), Special Actions, Security Police Activities, Security Police
Measures, Policework, Liquidations, Arrests and Liquidations, Executive
Activities, Executive Measures, Executions and Other Measures, Actions
Against Functionaries, Agents, Saboteurs and Jews, Actions Against Jews,
Measures Against Criminals and Plunderers, List Concerning the

Liquidations (Aufstellung über die Liquidierungen), Police Matters, Security Police Observations and Measures, State of Security Policework, and Shootings. These captions served as headings either to separate sections or were subheadings as part of more comprehensive reports that involved other types of information. In addition, killings were ubiquitous throughout the reports of antipartisan operations, which was often the setting for killing Jews.

An examination of the reports found in the sections just cited soon reveals that there was no uniform methodology in the way the killings were presented. Just as discussion of the killings materialized under a variety of headings, several methods were followed by the Security Police throughout the entire series and were used in combination within individual reports. We will begin our analysis by considering the manner of presentation from two perspectives: that of the victims, and that of the Einsatzgruppen themselves. With regard to identifying groups or categories of people killed, the manner of description may be summarized in the following ways:

1. The exact number of victims was mentioned in the course of a report. This method listed a specific group individually, Jews, Gypsies, communists, and so on, and gave a precise number of persons killed. This method was the most prevalent one throughout the reports. Almost all reports which listed liquidations have examples of this type of description. Jews were the primary target of the Einsatzgruppen. They were almost always listed separately as a group in the Einsatzgruppen tabulations. (This is the case even in the reports on antipartisan operations found in the Reports from the Occupied Eastern Territories.)

2. The number of victims of a specific group was listed as an approximate or rounded off number. For example, Operational Situation Report 143 mentioned fifteen thousand Jews were killed in Rovno on 6 and 7 November 1941.[9] This method indicates that the exact number was either not known by the Einsatzkommando, or because of the circumstances of the execution operations, it was not possible or desirable to undertake an exact count.

3. The number of persons killed was not mentioned either exactly or approximately. For example, many reports mentioned that an area was "free of Jews" or that a whole village was liquidated, without giving figures. Also, some reports stated that "a number" or "a handful" of Jews were killed, without being more exact. These methods are to be distinguished from the previous one in that here the number is unknown, and we are not really able to form an approximate total figure from what is described.[10]

4. Specific groups or types of victims were not singled out numerically but were mentioned as being included or combined with other groups or categories of victims. For example, Operational Situation Report 184 mentioned that south of Karasubasar eight hundred Gypsies and insane people were "rendered harmless." The report was not more specific as to how many persons in each of these categories were killed.[11]

5. A total number of persons killed was given and this number was then broken down as to category of victim. For example, Operational Situation Report 190 stated that in the second half of March 1942, Einsatzgruppe D killed 1,501 people, and that this number included 588 Jews, 405 communists, 247 partisans, and 261 asocial people including Gypsies.[12] This method differs from that of point 1 above only in the fact that a total was given, which was further broken down. These two methods were by far the most frequently used in describing the killings.

6. Some reports gave imprecise or no information concerning victims other than the number and the location of the executions or other limited data. A report by Einsatzgruppe A described screening operations in Tosno on 20 October 1941. During the period from October 15 to 23, 156 persons were shot. The report did not inform as to what category these 156 persons belonged. The numbers cited in this fashion, therefore, might have included several types of victims.[13]

The above six categories indicate that there were essentially two points of reference with regard to the victims: who they were—they were either known or unknown as a group (points 1, 2, 3, 4, 5, 6); and how many there were—this was known exactly or approximately (points 1, 2, 4, 5, 6) or was not known (point 3). The categories also indicate a measure of inconsistency of detail in the reports concerning the victims in spite of the reasonably high level of precision in some respects.

Who were the victims of the Einsatzgruppen killing machinery, and how were they characterized in the Operational Situation Reports? A by no means complete list of victims, as characterized in the reports, would include the following: Jews,[14] intellectual Jews,[15] Jewish activists,[16] wandering Jews,[17] rebellious Jews,[18] partisans,[19] Gypsies,[20] communist party members and functionaries,[21] politruks,[22] commissars,[23] NKWD agents,[24] Asiatics,[25] Krimtchaks,[26] guerrillas,[27] Bolshevists,[28] hostages,[29] prisoners of war,[30] saboteurs,[31] agitators or political agitators,[32] public nuisances (Volksschädlinge),[33] neglected juveniles (Verwahrloste Jugendliche),[34] unreliable elements,[35] racially inferior elements or inferior elements,[36] hostile elements,[37] asocials or asocial elements,[38] suspicious elements,[39] undesirable elements,[40] criminals or criminal elements,[41] politically suspicious persons,[42] terrorists,[43] delinquents,[44] murderers,[45] snipers,[46] plunderers,[47] spreaders of propaganda,[48] mentally inferior persons or mental patients,[49] spies,[50] informers,[51] instigators,[52] accomplices,[53] forgers,[54] civilians,[55] pests (Schädlinge),[56] collective farm leaders,[57] and arsonists.[58] This list contains two types of victims: victims, such as Jews, Gypsies, and communist functionaries, who, a priori, were designated as victims and who were killed simply because the decision had been taken to kill them; and others, whose designation carried implicitly the "reason" for their killing—saboteurs, plunderers, agitators, and so on. The latter category included many types of victims, often not clearly defined in the reports.[59]

Shifting attention from the description of the victims to that of the perpetrators, the Einsatzgruppen and Kommandos themselves, again an inconsistency of presentation may be seen. The following methods may be distinguished:[60]

1. Some reports indicated that an Einsatzgruppe had killed a number of people in a city or area, but no Einsatzkommando or Sonderkommando of that Einsatzgruppe was specified as having carried out the operation.

2. Some reports mentioned that a particular Einsatzkommando or Sonder-kommando had carried out the killing action.

3. Some reports gave an exact date or time period of operations carried out by an Einsatzkommando, including the total number of victims, with or without the location where these events took place.

4. The number of persons killed over a lengthy period of time by an Einsatzkommando or an entire Einsatzgruppe was given in some reports.

5. A report sometimes included mention of an Einsatzkommando's operations and included those who acted as collaborators (Ukrainians, Latvians, Lithuanians, Wehrmacht, Waffen SS, other police units).

6. Some reports did not mention any collaboration with an Einsatzkommando, but on closer examination, it becomes evident that such collaboration likely did occur. Examples of this were found in reports where day to day workings of a particular Kommando indicated help from auxiliary units on one day, and then on the next day they were not mentioned. It was probable that the Kommandos were assisted on other days as well. In fact evidence would suggest that the true extent of collaboration with the Einsatzgruppen by local groups was not fully documented in the reports.[61]

The reports were thus marked by variations in the way the killings were presented concerning both victims and Kommandos who carried out the killings. This rather loose presentation was also reflected in statements about the time when events were said to have occurred. Events were either dated exactly, or not at all, or were said to have happened within some time period. There was a time lapse between the events and their appearance in the reports. At first, in the earliest reports, this gap was very short. Operational Situation Report 11, dated 3 July 1941, disclosed events of the previous as well as the same day.[62] In a report issued eight days later the gap had widened to more than a week.[63] As time passed and the Kommandos moved further east, their operations expanded and intensified. The greater distances,[64] plus the ever-increasing amount of information sent to Berlin, made even greater the time lapse between the events and the final reports. Both these factors, the distances and problems of communication, and the sheer bulk of the incoming reports and the time it took to evaluate the material, made it difficult for the editors to keep pace with the activities of the Einsatzgruppen. Eventually one could expect about two weeks or more to have passed before reading about an operation in the reports.

Yet even this was not always the case. The time difference could be even greater. Operational Situation Report 154, dated 12 January 1942, described the killing of 402 people in Vilna on 12 December 1941, exactly one month before.[65] The separation in time was sometimes even greater than a month. Report 156, dated 16 January 1942, included events that took place on 18 October 1941, November 23 and 26, and 1–7 December 1941.[66] It still happened as well that more recent events appeared in the reports. Report 157, dated 19 January 1942, mentioned shootings carried out during the period from January 1–15, only four days earlier.[65] The landing of three Russian parachutists during the night of March 1–2 appeared in a report issued only two days later.[68]

In general then, there was no exact uniformity of pattern to the gap between events and their materialization in the final reports, nor was there any regularity in the time span covering events described in the reports themselves. This might vary from a short period in the early reports, or a period covering about a month,[69] or a period ranging over several months.[70] Other reports give little or no indication when operations took place.[71]

Descriptions of the four Einsatzgruppen's operations appeared reasonably concurrently with each other. In spite of the irregular arrival of reports from the Einsatzgruppen, a relatively chronological sequence of events unfolded in the reports. Yet this chronology, too, was not always strictly maintained. In Operational Situation Report 154, dated 12 January 1942, mentioned above, Einsatzgruppe A reported the killing in Vilna of 402 persons. These killings took place on 12 December 1941.[72] Operational Situation Report 156, also mentioned above, issued four days later on 16 January 1942, described the shooting in Riga of ten thousand six hundred Jews on 30 November 1941—almost two weeks before the Vilna killings described in the earlier report.

These observations concerning victims and Kommandos will be expanded upon later when specific differences in the way each of the Einsatzgruppe's killing operations were presented will be analyzed in more detail.[73]

So far our attention has been directed to what is actually in the reports concerning the killings. We might now mention what is *not* in the reports— any description of the killing operations themselves. The circumstances surrounding the actual executions are known to us only from other sources, from trial affidavits and evidence of Einsatzgruppen and Kommando leaders, from members of the execution squads, from eyewitness accounts of soldiers and civilians, from letters captured after the war, from Jews who survived these operations, and from photographs and films of the executions that have survived. In the Operational Situation Reports, however, there was no mention of the killings in any detailed, graphic way beyond the fact that the victims were shot, executed, liquidated, or any one of the many euphemisms for murder that were used in the reports. On the other hand, other surviving SS documents, for example, the diary of the SS Leader in Libau, although similarly succinct as the Einsatzgruppen reports, did include description of the weather during some of the mass shootings and the state of health of the executioners.[74] Beyond the mention that large pits were prepared,[75] nothing in the Einsatzgruppen reports indicated the mechanics of the shooting operations. Nothing disclosed the extreme horror that attended these mass killings. This was to be expected, of course. There was no place in SS reports for Jewish suffering. Any sympathy expressed in these reports, and there were a number of instances when this occurred, was directed to the executioners themselves. The reports spoke of the "difficult task" that had to be done.[76] On 18 October 1941 the killing of three hundred Jewish mental patients in Kiev by Einsatzkommando 5 "represented a particularly heavy mental burden for the members of Einsatzkommando 5."[77] Many of the reports mentioned the difficult problems of bad weather, poor roads, shortage of vehicles, petrol, and manpower faced by the Einsatzgruppen. All of these difficulties found their way into the reports, but of the suffering of those executed not one single word can be found. The depersonalization of the Jews, which began in Germany in 1933, did not terminate with their death and burial in the mass graves throughout the eastern territories. The depersonalization did not even end in the exhumation and burning of the corpses carried out under Paul Blobel's direction.[78] It ended in the anonymous lists of statistics that comprised the Operational Situation Reports.

The deaths of thousands upon thousands were tabulated, yet one rarely ever encounters the actual name of a victim, especially Jews.[79] To single out an individual Jew would have given undue importance to that person, would have raised him to a level above that of "Untermenschen." Thus the compilers of the reports were not only following the exigencies of succinct police reporting but also the dictates of National Socialist ideology.

Shooting was the usual method of execution. When any of the other substitute words for shooting were used in the reports, it can be assumed that shooting was meant. Death by hanging, if it was the method of execution used, was usually mentioned as such. Hanging was often carried out in public and was used as a terror tactic on the local population. An Einsatzgruppe B report, dated 9 October 1941, described one such hanging operation. Sonderkommando 7a had noticed that a great deal of partisan activity was taking place in the forests southeast of Demidov. All males in the area aged fifteen to fifty-five were put into a camp in Demidov to be screened by Sonderkommando 7a. This screening brought to light seventeen partisans and communists within this group. It was claimed that some of the local Kolchos farmers had supported the partisans, and thus four hundred of these farmers were assembled to witness the hanging of five partisans who had "murdered" fourteen German soldiers. The remaining captured partisans were shot by Sonderkommando 7a.[80]

The Einsatzgruppen killed people by another method—by using gas vans. This involved first leading people into the back of a sealed truck, then by turning on the engine, the exhaust fumes were piped directly to the compartment containing the people, who perished within minutes. According to eyewitnesses, the first use of gas vans for killing Jews took place in Poltava by Sonderkommando 4a in November 1941.[81] It is also known that Einsatzkommando 5 received a gas van shortly before Christmas 1941 and that the other Einsatzgruppen received vans after the New Year.[82] The gas vans were not specified in the Operational Situation Reports or the Reports from the Occupied Eastern Territories as a means of killing people. The numbers killed by this method were thus part of the summary figures for this period in the reports.[83] One must seek elsewhere beyond the reports for descriptions of their use.[84] (It is clear that at least fifteen thousand deported German and Austrian Jews were killed by gas vans and by shooting at Trostinez near Minsk between May and October 1942.)[85] The gas vans do not seem to have been used with the enthusiasm hoped for originally. They were introduced, apparently on Himmler's order, for the killing of women and children in "a more humane" fashion. In general the vans were not popular with the Einsatzgruppen. According to the testimony of Erich Naumann, the leader of Einsatzgruppe B, his Einsatzgruppe did not use the vans, but forwarded them on to Einsatzgruppen C and D.[86] The vans kept breaking down and were not always reliable. The poor state of the roads limited their use and the unloading of the corpses at the burial pits presented too great a mental strain on the members of the Einsatzkommandos.[87]

6
Examples of Killing Operations

We have already cited a number of killing operations carried out by the Kommandos. We will now look at further specific examples of such operations as found in the reports. Due to the restrictions of space, our inquiry will be limited to a few such examples, but from these some sense of the magnitude of these killings and the manner in which they unfolded will be obtained.

Upon arriving in an area the Kommandos of the Einsatzgruppen would often attempt to set up and direct pogroms against the Jews and communists. This was a deliberate tactic. It was also one that had been used before. A memorandum prepared by Section II 112 of the SD that was presented to Heydrich in January 1937, recommended violent attacks as a way of dealing with the Jews.

> The most effective means for depriving the Jews of their sense of security is the rage of the people manifesting itself in violent outbursts. Although this method is illegal it has a considerably long-lasting effect—so much so that even Jews from Palestine no longer dare to come to Germany. This reaction is readily understandable from a psychological standpoint, since the Jew has learned quite a lesson from the riots and pogroms of the last centuries and nothing frightens him more than a hostile atmosphere that could spontaneously turn against him at any moment.[1]

The pogroms in the east were carried out either by anti-Semitic members of the local population or by local police units organized for this purpose. It was the intention of the Germans to put the blame for these initial "self-cleansing" actions on the local population.[2]

The earliest and largest pogrom took place in Kovno (Kauen) on the night of June 25–26, where, under the command of the Lithuanian partisan leader, Klimatis, more than one thousand five hundred Jews were killed and synagogues and many Jewish houses were destroyed. In subsequent pogroms two thousand eight hundred Jews were also killed. Throughout Lithuania other smaller pogroms erupted that numbered communists among the victims.[3] In Riga, Einsatzkommando 1a set up an auxiliary police force of about four hundred men, under a man called Neiss, for the purpose fo helping to "protect" the city. Two other units were set up for carrying out pogroms, and as a result, all of the synagogues were soon destroyed and four hundred Jews were slaughtered in the blood-bath.[4]

In addition to those in Riga and Kovno, pogroms took place in Lvov[5] (Lemberg), Vilna,[6] Tarnopol and Chortkow,[7] Minsk,[8] Kremenez,[9] Dobromil, and Sambor, where fifty Jews were killed by an "enraged crowd,"[10] and Hitzu, where one thousand five hundred and fifty Jews were disposed of.[11]

These pogroms were short-lived; they could not be extended for any length of time. A number of reports indicated that in many places the inhabitants, in spite of their strong anti-Jewish feelings, could not be persuaded to enact "spontaneous demonstrations" against the Jews.[12] In one report complaining of the lack of success in starting pogroms in the Ukraine, Einsatzgruppe C gave as the reason for this inaction the belief that the Ukrainian population feared "the strong position the Jews had held formerly and are still afraid of a possible return of the Soviets."[13] This fear was to be a recurrent one throughout the reports.

No further pogroms were attempted once the Kommandos had established themselves in an area. The annihilation process then fell directly into the hands of the Einsatzgruppen. In Kovno the Lithuanian partisans were disarmed on June 28 by order of the German Field Command. Immediately from the ranks of these partisans a five-company auxiliary police force was set up. Two of these companies came under the control of Einsatzgruppe A. One guarded the Jewish concentration camp in Fort 7 and carried out executions; the second was to assume security police tasks under the leadership of the Einsatzkommando.[14]

The general procedure of the Einsatzgruppen Kommandos was to clear the rural areas of Jews as quickly as possible.[15] Jews remaining in the larger urban areas, who survived the pogroms and the first liquidations, were placed in ghettos and utilized for labor by the various German agencies. By January 1942 it was reported that the only Jews left in Latvia were in the Riga and Dwinsk (Dünaburg, Daugavpils) ghettos.[16] In Lithuania the breakdown of surviving Jews at this time was as follows: Kovno (15,000), Vilna (15,000), and Shavli (Schaulen) (4,500). White Russia, or, as the Germans called it, White Ruthenia, still had about one hundred thirty-nine thousand Jews. In Estonia it was reported that about one thousand leading communists had been seized and shot and that 5,377 were put into concentration camps. Of the Jews remaining in Estonia when the Germans arrived (some had fled or had been deported by the Russians), all were either killed or put into labor camps.[17]

The killings proceeded at a much faster rate in the northern parts of the occupied territories.[18] Long after ghettos had been established in the Baltic States, White Russia, and the Ukraine, and hundreds of thousands of Jews and others had been annihilated there, Einsatzgruppe D had still not combed the area of the Crimea at least once.[19] Operational Situation Report 170 stated that the intended target date for accomplishing this was the end of February 1942. By 14 April 1942 it was declared that this goal had been achieved.[20]

Virtually every report routinely cited mass killings, giving numbers of dead in the tens, hundreds,and thousands. Reading the reports, one can soon get used to these figures; one can almost accept them as a matter of course. The impersonal format, the constant repetition over and over of killings can easily allow the mind to become dulled to the terrible significance of these numbers. Yet every now and then particularly large-scale operations were included that were so enormous that one is suddenly jolted out of any lethargic acceptance that may have set in. These large-scale operations were those that occurred within a very short period of time, either one or two days, and that involved numbers of victims in five figures.

On 29 and 30 September 1941, in a ravine called Babi Yar in Kiev, the Gruppe Staff and members of Sonderkommando 4a, with two Kommandos of Higher SS and Police Leader Friedrich Jackeln's Order Police Regiment South, killed a total of 33,771 Jews.[21] This, one of the most notorious actions carried out in the eastern territories, was by no means the only massive shooting operation. It was also not the largest. The largest massacre took place in Odessa, where an estimated 75,000–80,000 Jews were killed, mainly by Rumanian soldiers with the help of the Einsatzkommandos.[22] During a three-day period, 23,600 Jews were also shot in Kamenez-Podolsk by a Kommando of the Higher SS and Police Leader Jeckeln.[23] Higher SS and Police Leader Jeckeln led his forces, including members of the Einsatzkommando 2, in an extensive operation that took place on 30 November 1941. Jews from the Riga ghetto as well as a transport of German Jews were shot. This operation marked an early example of the shooting of Jews deported from the Reich.[24] The extent of the killings by the Higher SS and Police Leaders was further evidenced by the killing of ten thousand Jews by a unit of these forces in Dnjepropetrowsk on 13 October 1941,[25] and by the fact that during the month of August 1941 alone, Higher SS and Police units shot 44,125 people, mostly Jews.[26]

These killings, carried out very quickly and ruthlessly, prepare one for the even more heinous crimes mentioned throughout the reports. These were the occasions when the entire Jewish and/or non-Jewish population of a village was killed and/or the whole village was then burned down. The intention to carry out these acts appeared in Operational Situation Report 60, in which Einsatzgruppe C stated, "it is intended to round up the Jews in certain villages, to liquidate them and to raze the village to the ground."[27] That this plan was carried out with relentless consistency is indicated by the following examples. In the ghetto in Nevel it was reported that a scabies epidemic had broken out, 640 Jews were rounded up and liquidated, and the houses were burned down to prevent "further contagion."[28] This same report mentioned a similar action that was carried out in Janowitschi, where, to prevent the spread of a contagious disease, 1,025 Jews were given "special treatment."[29] All the Jews in three villages, Kujajschitsche, Krupka, and Scholopanitsche, were killed by Einsatzkommando 8. They had been accused of supporting the partisans and parachutists in the area.[30] Giving assistance to partisans was the reason advanced for other liquidations. The entire population of Audrini was killed, and the town was burned down. As a warning to the population, this action was described in newspapers and on posters throughout Latvia.[31] A detachment from Einsatzgruppe A exterminated all the inhabitants of Ussaditsche and burned the village. It had been discovered that ski tracks of partisans led to the forest from the village.[32] The people of Laki were suspected of giving food to the partisans in that area, and so on 23 March 1942 the whole village was burned down and fifteen leaders, including the mayor, were shot by Einsatzgruppe D.[33]

Throughout the reports example after example appeared where towns and entire regions were declared to be "free of Jews" or "cleared of Jews." This was the case especially in reports issued after September 1941. By then the liquidations were well under way, and thousands of Jews had been killed. A report dated 19 September 1941 announced that as the result of operations carried out by Einsatzkommando 3 with help from Lithuanian auxiliary forces, the districts of Raseiniai, Roskiskis, Sarasai, Perzai, and Prienai were "cleared of Jews."[34] Einsatzgruppe A reported that there was no longer any Jewish population in the Siverskaja area,[35] and that Estonia was "free of Jews."[36]

The limitations of space prevent citing further examples of these gigantic extermination actions. It is enough to point out that each Einsatzgruppe reported cities and areas within its range of activity where the Jewish question had been solved.[37]

Other Victims

In Chapter 5 we enumerated the categories of persons killed as they were found in the reports. Jews, especially, as well as communist officials, figured prominently in the lists. Yet Jews and communist officials, although the primary target of the extermination squads, were not the only victims. The entire population of the occupied eastern territories was in the firm grasp of the Kommandos. Anyone within this grasp could be done away with on the slightest pretext. The Operational Situation Reports are replete with massacres of groups other than Jews and communists. Let us take note of some of these other victims.

The first group to be considered were the Gypsies.[38] At Nuremberg Otto Ohlendorf stated that in Pretzsch the leaders were ordered to kill Gypsies, as well as Jews and communist functionaries.[39] The Gypsies were to be "treated in the same way as the Jews" because they were regarded as "antisocial elements" who, as one leader put it, would spread infectious diseases and who were also "politically unreliable."[40] Many reports offered evidence of the killing of Gypsies. These killings were either mentioned separately or were included in other summary figures for a given period. For Instance, it was reported that in the Siverskaja area between 16 November and 15 December 1941, Einsatzgruppe D killed 824 Gypsies for "causing trouble."[41] A report issued a week later declared that in the area of Einsatzgruppe D the "Gypsy question" was solved.[42] This was actually not the case, however, since later reports also indicated that many more Gypsies were killed in the Crimea[43]

A group of native Crimean Jews called Krimtchaks were also massacred in great numbers. In 1939 the Krimtchaks numbered about three thousand in all.[44] They were found in the following locations with this approximate numerical distribution: Karasubasar (2,000), Simferopol (500), Feodossija (300), Sevastopol (200). The Krimtchaks spoke a dialect of the Eastern Turki language transcribed into Hebrew letters.[45] They did not have the general appearance of Jews, and it was necessary for the Einsatzgruppe to consult with Berlin in order to decide what to do with them. Otto Ohlendorf stated at his trial that it was not for reasons of religion but of race that the Krimtchaks were killed.[46] They were usually referred to in reports together with Gypsies. Thus Einsatzgruppe D reported that in Simferopol, "apart from Jews, also the Krimtchak and Gypsy question was solved." It was alleged that the local population "generally welcomed the elimination of these elements."[47] Einsatzgruppe D reported on 8 April 1942 that no Jews, Gypsies, or Krimtchaks were left in the Crimea.[48] The references to the Krimtchaks were usually confined to these types of statements, with little specific reference to this group in itself or to precise figures. One exception to this was found in Operational Situation Report 150, which reported that during the period from 16 November to 15 December 1941, Einsatzgruppe D shot (among others) 2,504 Krimtchaks.[49]

A report of 19 January 1942 gave some indication as to the attitude of the population of the Crimea to the killing operations of Einsatzgruppe D. The report mentioned the negative effect that "the evacuation" of Jews, Gypsies, and Krimtchaks had had on the inhabitants.

The absurd fear that the Germans were going to exterminate the entire population, had vanished entirely a few weeks after the occupation of the Crimea. This fear was revived to a greater extent when in the beginning of December preparations were started for the evacuation of 12 to 13,000 Jews, Krimtchaks and Gypsies. . . . The evacuation of Jews, Krimtchaks, and Gypsies, with only a few exceptions, is welcomed by everybody. Also in this the general antipathy against the Jews on the part of the rural population and that of the city is being confirmed. That the Jews and the Krimtchaks receive the same treatment is considered as a matter of course, as the Krimtchaks are generally being looked upon as Jews. . . .[50]

In Operational Situation Report 145 it was stated that the operations against the Jews were "complicated by the Karaim, Krimtchak and Gypsy problem." The Karaim, or Karaites, were a group who observed a modified version of Jewish religious practices, and as in the case of the Krimtchaks, it was difficult for the Einsatzgruppe to decide whether or not to kill them. In the end they were spared.[51] It is noteworthy that in order to determine whether or not the Karaites were to be killed, the Germans not only examined literature on the Karaites, but also even consulted with Jewish scholars. The latter included Zelig Kalmanovitch of Vilna, who, realizing the consequences of the information he was to provide, told the Germans that the Karaites were not connected with the Jewish religious community and that they were not related to the Semitic race. As the result of their research the Germans decided not to kill the Karaites.[52]

Another group of victims designated as a specific category and who numbered in the thousands were the mental patients killed by the Kommandos. Bearing in mind that a precedent had been set with the euthanasia program established in 1939 in Germany itself,[53] it comes as no surprise that the untrammeled liquidation of "mentally deficient" persons was carried out extensively by the Einsatzgruppen. We have already mentioned the killing of three hundred Jewish mental patients in Kiev by Einsatzkommando 5 on 18 October 1941.[54] The "heavy mental burden" that was borne by Einsatzkommando 5 in carrying out these shootings in Kiev could not have been as great for the members of the Einsatz-kommando 3 when they killed the 544 inmates of the Aglona asylum on 22 August 1941. They shared the burden of this task with a Latvian self-defense unit. The nursing staff at this asylum was to be used thereafter to serve the medical needs of the German troops.[55] This problem of the "heavy mental burden" that plagued Einsatzkommando 5 in Kiev illustrates the twisted thinking of these men. The premise operating here would seem to be that it was much easier to kill people who were sane.

In Chernigov Sonderkommando 7b obtained information to the effect that the Russians had let out the patients of the asylum and had armed some of them. These patients were marching up and down the streets "marauding." The result of all of this was that twenty-one patients were caught and killed, while the others escaped to the surrounding villages. The report continued, "The population is cooperating with regard to the capture of the insane persons, so that soon again there will be quite a few in the asylum. Then, they will be treated according to the usual procedure."[56]

The killing of so-called "armed" insane persons was not confined to the above example. Another report mentioned that Kommandos of Einsatzgruppe A killed eighty-seven insane persons who had "armed themselves" and who were "incited" by eleven communists, including six Jews.[57] Still another report described how Einsatzkommando 5, during the systematic combing of villages throughout a large area, shot several Bolshevist mayors and "mentally handicapped" persons, who had been ordered to carry out sabotage by the NKWD. This report continued: "It seems that the NKWD favoured mentally retarded persons in the distribution of these kinds of tasks who, nevertheless, in spite of all inferiority summoned enough energy for their criminal activities."[58]

Other killings of mental patients were described in several reports.[59] From among these the killing in Poltava of 565 patients from the local asylum might be cited. The farm next to the asylum had been used for feeding the patients, and with their murder, its produce then became available to the German soldiers. This operation was done in agreement with the 6th Army and the local commander of the Wehrmacht.[60] Finally, three reports outlined the preparation and systematic killing of about one thousand and five hundred mental patients from the Igrin Hospital near Dnjepropetrowsk.[61]

It was common practice for the Einsatzgruppen to shoot hostages. This was probably carried out much more extensively than was mentioned in the reports. The Wehrmacht was often directly involved in these operations as well.[62] A top secret directive issued on 16 September 1941 and signed by OKW Chief Wilhelm Keitel stated in part:

In each case of revolt against the German occupation force communist sources are to be suspected regardless of what the individual circumstances are. ... Attention should be paid to the fact that a human life in the countries concerned often means nothing and only by unusual severity can a deterrent effect be achieved. In these cases the life of one German soldier must be atoned for by the death sentence of 50 to 100 communists, as a rule. The manner of execution shall further increase the deterrent effect ... prizes and rewards should be lavishly offered to the population in order to ensure its cooperation in a suitable way.
The death penalty is the only effective one.[63]

The order, which was issued partly in response to the increased resistance to the occupying forces, reflected the already prevailing ruthlessness of the German will to crush all resistance by every possible means. Clearly illegal in its willingness to place blame for resistance on "communist sources" (which could mean anything) regardless of the circumstances, Keitel's order further sought to justify such measures with the reprehensible claim that Russians did not understand the value of human life. Presumably, the shooting of Russians in the ratio prescribed would help the Russians acquire the understanding that they lacked.

A few examples will be given here of victims designated as hostages in the reports. On 25 October 1941 in Tosno a sawmill burned down. This sawmill had been preparing building materials for five German army divisions. The guards at the mill were blamed for this suspected arson. "In the presence of representatives of the community 13 hostages were shot dead. The names of these hostages were already previously established for the eventuality of acts of sabotage."[64]

Attacks against Wehrmacht personnel and military vehicles and railroad lines were numerous and were the reason for many hostage shootings. Examples of this appeared in several reports.[65] Einsatzkommando 10a of Einsatzgruppe D reported one particularly extensive action. As the result of "attacks" against the Wehrmacht, the Kommando carried out raids against the Jews. In all, ninety-seven Jews were shot and 1,756 hostages were taken. The report said that "Hostages are taken in each new place, and they are executed on the slightest pretext."[66] In Kiev the town commandant announced that hostages would continue to be shot if arson and sabotage were not stopped. He ordered that the population was to report "without delay any suspicious observations." The same report stated that between 2 and 8 November 1941 Einsatzkommando 5 shot 414 hostages in agreement with the above mentioned directive.[67] It is interesting to notice that an earlier report also gave a figure of 414 hostages shot for the period between 26 October and 1 November 1941.[68] Since the same number appeared in both reports, this gives rise to the question—was this a coincidence or an error on the part of the RSHA editors? Was there a mix-up in the dates and the figures were simply repeated? (Other statistics presented in both reports were different, which may indicate that the repetition of the 414 figure may have been merely a coincidence.)

Another group of victims, which for our purposes here may be regarded as a separate category, was that of women and children. The Operational Situation Reports included many examples of the murder of women and children. It would seem that there probably was an initial reluctance on the part of the Kommandos to shoot women and children. This reluctance was suggested in Himmler's speech given in Posen to the Reichsleiter and Gauleiter on 6 October 1943. Himmler stated that "We faced the question: what about the women and children? I have decided to find a perfectly clear solution. I did not consider it justified to exterminate the men—that is to kill them or let them be killed—and allow the children to live as avengers, for our sons and grandchildren. ...." Whatever qualms that may have existed were soon overcome. By the middle of August 1941 Einsatz-kommando 3, for instance, was shooting Jewish children en masse almost daily. Women and children were killed as part of the liquidation of Jews but were not always singled out in the summaries. The reports did give examples where this was done, however. When this was the case, almost always there was a "reason" given for the killings. It was as if even within the deadly world of the Einsatzgruppen, and in spite of the acceptance of the need for the killings, it was still necessary in the case of women and children to take special pains to present an explanation for these executions.

The killing of women ranged from individual women[69] or relatively small numbers,[70] to larger operations involving hundreds of women. It is instructive to take note of the manner of presentation of some of these killings. In Witebsk for instance, Einsatzkommando 9 reported that three German soldiers had been killed and a "Wehrmacht pacification action" was then carried out. The result was that nineteen Jews, including women, were caught in the forest where the murders had occurred. The report went on to say that the Jews "were executed on the strong suspicion of having taken part in the attack and because they had been found having committed arson in Witebsk."[71] The excuse of the "strong suspicion" of engaging in attacks and arson was matched in another report by an excuse of comparable validity. Near Mogilev twenty-eight Jewish women were shot for being "extremely obstinate" and for not wearing the required Jewish badge. This report also said that again in Mogilev, for spreading false rumors and sabotaging regulations, a further 215 male Jews and 337 Jewish women were shot.[72] In Berditschew on 1 and 2 September 1941 a large massacre took place. This was carried out by a detachment of forces of the Higher SS and Police Leader. In all, 1,878 Jews were killed including 575 Jewesses over twelve years of age.[73]

The killing of adolescents and children appeared in the reports along with the statistics concerning women.[74] Einsatzgruppe D reported that seventeen women and children were killed as the aftermath of arrests made during four raids undertaken with the help of the Wehrmacht.[75] Often in reports arrests were listed as having been made, but no further information was given as to the subsequent fate of those arrested. For example, in Radomyschl on 13 September 1941 three adolescents were arrested by Sonderkommando 4a and were convicted of espionage.[76] One need not speculate too long as to their fate.

Scattered throughout the reports were many references to so-called "Asiatics" who were also killed. Never clearly defined, they fell within the Nazi racial category of "undesirable" or "inferior elements" and as such were to be treated in the same fashion as the Jews. Again as in other groups of victims at times it sufficed to simply report that all Asiatics apprehended were killed after searches on the highway,[77] for example, or after searches through civilian camps.[78] The reports sometimes also presented justifications for the killings as well as in the case of Operational Situation Report 92, which announced that eleven Asiatics and two Jews found by the Wehrmacht were killed for planning sabotage.[79]

Discussion of ethnic Germans living in the conquered territories was a continuous feature of the reports. These people were a significant ingredient in Himmler's plans for the vast restructuring and resettlement of eastern Europe along ethnic lines.[80]

Ethnic Germans living in the territories of the east were very often the beneficiaries of preferential treatment and the spoils of war taken from the murdered Jews.[81] Not all members of this group shared the ideals of the invaders, however, and occasionally ethnic Germans were included among the lists of victims of the Einsatzgruppen.[82]

Many Ukrainians played a significant role as collaborators with the Einsatzgruppen.[83] Yet, Ukrainians were also killed by the Kommandos and this, too, was reflected in the reports. The statistics of Ukrainian victims in these references were generally quite low and undoubtedly did not reflect the full numbers even for the period of the Operational Situation Reports. Ukrainians killed tended to be either suspected communists or members of nationalist resistance groups. One entry concerning Ukrainians occurred as part of a report on the Ukrainian Resistance Movement. In Kiev on 25 February 1942 three Ukrainian drivers were arrested for "endangering the safety of the columns of municipal trucks and the orderly food supply for the city of Kiev by their disobedience to existing orders and neglectful conduct."[84] This passage illustrates that the same trumped up, ridiculous charges leveled at the Jews could also be directed at others.

The same report included other actions against Ukrainians. In Shitomir the Bandera organization, a Ukrainian nationalist resistance group, had been "cracked" in late February 1942. Twelve of its members were arrested between 10 and 13 March 1942. On March 10 four former Ukrainian prisoners of war were killed. They were blamed for trying to give information to the Soviets.[85] Other anti-Bandera operations occurred in Krementschug, Stalino, and Kiev during March 1942.[86] On 12 March 1942 two Ukrainian workers were hanged in Potschanowka as a reprisal for stopping work at a railroad construction site. It was reported that this hanging "had an extremely favorable effect on the work at the site." Similarly two Ukrainians were hanged by Sonderkommando 4a in Charkov for attempting to organize a strike at a forge in the Todt Organization.[87]

Later in this study the attitude of the local populations, as reflected in the Operational Situation Reports, will be looked at in greater depth. For the moment, concerning the shooting of Ukrainians, one final report can be mentioned. This report dealt with the problems with the population vis-à-vis the shooting of Ukrainians and Russians. The Kommandos perceived that in the popular mind the Gestapo had come to be considered in the same light as the NKWD. This was not what they desired. This report stated:

> We have great interest in preventing such opinions from becoming deeply rooted and in spreading the convictions that all cases are closely investigated and tried with justice on our side. For these reasons, Einsatzkommando 6 carried out

executions of Ukrainians and Russians always in such a way that nothing about them would be known to the public.[88]

The report went on, stating that on some occasions the population was told that a man was a communist official and was guilty of more than one "deed" and that he had to be shot. The population, it was claimed, understood this. "Executions of Jews are understood everywhere and accepted favorably. It is surprising how calm the delinquents are when they are shot, both Jews and non-Jews. Fear of death seems to have been dulled by 20 years of the Soviet regime. . . ."

The report continued with the admonishment that everything was to be done to avoid the impression in the population's mind that the "German Security Police arrests and executes people merely on slight suspicion or haphazardly as far as Russians and Ukrainians are concerned."[89]

The final category of victims to be considered here were the Russian prisoners of war.[90] We will examine first the background for these killings very briefly. As the result of talks that ended on 16 July 1941, Heydrich reached an agreement with Generalleutnant Hermann Reinecke, chief of the General Armed Forces Office (Allgemeines Wehrmachtsamt). The next day Heydrich issued the previously quoted Operational Order 8 (which was essentially a repeat of a June 28 directive).[91] This order outlined the procedures for the identifying and shooting of certain groups found in the prisoner-of-war camps. The detachments from the Kommandos who were to screen the prisoners usually consisted of one officer and four to six men.[92] They were to work "independently according to special authorization" within the "limits of the camp organizations." They were to "keep close contact with the camp Commander and the defense officers assigned to him." The task of the Kommandos was to find trustworthy persons among the prisoners, who, even if they were communists, could be of use to the Germans for intelligence and administrative purposes. As well, the Kommandos were to find those considered untrustworthy. The untrustworthy elements were to include the following:

All outstanding functionaries of the State and of the Party, especially Professional revolutionists Functionaries of the Comintern.

All leading Party functionaries of the Russian Secret Police and its fellow Organizations in the Central committees, in the regional and district committees.

All Peoples-Commissars and their Deputies.

All former Political Commissars in the Red Army.

Leading personalities of the state.

Authorities of central and middle regions.

The leading personalities of the business world.

Members of the Soviet-Russian intelligence.

All Jews.

All persons who are found to be agitators or fanatical communists.

Anyone in the above categories was to be executed. The prisoners were not to be killed inside the camp or within the immediate vicinity of the camp.[93]

According to one statement, a special department attached to Group IV A 1 of the RSHA, led by Franz Koenigshaus, was responsible for prisoners of war. Koenigshaus prepared the execution orders and submitted them to Müller for signature. One order was sent to the agency making the request for execution, that is, the prisoner-of-war camp, and another was sent to the concentration camp where the execution was to take place. At first the prisoners were formally released from prisoner-of-war status and then were transferred and executed.[94]

The handing over of prisoners of war to the Security Police Kommandos continued as late as July 1944.[95]

While these prisoner operations generally functioned smoothly, they were not without their problems. In the summer of 1941, soon after these operations had begun, a meeting took place to discuss these problems. Objections had been raised concerning the bad effect the killings were having on the army personnel, the difficulty in finding informers among the prisoners, the arbitrary nature of the selection process the led to "mistakes," where members of other ethnic groups were killed in the belief that they were Jews, and the now greater reluctance on the part of the Red Army soldiers to surrender.[96]

Consequently Heydrich issued a directive on 12 September 1941, which ordered that the screening procedure be done more carefully. It was reiterated that the executions were to be held in secret.[97]

In the Operational Situation Reports there is some indication of the tensions that had developed between the Wehrmacht and the Kommandos concerning the prisoners. For example, in Winnitsa (Winniza), the camp commander had objected to the transfer of 362 Jewish prisoners of war. When these Jews were handed over by a deputy, the camp commander put the deputy and two officers under court-martial. These difficulties were soon overcome. The army was obliged to "cooperate." The report stated that Field Marshal von Reichenau had "repeatedly praised the work of the Einsatzkommandos highly."[98]

Other reports mentioned much smoother liquidations of prisoners. Operational Situation Report 132 indicated that Sonderkommando 4a executed many Jewish prisoners of war who had been handed over by the Wehrmacht. In Borispol on 10 October 1941 the men of Sonderkommando 4a shot 357 Jewish prisoners of war, and four days later they shot 752 more. These actions were carried out at the "request" of the commander of the Borispol prisoner-of-war camp, and included seventy-eight wounded Jews who were handed over by the camp doctor, as well as a number of commissars. The report pointed out that "it was largely due to the energetic help of the Wehrmacht authorities in Borispol that the Borispol activities were carried out smoothly.'' In this same report it was stated that another detachment of Sonderkommando 4a in Lubny killed "without any interference" among others, fifty-three prisoners of war and a few Jewish riflewomen.[99]

Other examples of the killing of prisoners of war included the shooting between October 31 and November 5 by Sonderkommando 4b of 740 prisoners during "clearing out" operations in the camp at Losovoya[100] (Losowaja) and the killing by Einsatzgruppe B in Witebsk of 207 Jewish prisoners of war and 117 Jewish prisoners in Wjasma.[101]

The foregoing discussion, though limited, nevertheless underlines not only the extent of the mass shootings in terms of numbers, but also the degree to which these actions merged as one, German racial, ideological, and military goals. Within the broad spectrum of Nazi racial/ideological/ security policy, all the victims cited—Gypsies, Asiatics, communist officials, women, children, mental patients, as well as Jews—could be killed. Any category among the victims fell easily within this paradigm. Moreover, the system was a flexible one. Gypsies were killed because they could "spread disease" or "cause trouble," or because they were "politically unreliable." Nor was the killing of mental patients confined under the obvious framework of racial inferiority. Their destruction could be bolstered by the concept of security as well. Mentally ill persons were therefore said to have posed a physical threat since they had "armed themselves" and were carrying out "criminal activities," "incited" by communists. Such feeble attempts at placing blame of this sort could just as easily be dispensed with, as was the case of Poltava, where the reporters stated the 565 mental patients were killed because the Germans needed the produce of the adjacent farm for themselves. Similarly, the cited Wehrmacht directive of 16 September 1941 implied that maintaining security was not the only consideration for the justification for shooting hostages in great numbers. It was inferred also that the people "in the countries concerned" must be inferior since a human life meant nothing to them. Again, security and racial concepts were present. In the chapters that follow, more examples of the Einsatzgruppen crimes will be examined. In all of these, as we have already seen in the material, we will note the attempt is made to justify the killing in some way. It is this attempt at rationalization on the part of the Einsatzgruppen reporters that will now be examined.

7

Reasons and Justifications for
the Killings

The Einsatzgruppen reporters for the most part did not simply record the killings, but felt the need to use euphemisms in their reports to cover up the act of murder. In the same way they also gave "reasons" for their actions in order to justify them. We have already noticed this practice in the killing operations cited in the previous chapters. The use of euphemistic language to color unpleasant activities or concepts was by no means an invention of the National Socialists. Governments, before and since Hitler's, have made use of euphemisms to disguise the unacceptable or at least render it more palatable. In the case of Hitler's Reich, however, given the nature of its fundamental philosophy and activities, the German bureaucracy's practice of covering up went well beyond that of other nations. In a regime where criminal activities formed a significant part of its daily operations, the tactic of evasion was no mere accretion, but was essential to the normal routine.[1]

For the Einsatzgruppen the need for this covering-up stemmed from two separate, but closely related ideas. The first was the fact that in presenting justifications for their deeds, the Einsatzgruppen leaders believed they were thereby providing themselves with a "legal" basis for the killings. While they may have believed that it was correct to annihilate the Jews, such a belief certainly had no foundation in law. With an eye to the future, and a possible, although unlikely, occasion when they might be held to account for their activities, the Einsatzgruppen constantly depicted the executions as reprisals against so-called criminal acts of Jews, partisans, and others. This was a way of cloaking their work in a shroud of legality. This "legal" self-protection was therefore outward-looking, a means of defense against external scrutiny. The second idea was subtler, and was directed more at the psychological problems of the Einsatzgruppen personnel themselves. It involved the use of camouflage words to disguise the reality of what was being done. It also involved the legal justifications just described, but here these tactics functioned for the more immediate benefit of the killers themselves. It was a way of coping from day to day, of making acceptable to themselves the measures they were undertaking against defenseless people.[2] These two points of view will now be examined more closely.

The shooting of hostages as reprisal measures against a conquered population was, under certain very strict conditions, permissable under existing international law. The Hague Rules of Land Warfare outlined that certain rules had to be followed in order for the shooting of hostages to be legal. These rules sanctioned the use of reprisals only when an unlawful act of warfare had been first committed by the enemy. Shootings were to be used only as a last resort when all other means of preventing the illegal acts had been explored. Public warnings were to be issued to the population that in the event of the recurrence of the illegal acts the hostages would be shot. There was to be a definite connection between the unlawful acts and the persons who were designated as hostages. No one—partisan, spy, or civilian, was to be executed without a proper court-martial or military court trial to determine their guilt. Above all, there was to be a reasonable relationship between the reprisals and the acts they were intended to stop. The number of persons shot was not to be so great as to exceed what was necessary for achieving this end. If these measures were not observed, the use of reprisals was considered a war crime.[3]

It was within this context of accepted legal procedure that the Einsatzgruppen leaders claimed to possess the necessary legal armature to justify their actions. The strictly limited perimeters outlined in The Hague Convention became the basis for the killings by the Kommandos. The degree to which this was conscious or not on their part cannot be determined. At the trial of the Einsatzgruppen leaders, many of these men maintained that the executions were simply "counter measures" against the continued unlawful acts of partisans, Jews, communists, and other "dangerous" elements. The danger to security was thus advanced as the motive for executions.[4] The fact that lawyers formed a sizeable percentage of the Einsatzgruppen leadership as well as the RSHA personnel should not be forgotten. These legally minded officials were automatically aware of the necessity for the appearance of legality.

Consideration of the validity of the reprisal argument need not detain us very long. None of the strictures put forward in The Hague rules were followed by the Einsatzgruppen.[5] The shootings were part of a planned program of extermination, which had been decided upon before the war against Russia had even started. Also, the intended goal of the systematic and complete destruction of the Jews was repeatedly referred to throughout the reports without any attempts at disguising this purpose. The killings, therefore, could not possibly be seen simply as measures of retaliation. Even the antipartisan warfare was used as an opportunity to disguise the killing of Jews and other "undesirables." As proof of this, one has only to recall Hitler's cynical comment made in July 1941 that the partisan war was a good thing because it offered the chance to wipe out anyone who opposed the Germans.[6] The constant destruction of whole villages by the Kommandos and the immense numbers of persons killed renders quite preposterous any claims that these operations were legal acts carried out solely in response to actions by the indigenous population.

However specious this argument of legality may have been, and to whatever extent it may have been accepted by the Germans, it certainly was an important feature of the reports. Obviously it was deemed necessary to record in writing reasons for the executions. Whether believed or not, the façade of legality had to be present.

Concerning the use of reprisals and excuses to explain the killing of the Jews, Helmut Krausnick has suggested that their use was probably the result of a directive from Heydrich. In other words, Heydrich likely handed down "language rules" (Sprachregelung) that were to be observed in the reports. Krausnick has pointed out that during July of 1941 the reports of Arthur Nebe, the leader of Einsatzgruppe B, unlike the reports of the other Einsatzgruppen, did not attempt to justify the shootings of the Jews. (In Operational Situation Report 21, for example, Einsatzgruppe B reported without further qualification that in Minsk 1,050 Jews had been liquidated, that in Vilna the liquidation of the Jews was underway, and that five hundred Jews were shot daily.)[7] Krausnick has noted that in Activity and Situation Report 1, of 31 July 1941, which summarized the events of the month of July, it was reported that the shooting of eight thousand persons by Einsatzgruppe B was done as retaliation for alleged crimes. Clearly the new emphasis on justifying the killings in Activity and Situation Report 1 was the result of editorial decision in the RSHA. As Krausnick has underlined, the RSHA did not want it expressed at such an early time that the Jews were being exterminated purely for racial reasons. This was especially the case with the Activity and Situation Reports, which were distributed to a wider readership than the Operational Situation Reports. The use of palliative methods in the reports of Einsatzgruppe B from this point on suggests that Nebe was probably told to bring his reports in line with the required formula.[8]

If Heydrich *did* pass on specific guidelines for reporting "reasons" for the shootings, this was a practice not without precedent on his part. In his letter to the Einsatzgruppen leaders in the occupied Polish territories on 21 September 1939, Heydrich had specifically ordered the leaders to say that the Jews were to be concentrated in certain centers because they had started riots and had engaged in looting.[9] The uniform use of the justifications by all four Einsatzgruppen after July 1941 would indicate a general directive was given. Whether the result of a directive, or the inclinations of the reporters individually, the ultimate purpose was the same—to cover up the reality of mass murder based on ideological reasons.[10]

The second aspect of the covering-up process involved the use of euphemistic language and justifications in order to lessen the impact of their deeds on the minds of the Einsatzgruppen members. This would seem to be a contradiction of the previous aspect. After all, if the killings were "legal," why attempt to cover them up? It should be pointed out that these devices were not used in the Einsatzgruppen reports only. As just mentioned, they were part and parcel of all forms of German communication, of correspondence, of speeches, or orders. They were even used in private conversation.[11] This employment of euphemistic language to disguise the killings and explanations to justify them was a very complex phenomenon within the Nazi world. It resulted in more than a mere stating of what happened, when, and where. The requirements of this straightforward type of reporting would have been met by simply recording numbers of victims and locations of executions. Since the reports were highly secret, the Einsatzgruppen bureaucracy did not really have to include reasons for its actions, but it did. As one historian has suggested, it did so as the result of the desire to conceal the killing process "not only from all outsiders but also from the censuring gaze of its own conscience."[12]

The men who were implementing mass murder could hardly be expected to call what they were doing "murder" or "mass killing" in their reports. Human beings, however depraved they may be, cannot usually sustain for long the thought that they are carrying out murder. The Einsatzgruppen even accused the Soviet leadership of a planned program of murder and constantly blamed the Jews for atrocities.[13] That they were undertaking such a program themselves was something not to be compared with the deeds of the enemy.[14] They were shooting thousands of people. If one was a convinced Nazi, one "had" to accept the ideological basis for the shootings. Yet it was inconceivable to describe this as murder. Other terms had to be found as substitutes for the obvious. What were these substitute terms?

Confining ourselves simply to the terms used in the reports to disguise the act of killing, we obtain the following representative list: action, special action, or large-scale action,[15] reprisal action,[16] pacification action,[17] radical action,[18] cleaning up or cleansing action,[19] overhauling,[20] cleared or cleared of Jews, or freeing the area of Jews,[21] special treatment or special measures,[22] handled appropriately,[23] liquidated,[24] rendered harmless,[25] Jewish problem solved,[26] handled according to orders,[27] ruthless collective measures,[28] executive tasks,[29] severe measures,[30] elimination,[31] evacuation,[32] eradication,[33] and treating according to the previous procedure.[34]

Combined with these camouflage words were the rationalizations that sought to justify the killings. In this way the mass shootings were reduced "to an ordinary bureaucratic process within the framework of police activity."[35] These justifications generally took two forms. The first involved a brief description of the details surrounding the so-called criminal activities of the persons shot. The second was even shorter. It was simply the use of the label that identified the crime. These labels characterized persons as looters, saboteurs, agitators, and so on,[36] and the labels in themselves implied the "reasons" why these people were guilty and why they had been executed. The labels justified the executions in the same way the more elaborate explanations did. The labels were not drawn up as a response to the existing situation in the east, but had been formulated earlier, and were included, for instance, in the "Guidelines for the Conduct of the Troops in Russia" issued by the German High Command prior to the attack on the Soviet Union.[37]

Jews, commissars and communist functionaries were to be killed automatically as a matter of policy. In their case it generally sufficed to present the numbers executed without further comment. As Adolf Ott, leader of Sonderkommando 7b during 1942 testified, the orders were to kill every Jew who was apprehended. It did not matter if he had committed any offense or not.[38] While it was not really necessary, as we have seen, explanations were also very often provided to justify the killing of Jews and communist officials. It was assumed that no trial was required to determine the guilt of the persons captured. To be a Jew or a communist official was to be guilty of a crime that warranted execution. The same thing held for other "crimes." Nothing more was needed to permit the shooting of these people. They were guilty and that was that. (At Nuremberg many leaders insisted that the guilt of the people shot had always been determined by proper investigation, and thus the shootings were legal.) The list of offenders and offenses included in the various labels and explanations was so all-embracing and at times so vague, that in practice it allowed the Einsatzgruppen to get rid of anyone they pleased. Even in wartime it is highly questionable that being guilty of looting is sufficient reason for being shot, let alone for being shot as a "neglected juvenile" or an "unreliable element." Of course, such normal considerations of legality were not within the thinking of the Einsatzgruppen. Furthermore, the assumption here is that people had actually carried out the crimes for which they had been executed. Not only the questionable presentation of the reports, but other direct evidence indicates that such accusations of criminality were simply manufactured by the Germans. At the end of July 1941 the SS Cavalry Brigade under Higher SS and Police Leader Bach-Zelewski was specifically ordered to refer in its reports to murdered Jews as "looters" or "partisans."[39] Additional written instructions have survived specifying that in the Ukraine members of the Bandera movement were to be arrested and secretly liquidated "as looters."[40] The untruth of such charges levelled by the Germans is therefore clearly proven.

This use of justifying labels and explanations and euphemistic descriptions to cover up the killings raises certain questions. Although part of other methods of Nazi communication, the use of these devices was of particular importance in the Operational Situation Reports. In them the subject was so obviously murder and was so all-pervasive that the cover-up tactics had to be used more so than in most other circumstances. The need was clear. The killings had to be faced. They had to be disguised. Disguised—but for whose benefit? No outsiders would ever see the reports (or so it was believed). And so if the obscuring and justification were there only for the Germans themselves, for the Einsatzgruppen officials, the Kommando leaders, for the RSHA officials, for the typists who typed the reports, and for the recipients of the reports, one still must ask certain questions. Did all this camouflage actually work? Did the officials reading these reports really take these justifications at face value? Did anyone see in them anything other than what in fact they were—descriptions of outright murder? Who could have really convinced himself otherwise? What poverty of mind would have led anyone to not realize that hundreds of thousands of human beings were being annihilated in the east?[41]

But if for the moment one accepts the unlikely conclusion that the camouflaging and justifications did fulfill their purpose and that the eyes of the officials were blinded and their consciences were not disturbed by what they read, then one still is faced with another question. If these methods worked, why were they not universally used throughout the reports? The ambiguous terms were often found under the unambiguous headings Executions or Liquidation.[42] Why does one find right beside such terms as "special treatment" or "rendered harmless" such unequivocal terms as shot, liquidate, or annihilate? This question provides an example of the inexplicable and irrational quality inherent in much National Socialist thinking and methodology. One discovers in the reports, therefore, three phenomena: first, the very extensive use of rationalization and camouflage language to both justify and repress the killings; second, more direct and unadorned reportage of the killings and a frequent direct reference to the desired goal of destroying the Jews; and third, an inconsistency in the use of either of these methods.

On one level this lack of consistency can perhaps be explained. The Einsatzkommandos were not concerned with the niceties of literary style or a balanced, careful ordering of the material they were constantly sending to Berlin. They had no time for this. Time was a factor as well for the busy RSHA editors in Berlin. It is unlikely, therefore, that consistency was a real concern in this matter. Within the general guidelines laid down, a way of reporting developed that got the job done as quickly as possible. Thus the necessity of pure expediency likely came to bear as much as anything on the way the reports were drawn up.

But in the reports there was so much overlapping and combining of categories (Jews and communists were also described as plunderers, terrorists, saboteurs, agitators, and so forth) that one doubts the seriousness with which these characterizations were given or that they had any real meaning. Ultimately one senses a desperate and pathetic attempt to come up with plausible reasons for mass murder. It is the constant repetition of the same handful of terms over and over again that robs the attempts at justification of any real believability. To cite only one example, Einsatzgruppe B frequently employed the heading, Actions Against Functionaires, Agents, Saboteurs, and Jews. This heading was used throughout without ever altering the order or omitting any of the categories.[43] All the categories were viewed as one. The presentation was a mere formula. Again we must ask the question, why in the many breakdowns of numbers were victims always depicted as saboteurs, plunderers, and so on, *and nothing else*? Could so many victims have been only these few things?

A mindless process of presentation permeates the reports, a kind of hurried, easy shorthand that, by its crudeness, almost does not expect credulity on the part of the reader. The continued practice of stating "reasons" for the shooting of Jews alongside undisguised statements about their wholesale extermination became more incongruous as time passed, especially when the latter type of statements appeared more frequently, and the statistical record of the killings rose beyond any plausible association with the norms of mere policework.[44] Quite apart from very obvious references to the total extermination of the Jews (which will be discussed later), one encounters almost inadvertent admissions of what was really intended in reports dealing ostensibly with other matters. For instance, in a discussion of the need for the services of Jewish tradesmen, Einsatzgruppe C said it was necessary to exclude the "older Jewish skilled workers from the executions."[45] It is apparent that "the executions" in question were not connected whatsoever to any alleged crimes. Had these Jews not possessed knowledge required by the Germans, they would have been shot. The practice of simply supplying numbers of Jews killed combined with "reasons" for the execution of others became firmly entrenched by the fall of 1941. Yet, as just noted, this practice was not consistently applied. Operational Situation Report 143 followed this method, but in Operational Situation Report 148, for instance, one finds many pretexts for the shooting of the Jews. This façade of pretense continued to linger throughout the reports, although it was apparent to all that the measures against the Jews were something special. As for the RSHA officials, it is unlikely that they could have really believed what they were writing. No doubt some people were killed because they had actually committed the offenses described. But what rational person would believe this was the case to the extent given in these reports? Jews were to be killed, but not for the reasons advanced in the reports. Even the most ardent Nazi or the most gullible official could not have deluded himself as to their meaning. He may have accepted the justification, but if so, he did as the result of prior blind conviction and not because of the tactics presented in the reports. As one writer has put it, "reality was reinterpreted to fit preconceived rationalizations to justify a mass murder that had been decided upon independently of any reasons or causes."[46]

We may conclude from this discussion that two factors came to bear on this aspect of the reports. The first was the immediate attempt to ease the conscience of the people involved. The second was the gnawing fear of a possible discovery of the nature of their actions. It was hoped that the "paper legality" would offer protection against such an eventuality. There came a point later when even the euphemism "Sonderbehandlung" (special treatment) was no longer considered acceptable. On 10 April 1943 Himmler ordered that this term be replaced by the phrase "transported to the east."[47]

We will mention here only a few examples of the reasons for the killings given in the reports. Further examples will be seen in reports discussed in later chapters. Rather than cite examples of the more commonplace type (sabotage, looting, spying, etc.) that were ubiquitous throughout the reports, we will restrict ourselves to more unusual examples, those that called for more "imagination" on the part of the reporters. They indicate the extent to which the Einsatzgruppen went to justify their deeds.

To begin it must be repeated that the Jews were constantly blamed for alleged atrocities. Thus in Zborow the Waffen SS killed six hundred Jews as retaliation for "Soviet atrocities."[48] Similar measures were carried out by Sonderkommando 4a in Luck, where two thousand executions took place as "counter measures" for the killing of Ukrainians.[49] Retaliation for "inhuman atrocities" was the reason for the killing of about seven thousand Jews in another report, which also included the shooting of fifteen Jews who were blamed for the murder of thirty-two Ukrainians.[50]

Jews were also blamed for arson. In particular the bombing and fires in Kiev on 20 and 24 September 1941 were attributed to the Jews.[51] In Nevel, arson was blamed on the Jews, and as a reprisal Sonderkommando 7a shot seventy-four Jews as well as communists and "intellectual" Jews in the smaller villages in the area.[52]

The spreading of rumors was thought by the Einsatzgruppen to be a very insidious type of crime, particularly the rumor that the Russian army was advancing. Instances of this happening occurred in Minsk where Einsatzgruppe B shot ten persons[53] and in Choslawitschi, where, according to the local Russian population, the Jews had spread this rumor. Consequently, Vorkommando Moscow sent a detachment there and killed 114 Jews. The same report stated that as a result of "false" rumors and "hate" propaganda against the German authorities in Mogilev and Bobruisk, 1,932 persons, mostly Jews, were killed by Einsatzkommando 8.[54] A favorite type of description of rumor spreading was the so-called "whispering propaganda." It surfaced frequently in the reports. Here one example might be presented. In the Minsk ghetto the Jews were accused of "anti-German whispering propaganda which was especially effective with the rural population, who tried to sell their products in the ghetto."[55]

The spreading of "Bolshevist propaganda" was another commonplace of the reports. The following is one such example. In Orel, a number of Jews were arrested and shot. They were accused of spreading communist propaganda and "in an evil way had incited hatred against the German Wehrmacht."[56] This passage is interesting as it is typical of the literary style of much of the reports. The adjective "evil" in this context is meaningless. No doubt it was never considered under what circumstances hatred can be incited in a way that is *not* evil. Another questionable, but characteristic turn of phrase was found in a report dealing with Einsatzkommando 8 in the town of Talka. The Kommando had killed 1,218 Jews who had spread anti-German propaganda and had "continuously terrorized" the people of Talka with "usury."[57] Just how the 1,218 Jews had accomplished this was not explained.

Many reports described reprisals for not following various German regulations,[58] for "loitering,"[59] for not wearing the Jewish Star,[60] for "refusal" to work,[61] and for escaping from the ghetto.[62] Jews were often accused of certain negative attitudes without further description of what form these attitudes took. One report spoke of "Jewish sadism" and "revengefulness."[63] Jews were guilty of "hostile" and "provocative" conduct.[64] In Cybulov, on 25 September 1941, Einsatzkommando 5 shot seventy-eight Jews because the Jewish population there had been "particularly insolent to the Ukrainian population."[65] In Chmielnik, 299 Jews were "taken care of" by the same Kommando because the area had "suffered from Jewish terror."[66]

The Kommandos often carried out executions of people who were merely "suspected" of having committed a crime. In Smolowicze Jews were suspected of blowing up railway lines and so Einsatzkommando 8, helped by the rear Kommando for Minsk, shot 1,401 Jews. The same report mentioned that nineteen Jews under "suspicion of having either been communists or having committed arson were executed."[67]

Active participation in the fighting against the Wehrmacht led to the killing of many Jews. This fighting took a number of forms, such as direct combat with German troops and military vehicles,[68] and involvement in various partisan operations.[69] One example was of an attack on the Security Police headquarters in Vilna. This reference is important in that it gives some indication of the continuous nature of the killings carried out by the Kommandos. The report stated that the attack mentioned necessitated a special liquidation, one that brought the numbers above the normal "daily liquidation quotas."[70]

One of the most frequent excuses given in the reports for liquidations was the so-called "danger of epidemics." This excuse was in keeping with the Nazi perception of all Jews as bearers of disease and vermin.[71] While many examples of this were offered in the reports, only two will be cited here.[72] The first was included in the final Operational Situation Report. This report described the massacre of 983 Jews who "had infectious diseases or were so old and infirm that they could not be used any more for work."[73] The second reference, in a report by Einsatzgruppe B, is perhaps the most vile attempt at justification for killing in all the Operational Situation Reports. It took place in Schumjatschi, where sixteen mentally ill Jewish and Russian children were found. It was reported that they had been placed in

a children's home, which had been left in a completely neglected condition by the Soviet authorities. In part, the children had been lying in their dirt for weeks already, and all had severe exema on their bodies. The German Oberstabsarzt from the hospital in Schumjatschi, who had been called in for consultation, declared that the children's home with its inmates represented a center of an epidemic of the first degree, and that therefore their shooting was called for.[74]

8

Factors Affecting the Rate and Extent of the Killings

The rate and extent of the exterminations were not uniform throughout the eastern territories. Many factors determined the course of the operations of the Security Police, and these factors came to bear in different ways in the very different situations that existed in each of the areas occupied by the four Einsatzgruppen. To deal comprehensively with the full range of these factors would require detailed examination of each area and an analysis of a host of questions, events, documents, and personalities. Such an analysis is well beyond the limitations of this study. In this chapter, therefore, we will confine our inquiry to a few key factors that had an overall effect on the rate and extent of the killings generally, and note the treatment of these themes in the reports.

We must bear in mind that the shootings in the east were done during the course of the German-Soviet war, arguably the most bestial war in history. The unprecedented horror of this war in itself cannot be forgotten. The casualties[1] suffered by both sides alone indicates the truth of Hitler's prediction on 30 March 1941 that this war was to be very different from the war in the west.[2] The awesome nature of the overt destruction resulting from the course of the war, however, should not in any way detract from the equally grim reality of the atrocities carried out for reasons quite separate from "accepted" military goals. The massacre of the Jews began, therefore, in the context of this war against the Soviet nation and system— the destruction of Bolshevism, with which the Jews were constantly identified in Hitler's mind, being the first and foremost goal.

Because it was undertaken within the framework of the war, this destruction was largely affected by the circumstances and the unfolding course of this war. A critical factor in the Einsatzgruppen success was the close proximity of the Kommando units to the front-line area. Originally the Kommandos had been mandated to work behind the front-lines. This was soon abandoned in practice, as the reports cited below indicate. The summary report for the month of July 1941 stated:

For this reason the principle of having the Einsatzkommandos operate chiefly in the rear area of the army had to be partly abandoned by agreement with the army groups. In view of the originally uncertain combat situation, the advance of the Einsatzgruppen depended principally on the military operations.[3]

Stahlecker's summary report also mentioned the necessity for the Kommandos to move closely with the army:

> At the start of the Eastern Campaign it became obvious with regard to the Security Police that its special work had to be done not only in the rear areas, as was provided for in the original agreements with the High Command of the Army, but also in the combat areas, and this for two reasons. On the one hand, the development of the rear area of the armies was delayed because of the quick advance and on the other hand, the undermining communist activities and the fight against partisans was most effective within the area of actual fighting especially when the Luga sector was reached.
>
> To carry out the duties connected with Security Police, it was desirable to move into the larger towns together with the armed forces.[4]

Stahlecker indicated that when Kovno, Libau, Mitau, Riga, Dorpat (Tartu), Reval (Tallinn), and the suburbs of Leningrad were captured, the Security Police units were there.[5]

The presence of the Kommandos in the vanguard of the attack had devastating consequences for the Jews. In addition to this immediate Einsatzgruppen presence, perhaps the most conspicuous factor that determined the killing statistics was the actual number of Jews within the various areas of the east when the Germans attacked in June 1941. Those areas with the largest Jewish population had the greatest number of victims. Closely related to this was the speed with which the Germans conquered each region. The time it took to overrun the territories played an important role in determining how many Jews were able to escape. Once the Germans had taken over an area, escape was virtually impossible.

In Lithuania at the time of the German occupation the number of Jews was between 220,000 and 225,000.[6] Latvia had approximately 95,000 Jews,[7] Eastern Poland 1,350,000,[8] Estonia 5,000,[9] White Russia and the Ukraine 1,908,000, Bukovina and Bessarabia 300,000, and the Crimea 50,000.[10] Thus about four million of the five million Jews in Russian territory were living in the western part of the country, in the very regions conquered by the Germans. Most of these Jews lived in the major urban centers. It has been estimated that one and half million of these four million Jews escaped before the Germans arrived.[11]

The German assault was swift and powerful. For their part the Soviets, despite warnings, were unprepared for the attack.[12] During the first days of the invasion, the German planes raided more than sixty Russian airfields, mainly those that housed modern planes. In the western areas the Soviet Air

Force was essentially destroyed on the first day of the attack.[13] The German advance was so rapid that by July 3, Franz Halder, the chief of the General Staff, recorded in his diary "It is thus probably no overstatement to say that the Russian campaign has been won in the course of two weeks."[14]

The speed of the attack sealed the fate of hundreds of thousands of Jews. Just noted was the fact that it was the desire of the Kommandos to enter a conquered city or area with the army forces. This allowed little or no time for the Jews or communist officials to escape. Operational Situation Report 94, for example, mentioned that an agreement with the army guaranteed that Kommandos of Sonderkommando 4a would "march into Kiev with the advance guard after the fall of the town." This happened on 19 September 1941, and soon after a fifty-man unit of Sonderkommando 4a was in Kiev. Paul Blobel, leader of this Kommando, arrived two days later and the main Kommando members and Gruppe staff arrived on September 25. Within four days preparations were completed and on 29 and 30 September, 33,771 Jews were shot.[15] Other occasions illustrating the rapidity of conquest and extermination could be given. The city of Kovno was captured on the second day of the war, June 23. On the night of June 25 to 26, the already cited pogroms resulted in the death of one thousand five hundred Jews. Within the first weeks four thousand Jews were killed in pogroms by Lithuanians in the Kovno area. Vilna fell on June 24. All of Lithuania was under German rule within five days.[16] During the period from June to November 1941 approximately 173,000 to 177,000 Jews had been killed in Lithuania, that is, more than 80 percent of the Jewish population there.[17]

On the second day of the campaign the Germans had already entered Latvia.[18] The country was captured in two weeks. Dwinsk fell on June 26, and by the beginning of July Riga and Libau were in German hands.[19] Farther south in White Russia the pace was equally impressive as the Germans encircled the Red Army divisions. Slonim was occupied on June 25,[20] and within five days Minsk was captured.[21] In the Ukraine by July 9 Shitomir was captured,[22] and by August 29 the Germans had reached as far east as Charkov.[23]

The progress of the military operations was decisive in relation to the work of the Einsatzgruppen. The reports offer indications of the effect produced by a slowing down or pause in these operations. The Kommandos had to stay put and await orders while the front was secured. The most immediate result of this situation was that the advance of the Kommandos was delayed temporarily, and this gave more time for potential victims to escape.

In the area of Einsatzgruppe B the advance of Army Group Center was delayed by the determined fighting of the Soviets. The area around Orscha and Smolensk proved to be particularly difficult. While Minsk had been captured in five days, by mid-July the Germans were stuck at Smolensk. Einsatzgruppe B gave indications in the first weeks of the war of the already growing threat of partisan operations in the Orscha district. The road to Smolensk was not yet secured. Any further advance beyond Smolensk was inadvisable. The report warned that, "Not only men but also the vehicles may be lost at any time as a result of the strong enemy activity."[24] The battle of Yelnyia, southeast of Smolensk, raged on throughout the month of August. On September 5 it was recaptured from the Germans (until October 1941) and represented the first victory of the Red Army over the Germans.[25]

Einsatzgruppe D had to cover a much greater distance in order to reach Bessarabia/Bukovina. As a result the Kommandos were slower in reaching their initial area of operations.[26] Breakdowns of vehicles also hampered their progress eastward.[27] To these delays caused by distance and problems of transportation were added those related to the military situation. In Belzy (Balti), for example, because fighting was still going on there, Sonderkommando 10a was not able to enter the city until July 9.[28]

Delays caused by the military situation, while they prevented the Kommandos from moving forward and capturing new victims, also enabled the Kommandos to consolidate more carefully their security work within the areas already under their control. Thus Einsatzgruppe B reported on 23 September 1941 that the time caused by the unchanged military situation allowed "for a more thorough SD overhauling" of the area.[29] Communist officials and partisans in the area, who had hitherto escaped detection, were now arrested by the Kommandos. The fact that the rapid advance of the Germans had forced the Einsatzgruppen to move too fast to comb the rear areas completely was recognized very soon by the Einsatzgruppen leaders.[30] The Germans ensured that areas left behind were combed for undesirables by backing up their own work with that of other units. As a consequence, Kommandos from Tilsit carried out shootings in July in the border regions of Lithuania.[31] Similarly, Security Police Kommandos from Krakow (Krakau) set up headquarters in Lvov (Lemberg), Brest-Litovsk, and Bialystok and carried out actions in areas of eastern Poland.[32] Ironically, by having to remain in one place for a longer period than was anticipated, the Kommandos were given the opportunity to "clear up" that area to a much greater degree than would have been possible had they advanced further right away. Either way, by staying put or pushing forward, they captured victims.

Delays resulted from other reasons as well. A report by Einsatzgruppe C mentioned that in Charkov a major action against the Jews was to be undertaken by Sonderkommando 4a. The Kommando had to delay the beginning of the action until "arrangements for the accommodation of the Kommandos" had been made.[33] (The delay in this particular case was not long. The next report by Sonderkommando 4a concerning Charkov appeared just over two weeks later, and mentioned the evacuation of the Jews and preparations for their shooting. The report stated that 305 Jews had already been shot.[34]) The front line often fluctuated back and forth between the opposing sides. Retreats were not uncommon. Einsatzgruppe D was forced to leave Belzy because of the return of the Soviets.[35]

The unfolding of the battle for Kiev had repercussions for the Kommandos of Einsatzgruppe C. A report, dated 23 August 1941, stated that a Teilkommando of Sonderkommando 4b had arrived at Kirovograd. The rest of the Kommando would follow by September 14. The report then mentioned that "The advance detachment of the group that started for Wasilkow was recalled in the meantime since the attack on Kiev has been discontinued and further offensive actions against Kiev are not expected to take place in the near future."[36] (Kiev was not captured until September 19.)

Another example of having to change the plans of the Kommandos as the consequence of unexpected setbacks or delays at the front occurred in the area of Einsatzgruppe A. It had originally been planned to use units of Einsatzkommandos 2 and 3 in Leningrad, and for this purpose they were sent to Nowoselje. The advance to Leningrad did not take place, so these units at Nowoselje "were used for extensive operations of cleaning and pacifying in the area of Panzer-Group Four."[37]

In spite of the rapid thrust of the German forces throughout much of the eastern territories, reports indicated that in many areas many Jews had escaped before the arrival of the Germans. Mainland Estonia, for instance, was not completely conquered for two months, and the islands off Estonia were able to hold out until the middle of October. This allowed time for about half of the approximately five thousand Jews in Estonia to escape.[38] Many of the Operational Situation Reports gave evidence that in addition to Jews, many communist officials had also escaped.[39] One report from Einsatzgruppe D announced that in Nikolajew and Cherson no leading communists were left in the area as they had left with the Soviets.[40] Another report, issued almost two weeks later, declared that the same two towns were free of Jews and that the "remaining officials" were "appropriately treated." The report stated that "the high communist officials had taken themselves to safety. It was mostly leading partisans or leaders of sabotage detachments who were seized."[41] A later report, also by Einsatzgruppe D, reiterated that in the Crimea, as elsewhere, leading communists had escaped. Also because of the long time it took to occupy the Crimea, food, cattle, and grain had either been destroyed or taken away by the Russians.[42]

The extent and manner of the evacuation of the Jewish population throughout the east has been a matter of controversy among historians.[43]

The Operational Situation Reports would seem to indicate that significant numbers of Jews did escape on their own or were evacuated as part of systematic evacuation procedures in some areas. These escapes, whether organized or not, were widespread, and significantly reduced the numbers of victims who otherwise would have been captured.

Upon arrival in Mogilev-Podolski, Einsatzgruppe D found that no security police measures were necessary since the Russians had evacuated the entire population and had destroyed the village completely.[44] Other evidence confronting the Einsatzgruppen indicated that large-scale evacuations had occurred. In the Welikije-Luki-Gomel-Chernigov regions, Einsatzgruppe B discovered that "organized evacuation to a larger extent than in previous cases was prepared by the Soviets and actually also carried out."[45] Einsatzgruppe B also reported that in many towns along the Smolensk-Moscow road the Soviets had evacuated the entire Jewish population.[46] Operational Situation Report 133 stated that "the Jewish population has run away without exceptions as far as could be found out up to now, and the same is the case as regards the members of the communist party and skilled workers." The report said that SD reports had shown that the population had been told to move to the Volga and Ural districts and that trains had been provided for this purpose.[47] Another Einsatzgruppe B report noted "the continuing flight-exodus" of the Jews eastward. The towns of Orel, Medyn, and Malojaroslawec were cleared of Jews when the Kommandos arrived there.[48] Einsatzgruppe C reported that when their Kommandos arrived in Dnjepropetrowsk about seventy thousand of the approximately one hundred thousand Jews there had escaped.[49]

In the central and eastern Ukraine, Einsatzkommando 6 reported the Jews had fled after hearing what was in store for them. Not disappointed at this loss of more victims, the Kommando added boastfully,

This may be considered as an indirect success of the work of the Security Police, as the gratuitous evacuation of hundred thousands of Jews—as we hear mostly to the other side of the Ural—is a considerable contribution to the solution of the Jewish question in Europe.[50]

When reports pointed out that Jews were not found in a city upon the arrival of the Kommandos, it did not always mean that the Jews had escaped outright. Often it simply indicated that they were in hiding in the surrounding area,[51] and were waiting for the situation to settle down or for the departure of the Kommandos before they would return. This was soon apparent to the Einsatzgruppen, who then used it as a method of capturing the Jews. Large-scale actions were postponed. The Einsatzkommandos looked for confidential agents from among the Ukrainian and ethnic

German population and waited. In the meantime, many Jews, believing it was safe to return, came back to their homes and were caught.[52]

In the southern area of Einsatzgruppe C the Kommandos arrived into "empty space" with few Jews to be found. As the military operations were too close, the "fugitives" had not yet returned in sufficient numbers.[53] Another report by Einsatzgruppe C issued eight days later also mentioned the lack of Jews in the southern part of its operational area. As a result, here the activities of the Kommandos centered on smaller individual investigations, while in the Berditschew-Shitomir region there was more "opportunity for actions on a larger scale."[54] It is interesting that in view of the differences just cited, the Kommandos considered it necessary to explain that these differences were the reason why there was such a discrepancy in the number of victims reported by each Kommando. This almost apologetic tone was repeated later in the report, where the reporter reminded that "the procedure against the Jews is necessarily different in the individual sectors, according to the density of their settlement." In the northern areas of Einsatzgruppe C, the return of many Jewish refugees presented a problem with regard to the food situation. The often repeated "danger of epidemics" was then given as the excuse for a "thorough clean-up" of the areas.[55]

In summary, while the Operational Situation Reports in themselves do not give any really precise figures as to the number of Jews (and communist officials) who escaped, they do point very strongly to the fact that large numbers did manage to flee and elude the grasp of the killers, even if, in many instances, escape was only temporary.

The Germans had essentially two immediate goals with regard to the eastern territories. The first was the complete destruction of the "Jewish-Bolshevist" regime and the concomitant extermination of the Jews. The second was the economic exploitation of the land and resources of the region for the German war effort.[56] These two goals came into conflict with each other when the Germans realized their pressing need for Jewish labor in order to achieve the second goal. This need for Jewish labor was felt especially by the Wehrmacht and by the various civilian agencies throughout the territories.

The Einsatzgruppen frequently reported the necessary preliminary measures that were taken to exploit the labor forces of the Jews—the establishing of Jewish councils, the registration of the population, the wearing of the yellow Star, the confinement of the Jews to ghettos, and the formation of labor brigades.[57] The importance of Jewish manpower was reflected very early in the Operational Situation Reports. The war was just over a week old, when, in a report, Einsatzkommando 2 stressed the necessity for Jewish labor "in order to keep the war plants and the plants vital for the population in operation."[58] In Estonia, Jews, mostly female, who survived the initial liquidations, were placed in camps and were used for farm work and for peat cutting.[59] By 5 January 1942 it was reported that all the Jews still alive in Latvia and Lithuania were in ghettos and that the Jews of the Riga ghetto were being used for military labor.[60]

German rule in the Russian territories was by no means a smoothly running organizational machine. The assumption had been that the war would be over quickly—in about three months. It was felt that there was no need for any detailed planning with regard to the political management of the territories. Political factors and propaganda were not considered to any great degree.[61] There was little coordination and much antagonism between the various German agencies operating in the east.

One of the central issues, and one that had great bearing on the extent of the destruction, was this issue of Jewish labor. This subject involved much disagreement and wrangling among the various agencies. Were the Jews to be exterminated or were they to be exploited as labor? In other words, did economic and military considerations have priority over the great ideological one, the total destruction of the Jews? It is not our purpose here to analyze this debate in detail. We will merely take note of a number of references to this problem found in the reports.

The antagonism against the principal recruiter of Jewish labor, the Wehrmacht, is observed in many reports. Often it is felt smoldering just beneath the surface of the reports. In Shlobin, Einsatzgruppe B reported that the Wehrmacht had employed Jews for board and wages. At the same time a good part of the local Russian population was still unemployed. The Einsatzgruppe complained that "These measures can very easily be interpreted as a preferential treatment of the Jews." After voicing this complaint, the report then stated that by "contact" with the local Wehrmacht agencies the matter was resolved.[62] Einsatzgruppe A, in a report issued two days after the report just cited, also had strong words concerning the employment of Jews as labor. Jews were employed in the cities, the report stated,

> by all German agencies as upaid manpower. Difficulties with such employing agencies are everyday occurrences if and when the Security Police must take steps against working Jews. Economic agencies have repeatedly even filed applications for exempting Jews from the obligation to wear the Star of David and for authorizing them to patronize public inns. This concerns mostly Jews who are designated as key personnel for certain economic enterprises. Such efforts are of course suppressed by the agencies of the Security Police.[63]

A strong difference of views is seen here as to how the Jews were to be treated. Naturally the Security Police presented what they thought to be the "correct" attitude—the suppression of such preferential treatment of the Jews. Yet later in the same report Einsatzgruppe C recognized the fundamental fact that without the Jews, the Germans would be deprived of the skilled labor that they urgently required.

> Difficulties have arisen in so far as Jews are often the only skilled workers in certain trades (i.e. harness-makers, tailors, carpenters, locksmiths). The cause of this shortage of skilled workers is to a large extent to be found in the unlimited compulsory evacuation of skilled Ukrainians by the Soviets. In order not to endanger reconstruction and the repair work also for the benefit of transient troop units, it has become necessary to exclude provisionally especially the older Jewish skilled workers from the executions.[64]

This argument for the use of Jewish labor had in fact been even more forcefully put forward in an earlier Einsatzgruppe C report. This report read in part as follows:

> In the western and middle Ukraine all urban workers, skilled mechanics, and traders are Jews. If the Jewish labor force is entirely discarded, an economic reconstruction of the Ukrainian industry and the extension of the administration centers of the cities is almost impossible.
> There is only one possibility, which the German administration in the General-gouvernement has been familiar with for a long time: solution of the Jewish problem by extensive labor utilization of the Jews. This will result in a gradual liquidation of Jewry—a development which corresponds to the economic conditions of the country.[65]

This excerpt is noteworthy in that it proposes to solve the labor versus extermination issue by merging the opposing procedures together. Jews are to be utilized for labor, but at the same time are to be worked to death gradually. Thus the Germans will have it both ways, since the desires of the advocates of both sides of the issue will be satisfied. It is also interesting to compare a non-SS document on the subject of labor. In a letter to the chief of the Industrial Armament Department in the Ukraine, Dr. Thomas, the strong complaint was voiced that the massacre of the Jews was "horrible" and that "no consideration was given to the interests of the economy." After noting that hundreds of thousands were killed or allowed to starve to death, the writer of the letter adds: "Who in the world is supposed to produce something of value here?"[66]

The conflicts between those agencies that sought to give priority to the extermination of the Jews and those who placed the economic needs of the war first were never really resolved.[67] This was true even after the often quoted clarification of this question was sent by Otto Bräutigam on 18 December 1941 to Reichskommissar for the Ostland, Hinrich Lohse. The letter said as follows:

> Economic considerations should fundamentally remain unconsidered in the settlement of the problem. Moreover, it is requested that questions arising be settled directly with the Higher SS and Police Leaders.[68]

The liquidations continued, but the need for labor continued as well. That conflicts over the Wehrmacht's recruiting of Jewish labor did not abate after the Bräutigam pronouncement was shown by a letter deploring that German soldiers had been going into the Riga ghetto and rounding up Jews without proper orders. The letter complained as follows:

> The Jewish police is doing well with the daily commitment of about 4000 Jews. Therefore it must be prevented that the Germans attack Jewish policemen in the presence of thousands of Jews.

The letter further suggested that a German policeman capable of preventing the German soldiers from seizing the Jews illegally be placed at the entrance of the ghetto from 5:30 to 8:00.[69]

In one of the last Operational Situation Reports it was reported that Fritz Sauckel, Plenipotentiary for Labor, had ordered White Russia to produce one hundred thousand workers to be sent to Germany. To date only seventeen thousand had been shipped. The report declared that in order to get the right number "the principle of voluntary recruiting is abandoned and compulsory measures will be adopted."[70] (The reference here was to non-Jewish labor, but it indicates the dimensions of the problem of labor confronting the Germans. Even greater numbers were conscripted later.)

To conclude this discussion of Jewish labor in the eastern territories, it must be noted that even after Himmler's order of 21 June 1943 liquidating the ghettos in the Ostland and the setting up of concentration camps, and when, as a result, great numbers of "useless" Jews were killed, the conflicts over Jewish labor remained. The civilian administration authorities had no wish to give up to the SS the not inconsiderable source of income that the Jewish workers provided for their treasury. With the collapse of the military situation the Germans had even more desperate need of the Jewish workers.[71] In summary the need for Jewish labor by the Wehrmacht and civilian agencies and their strong advocacy of this viewpoint against the ideological claims of Himmler's troops allowed many Jews to escape annihilation although the demand for labor merely postponed death temporarily for hundreds of thousands of others. Labor meant a slow and painful death under the inhuman conditions of the work camps, but in the long run, it also enabled thousands of Jews who otherwise would have been killed outright to survive the war.

9

Comparison of Methods of Reporting and Statistics of the Four Einsatzgruppen

The manner in which details of the killings were presented in the Operational Situation Reports was summarized in general terms in Chapter 2. To be considered briefly now are differences in the way this information was presented specifically by each of the four Einsatzgruppen, as well as a comparison of the total number of persons killed within the areas of each Einsatzgruppe during the period up to the end of 1942.

It is not easy to obtain a clear picture of any distinct features that may have characterized the reports of individual Kommandos and Einsatzgruppen themselves. Of the original reports sent to Berlin, which may have enabled us to do this, few have survived. Therefore it cannot be determined exactly how Müller and the RSHA officials may have altered the material they received.[1] The reports of the four Einsatzgruppen were structured in basically the same way. This general sameness of format may have allowed nuances of presentation to be "lost." There was no desire for any individualization in the presentation of the killing statistics. In the absence of original reports, definite conclusions cannot be made on this point. It can be assumed, however, that there was a reasonable correlation to the original reports and that the Operational Situation Reports probably reflect a *reasonable* picture of how the information was presented to Berlin in the reports sent by the individual Einsatzgruppen.

In our earlier general examination of the reports it was noticed that there were inconsistencies in the way attention was given to details of the operations. Variations prevailed as to the inclusion of dates, locations of killings, who was responsible for the actions, and the precision as to statistics, and so on. There was often a lack of uniformity within each report and within each Einsatzgruppe itself. In spite of these inconsistencies certain patterns emerge that permit us to risk a number of generalizations about each of the Einsatzgruppen, although the reasons for any distinctions among the reporting methods cannot be ascertained with any certainty.

It is apparent that both Einsatzgruppe B and Einsatzgruppe C tended to give more detailed information regularly as to the killings, including more specific data concerning numbers killed and times of the killings on an individual Kommando level. They also included breakdowns of victims by category roughly to the same degree. With regard to dates of the operations, both Einsatzgruppe B and C included dates, and described killings without providing any date when these occurred as well. In general Einsatzgruppe C was somewhat more regular in giving both exact dates or time periods when its Kommandos carried out shootings. While both Einsatzgruppen failed to present dates of many of their actions, Einsatzgruppe B offered more examples of this generally. Comparing these same two Einsatzgruppen from the point of view of place description, it is seen that both tended to be quite clear in this respect. Einsatzgruppe B had the edge in this regard. Seldom were executions mentioned in the Einsatzgruppe B reports without including the locations where they occurred.

Einsatzgruppe A included the above details in its reports, being somewhat more exact with regard to locations than dates. It was often not made clear which Kommando carried out a particular operation, and in order to determine this, one has to refer to the Locations and Lines of Communications list. (It is probable that it was assumed that this would be done by the reader.)

Summary figures for numbers executed by each Einsatzgruppe up to a certain point appeared from time to time throughout the reports. All four Einsatzgruppen included their totals in addition to the day-to-day statistics of individual operations. The totals presented by Einsatzgruppe A and Einsatzgruppe C were totals on the level of the Kommandos, mainly Einsatzkommando 2 and Einsatzkommando 3 of Einsatzgruppe A, and Sonderkommando 4a and Einsatzkommando 5 of Einsatzgruppe C. Cumulative numbers relating to other Kommandos appeared too, but these were partial figures that were not continued regularly throughout the series. Einsatzgruppe B was the most precise in reporting these totals. The figures that summarized the totals of Einsatzgruppe B as a whole always included a breakdown of these numbers for every Kommando. For this reason the statistical progress of Einsatzgruppe B's killing operations can be followed more closely on both levels, although this is limited mainly to the period up to 14 November 1941. (See tables 1 to 6.)

The reports of Einsatzgruppe D were usually much less informative about details on the Kommando level. Information as to locations of killings was fairly definite, but it was not often clarified in the text which Kommando was responsible for the operations. Again one is forced to consult the Locations list for help. The Einsatzgruppe D reports were also somewhat vague as to dates of the shootings. Most reports, especially from Operational Situation Report 89 on, gave time periods of roughly two weeks during which operations were said to have occurred. In many other reports no dates were given for the Einsatzgruppe's activities. The periodic totals included in the Einsatzgruppe D reports were a steady account of the numbers killed by the entire Einsatzgruppe. These numbers were never broken down by Kommando, although sometimes a breakdown was included of a large number by category of victims in the day-to-day tabulations.

If the bottom line of our inquiry into the killing operations is to discover to the greatest degree possible how many people were killed, when, where, and by whom, then the irregularity of the reporting frustrates us at every turn. From Einsatzgruppe D a clear picture emerged of the overall numbers of the entire Einsatzgruppe for the period until April 1942, but relatively little can be learned about numbers for individual Kommandos of this Einsatzgruppe. On the other hand, totals on the Kommando and the Einsatzgruppe level, when provided by the other Einsatzgruppen, are limited to certain time periods. For example, the last total for Einsatzgruppe C as a whole was found in Operational Situation Report 128. In the case of Einsatzgruppe B the final total for the Kommandos and the Gruppe was published on 14 November 1941 in Operational Situation Report 133. This coincided roughly with Nebe's departure as leader of Einsatzgruppe B.[2] The precision with which totals for Kommandos and the entire Einsatzgruppe B were recorded during Nebe's time disappeared with his departure. Only in three subsequent reports in the series did Einsatzgruppe B include detailed discussions of its shootings.[3] And not until Operational Situation Report 194 do we again see the familiar breakdown of statistics by Kommando, although no cumulative total for the Einsatzgruppe to date was given. This report indicated that 3,733 people were "specially treated" during the period from 6 March to 30 March 1942.[4]

It is difficult to generalize as to the reasons for these variations in the method of reporting. The character of the incoming reports resulted from conditions at the Kommando level. The reports on these events reflected the perceptions of the local leaders. Whether factors other than personal idiosyncracies of the reporters were at work here cannot be determined from the reports alone. We can only speculate, too, on the considerable discrepancy in the representation of the four Einsatzgruppen in the Operational Situation Reports. Each Einsatzgruppe sent in reports more or less constantly, but reports of all four Einsatzgruppen were not included in every final report. In fact the great majority of individual reports dealt with the reports of only two or three Einsatzgruppen, and a fair percentage of the 195 reports dealt with only one Einsatzgruppe.[5] Also, depending on the situation, not every Kommando was represented in the reports of its own Einsatzgruppe included in the report. As noted earlier, the individual Kommandos often filed separate reports directly to the RSHA, and these reports appeared frequently on their own, independently of other reports from their Einsatzgruppe.

Reports of Einsatzgruppe A appeared in 103 Operational Situation Reports. This constituted the greatest representation by the four Einsatzgruppen. Einsatzgruppe D received the least representation, being featured in only sixty-three reports, followed closely by Einsatzgruppe B with only sixty-four. Reports of Einsatzgruppe C appeared in seventy-seven reports in the series. Since evidence suggests that only what was deemed worthy was included in the final reports, it is entirely possible that a good deal of the information sent by the Einsatzgruppen was not included. Therefore it can be assumed only with a certain caution that there was a correlation between the amount of material sent in by the Einsatzgruppen and the extent of their inclusion in the Operational Situation Reports.

Another puzzling feature of the reports were the large gaps that appeared occasionally between entries of a particular Einsatzgruppe. Einsatzgruppe B, for example, was not mentioned in Operational Situation Reports 35, 37 to 42, 46 to 49, and in particular, Operational Situation Reports 51 to 64. In Operational Situation Report 50, the Einsatzgruppe B entry covered a long period of time, and no specific Kommandos were singled out in the descriptions. Therefore within the period covering Reports 34 to 65, Einsatzgruppe B was represented only five times. No doubt gaps in the final reports reflected gaps in the actual sending and receipt of reports. There was no regularity in the quantity of reports reaching Berlin, and since it was considered very important for the reports to be long in order to document all aspects of the operations, it was Knobloch's practice to put aside information on days when many reports came in for days when fewer arrived.[6] Here again we can only speculate as to why these gaps were present. The pressing tasks at hand may have been affected by a variety of circumstances. For example, the increasing partisan operations in their area may have forced the members of Einsatzgruppe B to devote more and more attention to this problem, and this may have influenced the frequency of their reports to Berlin. These factors may also have affected the gathering of material by the SD men for their reports, a practice that no doubt took time under the best of circumstances. According to one statement, Einsatzgruppe D apparently did not send reports during periods when Ohlendorf was absent from staff headquarters.[7] This may have been the case with other Einsatzgruppen. Gaps may also have resulted from the many periods when a Kommando was in transition from one location to another, or was held up in its operations by the military situation. The reports of Einsatzgruppe D figured in the final reports only seventeen times up to Operational Situation Report 88. Present in this period was a gap of twenty consecutive reports (Reports 68–87) where no Einsatzgruppe D material was included, a period that coincided with the shift of the headquarters from Ananjew to Nikolajew.[8] The telephone and teletype lines were constantly being sabotaged by the partisans, and this prevented or delayed the sending of messages via these methods. Poor weather conditions as well often hampered the courier service. In general the fact that not every Einsatzgruppe appeared in every report allowed more "space" for those Kommandos whose operations were included. Knobloch's method of putting aside material came about from the need to have something to offer. A report of some sort had to be compiled. Yet, in spite of these precautions, it was not always possible to issue reports with sufficient material on even one Einsatzgruppe. Other than mention of their locations and lines of communication, seventeen of the Operational Situation Reports contained no reports on any of the Einsatzgruppen.[9] These reports consisted solely of reports from other Security Police officials from areas of the Reich, the Generalgouvernement, and other occupied territories as well as the short military reports.

To conclude, while at first glance the Operational Situation Reports seemed to offer the same details surrounding the killings, on closer inspection it was clear that a fair amount of variation in the presentation of these details prevailed. This lack of uniformity probably characterized the reports as they reached the RSHA, and it was perhaps not considered necessary or possible to bring this information into a more regular format. These differences in the pattern of reporting were also paralleled in the differences in the total numbers of victims reported killed by each Einsatzgruppe, a subject that will now be examined.

In order to compare the statistics of all categories of victims killed in the area of each Einsatzgruppe, it will be necessary to include some sources beyond the Operational Situation Reports as the latter are incomplete. Tables 1 to 6 list the important statistical information concerning killings found in the Operational Situation Reports, and combine them with figures from other reports and sources. This tabulation is limited to the period up to the end of 1942.

A brief explanation of the tables is in order. The column on the left includes the report or other documentary evidence that constitutes the source for the statistics presented. In tables 1, 4 and 5, the middle column indicates the particular Kommando or Higher SS and Police Leader units and the numbers killed by these forces. The right column includes known totals for each Einsatzgruppe as a whole. (In arriving at the final totals great effort has been made to avoid overlapping in the tabulations, in particular with respect to totals of individual Kommandos and those of an entire Einsatzgruppe. In spite of this effort, given the manner of reporting, one cannot always be certain that in some cases overlapping of numbers is not present to some extent, especially in the case of Einsatzgruppe A and C.) Rather than just cite final totals for the Einsatzgruppen or Kommandos (where possible) earlier figures and cumulative totals given in the reports are included in the tables. This is done to offer the sense of the extent of the killings as time passed.

Totals used to calculate the final overall statistics for the area of each Einsatzgruppe are marked with an asterisk. The other numbers in the tables are of two types: 1) cumulative numbers marked (cum.); 2) available numbers for individual Kommando, Higher SS and Police Leader unit, and Einsatzgruppen Operations given in the reports. Included in the latter category are estimates of killing statistics derived from reports where no total was presented. As these estimates are conservative, these figures are qualified with the words "at least."[10]

Tables 2 and 3 include, under the heading of Einsatzgruppe A, the three reports that furnish statistics concerning killings by Einsatzgruppe A personnel. The two so-called Stahlecker reports (tables 2 and 3) give numbers on the basis of geographical areas. The report by Karl Jäger (table 3) provides a total of those people killed by Einsatzkommando 3 until 1 December 1941. The monthly totals given here are those listed separately by month in the first part of the statistical section in the report. For August, September, October, and November, the numbers actually are greater for each of these months, since there was an overlapping from one month to the next in the presentation of some of the statistics. The figure 47, 288 presented here is the total of killings by detachments of the Kommando carried out in various cities from 13 July to 25 November 1941 as found in the latter part of the statistical section. The entries for these numbers provide specific dates as well as time periods for killings. (See Chapter 12 for a further discussion of the statistics of Jäger's report.)

Two things become apparent from a study of these tables: a real sense of the great numbers of victims involved; and the realization that these numbers, great as they are, are incomplete. It is evident that it is not possible from these reports alone (and the later Reports from the Occupied Eastern Territories) to obtain a true total of people liquidated by the Einsatzgruppen. One is even unable to distinguish clearly between those actions carried out by mobile formations and those of the more stationary units established in areas under civilian administration.[13] Thus any total number of victims arrived at can only be approximate. Let us examine these numbers and see the reasons for this.

Attempts at arriving at comprehensive figures of those people killed by the Nazis are plagued with great difficulties.[14] This is also true even when narrowing one's attention, as we are, only to the Einsatzgruppen. It was noted earlier that the numbers in the reports were often not known or stated precisely, as when an area was declared "free of Jews" or that in an action a "number of Jews or communists" were executed. Such uncertainty may affect some of the subtotals in the above lists. It was also seen that frequently the numbers given were only approximate or were rounded off. There is also evidence to suggest that some of the Einsatzkommando and Einsatzgruppen leaders deliberately exaggerated the numbers of persons

Tables of Killing Statistics

Table 1

Einsatzgruppe A

Document	Kommando		Einsatzgruppe A as a whole
Operational Situation Report (OSR) 88	EK3 —	46,692 cum.	85,000
OSR 94	EK3 (area) — about 75,000 cum.		
OSR 131	EK2 —	31,598 cum.	
OSR 155			33,210 Jews in White Russia since EGA took over this area.
OSR 156	EK2 —	33,970 cum.	
	HSSPL —	10,600	
OSR 163	EK2 —	34,193 cum.	
OSR 165–195			At least 23,732* more persons.
Letter of Kube to Lohse (31 July 1942) PS-3428	Mentions killings during last ten weeks of approximately 65,000* people.[11]		

Table 2

Einsatzgruppe A

Document	Area		
Report of EGA up to 15 October 1941 (Stahlecker report) L–180	Latvia —	31,868	
	Lithuania —	81,171	This number includes about 42,000 people in Shavli who were killed by EK2 before EK3 took over this area on 2 October 1941.
	Estonia —	1,158	
	White Russia —	7,620	
	Additional actions, pogroms, etc. —	13,750	
	Total	135,567	As of 15 October 1941.

Table 3

Einsatzgruppe A

Document	Area		
EGA report	Estonia —	2,000	
Winter 1941–42 (Second Stahlecker report) PS–2273	Latvia —	71,184	
	Lithuania —	136,421	
		5,000	Pogroms
	White Russia — 41,000		
	Estimate of Number shot in White Russia by Armed Forces (Not included in above figure) —	19,000	
	Total	274,605*	(Total Jews shot 229,052)

Document	Kommando	
Jäger report (December 1, 1941)	EK3 — 137,346 (SIC)	As of 1 December 1941, including pogroms.

Breakdown by Month

July	—	4,400
August	—	38,324 (SIC)
September	—	23,435
October	—	13,281
November	—	6,618

And detachments of EK3 in various locations from 13 July to 25 November 1941 — 47,288 (SIC)

Table 4

Einsatzgruppe B

Document	Kommando		Einsatzgruppe B as a Whole
OSR 31			7,620 cum.
OSR 43			11,084 cum.
OSR 73		(as of August 21)	16,964 cum.
OSR 92		(as of September 23)	23,804 cum.
OSR 108		(as of September 28)	30,094 cum.
OSR 125			37,180 cum.
OSR 133			45,467 cum.
OSR 146–149		at least	18,522
OSR 194			3,733
	Total for Einsatzgruppe B for the period of the Operational Situation Reports	at least	67,722
	Total for Einsatzgruppe B as of December 1942		134,000*

Table 5

Einsatzgruppe C

Document	Kommando	Higher SS and Police Leader South	Einsatzgruppe as a Whole
OSR 37	SK4a — 2,531 cum.		
OSR 80	SK4a — 7,152 cum. (as of August 24)	23,600	
OSR 86	SK4a — 6,584 cum.	511	
OSR 88	SK4a — 11,328 cum.	1,878	
OSR 94		44,125 killed in August 1941 (Includes above 23,600)	
OSR 101	SK4a and Police 33,771 (Kiev)		
OSR 111	SK4a — 51,000 cum.		
OSR 128			80,000
OSR 132	SK4a — 55,432 cum. (as of October 20) EK5 — 15,110 cum.		
OSR 135	EK5 — 21,258 cum.	10,000	

Document	Kommando	Higher SS and Police Leader South	Einsatzgruppe as a Whole
OSR 143	SK4a — 57,243 cum. (as of November 8) EK5 — 29,644 cum. (as of November 10)	15,000	
OSR 156	SK4a — 59,018 cum. (as of November 30) EK5 — 36,147 cum. (as of December 7)		
OSR 190		(During 1 March to 3 April 1942)	1,315
(all OSR)	SK4b — 6,329 at least	— extracting totals where possible.	
OSR 173 and 177	EK5 — 9,955 at least		
OSR 1 to 195	EK6 — 5,577 at least		
	at least	71,514*	118,341*† at least
			†(includes Kommando totals cited)
Report 51 HSSPL Prützmann		363,211* (Jews killed August to November 1942)	

Table 6

Einsatzgruppe D

Document		Einsatzgruppe D as a Whole
OSR 89 and 95		13,315 cum.
OSR 101		35,782 cum.
OSR 117		40,699 cum.
OSR 129	(sic?)	31,767 cum.
OSR 145		54,696 cum.
OSR 150		75,881 cum.
OSR 153		79,276 cum.
OSR 157		80,160 cum.
OSR 170		86,652 cum.
OSR 190		91,678 cum.
OSR 193	(at least)	50
total		91,728*

Note: approximately 60,000 Jews killed in Odessa at the end of October 1941 are not included in the above calculations. The Kommandos of Einsatzgruppe D were not always able to determine exactly the numbers killed by the Rumanian soldiers.[12]

shot for their own self-aggrandizement.[15] This would make even more difficult a truly correct tabulation. If these exaggerations existed, there is no way to determine by how much and where the numbers were embellished. Totals may in fact be greater than those presented in the reports, as operations by collaborators, either army, or SS units or civil agencies are very often absent from the reports. Figures related to Higher SS and Police Leader operations tend to be incomplete and when included, are often only approximations.[16] The reports do not take into account deaths by natural causes, or deaths in ghettos or elsewhere by disease, cold, or starvation.[17] The use of gas vans in the east had begun by the end of 1941 but were not specified in the Operational Situation Reports. Gas vans were also not mentioned in the Reports from the Occupied Eastern Territories, nor is it possible to ascertain to what extent these numbers may or may not have been subsumed in the fragmentary later figures available. The totals taken directly from the reports may suffer as well from the above uncertainties, nor does there often seem to be a relationship between the periodic totals and the day-to-day tallies. Unfortunately, all that one can do is work with the figures at hand and assume that the Germans' arithmetic is correct.[18]

The impossibility of determining an exact total becomes even more obvious when one examines closely the numbers given in the tables. The totals given in the reports are for different time periods and thus do not include all the killings up until the end of 1942. The dates of the last Operational Situation Reports, which contain total figures for each Einsatzgruppe as a whole, are 19 September 1941 (Report 88) for Einsatzgruppe A; 14 November 1941 (Report 133) for Einsatzgruppe B; 3 November 1941 (Report 128) for Einsatzgruppe C; and 8 April 1942 (Report 190) for Einsatzgruppe D. Anything approaching a final total for the entire period of the war cannot be realized. Yet we are faced with difficulties even if we limit ourselves solely to the period of the Operational Situation Reports, that is, from June 1941 to the end of April 1942.

Let us take the numbers of each Einsatzgruppe in turn and examine them briefly.

As already noted, the statistics for Einsatzgruppe B and Einsatzgruppe D are cumulative and cover different periods of time. We will accept these totals as given, and will not speculate here as to their accuracy. In table 1 (for Einsatzgruppe A) the Operational Situation Reports mention totals for Einsatzkommandos 2 and 3 only. Operational Situation Report 88 gives the only total for the entire Einsatzgruppe as eighty-five thousand[19] as of 19 September 1941. A later report (Operational Situation Report 155) gives a figure of 33,210 Jews killed by Einsatzgruppe A during the period since it took over the area of White Russia. These numbers, plus the 10,600 killed by the Higher SS and Police Leader units given in Operational Situation Report 156, and the 34,193 killed by Einsatzkommando 2 listed in Operational Situation Report 163, yield a total of 163,003 for the area of Einsatzgruppe A by 2 February 1942.[20] When a comparison is made between this total and that given in the Einsatzgruppe A draft report (table 3), we encounter a problem that is found throughout these tables. This is the discrepancy between the figures from two sources even when the time period is roughly the same for both.

The Einsatzgruppe A draft is not dated. From its content we can assume it dates from the winter of 1941–42, approximately until the same period of time as covered up to Operational Situation Report 163. (2 February 1942). This report states that, to date, 229,052 Jews had been killed. There is a big difference between this total and that of 163,003 just cited, even bearing in mind that the latter number must be incomplete. There is a further problem with this report. When we add up the totals that are given in this report by area, we get a total of 274,605 persons killed, including the pogroms in Lithuania.

The Stahlecker report dated 15 October 1941 (table 2) and the Jäger report (table 3) do not correspond as to time or method of compilation. The former provides a total for the entire Einsatzgruppe A as of 15 October 1941. The latter gives a total for Einsatzkommando 3 as of 1 December 1941. Further complications result from the fact that the 81,171 persons killed in Lithuania (table 2) no doubt includes about forty-two thousand Jews in Shavli, who were killed there by Einsatzkommando 2 before Einsatzkommando 3 assumed control in the Shavli area on 2 October 1941. This number is therefore not included in the Jäger report total since this report concerns only the activities of Einsatzkommando 3.[21] When one is able to compare the cumulative figures for the same Kommando for the same time period, the figures sometimes do seem to match. For instance, Operational Situation Report 94 (25 September 1941) stated that about seventy-five thousand persons were killed in Einsatzkommando 3's area. Adding the totals listed in the Jäger report up to the end of September, one arrives at a total of 75,159.[22]

The Operational Situation Reports give a clearer, if incomplete, picture of the numbers for Einsatzgruppe B. We can trace the steady rise in numbers by the Einsatzgruppe as a whole as well as those of the individual Kommandos since this breakdown by Kommando appeared with almost every summary figure.[23] These cumulative totals end, however, on 14 November 1941. Einsatzgruppe B, up to 21 April 1942, killed at the very least a further 22,255 people according to subsequent Operational Situation Reports. A later report gives a total figure for Einsatzgruppe B as one hundred thirty-four thousand persons killed by December 1942.[24]

In comparing the totals for Einsatzgruppen A and B, the enormous difference of pace and numbers is seen. Einsatzgruppe B got off to a relatively "slow" start, but as the numbers of victims increased, so did the rate. By the period roughly from the month of September to the beginning of October 1941 (Operational Situation Reports 73 and 108) and from mid-October to mid-November (Operational Situation Report 108 to 133) the increase reached an average of about fifteen thousand in each of these periods of time. The difference in the two Einsatzgruppen is made especially clear when we realize that by mid-November 1941 Einsatzgruppe B as a whole had reported 45,467 executions, whereas Einsatzkommando 2 alone was already responsible for killing 31,598 people, and as of a couple of weeks later (1 December 1941), Einsatzkommando 3 reported the shooting of 137,346 people. The 45,467 mentioned in Operational Situation Report 133 is incomplete since it does not include earlier operations carried out by Einsatzkommando 9 in areas later taken over by Einsatzgruppe A.[25]

The latest overall totals for Einsatzgruppe C (table 5) are for the period up to 7 December 1941. (Operational Situation Report 156, 16 January 1942). These numbers refer to Kommandos only. As of this date Sonderkommando 4a and Einsatzkommando 5 together killed 95,165 people. Again, as with the totals for Einsatzgruppe A, only two Kommandos were specified. In table 5 totals have been given for the other Kommandos as well as for Sonderkommando 4a and Einsatzkommando 5 after Operational Situation Report 156, but these calculations are incomplete for the reasons stated earlier. The numbers given are therefore absolute minimum totals of operations that can be pinpointed and quantified from the evidence of the Operational Situation Reports. (In the case of SK4b and EK6 there is the possibility of overlapping with the total for the whole Einsatzgruppe.) As for liquidation figures after the end of April 1942, given the large number of Jews living in the Ukraine, it is not surprising that Himmler reported to Hitler on 29 December 1942, that 363,211 Jews had been killed in the Ukraine, the Bialystok, and South Russian areas from August to November 1942.[26] While some of these killings took place in regions beyond the jurisdiction of Einsatzgruppe C, this total would indicate that the number of victims was extended greatly in late 1942.

A glance at totals in table 5 for Sonderkommando 4a in the reports that are roughly one month apart (Reports 111, 132, 143, and 156) reveals that the *rate* of *increase* of the killing actually went down during this period. This decrease is also true for Einsatzkommando 5 during those times that can be compared on a similar monthly basis (Reports 135, 143, and 156).

The totals for Einsatzgruppe D (table 6) are much more complete. While it is not until Operational Situation Report 89 that totals are given in a steady consistent manner (note that the total 13,315 is repeated in Operational Situation Report 95), the shootings listed in the reports as having taken place between the sets of totals seem to correspond with these totals. This is true at least up to Operational Situation Report 157. After this the numbers do not seem to be complete and do not correspond exactly with the cumulative totals given. Numbers in reports before Operational

Situation Report 89 tend to be incomplete, or at best minimum figures, and some reports discuss operations without providing numbers.[27]

Operational Situation Report 190 gives a final total of 91,678 persons liquidated. To this number can be added at least fifty more people until the last report. It can be assumed that this number is a more exact calculation than those given for the other Einsatzgruppen. The lateness of the report, the fact that the total is for the entire Einsatzgruppe with no breakdown by Kommando and thus with no omissions of Kommando numbers or *possible* overlapping of numbers, as was the case with Einsatzgruppe A and Einsatzgruppe C, the relatively fewer examples of Higher SS and Police Leader operations for this area and period, and the fact that Ohlendorf himself admitted that ninety thousand people had been killed by his Einsatzgruppe during the period of his leadership—all these factors indicate that the total (91,728) may be considered a reasonably complete one.

The Reports from the Occupied Eastern Territories concerned themselves mainly with antipartisan warfare and did not continue to describe liquidations of Jews and others. Of course the killings did not stop, and reports were certainly drawn up giving details of these operations. Fragmentary evidence does exist for later killings. In one of two reports by the SS statistician Dr. Richard Korherr summarizing statistics about the final solution of the Jewish question up to 31 December 1942, a figure of 633,330 Jews who had been "evacuated" in the Russian areas appears. This number, based on RSHA calculations, is probably a summary of total Einsatzgruppen killings to date. Yet Korherr admitted that this number was not complete since the statistics of the operations of the Higher SS and Police Leaders were not available to him, nor did the number include an estimate of the range of deaths that occurred in the ghettos.[28]

These totals, therefore, are incomplete. In themselves, the reports do not present us with an exact total of persons killed, even for the time that they covered. The lack of a coordinated system of reporting totals has made precise calculations impossible. In spite of these limitations, the reports do indicate clearly the scope of the killing. If we were to assemble the final numbers in the tabulations discussed above, none of which appear to overlap although this cannot be absolutely ruled out, we might arrive at the following minimum total for the period ending December 1942:[29]

Einsatzgruppe A	274,605 (table 3)
	23,732 (table 1)
	65,000 (table 1)
Einsatzgruppe B	134,000 (table 4)
Einsatzgruppe C	118,341 (table 5)
Einsatzgruppe D	91,728 (table 6)
Higher SS and Police Leaders	82,114 (tables 1 and 5)
HSSPL Prützmann	*363,211 (table 5)*
Total	at least 1,152,731 persons

This total refers to all categories of victims. Since the above numbers do not reflect the entire picture, the total arrived at is also a minimum figure. The numbers for the Higher SS and Police Leaders are certainly only part of their operations. The number given here is limited to those major operations of the Higher SS and Police Leaders that were included in the reports.[30]

The reports are essential to our understanding of the magnitude of the killing program in the east. On the level of day-to-day actions in specific locations, they give us a great deal of information. Precise totals elude our grasp. It is unlikely that historians will ever get beyond educated estimates as to the number of persons killed in the eastern territories as well as in other areas. We may conclude, given our own total cited above, and the fact that we have limited our inquiry to the end of 1942 only, that the estimate of Raul Hilberg that over 1,300,000 Jews were killed in the east by the Einsatzgruppen and other SS agencies and collaborators is probably as close to a true figure as we are likely to find.[31] Bearing in mind that Hilberg's total refers to Jews only, we recognize that the addition of numbers of non-Jews liquidated (many of which are included in our above total) would raise this number considerably higher.

10

Attitude and Collaboration of the Eastern Populations

We come now to a consideration of collaboration with the Germans, one of the most contentious subjects relating to the war in the east. We will examine here the following questions: What do the reports indicate regarding the general attitude to the Germans of the population throughout the occupied eastern regions, and in particular what do they indicate about the latter's attitude to the killing operations? How did these attitudes change with time? What evidence do the reports offer concerning active collaboration in the killing by members of the eastern population?[1]

When the German armies moved eastward they faced a vast area that included very different geographical, social, political, and demographic conditions. The territories comprised a mixture of Poles, Jews, Ukrainians, Estonians, Latvians, Lithuanians, Russians, Tartars, ethnic Germans, and other groups, all of whom, in turn, were divided into various political affiliations. In spite of these great differences, all four Einsatzgruppen had the same task to carry out, and they were confronted with the realization that they could not do it alone. They needed the help of the indigenous population in the Security Police work and the liquidation of the undesirable elements. To an astounding degree they received this help. How did this come about?

Many of the territories invaded on June 22 had themselves been occupied only recently by a foreign power. Poland had been divided in two on 28 September 1939, and the eastern half of the country had been under Soviet rule. The Baltic States, Estonia, Latvia, and Lithuania were annexed by the Soviet Union in June 1940 after having suffered the presence of Soviet military air and naval bases since 1939. This takeover had occurred in spite of assurances given by Molotov in a speech on 31 October 1939, that the sovereignty of these states would be respected.[2]

Throughout these territories the relationship between the Jews and non-Jews and their place in society was a complex one. It is beyond the scope of this study to delve into this subject in detail. Suffice it to say that with the exception of Estonia (perhaps as the result of the fact that only five thousand Jews lived there), Jews traditionally had experienced a considerable degree of anti-Semitism at the hands of the eastern populations. Long standing tensions, both political and religious, between the diverse elements of the society had led to antagonisms that deepened with time. In the popular mind there was a strong association of Jews with Bolshevism. This perception had its origins as far back as the Bolshevik Revolution and the years of the Civil War (1917–21).[3] To give an example, in Lithuania this association of Jews with Bolshevism was intensified during the period of Soviet rule between 1940 and June 1941 (and in Estonia and Latvia as well). During this period, while the Jews suffered economically as a result of Soviet nationalization of business and property[4] and spiritually as a result of restrictions on their cultural life, they also benefited from the outlawing of anti-Semitism and their increased participation in government, in education, in medicine, and other areas of Lithuanian life that had been largely closed to them previously.[5] When rumblings of war between Germany and Russia began to be felt in 1941, the Jews, aware of German actions against the Jews in Poland, quite naturally hoped that the Soviets, as the lessor of two evils, would remain in Lithuania.[6] Lithuanians (as did Estonians and Latvians) viewed the conquest of the Soviets as a tragedy. The loss of independence, the brutal deportations and the repressive measures caused them to look to Germany for deliverance.[7] The attitude of the Jews was seen as being procommunist by many Lithuanians.[8] In Lithuania local partisan groups were already organized to assist the Germans in the coming struggle against the Soviets.[9] These groups circulated proclamations that denounced the Jews and ordered their expulsion from the country. The final event that increased the animosity against the Jews was the deportation of 25,000–30,000 people (including 6,000 Jews). This was carried out by the People's Commissariat for Internal Affairs. Some Jews were numbered among its membership.[10]

Similar attitudes toward the German invaders existed in Estonia and Latvia where local fascist groups were also poised to assist the Germans. In the western Ukraine following World War I, the Jews had found themselves caught in a power struggle between Poles and Ukrainians.[11] Ukrainian nationalist elements during the 1920s and 1930s had established ties with German leaders and agencies and had absorbed some of the ideological thinking of the Nazis.[12] In April 1941 the resolution proclaimed at the Second General Congress of the Bandera faction of the Organization of Ukrainian Nationalists (OUN) included an unmistakably clear identification of Jews with the Bolshevik regime.[13] For their part, Ukrainians had good reason to view the Soviets as their worst enemy, given the suppression of Ukrainian independence in 1917–20, the destruction of their people by the famine of 1933, the repressive measures during the 1930s and between 1939 and 1941.[14] With regard to achieving an independent Ukrainian state, it is evident that certain leaders in Germany, especially Alfred Rosenberg, were in favor of such a concept.[15] Given this sympathetic attitude among certain German officials, it follows that Ukrainians (like the Baltic peoples) could look optimistically to the Germans to assist them in gaining independence. Yet Rosenberg's opinions concerning the Ukraine did not prevail. The Ukraine was exploited, not granted autonomy, and again, the Jews were caught in the middle.

This brief outline provides some background to the situation as it existed when the Germans invaded in June 1941. It also places in context the largely sympathetic attitude to the destruction of the Jews that was evidenced in many of the Einsatzgruppen reports. Before examining the subject at hand, however, the point of view of our inquiry must be considered. Given the obviously controversial nature of the subject, it must be stressed at the outset that our analysis is based on what the Einsatzgruppen reporters wrote in their reports. These were Security Police and SD reports. Events were seen from the perspective of these German agencies. This has advantages and limitations. The advantages resulted from the fact that, however limited the outlook was, it was still a reasonably detached one, that of an "external" source, the Einsatzgruppen, who had only their own interests to consider. This was the perspective of the outsider, who had no real obligation or desire to place the eastern people in a favorable light. (One cannot imagine the local populace viewing itself so critically.) The reports were top secret. They were to be seen only by Germans, and while it is likely that to some degree the presentation of a positive attitude on the part of the local population was desired by the SD members, they still had to put forward a reliable picture as they had been obliged to do in the earlier reports on the situation in Germany. In fact, of all the reporting agencies functioning in Germany before the war, the SD was probably the most consistently objective in its reporting. The SD had little vested interest in presenting a falsely optimistic picture, as had, for example, the various regional and district reporters of the Nazi Party.[16] In comparison to the party reports, the earlier SD reports in the Reich had been marked by a somewhat more varied and reliable presentation. This was true in comparison as well with the later Operational Situation Reports, given the greater facility in reporting in a nonwar environment. The resulting earlier reports, for example, those dealing with the German public's attitude to the Jews, were characterized by a subtlety and variety of detail and complexity of differentiation not found in the later reports.[17] Still, the Einsatzgruppen reports did include negative attitudes and analysis critical of German policy formulated in Berlin.

The limitations of the German perspective resulted from the methods used to gather the information. We cannot be certain exactly how the SD officials collated their information on the general mood, and therefore, we cannot determine with absolute precision the reliability of these sources. We do know that the Kommandos made contacts within the local population and used these contacts as informers relying mainly on them to furnish information and get wind of the attitude of the people. These secret methods of obtaining intelligence had long been a standard technique used by the SD before the war in Germany. The so-called confidence men, the Vertrauensleute or V-Männer, had been placed at the grassroots level in every village in Germany, and they, in turn, organized networks of informers who passed on the information they were able to uncover.[18] While this modus operandi reaped good results in Germany, it must be borne in mind that in the very different situation in the occupied east the unfamiliar environment, combined with the problems of fighting a war, probably did not allow for the same measure of reliability in the information than was the case earlier. It is not possible to gauge such a difference quantitatively. The contacts within the population passed on their information to the Kommandos who then submitted it to the Kommando leaders. The reports submitted by the Kommando leaders, in turn, formed the basis for more comprehensive reports drawn up at the headquarters. The Kommando reports were thus the source for opinions on the general morale of the population.[19] More overt public demonstrations of pro-German feelings were easily observed and these, coupled with the information obtained from the spies, enabled the SD to piece together a picture of the general mood. Yet we must recognize that it was always the more militant factions that made their views felt. In the situation in the east overt pro-German attitudes, because they were the only ones tolerated, would likely be felt more readily by the authorities than would passive anti-German ones. In general the more "captive" a people are and the more persecuted they may be for deviations from accepted doctrine, then the greater is the unlikelihood of them speaking their minds freely. This renders much more difficult the task of discovering the true sentiments of the population than would be the case in a more open society.[20] Of course it would be hard to imagine a more restricted environment than that imposed by German rule in the east. When reading these reports these limitations must be taken into account. One might do well to follow Wilhelm Keitel's instructions to his military subordinates when he ordered them to observe "extreme caution" in assessing the "credibility of statements made by enemy civilians."[21] It must also be remembered that even in the best of circumstances, it is often difficult to generalize accurately about a situation, and that certainly not all members of the eastern population shared the views described in the reports.[22] One must, therefore, recognize the restricted perspective of these reports.

Keeping in mind this caution, it must still be acknowledged that strong, deep-seated anti-Semitic and anticommunist feeling did exist in eastern

Europe, and that these two attitudes were closely linked. These beliefs were exploited by the Nazis by isolating the Jews in ghettos, and by virtually eliminating communication between the Jews and the local population, they made even worse already existing anti-Jewish sentiments.[23] The Nazis succeeded in this to a far greater degree than in western Europe, among other reasons, because of the extent to which these attitudes were entrenched in the fabric of society. Many of the nationalist aspirations of the eastern population were closely linked with the anti-Semitism that was endemic to eastern Europe. Furthermore, collaboration in western Europe was not motivated by a concern for the emergence of a national identity (as in the Ukraine) since these regions already existed as separate nations.[24] The program of systematic killing began in the east, and thus supplied there the terrible outlet for collaboration in genocide that did not exist earlier. It is significant that collaborators existed in the east in such numbers. They were not simply willing to fight as legitimate soldiers against the Soviets, and thereby rid themselves of oppressive Soviet rule; they were also willing to participate in the murder of thousands of men, women, and children.

One may rightly argue that in every society one will always find people willing to do this dirty work and that eastern Europe was simply another example of this. Yet, the extent and brutality of collaboration in the east must surely be some barometer of the anti-Semitism as it existed generally among the population. Of course being anti-Semitic was not the same thing as sanctioning or taking part in genocide. The generalizations given in the Einsatzgruppen reports were, therefore, at best, *some* measure of the reality of the various attitudes of the eastern population, or at the very least, the SD perception of this reality, however limited.

References to the favorable response of the local population to the occupying German forces materialized very early in the reports. One week after the war started, Sonderkommando 7b reported the "friendly" attitude of the population of Brest-Litovsk.[25] Such descriptions surfaced regularly in the reports. Operational Situation Report 23 quoted a telegram to Hitler from Ukrainians in Lvov that spoke of gratitude for their liberation and a pledge to assist in the rebuilding of Europe freed from "the bloody Jewish Bolshevist rule and plutocrat oppression."[26] In a report included as part of Operational Situation Report 19, Higher SS and Police Leader Hans Prützmann stated that "The attitude of the population of Lithuania is so far friendly towards the Germans."[27] "Positive and pro-German" were the words used to describe the Lithuanian population by Sonder-kommando 1b.[28] Very soon after their arrival, the Security Police noticed a difference in the Russian territories proper and the former Polish territory, which had been occupied by the Soviets since September 1939. Einsatzgruppe C, changed as of Operational Situation Report 19 to Einsatzgruppe B, explained that two years of Soviet rule had caused resentment against the Soviets. The German troops were "treated for the most part as Liberators, at least in a friendly neutral fashion by the Polish people as well as by the White Russian population."[29] The Kommandos reported that Bolshevism had not become a deeply entrenched concept in the minds of the population in many areas.[30] It was hoped that the "spiritual separation" of the White Russian people and Bolshevism would not be impeded by the actions of the Security Police. Thus only those White Russians who were unmistakably proved to be Bolshevist officials or agents were to be killed.[31]

These latter observations are early examples of the awareness on the part of at least some of the Einsatzgruppen personnel of the need to keep in mind the concerns of segments of the local population. It was deemed wise, whenever possible, to avoid antagonizing potential collaborators. Such careful manoeuvering would reap benefits in the long run. These early reports reflected the optimistic mood of the local population and the desire of the occupying forces for the easy exploitation of this frame of mind. The hopes of the eastern peoples were a case in point. Much ink was used in the reports to describe their national and political aspirations. It soon became plain that the various regions wanted autonomy, and it was evident that the SD had to monitor these developments carefully. The first Germans to encounter manifestations of local nationalism were the German soldiers, under whose administrative authority all newly conquered areas fell. A report issued on 2 July 1941 said that Lithuanian nationalists under Zakevizcius had formed a town committee, the Vilna City Committee, soon after the entry of the German troops into Vilna. The army field commander had recognized this committee "provisionally." The report announced that "Activists strive for independence similar to Slovakia. Point to their sacrifice in lives." "This matter" was to be cleared up by the head of the Einsatzgruppe in this area, Arthur Nebe, as the result of discussions to be held with Army Group Center.[32] The next report affirmed that this had been done, and that Army Group Center was issuing the appropriate orders immediately.[33]

At this time in Lithuania, a provisional government was set up, which the Lithuanians claimed to be the sole ruling power in occupied Lithuania. A report issued on July 9 stated that an attempt was being made to impress upon the German military leaders that this government was operational and that a Lithuanian army was also in existence. The report mentioned that the German army was tolerating this situation. The report continued by stressing the attempts of the Lithuanian activists to present a Lithuanian character to Vilna, although Lithuanians certainly did not form the majority of the city's population. Finally, steps were taken, in concert with the Wehrmacht, to circumscribe the political actions of the Lithuanians in order to prevent similar future problems. To further counterbalance the operations of the Lithuanians, the establishment of a White Russian Nationalist organization was approved.[34] Immediately thereafter, in a report issued on July 11, the following further reaction of the Germans to this Provisional government was recorded: "The Wehrmacht has received a new directive ordering it not to recognize the newly formed Lithuanian Government, but to make use of it.[35]

In pursuing this course, the Wehrmacht was following strict orders by Hitler that forbade the reestablishment of local noncommunist government. It was necessary, as well as prudent, because of manpower problems, to appear to offer to meet the aspirations for local self-rule and to grant the population some say in the administrative machinery.[36] By this means the Germans were able to gain a strong foothold by using the structures of government for their own purposes, and at the same time they pleased the local activists by offering them some degree of independence that could be controlled.[37]

In Riga at this time problems with regard to political aspirations of the Latvians were also developing. A committee had been set up, which hoped to be recognized by the Germans.[38] Within a week, concern was being expressed about this committee. A report dated 14 July 1941 stated:

> General von Bock, Chief of the rear army area, reports that the Latvian Council in the composition as visualized up to now is a failure and has outlived its usefulness. Only Col. Plenzner is, for the time being, active as liaison agent. Completely new situation now. In these circumstances the circles aiming at the restoration of inner political conditions before the arrival of the Russians are gaining. Revival of the Ulmanis-Clique. Increasing indignation of constructive and positive Lativian circles due to their being shelved completely. Impairment of German-Latvian relations necessarily the consequence in the near future."[39]

Again the desire of the eastern people to rule themselves was acknowledged. Also apparent was the intransigence of German policymakers in not allowing this to happen in any significant way. This problem remained to the end a critical one in the relationship with the population.[40] It was a major factor in the eventual turning against the Germans by the general population.

But we are anticipating events. All this time the Einsatzgruppen were methodically killing Jews, communists, partisans, and other "undesirables." Many indications of the population's attitude toward the Jews and their reaction to the shootings are found in the reports. Under the heading "The Jewish Question," a report by Einsatzkommando 6 on the situation in the Ukraine declared the following: "All experiences confirm the assertion made before that the Soviet state was a state of Jews of the first order." In every enterprise, the report maintained, the leading positions were held by Jews, the workers were Ukrainians. The report continued:

For these reasons, the Jewish question has become a burning problem for the Ukrainian people. Whenever this question is being discussed, enthusiastic approval can be heard. . . . The aversion of the population and the clear understanding of the Jewish problem increase when going from west to east, which means that in the districts of central and east Ukraine, where there are no deep-rooted Jews, as perhaps in Berditschew and Shitomir, the Jew is rejected with still greater exasperation than in the "old Jewish" districts where a greater dullness and a getting-used to the association with Jews took place in the course of the centuries.[41]

The report declared that in the Ukrainian districts the population was "always gratefully susceptible to the Jewish question."[42]

In Operational Situation Report 125 this evaluation of the effect of actions against the Jews was put forward by Einsatzgruppe C:

The flight of the Red rulers and of the majority of the Jews produced a relief among the population which was even increased by the actions of annihilation against the remaining Jews. All the feelings and impulses, of the proper nationality, hitherto suppressed became more free.[43]

In the Ukraine, the OUN, or Organization of Ukrainian Nationalists established in 1929, was no friend of the Jews either. In Lvov a letter was sent to the police headquarters. It was signed OUN and, as well as advocating the political autonomy of the Ukraine, advocated harsh action against the Jews. The letter read in part: "Long live greater independent Ukraine without Jews, Poles, and Germans. Poles behind the San, Germans to Berlin, Jews to the gallows." The letter also expressed doubt about Germany's ability to win the war without the Ukraine.[44]

In the area of Einsatzgruppe B, similar reactions were acknowledged. Einsatzgruppe B reported that the public execution in Witebsk of twenty seven Jews who had refused to come to work was "approved of" by the White Russian part of the population.[45] It was announced by Einsatzkommando 5 that in Chmielnik 229 Jews had been "taken care of" since the area had "suffered from Jewish terror." The Kommando stated that "The reaction of the population here to the delivery from the Jews was so strong, that it finally resulted in a Thanksgiving service."[46]

Other reports cited further examples of anti-Jewish feelings. Mention was made in one report of the "quieting" effect of public executions of partisans in Mogilev. This report noted the "indifference to the total liquidation of Jews," and the fact that the population "soon became used to the disappearance of the Jews without being influenced in either a positive or negative way."[47] Einsatzgruppe D characterized the Crimean population as "anti-Jewish," and presented the solving of the Jewish, Krimtchak, and Gypsy problem as a fact that was welcomed by the general population.[48] A later report by Einsatzgruppe D spoke of the "active cooperation of the population" in the combing out of the villages.[49] Einsatzgruppe D also reported the execution of ninety-four Jews as a countermeasure for the instigation of resistance to the harvesting that the local population had started on its own.

> The population was visibly relieved by these measures and hardly knows how to show its gratitude. This measure, as well as protecting the population from looting Rumanian soldiers, which was necessary in many cases, led to the fact that the population put absolute confidence into the Germans, which reflects itself by the number of people reporting for work."[50]

Einsatzgruppe C also proclaimed that the harvest was in full swing and that the population in its area had "expressed to the Wehrmacht its great satisfaction and gratitude that the SS had taken care so effectively of the most urgent requirements of the inhabitants."[51]

A further illustration of the reactions to the Einsatzgruppen operations was found in another report by Einsatzgruppe C. This report put forward the following:

> The activity of the Einsatzgruppe concerning the strong measures against the Jews and former members of the communist party had good results as to the public feeling in general. Not only the treatment of the Jews, but also the actions against persons causing the unrest are accepted with understanding."[52]

This passage is significant in that it distinguishes, perhaps inadvertently, between Jews and those "persons causing the unrest." Contrary to the doctrine constantly repeated throughout the reports, there is here an admission that Jews were, in fact, not the ones responsible for the "unrest" in the east.

Einsatzgruppe A also reported anti-Jewish feelings within its area. A report dated 9 March 1942 set forth the following observations:

> The March 2 and 3 action against the Jews had led the Minsk population to expect further actions on a large scale in all of White Ruthenia within the next few weeks. The population greeted the actions which were introduced, for they have grown angry, that the Jews are relatively well supplied in regard to food, which could be determined again and again when looking over the Jewish apartments which have become empty.[53]

Many of the reports dealt in detail with the question of the Jews, their place in Soviet life, and the attitude of the population toward them. These discussions were generally little more than a trotting-out of accepted Nazi anti-Semitism under the guise of investigative reporting. We may refer to one example here as it is characteristic of many such reports. On 5 November 1941 the report of Einsatzgruppe C included an examination of the Jewish influence in Soviet Russian spheres of life. The customary dogma of Jews as the originators of Bolshevism and controllers of all levels of Soviet life was reiterated. This report, typical of many of the reports, was filled with a number of glaring inconsistencies. On the one hand, it was propounded with confidence that everything was controlled by the Jews, and on the other, that no exact statistics could be given on this question because the files were "lacking or were destroyed or removed." The report continued by dismissing the need for official Soviet statistics concerning Jews since they would be of doubtful value anyway, and with the statement that the "so-established facts of an organized desire for power on the part of the Jews are perhaps so convincing" as to make official figures unnecessary. What these so-called "established facts" were and how they were obtained was not demonstrated in the report. This passage is a textbook example of advancing a conclusion as an argument for that conclusion. The report also described the particular form of anti-Semitism as found in the Soviet Union. It was not an attitude based on racial antagonism (the stock and trade of Nazi ideology), but it resulted from the "better economic position" of the Jews and "in the undoubted Jewish leadership in Bolshevist ideologies and in the oppression and terrorism provided by them as a whole." More than 80 percent of all communist party positions were filled by Jews, "according to assurances made by Aryan Soviet citizens." Similar leading positions in other areas of Soviet life were controlled by Jews and were outlined in like fashion throughout the report. Again, when discussing the fact that Jews tended to live in urban areas, the report maintained: "The high percentage of the Jewish populations in towns, even compared with that of the Czarist era, gives evidence for this (exact figures cannot be furnished here either since all the files are lacking)."[54]

The few excerpts given above furnish us with some idea of the general tone and content of much of the SD opinions in the reports as to the Jewish problem and the relationship of this question and the attitude of the local population. The qualifications stated earlier concerning the reliability of this opinion gathering should be taken into account when reading these reports. The "assurances of Aryan Soviet citizens," if they were indeed the yardstick by which public feeling was gauged, are to be taken with great circumspection. We must attempt to distinguish between blatant ideology, SS wishful thinking, and those opinions that were, in fact, a reasonable assessment of the situation as it existed.

In spite of the apparent "success" of the measures carried out by the Einsatzgruppen with the local population, as claimed in the above examples, it was recognized that such measures were in themselves not enough to win the support of the population. It became common practice for the Kommandos to distribute clothing, food, property, furniture, etc., of the liquidated Jews to the local population.[55] Such crass tactics likely found favor with the recipients of these stolen goods, yet the reports indicate that, despite favorable reaction to the anti-Jewish measures, it was more often the practice to carry out the shootings as unobtrusively as possible. As a result, we must conclude that a sizeable part of the population was probably not aware of the ultimate fate of the Jews. This was so to the extent that Einsatzgruppe A reported that "In the population and even among the remaining Jews the impression prevailed that the Jews had been resettled in other parts of the eastern territory."[56] In Kiev Einsatzgruppe C reported that the local population believed that the Jews shot on 29 and 30 September 1941 had been relocated elsewhere.[57]

The content of the SD reports, however, was not confined to the rather simplistic one-sided opinions outlined thus far. Whatever reservations one may have about some of the reports, it must still be acknowledged that they included criticism of many aspects of German operations in the east. They also included examples of negative attitudes on the part of the population. This presence of differing shades of opinion would seem to give some weight to the validity of those opinions that were obviously positive or pro-German. Side by side with comments describing the approval of the local population to the Einsatzgruppen operations were reports on the lack of sympathy to these actions. While the population may have approved of the Einsatzgruppen actions, it was quite another matter to get them to carry out violence against the Jews on their own. Einsatzgruppe B, in exasperation, complained that the White Russian population could not "make up their minds to incite pogroms" against the Jewish population.[58] A short time later Einsatzgruppe B repeated this same complaint and offered an explanation. The Einsatzgruppe reported, "In general the population harbors a feeling of hatred and rage toward the Jews and approves of the German measures." The population does not "by itself take the initiative in regard to the treatment of the Jews. Altogether it can be said quite generally that the population is lacking in activism; the reason for this fact is probably to a certain degree the treatment by the Soviets. This is disclosed among other things in the self-administration."[59]

In the reports, in addition to the flattering reports of the local population's mood, the sober realization appeared of the means necessary to ensure their continued support. It was seen that it was "expedient to support not only the national movements in these regions but also the national ambitions of other peoples, when they are reached, in order to split up the Russian feeling of unity." Problems of local politics and economics facing the population were to be taken up and practical economic reforms to deal with these issues were suggested. Above all, it was stated that those who greeted the Germans "joyfully" should be treated well,[60] and a distinction was to be made between the Russian people and the Soviet state.[61]

In the end, this and similar judicious advice was not heeded. The

Germans became bogged down in a war of widely differing policies constantly at cross purposes with each other. The increasingly brutal measures against the Jews, the local population, and the Russian prisoners of war led to a terrorizing numbing effect on the inhabitants. If it had ever been possible to begin with, the chance to win over the eastern population was soon lost by the Germans.[62]

As time passed the true intentions and methods of the occupying force became more obvious. The initial optimism gave way to a deadening inertia and fearful uncertainty. This change in the popular mood was reflected in the reports. In White Russia, for example, Einsatzgruppe A described the killing of fifteen thousand Jews in Rakow and Tscherwen as having resulted in a "feeling of insecurity and even anxiety in the population." The report warned that the more educated circles "were not used to such a procedure during the Soviet regime and that it was impossible to estimate the consequences of such measures."[63]

Yet the killings continued with little consideration of any consequences. In spite of the previously cited favorable attitudes to the killings, it was more likely the case that most of the people soon were in a state of numbed passivity. It was one thing to be anti-Semitic; quite another to assist in the killings. The fear of ruthless German reprisals (for helping Jews) and possible Soviet reprisals (for killing Jews) were an ever-present reality, and this led to a kind of neutral detachment by the population. There was the constant realization that at any time they too could become the next victims of the German killing machine.[64]

Another Einsatzgruppe A report, issued about the same time as the one just mentioned, attested to the "deterioration of the popular mood" in the Loknja area as a result of the fact that the Wehrmacht had again taken cattle from the villagers.[65] This report indicated that the Security Police were aware of the importance of economic issues in the minds of the population. The land reforms, the redistribution of the farms to the people, the availability of consumer goods, of food—these were matters of great concern to the local population. As well as mentioning better economic conditions, one report noted that the people hoped for "an existence worthy of a human being."[66]

One particularly frank report by Einsatzgruppe A gave this assessment of the situation within its area: "Generally speaking, it may be said that the civilian population will side with those who wield the power in the area." In areas where partisan or Red Army power was still strong, the "Russian inhabitant will obey the orders of his former rulers who naturally aim at disrupting supply and transportation and at harassing and injuring the German troops."[67] The inhabitants were caught in the middle. In the Minsk area the rural population complained of the partisans operating in their region. They refused to work on the collective farms in those areas unprotected by the Wehrmacht or police.[68]

Einsatzgruppe B also noticed that partisan activities had put local villages in a panic. They were not inclined to "defend" the collective farms, but hoped they would be eliminated and the land divided. Some of these measures had been undertaken, and it was hoped that as a result the country population would change its attitude and defend their property against the partisans.[69]

The economic situation was also uncertain, and this had an unfavorable effect on the morale. Bartering had long been the means of trade among the population.[70] Many people refused to work since the cash they received for their work could not pay for the things they needed.[71]

Another source of local uneasiness was the forced conscription of inhabitants in the district of Brjansk by the labor offices. The situation had created such a serious problem that it required representations by the Sonderkommandos and the Ic of the Korücks, or army rear area, in order to put it right.[72]

Much attention was given to the subject of propaganda in the reports. The dropping of leaflets by the enemy near Witebsk caused the Einsatzgruppen to evaluate German propaganda in the eastern regions. It was remarked that in the past the population had ignored these enemy leaflets, but now they were being "passed from hand to hand." The report described the lack of adequate German propaganda. It later went even further by declaring as follows:

> It is generally put on record that the German Wehrmacht reports, for example, make hardly any impression on the population. In these reports the population misses above all mention of localities and figures concerning the eastern front, and points out that far more detailed reports are made about other fronts (Africa).[73]

In Operational Situation Report 183 this criticism of German propaganda was put forward:

> Due to the lack of an extensive German enlightenment and propaganda program, the population is but little impressed by the slow but constant advance of the German troops. Soviet propaganda is considerably more active.[74]

Another report issued soon after also warned of the increase in enemy propaganda, and the effect such propaganda hoped to have on the population. The enemy propaganda campaign:

> tried by way of intimidations and threats to influence in an unfavorable way the willingness of the Ukrainians to help the Germans. The propaganda is carried on

first of all by party members who are receiving directives from couriers. It is tried by all possible means to ferment dissatisfaction within the population, and to induce the population to offer passive and active resistance.[75]

Suggestions for a more effective use of "enlightenment" and propaganda had been made earlier. For example, in July 1941 Sonderkommando 7b had reported that the leaders of the collective farms (Kolchos) were not working, but were waiting for instructions. The Kommando warned that the harvest would be lost unless the peasants were "enlightened" and directives issued.[76] Einsatzgruppe B had noticed that the Soviets were using fourteen- to sixteen-year old boys as agents for espionage. The suggestion was made that propagandistic use be made of this abusive treatment of juveniles by the Soviet intelligence service.[77] The Einsatzgruppen also exploited for propaganda purposes the fact that the Soviets had murdered civilians before their retreat. The propaganda units of the Wehrmacht and even the foreign press took part in the reporting of these killings.[78]

The importance of effective propaganda was thus clearly recognized, as were the shortcomings of the German achievements in this field. Above all it was evident that enemy propaganda was having a negative impact on the feelings of the eastern peoples. Rumors of the military situation and the strained food situation favored the acceptance of this propaganda. The civilians had been informed of the harsh measures enacted by the Soviets in the territories they reoccupied and this left the civilians in a state of anxiety, and as a result, they were certainly reluctant to side with the Germans.[79]

These and other later reports underlined the gradual disillusionment of the eastern peoples as their hopes for national autonomy, for an improved economic situation, and for a stability in the military situation (one way or the other) did not materialize. The waning fortunes of the German advance, the entry of the Americans into the war, the fear of Soviet reprisals, the increasing savagery of the Germans directed at a wider and wider range of victims, the lack of a clear-cut popular policy vis-à-vis the Russian population, the slow pace of land reforms—all were factors in this deterioration in the positive pro-German mood. The "friendship and enthusiasm" first shown to the Germans had declined tremendously.[80] Some measure of the more realistic feeling that was emerging in the minds of the population can be detected in a report issued in March 1942. On 23 February 1942, a document, written in Latvian, was found in a letter box in Riga. The document ended with the following comment:

We are ready to sacrifice everything for this common battle, but at first we want to know clearly and distinctly what our peoples will get out of it. Until this is promised to us unmistakably, no Latvian, who loves his people and his homeland, shall listen to false promises and follow secret or public invitations.[81]

Try as they might, the SD officials could not totally conceal the fundamental shifts in popular attitude. Behind the optimistic façade, still largely maintained until the end, can be detected the incipient collapse of the whole German edifice in the east.

*   *   *   *

From perceptions of the general mood we may now shift our attention to the evidence of the active collaboration with the Germans on the part of the eastern population. In doing this we are on somewhat more solid ground in the sense that we leave the realm of generalized opinion gathering for that of the concrete statement of fact. The Einsatzgruppen reports are a major source proving the collaboration of members of the various eastern peoples. Earlier in our discussion the context of collaboration in the east was examined briefly. Collaboration in its largest sense is a complex subject and involves many shades of meaning. It is usually thought of as the willing cooperation with, and the assisting of, one's enemy, especially an occupying power. Such cooperation can assume many forms, many not easily defined as being criminal. For our purposes here we will restrict ourselves to a very narrow application of the term. By collaboration we mean any involvement with the Einsatzgruppen, or other German forces in the various stages of the killing operations. This would include participation in any of the following activities: involvement of the indigenous population in pogroms, in the searching for and rounding up and denouncing of Jews and others to the Germans, in the guarding of ghettos, camps, and prisons, in the escorting of Jews and others to places of execution, in the active participation in the shooting of victims, and in the receiving of property, food, clothing, money, and positions of the people executed.

We have just traced the general attitude of the population. However accurate these reports may or may not have been, they reflected the perceptions of the Einsatzgruppen reporters. In spite of the difficulty of precisely gauging such sentiments, the reports described a high degree of anti-Jewish feeling. Given this climate of quite extensive anti-Semitism, it is not unusual that some segments of the society took the next logical step and participated in the killings.

It is not clear what motivated individuals to collaborate in the killings. The reports only hint at what may have led people to take part in this horrific process. No doubt with the eastern population, as was the case with Germans themselves, fascist convictions, coupled with deeply ingrained anti-Semitism were held by some to a greater extent than others. The desire for political autonomy, for some at least, was to be won at any price. Personal power was certainly an important motivating force, as were the obvious immediate rewards that attended taking part in the killings—the plundering of Jewish property, extra alcohol and cigarettes, avoidance of other "nastier" employment such as heavy labor, or fighting at the front, etc. Revenge also motivated many collaborators. The Kommandos took care often to recruit auxiliary forces whose members had had relatives either murdered or deported by the Soviets.[82] Such acts were blamed on the Jews and provided strong incentive for helping the Germans carry out the shootings.

The pogroms, described earlier, which took place under the guidance of the Kommandos, were the first occasions of collaboration. These pogroms involved both members of the civilian population and auxiliary police forces established by the Germans. They represented the first violent assault on the Jews and communists and were featured prominently in the early reports.[83] The Einsatzgruppen realized at once that in addition to the desirability of pogroms carried out by the local people, it was essential to enlist local collaborators to assist in carrying out their work. Stahlecker, head of Einsatzgruppe A, in his report of 15 October 1941 to Himmler wrote:

> In view of the extension of the area of operations and the great number of duties which had to be performed by the Security Police, it was intended from the very beginning to obtain the cooperation of the reliable population for the fight against vermin—that is, mainly the Jews and communists. Beyond our directing of the first spontaneous actions of self-cleansing, which will be reported elsewhere, care had to be taken that reliable people should be put to the cleansing job and that they were appointed auxiliary members of the Security Police. The difference of the situation in each part of the area of operations also had to be taken into account. In Lithuania activist and nationalist people formed themselves into so-called partisan units at the beginning of the eastern campaign in order to take active part in the fight against Bolshevism. According to their own report they suffered 4000 casualties.[84]

The so-called partisans in Kovno and surrounding areas were disarmed on June 28, and an auxiliary police force of five companies was organized to assist the Germans. Two companies were put at the disposal of Einsatzgruppe A and helped in every aspect of the work.[85] A report by Higher SS and Police Leader Prützmann included in a report dated 11 July 1941, less than three weeks after the beginning of the war, described the general cooperation that the Germans were receiving.

> The attitude of the population of Lithuania is so far friendly towards the Germans; they help the German soldiers, the officials of the police and other organizations functioning in this area as much as possible. Their cooperation consists chiefly in the search for and turning over of Lithuanian communists, members of the Red Army who have been separated from their units, and Jews.[86]

The report acknowledged that two thousand five hundred Jews had been killed in Kovno by the population during "a spontaneous uprising" and that a further rather large number of Jews was shot by the auxiliary police making a total of seven thousand eight hundred Jews killed so far. In addition a Sonderkommando of two hundred and fifty Lithuanian partisans were "being employed for possible executions outside the town."[87] A report issued two days later attested to the existence of a similar situation in Vilna where Lithuanian police units were "instructed to take part in the liquidation of the Jews." One hundred and fifty Lithuanians were appointed for this purpose. They arrested Jews, and put them in concentration camps where, on the same day, the Jews were shot. The report informed that the daily toll of Jewish victims amounted to five hundred.[88]

This report reiterated the pressing need for help from local police units. In Bialystok the security of the city and environs was not completely guaranteed because of the presence of so few White Russian police forces. The original police officials functioning there in 1939 had been replaced by new officials, and these had left with the Soviets, destroying documents and files in the process. Thus it was necessary to form an auxiliary police force from the White Russian and former Polish Criminal Police officials. This force, too, was subordinate to the Kommando in Bialystok.[89]

In Latvia auxiliary forces were also established in Riga.[90] It was hoped that these forces would "not turn into a Lithuanian militia."[91] An earlier report had said that the Latvians were eager to organize themselves nationally. The report recognized that the Wehrmacht had been forced to use Latvian troops in order to help capture Russian soldiers hiding in the woods. The Kommando leader had urged restraint.[92] Here was a problem which plagued the Germans throughout the war. On the one hand they needed the help of the local units; on the other they were reluctant to become too much in their debt and thus be obliged to grant autonomy to them.

In Dwinsk on 3 July 1941, the Latvians had also formed a police force and a town administration, both of which were led by a Latvian by the name of Perssons. The Latvians in this group were former army members, policemen, and members of the former Aizsargi organization (organization for self-defense) that had been formed in 1934. Sonderkommando 1b had used this 240–man police force. The Latvians were on duty in the six police districts set up thus far and were arresting Jews and evacuating them from their homes. In Dwinsk, as of July 7, 1,150 Jews had been shot and buried in prepared graves.[93]

In Latvia and Lithuania the organizing of collaboration was the same. After the initial pogroms had occurred, the auxiliary forces were established mainly from various police units already present in combination with individuals harboring very strong anti-Jewish and anticommunist views.

In Estonia the situation was somewhat different. Here no "spontaneous demonstrations against Jewry" were reported. This, it was claimed, was due to the relatively small number of Jews and the total lack of "substantial enlightenment" of the population. The local collaborators, the Estonian Self-Protection Movement (Selbstschutz), confined themselves at this stage to simply arresting Jews and killing "only some individual communists whom they hated especially." Under the supervision of Sonderkommando 1a, Estonian self-protection units shot 440 male Jews over sixteen years of age. The remaining Jewesses, estimated between five hundred to six hundred, who were fit for work, were placed in work camps.[94]

In the Baltic countries, therefore, collaboration in the killing operations was immediate and extensive.[95] Aside from the occasional mention of numbers cited in the above examples, the reports do not provide much in the way of details as to personnel and so on. The units were simply designated as auxiliary forces, self-protection forces, militia, or partisan forces, as in the case of Lithuania. Mention of the participation of these groups did not always appear in the reports, even though it is likely that such participation did take place. Stahlecker reported that in Lithuania the proportion of Germans to auxiliaries in the firing squads was one to eight.[96] If this was the case, then the collaborators' share in the killing of the 136,421 Jews cited in this report was considerable, but we must always keep in mind that the number of collaborators is not the only issue. Apologists for the people of eastern Europe often emphasize the relatively small numbers of collaborators in relation to the overall population. While this is certainly true, one must remember the terrible consequences of this collaboration brought about by these small numbers of people. Indeed, the four Einsatzgruppen themselves numbered only about three thousand men. This, too, was a relatively small number when compared, for example, to the regular army forces fighting in the east. Yet the Einsatzgruppen, together with other German police agencies and their collaborators, were responsible for the killing of more than one million people. Thus the numbers have little bearing on the magnitude of the killing. It was the particular murderous nature of the collaboration that proved so useful to the Germans; they found others to do their killing for them.

The draft report of Einsatzgruppe A (PS–2273) complained that in Latvia as a whole the pogroms had not been too successful. "Only a few thousand Jews" had been killed by the local forces on their own. This necessitated extensive mopping up operations, which were undertaken by the Einsatzgruppe with the help of Latvian auxiliaries. As of October 1941, thirty thousand Jews had been killed in this way.[97] Arrests and killings involving both Latvian and Lithuanians were reported throughout the summer and autumn of 1941.[98] In particular, one report described the slaughter on August 22 of 544 inmates of the Aglona lunatic asylum with the help of a Latvian self-defense unit. This report announced that as of the time of the report (19 September 1941) Einsatzkommando 3 and the Lithuanian units had already killed 46,692 people.[99]

Members of the population assisted the Einsatzgruppen in other ways. Many of the Jews who managed to escape the pogroms in Lithuania by fleeing to the countryside were frequently handed over to the German authorities by local farmers. Such cooperation with the Security Police in the rural areas sealed the fate of the Jewish population. The same reports that described the desperate situation of the Jews in the rural areas referred to active resistance on the part of the Jews, something not often encountered in the Einsatzgruppen reporting: "It is worthy of note that many of the Jews used force against the officials and Lithuanian auxiliaries who were carrying this out, and before their execution still expressed their Bolshevik convictions by cheering Stalin and abusing Germany."[100]

In the Ukraine a number of pogroms took place soon after the arrival of the Germans. The presence of long held anti-Semitic feelings crystallized into violence when the bodies of Ukrainians tortured and killed by the departing Soviets were found in several locations. The Jews were blamed for these atrocities, and this served as the excuse for some people to unleash brutality against them.[101] In Lvov, the prisons were full of murdered people. Sonderkommando 4b called these killings the "most awful atrocities."[102] Further details were set forth in another report:

According to reliable information, the Russians, before withdrawing shot 3000 inhabitants. The corpses piled up and buried at the GPU prisons are dreadfully mutilated. The population is greatly excited; 1000 Jews have already been driven together.[103]

In Luck, Sonderkommando 4a carried out two thousand executions as a reprisal for the killing of Ukrainians.[104] Einsatzgruppe C reported that on 5 July 1941 fifteen Jews had been killed for the murder of a Ukrainian leader. The local Ukrainian population had vented its rage by setting fire to the synagogue and to houses belonging to Jews.[105] In another report Einsatzgruppe C praised the "commendable activity" against the Jews of the Ukrainian population. In addition to the activities made known in previous reports, the "commendable activity" also involved the denunciation and subsequent shooting of forty men by the local population, as well as the capturing of 117 communists and agents in Sokal by the Ukrainian residents and militia. These 117 men were also shot on 29 June 1941, and a further 183 Jews were apprehended and shot in Sokal the next day.[106]

There is further evidence of specific killing operations carried out by the Ukrainian auxiliary forces. By August 1941 their operations were in full swing. In Korosten, 238 Jews who had been rounded up and taken to a special building were shot there by the Ukrainian militia. The report asserted that these Jews had been "a source of continuous unrest."[107]

One of the most horrific examples of collaboration in atrocities took place in Radomyschl on 6 September 1941. Here the overcrowding of the Jews had, according to the report, led to "intolerable" hygienic conditions. (The dreaded danger of epidemics appeared again.) As a result, Sonderkommando 4a shot 1,107 Jewish adults and let the Ukrainian militia kill 561 Jewish children.[108] An advance Kommando of Sonderkommando 4a, with the aid of reliable Ukrainians, killed 537 Jews in the town of Perejeslav on 4 October 1941. The Kommando reported that both the Ukrainian population and the Wehrmacht "saw this action with satisfaction."[109] Further references to the Ukrainian militia in the reports described their participation in arrests and subsequent shooting of Jews and communists in Lubny, Dnjepropetrowsk, Shitomir, Kosolec, and Ivankow.[110] The already cited shootings of 33,771 Jews in Kiev on September 29 and 30 was another operation involving Ukrainian collaboration. Posters put up by the Ukrainian militia in the city ordered the Jews to assemble on September 29 before eight o'clock.[111]

Denunciations by members of the Ukrainian population took place. Einsatzkommando 6, which had operated in the district of the Dnjeper bend since 5 October 1941, reported the

> immense number of denunciations with which the Einsatzkommando is simply swamped. Here the low level of the moral character of the population becomes apparent; almost every one of the inhabitants considers it necessary and of merit if, for selfish interests, he denounces his relatives, friends, etc., as having been communists to the German Police.[112]

Einsatzkommando 5 also reported that denunciations were received "daily in great numbers" from all classes of the population.[113] Such denunciations, wherever they occurred, invariably led to the death of those who were denounced. One report also stated, however, that some villagers who had travelled quite a great distance to denounce Jews, in fact, attempted to retract their information upon realizing that the Jews in question would be killed.[114]

Further south, the Rumanians, allies to the Germans in the war, also played an important part in the shooting operations. They did this largely on their own with little assistance from Einsatzgruppe D, which was the Einsatzgruppe operating within the orbit of the Rumanian forces. An early report said that there was a good sense of cooperation between Sonderkommando 10b and the Rumanian rural police. Sonderkommando 11, at this time located in Barlad, also spoke of the good relations with the Rumanian army.[115] In the town of Belzy, Sonderkommando 10a wrote that the Rumanian police were operating "in the political police field" under the Kommando's direction. It was also reported that the Rumanian police had acted "sharply" against the Jews.[116] In Czernowitz, 682 out of about one thousand two hundred Jews arrested were shot with the help of the Rumanian Police.[117] According to another report, on the suggestion of the Security Police, the Rumanian town commander in Kischinew established a Jewish ghetto in the old part of the town and nine thousand Jews were currently living there. They were used in rubble clearing and other work by both German and Rumanian agencies.[118]

The massacres in Odessa were described earlier. Some indication of the Rumanian participation in this slaughter appeared in Operational Situation Report 125, which pointed out that as a countermeasure for the bombing of the residence of the commander of the 10th Rumanian Division in that city, the Rumanians had "so far" killed about ten thousand Jews.[119]

Estonians, Latvians, Lithuanians, Ukrainians, and Rumanians all took part in killings. Cited here and there in the reports were other groups or segments of the society not identified on ethnic grounds who also participated. A report by Einsatzgruppe D on the Crimea stated the following:

> The population of the Crimea is anti-Jewish and in some cases spontaneously brings Jews to the Kommandos to be liquidated. The Starosts, (village leaders) ask permission to liquidate the Jews themselves.[120]

Einsatzgruppe A reported that twelve Russians and one Polish peasant, who were apparently engaged in partisan activity, were shot by the civilian population.[121] In April 1942 Einsatzgruppe B also reported that in the country the people were enthusiastically taking up the struggle against partisans operating in their area, and even refused the assistance of the Kommandos when they felt they could destroy the partisans themselves.[122] Einsatzgruppe B also reported that in Minsk it was the town authorities who arrested 142 Jews and shot them for loitering and for not wearing the Jewish Star.[123]

In some areas the participation of civilians in actual killings would seem to have been more prevalent than is suggested by the few cases given above. This is shown by the fact that it was necessary to issue a directive forbidding members of the eastern civil administration to take part in the shooting of Jews. Shooting of Jews was the duty of the Security Police and the SD.[124]

Not to be forgotten was the importance to the Einsatzgruppen of the networks of confidential agents throughout the territories, which supplied the Kommandos with information as to the names and whereabouts of Jews, communists, and other undesirables. Time and again the reports affirmed that the Soviets had destroyed or removed their files containing the

names of their agents and communist party members.[125] This made finding
these people more difficult. Therefore the Einsatzgruppen relied heavily on
their informers to obtain such information.[126] Obviously the Kommandos
took advantage of the fact that members of the local population knew the
immediate situation much better than they did. They knew the language, the
people, the area. They knew who were Jews, who were communists, where
they lived, who their friends were, who was helping partisans, and where
people were likely to hide in the area. These agents played a leading role in
the extermination process. The round up of victims would not have been
possible to the same degree without this help. This form of collaboration
led to the deaths of thousands. The reports provided example after example
of the range of this participation and its enormous impact on the success
of the operations.

Part of this intelligence network included the so-called information
stations, which, as one report asserted, "were established to induce the non-
Bolshevist population to take part in these search actions, and the people
were publicly invited to disclose the hiding places of their former
oppressors."[127]

In his report of 15 October 1941, Stahlecker provided a vivid picture of
how individuals in the villages could be persuaded to act as confidential
agents in the struggle against partisans. This involved a combination of
reward and terror. The report read, in part, as follows:

> In villages in the area where partisans had not been ascertained before, one
> behaved friendly towards the population. In view of the generally known shortage
> of bread one usually succeeded very quickly in finding one or several villagers who
> could be used as persons of confidence. They were promised to get bread provided
> they would give information concerning partisans or if they would inform the
> nearest units of the Germany Army or Police of any partisans appearing in the
> future. The network of information, thus built up yielded much information for
> the Einsatzgruppe, thus enabling them to surround more narrowly the quarters
> of the partisans.
>
> There was especially information concerning villagers who had given goods or
> provisional shelter to partisans. On the basis of these reports a great many villages
> were combed out. After a village had been surrounded all the inhabitants were
> forcibly shepherded into one square. The persons suspected on account of
> confidential information and other villagers were interrogated, and thus it was
> possible in most cases to find the people who helped the partisans. These were
> either shot off hand· or if further interrogations promised useful information,
> taken to headquarters. After the interrogation they were shot.
>
> In order to get a deterring effect, the houses of those who helped the partisans
> were burned down on several occasions. The population which had congregated
> was told of the reasons for the punitive measures. At the same time they were
> threatened that the whole village would be burned down if partisans were helped
> once more and if partisans appearing in the village were not reported as quickly
> as possible.

These tactics, to put terror against terror succeeded marvelously. From fear of reprisals, the peasants came a distance of 20 km and more to headquarters of the detachment of Einsatzgruppe A, on foot or on horseback in order to bring news about partisans, news which was correct in most cases.[128]

The network of agents gained in importance as the partisan activity expanded with time. References to their use in this regard increased. Einsatzgruppe B claimed that as more and more reports concerning partisans were received, the Wehrmacht realized the importance of the work of the SD and considered the "network of confidential agents the surest guarantee for tracking down the partisans."[129] On 8 March 1942, for example, after a meeting with Wehrmacht officials, a large joint anti-partisan operation was planned for the Bobruisk and Brjansk area. Einsatzgruppe B was to be used in the preliminary stages of the operation. Security Police and SD members from Einsatzkommando 9 and Sonder-kommando 7a were to prepare for the operation by the use of confidential agents in reconnaissance work.[130]

The reports of confidential agents were as devastating for Jews and communist civilians as they were for the partisan groups. While it is not possible to measure with exactness statistically the effect that this cooperation had, it was certainly a major factor in the capture of many Jews, communists, and others. Within three weeks of the German attack, there existed an already smoothly operating system of informants. In Bialystok, early in July, Einsatzgruppe B reported that a segment of the Polish population had "shown that it supports the executive activity of the Security Police by making reports against Jewish, Russian and also Polish Bolshevists."[131] In a report issued the next day Sonderkommando 10b of Einsatzgruppe D announced that it had completed its duties in Chotin. The Kommando, with the help of Ukrainian confidential agents, had been able to arrest rabbis, intellectuals, Jewish agitators, teachers, and lawyers. The Kommando reported (as was often the case elsewhere) that Jewish doctors were left at liberty to "administer the medical needs of the population."[132]

The Kommando leaders exhorted local mayors to report the presence of undesirables, such as former Soviet soldiers in civilian clothes, individuals with "bad political records," or other questionable people hanging about. Fugitive political functionaries were successfully apprehended by Einsatzkommando 5 with the help of agents.[133] Not only mayors but other administrative leaders played a part in this undertaking. Einsatzgruppe B reported that in Smolensk members of its network of agents were included in those officials appointed to the town administration.[134] The town commandant in Kiev, responding to earlier acts of arson and sabotage and continued reports of the Ukrainian population that further acts of sabotage were being planned, ordered the population to report "without delay any suspicious observations.''[135] Einsatzgruppe C, in another report, pointed out that its Ukrainian and ethnic German agents were paid with funds taken from Jews. Some agents were also given small farms from which they were able to obtain rations as payment. This report also asserted that on the collective farms the managers also worked as agents for the Security Police.[136]

These examples indicate that the Einsatzgruppen had at their disposal a powerful tool for their killing machine. The agents were a vital part in their security work and the destruction of their enemies. Stahlecker's report demonstrated that in each village "one or several villagers" were easily recruited to undertake this work. This was the case elsewhere in the cities. It did not require many people. A few were enough to give information that might destroy hundreds. One tends to focus attention on collaborators who participated in the actual killing of innocent people; many such killings would not have been possible without the help of these informers. The reports tell only a small part of this picture. No doubt the use of agents was far more extensive and the results more lethal than suggested by the reports. The reports do underline their importance within the total workings of the annihilation process.

In the course of their evacuation the Jews lost all of their possessions, and before they were killed, they lost even the clothes on their backs. Reports mentioned the seizing of money and property by the Kommandos.[137] Most of this stayed in German hands, but some went to the local eastern population.[138] That collaborators profited materially from the destruction of the Jews goes without saying. Ethnic Germans living in the eastern territories assisted the Kommandos in their tasks[139] and for their troubles received money, clothing, and food of the Jews killed, as well as other forms of assistance.[140] In the Ukraine the Jewish managers of the collective farms were shot by the Kommandos. Their positions were then taken over by Ukrainians.[141] Thus, the spoils of the destruction were reaped in several ways throughout the east. Again, the reports only give a glimpse of the extent of this profiteering. It is almost certainly the case that on a day-to-day immediate level of the operations, the corruption was far more extensive. Such behavior, by the German agencies especially, would, of course, not be referred to in reports, although reports did cite occasions when others took part in looting. It is likely, too, that frequent mention of benefits to local inhabitants was to be avoided. One is again forced to read between the lines of the reports to envision some measure of the scope of these activities.

As much as the Einsatzgruppen eagerly accepted the help of the local collaborators they were not without complaints against them. The Rumanians, in particular, came under fire.[142] Einsatzgruppe D, on the march through Bessarabia, complained that the Rumanian units lacked discipline and that the absence of a proper authority had led to large-scale looting by the civilians. The Rumanian attitude to the execution of Jews resulted in the following comment:

> There is no system in the way in which the Rumanians are dealing with the Jews. No objections could be raised against the numerous executions of Jews if the technical preparations and the execution itself were not totally inadequate. The Rumanians usually leave the executed persons where they have been shot without burying them. The Einsatzkommando has issued instructions to the Rumanian Police to proceed somewhat more systematically in this direction.[143]

In Belzy, Heinz Seetzen, the leader of Sonderkommando 10a, reported to the 11th Army that his unit had to finish off fifteen Jews left half-dead by the Rumanian soldiers.[144] Other reports described the Rumanian anti-Jewish operations as "desultory"[145] and "sporadic."[146] In addition Einsatzgruppe D characterized the Rumanian administration as being filled with an "ugly economy of corruption."[147]

One of the strongest complaints against the Rumanians concerned their brutal treatment of the Ukrainians within their territory.[148] The Germans viewed this situation with concern, as they looked upon the Ukrainians as allies whose assistance they were intent on exploiting to the fullest. A report issued on 14 July 1941 presented this assessment of the situation by Sonderkommando 10b:

> The Rumanians are inclined to exterminate the stratum of Ukrainian leadership in order to settle the Ukrainian problem in the North Bukovina once and for all, taking advantage of the present situation. Twenty-two Ukrainians are under Rumanian arrest in Czernowitz; Sonderkommando 10b has been given the following orders in this respect:
> (a) To influence the Rumanian authorities to take more severe measures concerning the Jewish question. Jewish meetings must be raided by us and conspiracies revealed in order to stimulate Rumanian activities also against the Jewish intelligentsia and to enable us to take a hand ourselves.
> (b) In order to protect or to exchange Ukrainians valuable to us, in particular OUN people, communists will be put at the disposal of the Rumanians.[149]

The situation concerning the Ukrainians got so serious that with Ohlendorf's approval, Einsatzgruppe C sent a squad of fifteen executive officials and fifteen Waffen SS members to Czernowitz. Their task, after the withdrawal of Sonderkommando 10a from the city, was to "take care of the interest of the absolutely unprotected and helpless Ukrainians."[150]

Another source of conflict between the Germans and their Rumanian allies was the problem of who was to deal with the great numbers of Bessarabian and Bukovinian Jews. In the summer and early fall of 1941, thousands of Jews were driven into the German area of operations. The

Germans did not want to deal with them, and despite Rumanian protests
thousands were driven back to Rumanian territory.[151]

The relationship with the Rumanians was not the only source of irritation
for the Einsatzgruppen. They had to deal with the often strained relations
that existed between the various indigenous groups under their control. It
was difficult enough to strike a workable balance with each group
individually. An added burden appeared when the antagonism between the
groups threatened to disturb the security. The tension between the
Lithuanians and Poles in Vilna was a case in point. The Lithuanians told
the Kommandos that during the Soviet occupation the Poles in Vilna had
formed armed organizations with a strength of twelve thousand men and
had stored ammunition in secret hiding places.[152] Another report touched
on the hostile situation in Vilna and noted that the presence of the
Wehrmacht had prevented outbreaks of violence between the two groups.
The report claimed that a secret Jewish organization had been discovered
whose aim was to reinstate Polish sovereignty by force.[153] Such bickering
among the groups asserting their own priorities certainly did not make
things easier for the Germans.[154]

The preferential treatment given initially to the Ukrainians, a subject of
disagreement among the Germans from Hitler down, backfired to some
extent. A large number of Ukrainian prisoners of war were released by the
Germans.[155] To its dismay Einsatzgruppe C discovered that many non-
Ukrainian prisoners of war were among those who had been discharged
simply because they claimed to be Ukrainians.[156] Further problems with
their Ukrainian collaborators surfaced in March 1942. It was discovered
that in its search for communists, Einsatzgruppe C realized that many
communists were to be found among the members of the Ukrainian
auxiliary police. These people were therefore purged for "political reasons"
and because of their "criminal record."[157]

Other allies also presented problems. The Hungarians had entered the
war against the Soviets on 27 June 1941.[158] The relationship with the
Hungarian troops was marked by occasional unpleasant incidents. In
Shitomir, for instance, the Hungarian army actually stopped a killing
operation by the local police.[159] In late August 1941 Einsatzgruppe D
complained that except for the area occupied by the Hungarians around
Swaniza, the region from Chotin to Jampol had been cleared of Jews.[160]
In the reports the Einsatzgruppen could find fault with their allies for more
mundane reasons than those already described. In a fit of pique, the
commander of Einsatzkommando 6 complained that the Italian and
Hungarian troops were engaged in the brisk business of selling German
cigarettes to the soldiers at exorbitant prices![161]

Complaints of a more serious nature appeared in a report in mid-March
1942. In their interrogation of captured partisans and communists the

Kommandos took care to obtain as much information as possible. Stahlecker himself had stressed the need for a thorough questioning of prisoners before liquidating them.[162] In the March report Einsatzgruppe A said that some auxiliary units were becoming very lax in this matter. Einsatzgruppe A observed the following in its report:

> The Lithuanian, Latvian, and Estonian companies employed in the area along the Loknja-Troiza-Chlavizy supply road by AK39 are operating satisfactorily, but it appeared that during their actions they frequently shot persons who might have given valuable information. Thus, in the course of a punitive expedition by a Lithuanian Hundertschaft against the village of Tshertesh, 10 km northeast of Yuchovo, amongst 23 partisans, 5 men were shot who wanted to give information on an espionage center in the Loknja district.[163]

The report put forward another example of the problems that could arise when different national groups were joined together.

> It could be observed that joint operations may lead to dissensions and to a weakening of the striking power of planned operations, as they give rise to a revival of envy and quarrels of a traditional nature between the Baltic nationalities.[164]

From the reports cited above it is evident that all was not always well between the Einsatzgruppen and their allies and that the Einsatzgruppen often entertained doubts as to the quality of their collaborators' performance and commitment to the task assigned them. Of course these doubts did not cause the Einsatzgruppen to decline the help offered to them. Such a move would have been unthinkable given the enormity of the undertaking, and basically their auxiliary forces got the job done. Whatever may have been the attitude of their leaders to the various indigenous groups at any given time, the Einsatzgruppen personnel were thankful for the assistance of the collaborators. The complaints that they did have were paradigmatic of the larger problems that faced the German administration in the east. Just as the Security Police were not always able to ensure that the auxiliary forces functioned in precisely the desired manner, so, too, the attitude and response of the population did not always conform to the expectations of the German policymakers. The Security Police and the SD were at the forefront in the east. The maze of varied national feelings, the complex range of reactions to the killing from stunned terror and indifference of the many, to the malevolent opportunism of the few, all this was known to the SD. They, as much as any Germans in the east, were concerned with these matters. Their reports presented a mixture of Nazi ideology, wishful thinking, outright lies, and sober pragmatism. They were not unaware of measures that could have improved the image of the

Germans in the east. These measures were not taken, or were taken too late. Ultimately, it was the Einsatzgruppen and the other police forces in the east that did the most damage to the fortunes of the Germans. It was they who were the most despised and feared by the population.[165] Yet they could not change, for the German policy of killing and exploitation was not to be changed. Hitler had deemed it so.

11

Army Cooperation with
the Einsatzgruppen

One of the most controversial aspects of the Russian war concerned the relationship of the Einsatzgruppen with the Wehrmacht. To a great extent the Wehrmacht and the SS were hostile bedfellows. The rivalry and enmity between them was deep and long-standing. The conservative military leadership had contempt for Himmler's minions and methods and viewed with suspicion SS military ambitions.[1] Early in the war in Poland the brutality and murder carried out by the SS forces was viewed with revulsion by many Wehrmacht leaders. By the time the war against Russia was about to begin, the Wehrmacht hierarchy had no illusions as to what would happen in the coming campaign.[2] While the army was not always pleased to suffer the presence of the SS troops within its domain, the cooperation that developed between them resulted in one of the blackest moments in the history of the German army. The centuries-old tradition of the German officer who fought with fairness, gallantry, and honor for his country was forever tarnished by the events in the east.

In spite of many postwar claims to the contrary by Wehrmacht leaders, what has clearly emerged from the various Nuremberg and other trials, as well as from subsequent research, is that not only were the Wehrmacht leaders aware of the activities of the Einsatzgruppen, but that regular army units actually took part in the killings. The extent of this collaboration between the Wehrmacht and the Einsatzgruppen has been analyzed in detail by a number of historians.[3] A brief consideration of the relevant documentation will suffice as background to this subject, and then a few important examples from the reports of army collaboration in killing operations will be presented.

Earlier agreements had spelled out the relationship between certain SS units and the Wehrmacht. Mentioned in Chapter 1 were the Verfügungstruppe, or Special Duty SS Troops. The decree of 17 August 1938, cited in Chapter 1, placed these troops under Himmler's control, independent of the Wehrmacht and the police. In wartime they were to come under the command of the army, although they remained a unit of the party politically. Hitler was to withhold, until mobilization, the decision as to the details of the integration of these forces into the wartime army.[4] In this 1938 decree, therefore, one finds the concept of SS troops being placed under army control while still retaining a measure of independence from the latter. This concept was to continue during the war against the Soviet Union. The friction between the SS units and the army, which had developed during the Polish campaign, made it desirable that suitable arrangements be made to avoid such problems during the upcoming operations. Consequently, in the months before the attack on the Soviet Union, negotiations took place between the Wehrmacht and the RSHA. The aim was to define clearly, before the war began, the areas of responsibility of Himmler's men and the relationship of authority with the army command. Each side hoped to limit the other's control over its operations. Then, a series of orders were issued before the war started. The key documents relating to this organization of authority were the following.

On 13 March 1941 a decree signed by Keitel, the commander-in-chief of the Armed Forces (OKW), offered this description of the task of the Einsatzgruppen:

> Within the field of operations of the army, the Reichsführer-SS, in preparing for the political administration, assumes, on behalf of the Führer, special duties which arise as a result of the struggle which must ultimately be carried out between two opposing political systems. Within the framework of these duties the Reichsführer-SS acts independently and on his own responsibility. In other respects, the executive power delegated to the commander-in-chief of the army and to authorities acting on his behalf is not affected hereby. The Reichsführer-SS will make certain that operations will not be disrupted when carrying out his duties. The supreme command of the army will arrange the details directly with the Reichsführer-SS.[5]

It is noteworthy that the Einsatzgruppen were not named as such in this decree, and that there was no mention of killing. In effect, the document gave Himmler the power to perform the "special duties" required of him by Hitler unhampered by anyone. He was restricted only in the sense that he was not to interfere with the purely military operations of the army. In matters of military consideration, the local army commander had supreme authority.

The further "details" to be decided upon were then worked out by the army and Heydrich. On 4 April 1941 Generalmajor Eduard Wagner sent a draft of an agreement (dated 26 March 1941) to Heydrich outlining the responsibilities of the Einsatzgruppen in Russia. This draft included the following:

> The Sonderkommandos of the Security Police and the SD carry out their mission on their own responsibility. They are subordinate to the armies in matters of the march, provisions and lodgings. Disciplinary and judicial subordination under the Chief of the Security Police and the SD is not affected thereby.

They receive their professional instructions from the Chief of the Security Police and the SD and, if the occasion arises, they are subject to restrictive orders by the armies as far as their activities are concerned. . . .

For the central direction of these commands a plenipotentiary of the Chief of the Security Police and the SD is appointed in the area of each army group. It is his duty promptly to inform the Commander-in-Chief of the army of the instructions issued to him by the Chief of the Security Police and the SD.

The Military Commander is entitled to issue to the plenipotentiary instructions necessary for avoiding disturbances of the operations; these supersede all other instructions.

The plenipotentiaries depend upon continuous close cooperation with the Commander-in-Chief; the command authorities may request the transfer of a liaison official between the plenipotentiary and the Commander-in-Chief. The Commander-in-Chief has to bring the tasks of the Sonderkommandos into accord with the military counter-intelligence, the activities of the Secret Field Police (GFP) and the exigencies of the operations.

The Sonderkommandos are authorized within the frame of their assignment to carry out on their own responsibility executive measures concerning the civilian population. They are hereby obliged to work in closest cooperation with the counter intelligence. Measures which may effect the operations require the approval of the Commander-in-Chief of the army.[6]

As in the earlier document, this one also avoided any mention of killing; the Einsatzgruppen were to carry out "executive measures concerning the civilian population." They were to perform their tasks in the army group rear areas and in the army rear areas, working closely with the army intelligence officers. The military commanders were to have control over them to the extent that military matters had precedence over everything else. This, no doubt was of paramount importance for the Wehrmacht leaders. It would have been unthinkable for the Einsatzgruppen to be allowed to operate unrestrained in the theater of war. Yet this restraint was itself limited. A double line of authority was to exist in that the Einsatzgruppen were to function under the control of the army *and* the RSHA. The regulations also called for a close cooperation with the Secret Field Police, who were to deal with matters relating to troop security and who were to provide the Einsatzgruppen with any information that fell within the sphere of the latter's operations.

During the course of the attack on the Soviet Union all areas captured by the Germans at first came under army supervision. With time, as the Germans pushed eastward, the territory under German control was divided into two types of administrative control: areas to the east under military government; areas to the west under civil administration.[7] Moving east to west the regions under army control were divided as follows: front-line and operational areas, army rear operational areas, and army group rear areas.[8]

The agreement of April 4 did not allow the Einsatzgruppen into the actual front-line area. This matter was of great concern for Heydrich. In May 1941 further discussions on these points took place between the army

representative Generalmajor Wagner, and Walter Schellenberg, then head
of counterintelligence (Group IV E) in the RSHA, who replaced the
arrogant Heinrich Müller as Heydrich's representative. In his memoirs
Schellenberg stated that Heydrich said that the presence of the
Einsatzgruppen in the front-line area would "strengthen our position in
relation to the Wehrmacht" and "would have a favourable effect on
questions of personnel and finance."[9] As noted earlier, the presence of
Sonderkommandos at the front was a critical factor in the swift capture of
Jews and communists. Agreement was reached and a draft was signed at the
end of May by Heydrich and Wagner. No copy of this agreement has
apparently survived. In an affidavit Schellenberg recalled its main features.
A preamble to the draft was inserted by Schellenberg himself. This
preamble was the "Führer's Order" that functioned as the legal basis of the
rest of the order, which was therefore a reflection of the Führer's will. In
the front-line areas, the Einsatzgruppen were to undertake their operations
in complete subordination in every respect to the army. In the rear
operational areas and the rear army areas, they were to be only sub-
ordinated to the army in an administrative sense and were to be under the
command and functional control of the RSHA. In the areas that had come
under civil administration, the same rules were applied as in the Reich. The
other obligations of the army to provide the Einsatzgruppen with food,
fuel, and the use of army communications referred to in the earlier
agreement remained unchanged.[10]

In his affidavit Schellenberg also stated that he was convinced that the
murderous nature of the Einsatzgruppen duties was known to the
Wehrmacht before the war against Russia commenced.[11]

The picture in the east was made more complex by the presence of the
Higher SS and Police Leaders (HSSPL). The position of the HSSPL had
been created by a decree of 13 November 1937. As Himmler's representatives they were created to promote SS and police integration and to provide
political direction. Also, in the event of war, a HSSPL in each military
district was to take charge of all police forces. Both within Germany and
in occupied territories there remained great ambiguity in the relationship of
the HSSPLs and the other administrative agencies.[12] The HSSPLs had
great power. Nomination for the rank of HSSPL outside Germany
constituted a reward for "dynamism and ruthlessness."[13] On 21 May 1941
an order outlined the functions and relationship to the army command in
the occupied territories. In this order Himmler said:

> The Higher SS and Police Leader is placed in charge of SS and police troops and
> also of the operational personnel in the Security Police in order to carry out the
> tasks allocated to him by me personally.[14]

This order concerning the function of the HSSPLs in the rear army zones was similar to the order dealing with the Einsatzgruppen. Therefore, the HSSPL forces were to carry out assignments in the "political" field, while remaining subordinate to the army commanders in terms of movement, supplies, accommodation, etc. One difference with regard to the Einsatzgruppen was that being the highest ranking personal representatives of Himmler, the HSSPLs were, in effect, superior in rank to the Einsatzgruppen leaders.

Since the Higher SS and Police Leaders were responsible directly to Himmler, this resulted in two chains of command being created for the Einsatzgruppen in the Russian territories. In ordinary matters the chain of command was passed from the RSHA down the ranks, while orders came directly from Himmler to the Higher SS and Police Leaders who passed them on to their subordinates.[15]

This then was the situation as it existed on the eve of the German attack.[16] Areas of responsibility were delineated but remained ambiguous enough so that in practice the extent of the application of these directives depended largely on the personalities and authority of the individual participants. It was obvious to the army leaders from watching SS brutalities in Poland in 1939 that the "executive measures" to be carried out by the Einsatzgruppen in Russia were to be even worse. The ruthless nature of the coming Russian war had been spelled out by Hitler in a series of speeches to the Wehrmacht leaders and its barbaric quality had been exemplified in the so-called Commissar Order issued on 6 June 1941.[17] In effect Soviet Political Commissars were not to be given the protection granted to prisoners of war, but were to be separated from other prisoners and shot. Here the Wehrmacht authorities had been confronted with the first palpably illegal order, which they were instructed to carry out without question. It is not surprising in this growing climate of illegality and incipient terror that the army leaders took advantage of the fact that the agreements with the RSHA allowed for a separate jurisdiction over security police matters, and enabled them to step aside and let Heydrich's men accomplish their dirty work. It was so much easier to look the other way, and as in the case of Röhm Putsch in 1934, not have one's hands soiled with the blood of civilians. It was so much easier to "understand" Hitler's call for new, ruthless measures in this fundamental war of ideologies. There were other more practical advantages. The presence of the Einsatzgruppen freed the Wehrmacht personnel to concentrate on simply fighting the war and left the police work in the rear to the Security Police and the SD.[18]

Despite the undoubted desire of many officers to the contrary, the military leaders thus began the first step in the collaboration with the SS by not offering any serious objection to the presence of Himmler's troops, knowing full well the consequences of such inaction. Their cooperation did not end with inaction, however. It soon took the form of active involvement of the German soldiers in the killing of civilians.

The OKW–RSHA agreement had called for a close working relationship between army and Einsatzgruppen forces. As soon as the fighting began, such rapport was much in evidence. The earliest Einsatzgruppen reports spoke of discussions on various matters of concern taking place.[19] Two reports issued within four days of each other offered examples of important decisions being made after consultation with army personnel. In the first, Higher SS and Police Leader Hans Prützmann announced that the army had offered to take over security measures in the Grodno, Kovno, and Baltic Sea area. Owing to the size of this area and the rapid expansion eastward of the front-line, an agreement was reached with the army rear area north that allowed for the commander of the ORPO in Königsberg, Prussia, to take over security police duties in this area with his own men.[20] The second report described a fruitful conference between Ohlendorf and Generaloberst Eugen von Schobert on 12 July 1941. Among other things, it was decided at this conference that Ohlendorf was to have a "free hand" in the deployment of the Kommandos and that the army was to use the Kommandos in "an elastic way," not only as "an alerted reserve."[21]

Such cooperation was routine throughout much of the eastern campaign, and while conflicts arose, they were usually cleared up, allowing the day-to-day operations to function smoothly.[22] Disagreements that did arise were seldom, with some exceptions, referred to in the reports. Joint decisions had to be constantly made concerning the daily operations of the Kommandos. The Kommandos could not move to an area until given permission to do so by the army commander. Movement was often restricted while the Kommandos waited for word from the army.[23] Close contact at the front-line with the army was essential. The Kommandos or detachments of Kommandos often reached a captured city along with the army.[24] This day-to-day contact between army and Einsatzgruppen personnel was summarized in a report dated 2 January 1942. This report declared that cooperation with the Wehrmacht was "sometimes so close that in the offices of the commanders of Einsatzgruppe A discussions take place regularly with the local commanders and other interested offices of the Wehrmacht on questions of local importance."[25]

Two reports by Einsatzgruppe C also illustrated the good working relationship with the army. The first report noted that the "Security Police is highly regarded, in particular by the army staff. The liaison officers stationed at the AOK are loyally instructed on the military operations, and apart from this they receive the utmost assistance."[26]

In another report, after describing actions against Jews, partisans, and communists in October 1941 in Borispol, Sonderkommando 4a reported that the success of these operations was mainly due to the "energetic help" of the Wehrmacht authorities in Borispol.[27]

The spirit of cooperation was present from the beginning. Yet, the "close, almost cordial" cooperation with General Erich Höppner that Stahlecker described in his report[28] soon went beyond matters of daily routine. It became participation in mass murder.[29] Both Einsatzgruppen and units of the army's Secret Field Police were immediately active in combing out towns, arresting and screening and shooting people.[30] On July 2 in Luck, one army infantry platoon assisted in the shooting of 1,160 Jews, who were killed as a reprisal for the death of ten German soldiers. Several hundred Jews were also killed in Zloczow by order of the Wehrmacht in retaliation for the killing of Ukrainians there by the Soviets.[31] The 10th Company of the 354th Infantry Regiment assisted in the combing of the area north of Borisov. This operation resulted in the killing of 118 persons. In Witebsk, following the death of three German soldiers, an army "pacification action" was undertaken which resulted in the death of nineteen Jews.[32] Sonderkommando 4b reported that "understanding" was shown by the Wehrmacht towards the Kommando's actions in Poltava.[33]

Quite often the reports described the screening of civilians held by the Wehrmacht, followed by the handing over of these civilians to the Kommandos for execution.[34] The coordination of the intelligence operations of the SD and the Secret Field Police had been provided for in the April 4 directive.[35] The results were mutually beneficial. Einsatzgruppe C reported that information was exchanged with the Secret Field Police "without any friction." The hope was expressed that the "pleasant relationship" would be continued in the future.[36] The Army Police detachments did not confine themselves to intelligence gathering. It was reported that in Fastov the Secret Field Police of the local army command shot thirty snipers and fifty Jews.[37] Secret Field Police units and Einsatzgruppe B Kommandos "combed out" the camp in Minsk, which had been set up by the army there. Thousands of Jews, criminals, political functionaries, and Asiatics were caught. Later in September 1941 Sonderkommando 9 also reported that in Minsk it was assisted in the shooting of 2,278 Jews over a three-day period by members of the Order Police and the Field Police.[38] In Shitomir General Hans Reinhardt's men assisted the men of Einsatzgruppe C in a combing out of this town.[39] The military police assisted in the shooting of two thousand two hundred victims in Gorki. The report announced they were shot as the consequence of "numerous complaints about their provocative behavior."[40] Another screening and shooting action that involved the Field Police took place in Tosno, where 156 persons were killed from 15 October to 23 October 1941.[41]

Einsatzgruppe C reported that as a result of complaints against the Jewish population in Shitomir a meeting was held on 18 September 1941 with the rear army authorities. At this meeting it was decided that all the Jews in Shitomir were to be killed. That night, sixty Ukrainian militiamen surrounded the area, and at four o'clock in the morning, the removal of the Jews began. The twelve trucks used to carry out this task were supplied by the rear army headquarters and the city administration of Shitomir. In all 3,145 Jews were registered and then shot.[42] In Topala it was reported that twenty-one German soldiers had been shot. As a reprisal two thousand one hundred Jews and Gypsies were killed solely by the Wehrmacht. In this operation the role of the Security Police was limited to rounding up the required number of victims.[43]

The killing of 595 mental patients in Poltava, cited earlier, was done with the agreement of the 6th Army and the local commander of the Wehrmacht.[44] Einsatzgruppe D reported that actions carried out by the Wehrmacht in the Karasubasar region had "rendered harmless" eight hundred Gypsies and insane people. In Feodossija a series of raids took place in March 1942 also with the help of over three hundred German soldiers. These raids resulted in the death of most of the persons captured.[45]

The army units not only assisted the Security Police in their work but received help themselves from the Einsatzgruppen. Activity and Situation Report 2 mentioned the close rapport with the various military agencies. The report went on to say that:

Mutual assistance during large scale actions is self-evident. Thus for instance a Kommando of the Security Police and the SD consisting of sixty men was put at the disposal of the 87th Division for use against Russian Cavalry.[46]

It is unnecessary to expand further the earlier discussion of army involvement in the killing of prisoners of war. We limited this discussion to the handing over of prisoners to the Security Police for execution.[47] The evidence made clear the role of the army in this enterprise. These killings were one of the most flagrant violations of international law and accounted for the deaths of thousands of Jews, communist officials, and others. The conference at which Erwin Lahousen protested on behalf of Wilhelm Canaris against these killings changed little. As a sop to the army's conscience, it was simply agreed that the killing of the prisoners was to take place away from the camps so as not to be seen by the soldiers.[48]

In the east the army found itself surrounded by a program of mass extermination. It happened frequently that many soldiers stumbled accidentally upon killing operations. It also happened that the soldiers took part in killings without permission to do so. This was not to be tolerated and an order was issued prohibiting this practice.[49] No doubt many officers objected to these killings, but the military leadership, who in the end were the only ones capable of mounting any sort of protest, did very little. It is significant that in May 1941, when General Halder first heard of Himmler's intentions for his SS troops in the east, he recorded in his diary: "SS units for rear areas: the missions requested by these units must be refused."[50]

But there was no refusal. On the contrary, what evolved was a partnership that enabled the killing machinery to function much more easily. Something of the measure of the importance of Wehrmacht participation in the killing may be best indicated by noting that the winter draft report of Einsatzgruppe A estimated that as of December 1941 "about 19,000 partisans and criminals, that is, in the majority Jews" had been killed by the Wehrmacht in White Russia alone.[51]

The above examples from the reports offer clear, but somewhat limited evidence of army collaboration in war crimes. Other sources must be consulted to obtain a full account of Wehrmacht criminality. Rather more plentiful in the reports were the expressions of the good spirit of cooperation that resulted from the collaboration of the army. These acknowledgements of the Wehrmacht's attitude do not always refer to specific incidents of killings, but indicate the general feeling of positive cooperation that prevailed. The reports mentioned the sometimes urgent requests of the army for the assistance of the Security Police.[52] The gratitude of the Wehrmacht for this assistance, especially in antipartisan operations, was much in evidence. Einsatzgruppe A reported that in the rear army zone the Security Police and the Latvian and Lithuanian auxiliary units had liquidated two thousand nine hundred partisans. The army commanders had "repeatedly expressed their special thanks for this achievement."[53] In another report Einsatzgruppe B stated that the SD suggestions for tracking down partisans were welcomed "unreservedly" and that SD Kommando participation with the army in small military actions had proved so successful that army leaders had invited them along for even bigger operations.[54]

One particularly glowing account of Wehrmacht appreciation of the Einsatzgruppen's work was found in a report dated 27 March 1942. This report, also filed by Einsatzgruppe B, described a conference held at the headquarters of General Max von Schenkendorff, the commander of the Central Communications Zone. The conference was held on 8 March 1942, and dealt with preparations for a large-scale Wehrmacht antipartisan operation in the Bobruisk and Brjansk areas. Schenkendorff ordered Einsatzgruppe B to use its forces to create the conditions "for the execution of the operation." With the help of units from Einsatzkommando 9 and Sonderkommando 7a, intensive reconnaissance work was to be carried out.

Schenkendorff expressed his "gratitude to Einsatzgruppe B for the work performed so far in the fields of Security Police and Security Service without which a successful operation by the Wehrmacht would not be possible." The desire for a close cooperation between Army Intelligence and the Security Police and SD was expressed.[55]

The relationship with the Wehrmacht was a fruitful one from both the Einsatzgruppen's and Wehrmacht's points of view. The role the Einsatzgruppen played in the security operations and the antipartisan war behind the front lines was of immense help to the army. On the other hand, the Einsatzgruppen profited from army involvement in the extermination process. Yet, as was the case with the local collaborators, the Security Police and SD were not always 100 percent pleased with their military confreres. The long-standing mutual antagonism was never very far from the surface. This, combined with the various policies emerging as the war progressed, led to problems, often serious ones. These problems received infrequent mention in the reports. Nevertheless, occasional examples appeared. The most serious conflict has been described earlier in this study. This concerned the Wehrmacht's need for Jewish labor. This conflict of interest led to strong complaints since the essential job of the Einsatzgruppen was to liquidate as many Jews as they could as quickly as possible.[56]

Another problem centered around the repulsive manner in which the killing and security operations were carried out, and the effect this was having on the local population and the German soldiers. Quite naturally little of this was included in the reports, which as we discovered earlier, tended to emphasize the positive reaction of the population.[57]

Einsatzgruppe C complained in one report that German soldiers had been engaged in looting the apartments of the Jewish population in Uman. As a result of these actions, Jews were warned and were able to escape, and only two NKWD officials were captured. The report charged that "Naturally, the systematic action of Einsatzkommando 5 suffered greatly by these planless excesses against the Jews in Uman." The report boasted that "these excesses were cleaned up immediately by Einsatzkommando 5 after its arrival." The "cleaning up" meant here was the more systematic shooting on 22 and 23 September 1941 of 1,412 Jews by Einsatzkommando 5.[58]

One of the concerns of both the Wehrmacht and the SS was the extent to which the secrecy of the killings was being undermined, particularly by the fact that so many soldiers witnessed them, took pictures of the executions, discussed them in letters, and in everyday conversations. A consequence of this lack of secrecy was that rumors of executions reached the Jews. Einsatzgruppe D complained that these rumors had made operations in Simferopol very difficult. Knowledge of these actions had become known, in part, as a result of the "unguarded talks of German soldiers."[59]

It is interesting to note that many objections of army officials to the Einsatzgruppen killings, objections that were voiced at the time or appeared in postwar statements, often gave as the reasons for the objection the danger to the troops, which resulted from a population aroused by the brutal killings, or the danger the killings presented to the morale of the German soldiers. Purely pragmatic considerations were stressed. There was often no mention of the terrible inhumanity to the victims themselves. One can understand pragmatic objections being raised during the war since moral arguments would have been of little use then. This type of criticism persisted even after the war, however. One is tempted to suggest that, had the danger to the security and the morale of the troops not existed, there would have been no objection to these killings.

Yet these were the statements of people who were against the killings. This apparent lack of moral perception, this seeming inability or unwillingness to confront directly the profound moral question of the exterminations, was characteristic of many army leaders in the east. The collaboration of the army and the Einsatzgruppen was a close one and deepened as time passed. The reports present only a small glimpse of this collaboration. The number of civilians killed with the direct assistance of the army cannot be determined. This collaboration played a decisive part in the workings of Hitler's plans. During the trial of the Einsatzgruppen leaders after the war, one of the major arguments of the defense lawyers was that the Einsatzgruppen were, in fact, simply an auxiliary security force for the army and were acting under the orders of the army commanders. The implication was that it was the army commanders who were responsible for the activities of the Einsatzgruppen.[60] This attempt to shift the blame for the crimes of their clients onto the shoulders of the army was an understandable legalistic move on the part of the lawyers. In the end it did not work because, of course, the basic premise of the argument was not correct. The fact that such an argument could be advanced at all showed the great extent that the activities of the armed forces were entwined with those of the Einsatzgruppen. In summary, many army leaders were as guilty of war crimes as the Einsatzgruppen leaders were.

12
Other Reports

We are now to consider, albeit briefly, the other Einsatzgruppen reports dealing with operations in the east. These reports, some of which have already been consulted earlier in our discussion, include the eleven Activity and Situation Reports, the fifty-five Reports from the Occupied Eastern Territories, the two reports prepared by Franz Walter Stahlecker, leader of Einsatzgruppe A, and the so-called Jäger report by the leader of Einsatzkommando 3.

We will begin with the Activity and Situation Reports. These reports were issued starting on 31 July 1941 and extended to the period ending on 31 March 1942. They covered the same time period as the Operational Situation Reports and were issued about twice a month (at first) and then on a monthly basis.[1] In effect, the Activity and Situation Reports were a summary of the Operational Situation Reports issued during the same period and were derived from them.[2] Apparently prepared at Heydrich's request, these reports added little to what had already appeared in the other reports. One encounters the same statistics of shootings, reports on the economy, culture, propaganda, agriculture, and the nationalist aspirations of the non-Russian segments of the eastern population. The reports consisted of highlights of significant information contained in the Operational Situation Reports. Few changes can be noted in this repetition of the material. It is often transcribed almost word for word. This pattern of direct lifting of information is readily seen by comparing the Activity and Situation Reports with the appropriate Operational Situation Reports issued within the corresponding time period. (For example, compare the killing operations in Activity and Situation Report 1 with the same events in Operational Situation Reports 20, 22, 24, 37; Activity and Situation Report 3, with Operational Situation Reports 61, 63, 64, 67; and Activity and Situation Report 6 with Operational Situation Reports 108, 111, 123, 124, 125.)

Some differences between these two series did exist, however. One structural difference was the use of a Table of Contents dividing the reports into several broad subject headings. The latter included, for example, the headings: Locations, Economic Situation, Police Tasks Carried Out,

Executive Activity, Attitude of Ethnic Groups, Police Resistance Movements, and so on. These headings had subsections and generally treated the information discussed as it applied to the different geographical areas. The Activity and Situation Reports, being summaries of the events covering two-week or monthly periods of time, were not as detailed as the Operational Situation Reports. They often did not include the dates of the actions, even when this information had appeared in the Operational Situation Reports. Typical in this regard were the events described in Zloczow and Belzy found in Activity and Situation Report 1 and the same events in Operational Situation Reports 24 and 37. The four areas of the four Einsatzgruppen were not always mentioned in the Activity and Situation Reports. Activity and Situation Report 6 does not describe events in the area of Einsatzgruppe D, for example.[3] The most salient difference between these reports was the expanded number of copies made as the result of a more extended distribution list. As many as one hundred copies were issued and sent to the commanders of the four Einsatzgruppen, the Kommando leaders, the Higher SS and Police Leaders, various SS and police leaders throughout the Reich and the eastern territories, and to various Reich Commissioners in various military districts.[4] Copies were also sent at Heydrich's request to the Foreign Office, where they apparently were summarized and read by a considerable number of Foreign Office personnel.[5]

More than the Operational Situation Reports, the Activity and Situation Reports seem to be characterized by the almost constant use of reasons to justify the executions. A possible explanation for this was the expanded distribution list, in particular, the including of Reich ministers and the possibility that unauthorized persons might get hold of the reports. Little evidence exists as to the reaction of recipients to these reports. It has been suggested that the Foreign Office may have expressed disapproval of the indiscretion of these reports.[6] Whatever the reaction may have been, there could have been no doubt in the reader's mind what was taking place in the east.

In Chapter 7 we recalled Helmut Krausnick's observation that in Activity and Situation Report 1 the presentation of Einsatzgruppe B's killing operations for July 1941 had characterized these operations as retaliatory in nature, an emphasis not present in the corresponding Operational Situation Reports. In the opinion of the RSHA hierarchy, this change was clearly necessary. We have just mentioned the somewhat obvious use of justification in the Activity and Situation Reports. There is further evidence to suggest that in preparing the Activity and Situation Reports, officials in Berlin, for reasons of their own, wished to suppress or emphasize certain information found in the Operational Situation Reports. One editor of the reports, Rudolf Fumy, has testified to this effect. In an affidavit given on

12 January 1948, Fumy specifically cites a detail in Activity and Situation Report 6 as an example of this editorial alteration. Fumy states as follows:

> If, in Activity and Situation Report 6, dated 25 November 1941, therefore, reports about demonstrations of the population against Jewry: "Spontaneous demonstrations . . . did not take place . . ." appear with the addition: "Spontaneous demonstrations against Jewry with *following pogroms* by the population were not noted"—then this addition has surely been added for some reason in Berlin.[7]

While the differences mentioned above were present in the summary reports, in the main, however, the Activity and Situation Reports were quite similar in content to the earlier reports. In sum, these reports were what they were intended to be, basic comprehensive overviews of the Einsatzgruppen activities.

The last Operational Situation Report was issued on 24 April 1942. On 1 May 1942 the first of a series of reports was issued, a series that eventually included at least fifty-five known reports, and that continued until 21 May 1943. These reports were called Reports from the Occupied Eastern Territories and were published once a week on Friday.

The surviving set of Reports from the Occupied Eastern Territories were discovered in four separate folders.[8] Included with some of the reports were a number of supplemental enclosures consisting of alterations and updates of the locations, personnel, and lines of communication of the Kommandos.[9] A feature of the reports, a carry over perhaps from the Activity and Situation Reports, but not used in the Operational Situation Reports, was the Table of Contents. This section amounted to a brief summary of the main points dealt with in the reports proper. Reports 1 through 6 included the Locations and Communications in the Table of Contents; after that it was dropped. Reports 7 through 55 only occasionally included in the existing copies the Locations list, and even some of these were incomplete.[10] The presence of these lists and the periodic corrections would indicate that these lists were a regular feature, but have simply been lost. The surviving set of these reports is virtually complete, although occasionally pages are missing,[11] or appear twice.[12]

These reports were stamped Geheim, a lesser degree of secrecy than the Geheime Reichssache marking of the Operational Situation Reports. As was true of the Meldungen aus dem Reich (Reports from the Reich), the surviving copies of the reports do not contain a distribution list nor any indication as to how many copies were made of each report. We are, therefore, not certain as to who received them. Copies of some of these reports have been found that bear the stamp "The Reich Defense Commissioner for the Wehrkreis XVII" or the "Vienna Reichsgau." The former was included in the distribution list of the Activity and Situation

Reports. This may indicate that the distribution list was the same as that of the latter reports.

The Reports from the Occupied Eastern Territories differed considerably from the Operational Situation Reports. It will be remembered that the Kommandostab had been set up by Heydrich in the autumn of 1941 to deal with the compilation of reports. At that time the Kommandostab consisted of the evaluation office of Group IV A 1 (headed by Lindow) of Office IV. After April 1942, the period of the Reports from the Occupied Eastern Territories, the Kommandostab consisted of the various officials from all the RSHA departments who met to summarize the reports from the east. All these reports appeared under the heading Der Chef der Sicherheitspolizei und SD- Kommandostab. This change in the method of drawing up the reports was accompanied by an immediate change in the character of the reports themselves. Liquidations of the Jews, which had played such a significant role in the Operational Situation Reports, were now almost completely absent from the new series. Most statements concerning the killing of Jews were connected with partisan warfare or anticommunist activities.[13] The victims in these reports were always described as partisans, partisan sympathizers, NKWD agents, or communists, etc. Reasons were always given for shootings, and the statistics of Jewish dead were often included in the figures concerning antipartisan and anti-NKWD operations. The killing of Jews as Jews, while not entirely absent, in these reports was treated as a subject that was taken for granted and required no further detailed repetition. Report 9 even resurrected the earlier concept of "the later intended Final Solution of the Jewish problem" in its discussion of the Jews in White Russia.

Two reports illustrate this avoidance of a direct treatment of this subject. Report 6 contained a discussion of the situation in Estonia and repeated information already months old that had appeared in earlier reports. Whereas the earlier reports had described the killing of the Estonian Jews, this report merely informed that the Jews had been "seized" thus "avoiding all unnecessary trouble in the economic life of Estonia." The report then proclaimed that today "there are no more Jews in Estonia." The reader is left to draw his own conclusion as to what happened to the Estonian Jews. Report 7 presented a similarly laundered description concerning Latvian Jews. After mentioning that about 3,750 Jews remained as specialized laborers in the ghettos of Riga, Dünaburg (Dwinsk), and Libau, the report said that with the exception of these Jews, Latvia had "become free of Jews in the meantime."

The Reports from the Occupied Eastern Territories therefore downplayed the killing of the Jews. Müller's office IV, whose representatives, among others, were responsible for the carrying out of these executions, received a less prominent place in these reports. Security operations by the Security

Police were primarily concerned with the ever-expanding war against the partisans and various forms of partisan resistance. Indeed, this war became the dominant concern, and almost every report dealt with it.[14] Consequently these reports remain an important, though limited, source for the study of the partisan war in the east from the German perspective. This was especially so in the case of partisan operations in the area of Army Group Center, where partisans were extremely active.

In general the Reports from the Occupied Eastern Territories were less specific about who did what and where. While usually separated according to the area of the Einsatzgruppen, most reports referred to events taking place in a fairly wide-ranging area, the Ostland, the Ukraine, the area of Army Group Center, and so on. Some statements referred to the eastern territory as a whole. Great prominence was given to the SD reports. As was true for the earlier reports, in addition to sections dealing with executive matters, antipartisan, and anticommunist measures, these reports were concerned with questions of the general situation in the east, but even more so than previously. As in earlier reports, these reports ranged from discussions of the general mood of the population, their reaction to the self-administration, to propaganda, cultural affairs, church matters, as well as to matters pertaining to education, the local economy, agriculture, the food situation, and labor. The reports reflected the growing concern that had appeared in the later Operational Situation Reports with regard to many of these subjects. The reports could be quite detailed and even included such information as monthly statistics of outbreaks of gonorrhea and syphilis.[15] Report 13 included an enclosure marked Anlage 5, a thirty-three page detailed report on the Caucasus. The attention had thus shifted away from the killing of Jews, which, of course, was still going on, to these more general topics.

We can only speculate as to why this change in emphasis took place. One reason was advanced by Gustav Nosske, leader of Einsatzkommando 12, who was in charge of the newly formed RSHA Group IV D 5 dealing with partisan warfare. In his testimony at the trial of the Einsatzgruppen leaders, Gustav Nosske stated that the "basic change" was brought about because the Operational Situation Reports were "unreliable, incorrect and inaccurate."[16] The new reports were to be sent out only once a week, thereby allowing for more time for the Kommandostab to prepare them. It was no doubt hoped that this would minimize the inaccuracies that plagued the earlier reports. Nosske claimed that after this change reports dealing with Hitler's Order to kill the Jews no longer were incorporated into the reports. Reports on these matters were sent to Eichmann's Group IV B 4.[17] Nosske related that "as a consequence of this, in the compiling of the reports, the individual contributions furnished by the various departments, as for instance, Jewish actions, could no longer be incorporated in the new Reports from the Occupied Eastern Territories." Nosske further testified that his department was instructed as to the form the reports were to take.[18]

Just how close Nosske's statements were to the truth cannot be determined. Understandably he wished to distance himself from the reports dealing with the annihilation of the Jews. It was also in his interest to describe the Operational Situation Reports as "unreliable" and "inaccurate." Even if his testimony was a correct explanation of how this subject ceased to be a feature of the reports, the suggestion that the reason for the general change in the reporting surely cannot be solely the one he advanced, that is, the errors found in the earlier reports. Inaccuracies might continue whatever form the reports took and whether or not liquidations were included. His reason alone does not satisfactorily explain the different character of the reports. No doubt the increased input that the other RSHA offices had in the newly revamped Kommandostab played some part in this change. From the available evidence it would appear that the manager (Geschäftsführer) of the Kommandostab, although deputized by Müller's department, did not have complete control over the content of the Reports from the Occupied Eastern Territories.[19] The concerns and priorities of the other offices of the RSHA would find greater expression than had been the case until April 1942.

Yet this, too, does not fully explain the matter. It is logical to assume that so fundamental a change had to be not just the result of internal administrative shiftings, but the result of a deliberate decision. This cannot be established with certainty, however, as enough conclusive evidence is lacking. It may well be that these procedural differences did largely account for the new tone of the reports, or it may have been simply more expedient to adopt the clearer structure of the reports and not have to worry about problems of chronology, events, and numbers that attended the accounts of the Jewish liquidations. The partisan danger had grown to such an extent that it became the main concern of the German forces in the east, short of the Soviet Army itself. The depth to which the Security Police were immersed in this war offered them the easy convenience of merging the antipartisan operations with the killing operations, as well as the opportunity of disguising the latter as a result. Also the need for safer, more neutral reporting may have been desired at this time since the next stage in the annihilation program was already under way in the killing centers established in Poland. The gassings in Treblinka, Auschwitz, Sobibor, and other places were treated with far greater secrecy than was the case with the Einsatzgruppen. It is possible that this newfound reserve vis-à-vis reports about the Jews had its source in this new situation. Whatever may have been the reason for the change, the Reports from the Occupied Eastern Territories were, as one historian has put it, "more discreet and offered the Nuremberg prosecution little material."[20]

Apart from details concerning the partisan war, the Reports from the

Occupied Eastern Territories do contain much valuable information as to the feelings of the local population on a variety of subjects. Naturally they are also indicative of the attitudes on the part of the SD reporters themselves concerning these subjects. Some of this material will be discussed later. It was, in fact, the perceived critical nature of the SD reports (in particular the Reports from the Reich) that apparently led Himmler and Goebbels on 12 May 1943 to cease issuing these reports in the form they had assumed up to that point. As with the Reports from the Reich, so, too, were the Reports from the Occupied Eastern Territories suspended.[21] The fifty-fifth report, dated 21 May 1943, was the last known Report from the Occupied Eastern Territories.[22]

The so-called Stahlecker reports and the Jäger report are especially important for two reasons: first, because of the wealth of information they contain, and second, because they were written not by RSHA officials in Berlin, but by an Einsatzgruppe leader and an Einsatzkommando leader, respectively. They are examples of summary reports unaltered by the editorial process that affected the other reports we have been considering. While admittedly these reports were the result of some editorializing and certainly reflect a high degree of precise organization, they do present events more directly from the perspective of these two leaders. Their personal opinions are much in evidence. The report written by Jäger is the best example we have of an extensive Kommando report "from the field," as it were. These reports contain criticisms, both implicit and explicit, of other German agencies, criticism that might not have made it past Müller's censoring eye, at least not in the form as found in these reports. In the absence of other surviving reports of this type during the 1941 period, we can only speculate as to how representative these reports were of material sent to Berlin from the Einsatzgruppen headquarters and from the Kommandos.

Franz Walter Stahlecker was born in Sternenfels on 10 October 1900. An administrative jurist (1921), who had joined the National Socialist Party in 1932, Stahlecker had held several important police positions. From 1934 he was leader of the Political Police in Württemberg, and in 1938 he became an SD leader inVienna. After serving as commander of the Security Police and SD (BdS) in the Protektorat of Bohemia and Moravia, in May 1940 Stahlecker became commander of the Security Police in Norway. He became an SS- Oberführer (major general) and Ministerialrat connected to the Foreign Office. In June 1941, after promotion to the rank of SS Brigadeführer and Generalmajor of Police, Stahlecker was appointed leader of Einsatzgruppe A.[23]

The first Stahlecker report[24] was a comprehensive report of the operations of Einsatzgruppe A up to 15 October 1941, and included reports of various dates written within this time period. In pencil at the top of the report was found the following: "Personal property of SS-Obergruppenführer. Wv.31.1 1942." This was followed by the rubber stamp marking Geheime Reichssache. This report bore Stahlecker's signature. It was over 130 pages long, far longer than the longest Operational Situation Report. Forty copies were prepared, the surviving copy being the twenty-third one. Stahlecker's report was a very thorough overview of Einsatzgruppe A operations during the first few months of the war in the east. It featured the familiar description of the eastward movement of the Kommandos, the establishment of contacts with the army commanders, the instigation of pogroms in various locations, the recruitment of local auxiliary forces, the actions against communist officials, the liquidation of the Jews, the setting up of ghettos, and the exploitation of Jewish labor. The report included eighteen enclosures that featured such things as a precise description of the total strength of the Einsatzgruppe A personnel, a breakdown of the Kommandos of the Einsatzgruppe, details of the strength and distribution of the auxiliary police,[25] the number of persons in prison,[26] antipartisan operations, the number and distribution of Jews within the population, information concerning the economy of the Baltic countries and the Jewish part in this economy, and so on. Above all, this report contained a detailed breakdown by country and major cities of the numbers of both Jews and communists executed by Einsatzgruppe A.

The second summary report[27] by Einsatzgruppe A was without date. As a Nuremberg trial document it consisted of eight pages (pages 56 to 64 of the original) and also included a map of the Baltic and White Russian areas illustrating with coffins and statistics the number of Jews executed thus far by Einsatzgruppe A. The original consisted of about 150 pages with nineteen additional enclosures and was to be distributed in fifty copies.[28] From its content and the cut-off date of 31 January 1942, which was mentioned, it can be concluded that it came after the first Stahlecker report, and was probably written in February 1942, or some time close to this date. As was often the case with the reports of the Einsatzgruppen, there was a lot of repetition of earlier material in this report. Comparing it with the summary report of 15 October 1941, we notice that much has simply been lifted with little modification from that document. No doubt common sources in the files of the headquarters of Einsatzgruppe A were used to prepare these and other reports.[29] Both reports stated that as the result of the "basic orders" received, the complete annihilation of Jews was to be achieved. The description of the Estonian situation, for example, was taken almost word for word from the earlier report. While the latter noted that the arrest of all male Jews over sixteen years of age was almost completed and that Estonia would soon be free of Jews, the second report announced that these measures had been completed. Similarly, the operations carried out in Latvia and Lithuania were recapitulated and brought up to date. A total of 229,052 Jews had been killed.[30]

In the first Stahlecker report it was stated that in Latvia and Lithuania, "an annihilation of the Jews without leaving any traces could not be carried out, at least not as the present moment." This was because Jewish skilled labor was indispensable for much needed repair work.[31] The second report, in describing the situation in White Russia, repeated the idea that to kill all the approximately one hundred twenty-eight thousand Jews remaining there was "fraught with certain difficulties." These difficulties— the need for Jewish labor, cold weather making executions difficult, transportation and fuel problems—would only delay the killing operations, however. This report simply said that two more months would be required to liquidate all the Jews.[32]

The report described the arrival in Riga and Minsk of Jews from the Reich. The first ten thousand sent to Riga were put in camps near Riga while the others were put "for the time being" into a separate part of the Riga ghetto. The report informed that only a small proportion of these Jews could work since most of them were women, children, and elderly people. The death rate among the Jews rose continuously, the report stated, as a consequence of "the extraordinarily hard winter." And then followed what is unique in all of Einsatzgruppen literature—the granting of faint praise for these Reich Jews:

> The amount done by those few Jews from the Reich who are fit for work is satisfactory. They are preferred as labor to the Russian Jews, because they are German speaking and because of their comparatively greater cleanliness. Worthy of note is the adaptability of the Jews with which they attempt to form their life in accordance with the circumstances.[33]

Stahlecker did not live to see the destruction of the remaining Jews within his territory. In fact, he survived the writing of his second summary report by barely a month. On 23 March 1942 he was killed by Estonian partisans.

The two reports just discussed were concerned with the activities of Einsatzgruppe A as a whole. Complementing these reports was one that dealt with one Einsatzkommando within Einsatzgruppe A. This was the report that summarized the killings by Einsatzkommando 3 for the period up to 1 December 1941. It was written by the head of Einsatzkommando 3, Karl Jäger. This report is of such importance in the world of captured Einsatzgruppen documents that we will examine it in some detail.

Born in Schaffhausen on 20 September 1888, Karl Jäger was fifty-three years old when, in 1941, he became leader of Einsatzkommando 3, somewhat older than the other Einsatzgruppen leaders. Jäger had joined the National Socialist Party in 1930, and two years later, the SS. He served in this capacity as an SS leader and in 1938 became SD section leader in Münster. By the fall of 1941, with the establishment of civil government in the east, Jäger assumed the position of commander of the Security Police and SD (KdS) for Lithuania. Jäger remained in this position until the fall of 1943.[34] Jäger was not among the defendants at the Einsatzgruppen trial in 1947–48; he committed suicide while awaiting trial on 22 June 1959.[35]

Jäger's report is only several pages long, but for cold-blooded horror, for a mind-boggling depravity that leaves one stunned and incredulous at the ordered recording of such atrocities, this report is without equal in all of the Einsatzgruppen reports. The report lists the murder of 137,346 people.[36] Yet the horror lies not only in the numbers killed, but also in the meticulous manner in which these killings were catalogued. In no other surviving document do we get as detailed a picture of the steady accumulation of victims. The six pages that encompass this macabre inventory offered to their reader a more exact description of the date and place of executions, numbers shot, and breakdown of victims by type than appeared in the Operational Situation Reports. It was pointed out earlier that the Operational Situation Reports were frequently inconsistent in the method of reporting this information. No such inconsistency can be found in Jäger's report.

The surviving original copy of this report, the fourth of five copies made, is today found in the Central Lithuanian Archives in Vilnius (Vilna).[37] The existence of this document was not known during the period immediately after the war, and thus it was not included in the documents at the Nuremberg Trials. There can be no doubt as to its authenticity.[38] A copy of this report was forwarded to Einsatzgruppe A headquarters and formed the basis of Stahlecker's draft report and of subsequent Einsatzgruppe A reports sent to Berlin. As evidence of this it might be mentioned that Jäger's report listed the figures for Jews still alive in Lithuania as follows: in Shavli, about 4,500; in Kovno, about 15,000; in Vilna, about 15,000. These statistics were repeated in the Einsatzgruppe A draft report, in Operational Situation Report 155, and in Activity and Situation Report 9. Another example from the Jäger report was the reporting of a Jewish "mutiny" during the shooting operations in Zagare on 2 October 1941. While not described in the Jäger report, the escape of at least fifty Jews on October 2 was mentioned in Operational Situation Report 155 and in Activity and Situation Report 9, where their recapture and shooting was described. In addition Jäger declared that Lithuania was now free of Jews, with the exception of those cited above in the ghettos in Shavli, Kovno, and Vilna. This declaration, too, soon turned up in the draft report and in Activity and Situation Report 9.[39]

Jäger's report began by saying that Einsatzkommando 3 took over Security Police duties in Lithuania on 2 July 1941. The Vilna area was taken over by the Kommando on 9 August 1941, and the Shavli area on 2 October 1941. Prior to these dates Vilna had been within the area of operations of Einsatzkommando 9 and Shavli within that of Einsatzkommando 2. The first victims listed in the report were the 2,977 Jewish men and women killed in Kovno on 4 and 6 July 1941, by Lithuanian partisans acting under Jäger's orders. At the end of the statistical part of the report, 4,000 Jews were listed killed in pogroms prior to Einsatzkommando 3's arrival. The remaining victims listed were killed by a mobile unit led by First Lieutenant Joachim Hamann and eight to ten trustworthy men from Einsatzkommando 3, with the help of Lithuanian partisans.

The exact dates of most of the killings were presented during the five months covered by the report. Some executions were listed as having taken place during certain time periods. For example, a detachment of Einsatzkommando 3 in Dwinsk killed 9,585 persons from 13 July to 21 August 1941. Also, several executions in different places were cited during a time period. For example, a detachment stationed in Minsk from 28 September to 27 October 1941, killed 3,050 persons in Pleschnitza, Bicholin, Scak, Bober, and Uzda.

In every instance (except the August 26 and 27 entries for the shootings in Kaisiadorys and Prienai) the numbers of those executed were broken down in some way, according to the number of men, women, and children, or other categories. These victims were the same as those mentioned in other reports. Jews formed the overwhelming majority of those killed, and their numbers were always separated according to sex. Jewish children were also listed separately in the breakdowns. With only two exceptions (14 July and 14 August 1941, where Jews killed were described as communists), this report distinguished Jews completely from communist victims. It is noteworthy that the victims included two Jews from the United States, a country that was still neutral at this time. In most cases the type of victims was simply listed, followed by the numbers killed. Occasionally, as was the case to a greater extent than in the Operational Situation Reports, "reasons" were given to explain the executions. Other national groups killed, such as Lithuanians and Russians, usually were designated as communists.[40]

Quite apart from the numbers presented in it, Jäger's report made clear the extent of the Kommando's operations. The thoroughness that characterized this destruction of human life was seen in the fact that over one hundred separate liquidation operations were included in the report. Seventy-one different locations were mentioned, and the Kommando, not content with visiting these once, actually carried out several shootings in some cities. Kovno, for example, was mentioned thirteen times; Mariampole, six times. The final entries for Vilna indicated that ten operations were undertaken there during October and November 1941 alone.[41] On several occasions detachments of the Kommando carried out killings in several locations on the same day. Thus, on 4 September 1941 executions were carried out in Praveniskis, Cekiske, Seredsius, Velinona, and Zapiskis; on 11 September 1941 in Leipalingis, Seirigai, and Uzasalis; and on 26 October 1941 in Seduva, Zarasai, Pasvalys, and Kaisiadorys. Between 28 August and 6 September 1941 during the cleaning up actions in Georgenburg, all 412 remaining Jewish men, women and children were exterminated there by Jäger's men.[42]

An examination of the numbers of persons killed reveals that for operations carried out on a single day the numbers ranged from one victim (July 22 in Panevezys) to 9,200 (October 29 in Kovno). After mid-July 1941 most of the executions numbered in the hundreds and thousands. The monthly totals for the five-month period covered by the report were as follows:[43]

July	20 entries	4,400 killed[44]
August	33 entries	47,906 killed
September	38 entries	41,097 killed
October	12 entries	31,829 killed
November	10 entries	8,211 killed

From these calculations it is evident that the numbers of victims rose sharply after July, when the daily entries consisted of relatively low numbers. The peak of the shootings occurred in August and September, then the numbers gradually declined as fewer and fewer Jews remained to be killed. The total given in the report encompassed all victims. As a result of the scrupulous breakdown of types of victim, one can separate from this total the number of Jews killed. This came to a total of 131,494. Adding to this the 4,000 Jews killed by Lithuanians in pogroms before the Kommando's presence, one arrives at a total of 135,494 Jews. It was not for nothing that Jäger boasted in his report that he considered the Jewish actions by his Kommando as virtually completed. Jäger's boast was premature, however. Executions continued to take place. For one thing, there were several smaller ghettos still in existence in addition to those in Shavli, Kovno, and Vilna mentioned in the report. As time went by these were gradually reduced by further actions.[45] Three months after this report, on 6 February 1942, Stahlecker requested that Kommando leaders Martin Sandberger (Sonderkommando 1a) and Eduard Strauch (Sonderkommando 1b) as well as Jäger, provide him with the number of executions by category carried out by their units. Apparently, Stahlecker received no reply from Sandberger and Strauch, but on 9 February 1942, in a handwritten reply, Jäger stated that as of 1 February 1942, his Kommando had killed 138,272 people. The breakdown of this total by category was as follows: 136,421 Jews, 1,064 communists, 56 partisans, 653 mental patients, 44 Poles, 28 Russian prisoners of war, 5 Gypsies and 1 Armenian. Of the total number of persons killed, 55,556 were women and 34,464 were children.[46]

The number of persons murdered was staggering. In reading Jäger's report it must constantly be kept in mind that this was the work of only one Einsatzkommando. The sobering thought also occurs that this was one of many such reports that were sent to Einsatzgruppen headquarters. If other reports were similarly detailed, it is clear that an enormous amount of information reached the Group staffs. There the editorial process came to bear on this "raw" material. We have seen how some of Jäger's report found its way into subsequent reports and while some details as well as his total figures were included, it was obviously impractical to itemize individual operations to the extent that Jäger did. No doubt this was true of other reports sent to headquarters, whatever the degree of detail contained in them. Thus, the "raw" state of Jäger's report may give us some indication of the selectivity and pruning that occurred during successive stages in the preparation of the reports. Finally, we recognize the special importance of Jäger's report in that it includes information concerning the operations of his Kommando that did not appear in earlier Operational Situation Reports.

Following the purely statistical section Jäger's report ended with a short description of the actual preparations involved in carrying out some of the executions. We will return to this part of his report later as part of a consideration of the general character of the Einsatzgruppen reports.

13

The Einsatzgruppen Reports as Legal Evidence

Since their discovery, the Einsatzgruppen reports, like thousands of other captured German documents, have essentially served two functions. First, they have been used as evidence in war crimes trials, in particular, the so-called Einsatzgruppen trial in Nuremberg and in later trials held in Germany. Second, they have been used as an historical source by historians writing about the Holocaust in eastern Europe and other aspects of German rule in this area during the war. The role of these documents for the lawyer and the historian is necessarily quite different. While both the lawyer and the historian would demand of a document that it be genuine, it is the function served by the document that embodies this difference. Used as legal evidence, the reports prove or disprove the guilt of specific individuals. It is the extent to which the reports perform this task that is of importance to the legal process. The historian is not restricted to this rather narrow use of the documents. While this legal function may be of interest to him, the historian may be concerned about other aspects of the documents. The historian's inquiries into the meaning of the documents are thus more varied and far ranging. For example, a document may contain exaggerations or deliberate errors and thus obviate its use as legal evidence. The historian, however, may inquire into the reasons why these exaggerations and errors are present in the document and what meaning this may have. Such meaning may shed light on the historical context which produced the document. As well, the questions that historians may ask of a document will vary as to their point of inquiry and the age in which they live.

In this and the following chapter we will discuss the use of the Einsatzgruppen reports from the legal and historical points of view, respectively.

On 15 September 1947 a trial began in Nuremberg. This trial, one of twelve held by United States Military Tribunals and known as Case 9, United States of America Versus Otto Ohlendorf et al., was the trial of twenty-four Einsatzgruppen and Kommando leaders. The trial was held under the authority of Control Council Law No. 10 of 20 December 1945.

Reinforcing this law were the following orders: Executive Order 9679 of 16 January 1946; United States Military Government Ordinances nos. 7 and 11 of 18 October 1946 and 17 February 1947; and United States Forces, European Theater General Order 301 of 24 October 1946.[1] The Einsatzgruppen leaders were charged with having committed crimes against humanity and war crimes, as well as having been members of the SS and the Gestapo, organizations that had been declared illegal by the International Military Tribunal. As was the case with the earlier Trial of the Major War Criminals, most of the evidence used in the Einsatzgruppen trial was based on documentation as opposed to the testimony of witnesses. This placing of emphasis on documentation had been a deliberate decision of the American prosecution team at the trial before the International Military Tribunal.[2] It was also the natural consequence of the great number of documents that were available. The tremendous volume of German documents uncovered in numerous locations at the end and after the war presented the allied prosecutors with an abundance of evidentiary material with which to advance their case. At the same time they were faced with the problem of how to organize this mass of documentation into a workable structure.

Captured documents were processed in preparation for their use as evidence in a manner that involved several stages. At first, specialized military personnel captured documents and placed them in temporary document centers. Here the Field Branch of the Documentation Division, Office of the United States Chief of Counsel searched for and screened documents that were likely to be of use for the prosecution of war criminals. These documents were given pretrial serial numbers and then forwarded to the Office of the United States Chief of Counsel. Here they were recorded, indexed, and sent to the Screening and Analysis Branch of the Documentation Division. They were reexamined as to their value as evidence. Documents considered of use were then sent to the Document Room of the Office of the United States Chief of Counsel and were assigned a trial identification symbol. In the case of the Trial of the Major War Criminals this indicated the source of the documents, that is, the Allied agencies that processed them. In the case of the twelve subsequent Nuremberg Trials, including the Einsatzgruppen trial, this symbol referred to the German organizations to which the documents pertained.[3] Within each series the documents were assigned a number that indicated the order in which the documents were accepted as evidence, not their actual chronological order. Documents that were accepted as evidence in a trial were given an exhibit number as well.

The next stage in the procedure involved an analysis that was called Staff Evidence Analysis (SEA). This analysis by members of the prosecution staff involved a description of the document, its date, the number of pages it contained, the source and location of the original, the persons or organizations mentioned in the document, a summary of its content, as well as the name of the person doing the analysis, and the date when the analysis was done. Photostatic copies were made of the original documents, which were then placed in a fireproof safe in the Document Room. From one of these photostatic copies an authenticated translation was made of the document. It was usually the set of copies of the original and the translations which were used during the trial proceedings. Unless the original was required for special purposes (for example, by the defense counsel for examination),[4] it remained in the Document Room throughout the trial.[5] No document or exhibit was offered as evidence unless a German copy of the document had been given to the defense counsel at least twenty-four hours in advance.[6]

During the Einsatzgruppen trial the prosecution did not put a single witness on the stand. The evidence presented by the prosecution consisted of 252 exhibits. All were documents of various kinds, SS personnel files, various reports, IMT and other court transcripts, orders, correspondence, minutes of meetings, addresses, publications, and charts. A large number of interrogations had taken place before the trials began. A significant part of the prosecution evidence consisted of forty-eight affidavits, thirty-four of which were by the defendants themselves. But it was above all the excerpts from eighty-two Operational Situation Reports, as well as excerpts from various Activity and Situation Reports and Reports from the Occupied Eastern Territories that formed the principal prosecution exhibits.[7]

The indictment[8] listed killings according to which Einsatzgruppe or Kommando had carried them out. The names of the defendants were not paired with these operations. The degree of detail as to place and time of the killings corresponded to that of the report from which the information was obtained. The report numbers were not mentioned after each charge. The indictment cited many examples of mass murder by the Einsatzgruppen, but stated that their crimes were not limited to these examples. Killings specified in the indictment were mostly those carried out against Jews, communists, and Gypsies. Shootings of partisans or "reprisal" killings tended not to be included, thus anticipating the arguments of the defense in this regard.

Concerning the reports, the tactics of the prosecution were quite simple. The reports, especially the Operational Situation Reports, were so damaging that little further evidence was needed to present the case. As the chief prosecutor put it, the proof was certainly "quite free of subtlety."[9] The locations, dates, numbers of victims, and descriptions of killings were so ubiquitous throughout the reports that the prosecution felt it sufficient to present the reports and simply prove that the defendants had been in

Table 7

Kommando	Report	Einsatzgruppe
SK1a	Operational Situation Report (OSR) 15, 111 (L–180)	*Einsatzgruppe A —* OSR 48, 130, 136,
SK1b	OSR 14, 24, 140, 150, 155 (184) (186)	140, 154, 155, 165,
EK2	OSR 24, 94, 31, 155, 163 (L–180)	168, 178, 181, 183,
EK3	OSR 19, 88, 94 (Jäger report)	184, 186 (L–180) (PS–2273)
SK7a	OSR 10, 34, 73, 92, 108, 124, 125, 133, 194	*Einsatzgruppe B —* OSR 21, 31, 43,
SK7b	OSR 73, 92, 108, 125, 133, 194	50, 67, 92, 133, 148, 149
V.K. Moscow	OSR 67, 73, 92, 108, 124, 125, 133, 194	
EK8	OSR 73, 92, 108, 124, 125, 133, 194	
EK9	OSR 17, 21, 24, 31, 73, 92, 108, 124, 125, 133, 194	
Trupp Smolensk	OSR 194	
SK4a	OSR 14, 19, 24, 37, 80, 86, 88, 94, 97, 101, 106, 111, 119, 132, 135, 143, 156, 183	*Einsatzgruppe C —* OSR 24, 47, 128, 183, 190
SK4b	OSR 19, 24, 47, 94, 173, 111, 132, 135, 143, 173, 177	
EK5	OSR 47, 60, 86, 88, 94, 111, 132, 135, 143, 156, 173, 177	
EK6	OSR 19, 81, 86, 94, 111, 135, 143, 156, 173, 177, 183, 187	
SK10a	OSR 37, 45 (hostages shot on slightest pretext)	*Einsatzgruppe D —* OSR 37, 40, 67,
SK10b	OSR 19, 22, 40, 150 (partisans), 157 (partisans), 165, 178	89, 95, 101, (107), 117, 129, 136, 145,
SK11a	OSR 45, 157 (partisans), 178	150, 153, 157, 165,
SK11b	OSR 45, 178	170, 178, 184, 190
EK12	OSR 165 (helped in combing out northern Crimea), 178	

charge of a particular Einsatzgruppe or Kommando at a certain time. This was easily done by consulting the names of the leaders of the Kommandos found in the Locations and Lines of Communication lists as well as the SS records of the defendants, their testimony, and their previously given affidavits. The reports thus formed the central core of the case against the defendants. Without question it would have been a far more difficult task to prove the specific details of the guilt of the defendants had copies of the reports not been discovered.[10]

Not all those persons who had been Kommando leaders for the 1941–44 period were defendants at the Einsatzgruppen trial.[11] Some had not yet been discovered and were tried in later trials. The evidence presented by the prosecution dealt with the criminal activities for the period between May 1941 and July 1943 only, and thus dealt with those defendants captured who had served during this time.

The proof of mass murder offered by the Operational Situation Reports was overwhelming. As we see in table 7, every single Kommando of the four Einsatzgruppen participated in killings. Table 7 simply lists examples of reports in which each Kommando was said to have done this. These examples deal essentially with killings not connected with antipartisan operations. Reports are only included where the Kommando is specifically named in the report as having carried out mass shootings. The column on the right consists of reports that described killings under the heading of the Einsatzgruppe, but that were not specific as to which Kommando carried out the killings.[12] It is obvious, therefore, that individual Kommandos were responsible for more killings that the left column alone indicates.

Table 8 connects individual Kommando leaders with Operational Situation Reports that give evidence of participation in killings of their Kommando or Einsatzgruppe during the period of their position as leader. Only the time span covered by the Operational Situation Reports is reflected in the reports listed. Guilt of individuals was established not only via these reports, but with other evidence too—affidavits, cross examination, etc. As was the case in table 7 other reports dealing with each Einsatzgruppe's activities may also indicate an individual Kommando's guilt, although it may not be clear. For example, the reports of Einsatzgruppe D usually emphasized actions on the Einsatzgruppe and not the Kommando level. Therefore, the totals given reflect all the Kommandos and their leaders, without a breakdown being included. (Table 8 includes some Kommando leaders who were not defendants during the Einsatzgruppen trial.)

Table 8

EGA	*Stahlecker*:	Stahlecker reports (L–180, PS–2273), all EGA reports up to mid-March 1942 (OSR 184)
	Jost:	OSR 184 to the end of the series
SK1a	*Sandberger*:	OSR 15, 111 and other EGA reports
SK1b	*Ehrlinger*:	OSR 14, 24, 140
	Strauch:	OSR 155, 184, 186 and other EGA reports
EK2	*Batz*:	OSR 24, 94, 131
	Strauch:	OSR 151
	Lange:	OSR 155, 163

EK3	*Jäger*:	Jäger report (1 December 1941) — OSR 19, 88, 94
EGB	*Nebe*:	All EGB reports up to OSR 133.
	Naumann:	All EGB reports after the period of the beginning of November 1941.
SK7a	*Blume*:	OSR 10, 34, 73
	Steimle:	OSR 92, 108, 124, 125, 133
	Rapp:	OSR 194
SK7b	*Rausch*:	OSR 73, 92, 108, 125, 133
	Ott:	OSR 194
V.K. Moscow	*Six*:	OSR 67
	Klingelhoefer:	OSR 73, 92, 108, 124, 125, 133
EK8	*Bradfisch*:	OSR 73, 92, 108, 124, 125, 133, 194
	Richter:	OSR 194
EK9	*Filbert*:	OSR 17, 21, 24, 31, 73, 92, 108, 124, 125
	Schäfer:	OSR 133
	Wiebens:	OSR 194
EGC	*Rasch*:	Reports up to the end of September 1941, including OSR 111.
	Thomas:	OSR 111 to the end of the series.
SK4a	*Blobel*:	OSR 14, 19, 24, 37, 80, 86, 88, 94, 97, 101, 106, 111, 119, 131, 135, 143, 156
SK4b	*Herrmann*:	OSR 19, 24, 47, (possibly 94)
	Braune, Fritz:	OSR 111, 132, 135, 143, 173, 177
EK5	*Schulz*:	OSR 47, 60, 86, 88, 94, 111
	Meier:	OSR 132, 135, 143, 156
EK6	*Kroeger*:	OSR 19, 81, 86, 94, 111, 135
	Mohr:	OSR 143, 156, 173, 177, 187
	Biberstein:	(Reports from the Occupied Eastern Territories)
EGD	*Ohlendorf*:	All EGD reports in the series.
SK10a	*Seetzen*:	OSR 45 and all other EGD reports in the series.
SK10b	*Persterer*:	OSR 19, 22, 150, 157, 165 and all other EGD reports in the series.
SK11a	*Zapp*:	OSR 45, 149, 150 and all other EGD reports in the series.

SK11b	*Müller, Bruno*:	OSR 45, all other EGD reports up to OSR 101.
	Braune, Werner:	All EGD reports after the period of October 1941.
EK12	*Nosske*:	OSR 165 and all other EGD reports up to February 1942.
	Müller, Erich:	All EGD reports after February 1942.

The case for the defense was put forward in a different way. Altogether 753 exhibits were presented by the defense lawyers. Two-thirds of these consisted of affidavits by individuals. As many as fifty-one witnesses took the stand. The defense took sixty-one days to present its evidence. Documents of various types were also presented, directives, publications, correspondence, charts, maps, personnel files, expert opinions, speeches, certificates of court cases, interrogations and photographs.[13] Excerpts from the Einsatzgruppen reports also figure in the defense evidence although, as we shall see, they were offered with a very different purpose in mind than that of the prosecution.

The defense counsel were faced with an uphill battle. The prosecution evidence, in particular the Einsatzgruppen reports, was utterly damaging in the extent and precision with which the Einsatzgruppen crimes were detailed. No trial had dealt with mass murder on such a scale, nor had mass murderers ever left such an astounding record of their crimes as they carried them out. No prosecution team had been able to present such incriminating evidence as was found in the reports. It was no wonder that the prosecution required only two days (29 and 30 September 1947) to present its evidence.

Faced with this formidable task the defense adopted a number of strategies to argue its case.[14] We cannot go into detail here concerning these arguments except to discuss those that were concerned directly with the Einsatzgruppen reports. Since the major portion of the prosecution evidence consisted of the reports, it was necessary for the defense to discredit the reports and thereby weaken the case against their clients. Let us examine the attempts of the defense lawyers to find fault with the reports.

The defense was unable to seriously challenge the authenticity of the reports.[15] There was not the slightest doubt that the reports were genuine and not forgeries. The reports were declared authentic by both Einsatzgruppen and Kommando leaders, as well as by RSHA officials and the very people who had compiled the reports in Berlin.[16] Minor objections were raised concerning errors in translation.[17] One defense lawyer wanted to see the original reports, not photostats,[18] while another complained that some documents were not signed.[19] All objections concerning these arguments were overruled.[20]

While the authenticity of the reports could not be doubted and minor complaints against the reports such as those just mentioned were of little consequence, the main thrust of the defense arguments against the reports centered on the probative value of the reports as evidence. The probative value of the reports was questioned not because the reports were not thought to be genuine, but because they were supposedly filled with errors and incorrect facts as well as exaggerated numbers of people killed. Also the defense demanded that the prosecution present a clear connection between the reports offered as evidence and the individual defendant to whom the reports referred.[21] Furthermore, the defense maintained that the mere contents of a report in itself was not sufficient to decide an individual's guilt and that it was essential that the nature of the defendant's part in these matters be examined carefully.[22] One defense counsel objected to the prosecution's claim that the latter could not be expected to assume the full burden of proving any defendant's foreknowledge of the criminal nature of the Einsatzgruppen's task.[23]

The main feature of the defense argument against the probative value of the reports concerned the errors that were to be found in the reports. These errors, the defense suggested, cast serious doubts on the validity of the documents as a means of deciding the guilt of the defendants. The inaccuracies in the reports were due to the manner in which the reports were compiled. The defense maintained that in order to judge the reliability of the reports, one had to ask how the final reports were arrived at and what were the possible sources and nature of errors that had cropped up during the various stages of their evolution.[24]

This questioning of the way the reports came into being formed the basis of the skepticism of the defense about the trustworthiness of the reports. We have already examined the method by which the reports were sent to Berlin and then compiled.[25] It will be recalled that generally the leader of the subunits of the Kommandos would summarize the reports sent to him by his subordinates. This draft would then be sent to the leader of the Einsatzkommando or Sonderkommando, who would then compile a more comprehensive report from the reports of the various subunits. From the Einsatzkommando staff this report would then be sent to the headquarters of the Einsatzgruppe, where it would be combined with others and used as part of a further summary report drafted at Einsatzgruppe headquarters. These reports were then sent by the Einsatzgruppe to the RSHA. We have also seen that reports often bypassed the Einsatzgruppe headquarters and were sent directly to Berlin.

The defense pointed out that each stage of this process provided opportunities for errors to occur. Each stage involved editorial decisions as to what was to be included in the subsequent content of the reports. At the Einsatzgruppe staff level it was not possible, for example, for men like

Willy Seibert of Einsatzgruppe D to verify the accuracy of the reports of the Kommando leaders.[26] They accepted their reports at face value.[27] Their job was to decide what sections of the Kommando reports were to be sent on to Berlin. These were arranged as a draft and submitted to the Einsatzgruppe leader, who signed and forwarded it on to the RSHA.[28]

The further evolution of the reports was affected by the circumstances present in the RSHA. These circumstances and the manner in which they came to influence the reports was summarized in the affidavits of defense witness Rudolf Fumy,[29] who was directly involved in the evaluation of the incoming reports and the compilation of the final reports. Essentially, Fumy said these reports contained errors, distortions, and omissions of various kinds. He stated that the reports: "should not be considered an exact description of the actual events and that they can be taken as a literal repetition of the original reports in a very limited scope only."[30]

The staff in Fumy's department was insufficient in numbers to deal properly with the increasing amount of material coming in, and the problem persisted in spite of the employment of additional staff. The result was "an ever-increasing superficiality in the entire work, which eventually was put up with as caused by the war." Fumy noted that Heinrich Müller played an important role in the preparation of the reports, and it was his practice, depending on the situation at the time, to emphasize or suppress material in the original reports that would affect either favorably or unfavorably other Reich agencies.

The manner is which the reports were sent to Berlin also led to problems. The official channel was not always followed. Local military field offices often sent a duplicate report directly to the RSHA. Delays because of distance (the reports sent by courier invariably took two or three weeks to arrive) combined with this and led to a confusion of dates in the mail arriving at Office IV. The radio and teletype messages were often mutilated, making difficult the correct arrangement of the information. Mistakes also occurred because reports were dictated directly from the teletype copy to the typist. This practice incorporated errors that may have cropped up earlier from an incorrect hearing of the original report. The enormous amount and variety of reports coming in, the lack of time and personnel to examine them properly, stenographers unfamiliar with their work—all these things, according to Fumy, made possible "only a very superficial selection and compilation of reports." Fumy stated that serious disputes with the reporting offices arose on several occasions as the result of incorrect accounts of events.[31]

The defense lawyers thus had cause to complain about the accuracy of the reports.[32] Other objections to the reports were raised as well. The final reports were compilations of material sent from the eastern territories; they were written by the men in the RSHA; and they were not written by the defendants themselves.[33] The defense therefore pointed out that the contents of the reports were not based on the direct observations of the men who actually compiled the reports, since they were in Berlin, not in Russia. The original documents that the final reports were based on were not known, nor were the final reports signed. It was not known whether the editor of the reports was a reliable person who carried out his task with the necessary care. Also it was not proven that the reports from the field were themselves prepared by persons who had observed the events firsthand. The reports, then, were simply hearsay evidence.[34]

From these observations at least one defense counsel claimed that it was doubtful that the facts contained in the Operational Situation Reports had actually taken place to the extent stated.[35] The defense noted that only about ten documents submitted by the prosecution could be described as "original reports, namely scattered reports to or from offices of the army." Even these reports, the defense declared, were "not free from errors of carelessness and deliberate misrepresentations."[36] It was not possible to establish the absolute accuracy of the reports since the original reports from the field were not available for comparison.[37]

Keeping in mind problems encountered by the men in Office IV, the defense lawyers pointed out that preparation of the reports got worse and worse as time passed. The hopelessness of putting any semblance of completeness into the final reports led to indifference on the part of the editors. It did not really matter to them how accurate the reports were. Only a portion of the incoming material was to be used. Who was to check the reports and who was to complain? The defense maintained that there was thus no compelling reason to verify the reports. It sufficed to make the reports reasonably coherent and presentable.[38]

The defense supplemented these general comments with specific examples of errors found in the reports. It was stated that the Locations and Lines of Communications lists included in the reports were filled with mistakes. There was some truth to this statement. The many examples where names and places were crossed out in the original copies indicated that the Locations list did not keep pace with the changing situation. When it finally became apparent that changes in personnel, their designation of rank, or the location of Kommandos had taken place, these changes were altered by hand accordingly. These corrections involved crossing out the names of leaders or places, and the writing in of the correct names or new locations.[39]

Erich Naumann's lawyer tried desperately to prove that Naumann did not become the leader of Einsatzgruppe B until the end of November 1941 rather than the beginning. He hoped to escape responsibility for killings carried out during November that were described in Operational Situation Reports 148 and 149.[40] It was argued that Office I of the RSHA had confused the date of Naumann's appointment (1 November 1941) with the date he actually took over as leader of Einsatzgruppe B. The Locations listing had been based on this faulty assumption.[41] It was testified that the defendant, Eugen Steimle, was on leave and replaced as leader of Sonderkommando 7a between 10 and 15 January 1942. The fact that in Operational Situation Report 186, dated 13 February 1942, he was still listed as the leader of this Kommando was explained by the fact that the appointment of his replacement was delayed by some weeks. It was stated that in the meantime Sonderkommando 7a had been led by a deputy, and that Steimle remained leader of the Kommando on paper only.[42]

The reports described events that had happened as much as a month or more earlier. In addition to this time gap, events did not always appear in chronological order in the reports. These two factors, the time lapse and incorrect chronology, were the result of the difficulties of wartime communication over great distances, and the methods used to transmit the reports. Reports sent by teletype reached Berlin faster than those sent by courier, even when they had been sent later. This led to anomalies such as the following: in Operational Situation Report 86 it was reported that as of the date of the report, 17 September 1941, Sonderkommando 4a and killed 6,584 people; yet Operational Situation Report 80, dated 11 September 1941, stated that as of 24 August 1941, Sonderkommando 4a had killed 7,152 people.[43] In some reports the statistics were sometimes repeated as part of another report. Operational Situation Report 47 indicated that six hundred Jews were killed in Tarnopol. This figure was found earlier in Operational Situation Report 19. Not only were statistics affected by these procedures, but events themselves often were duplicated in the reports. Operational Situation Report 165 stated that on 1 February 1941, in Loknja, thirty-eight Jews and one Gypsy were killed. In Operational Situation Report 181, issued over a month later, this information was repeated as part of an Einsatzgruppe A report on activities in the Loknja area. The same report concerning eleven persons who refused to work in Minsk appeared in both Operational Situation Reports 183 and 184.

Appraisals of the general situation would sometimes appear twice. Operational Situation Report 92 contained an Einsatzgruppe B report concerning the partisans. The report read as follows: "It is encouraging to find that the majority of the population is still hostile to the partisans."[44] Almost an exact repetition of this statement cropped up in Operational Situation Report 123, issued just over a month later.

An example of both a mixup of locations as well as duplication of information was pointed out by the defense counsel for Ohlendorf, Dr. Rudolf Aschenauer.[45] Aschenauer noted that in Operational Situation Report 89, under the heading of Einsatzgruppe D, Kikerino was listed as the headquarters of that Einsatzgruppe. This was incorrect. Kikerino was within the area of Einsatzgruppe A and not Einsatzgruppe D. Nikolajew had made its appearance as the headquarters of Einsatzgruppe D for the first time only in the previous report. This had followed a period when for twenty consecutive reports Einsatzgruppe D had not been included in the Operational Situation Reports. (See Appendix A.) It may well have been that the error was simply a slip, or the result of the unfamiliarity of the Berlin editors with this new location.[46] Operational Situation Report 89 also said that between 19 August and 25 September 1941, 8,890 Jews and communists were shot, bringing the total number of persons shot thus far by Einsatzgruppe D to 13,315, and that in Cherson and Nikolajew the Jewish question was being solved by shooting five thousand Jews in each of these cities.[47] These facts and figures appeared again in Operational Situation Report 95, this time under the correct Einsatzgruppe D headquarters location (Nikolajew).[48]

One basic objection to the prosecution evidence was the claim that the numbers of persons killed by the Einsatzgruppen were exaggerated in the reports. Implied in this argument was the notion that it somehow made a difference to the guilt of the defendants that they had collectively killed, say, only one million people and not one-and-a-half million. The defense claimed that the various stages in the reporting process had provided opportunities for increasing the numbers. We have seen that it was not always possible for the reports of the Kommandos to be exactly verified at the headquarters of the Einsatzgruppen.[49] Ohlendorf himself had apparently warned his Kommando leaders not to exaggerate figures.[50] In an affidavit, Ohlendorf stated that:

> I tried to keep the number secret in order to prevent the Kommando leaders from making a contest out of it and reporting larger numbers than had actually been executed.[51]

At the trial before the International Military Tribunal, where he appeared as a prosecution witness, Ohlendorf had admitted that his Einsatzgruppe had killed ninety thousand people between June 1941 and June 1942.[52] At his own trial, however, he changed his mind and said that this number was not correct.

> If, of course, the figure ninety thousand was named by me, I always added that of this, fifteen to twenty percent are double countings. That is on the basis of my own experiences. I do not know any longer how I could remember the number of just ninety thousand because I did not keep a register of these figures.[53]

Thus while he tried to prevent the numbers from being exaggerated by his Kommandos, Ohlendorf stated that he had to rely on their reports and could not double check them. He admitted that he knew that wrong numbers were reported to him on occasion by his subordinates.[54]

During their testimony, Ohlendorf, Willy Seibert, and Heinz Schubert all maintained that no total figures for Einsatzgruppe D existed, only totals that were reported by the Kommandos for a certain period. These periodic totals were kept secret and were sent to Berlin regularly by the signal officer Willy Fritsch. They did not appear in the written reports.[55] The inference here was that only the RSHA officials knew the overall total numbers and that their reliability in the final version of the reports was at the discretion of these officials.[56]

Concerning exaggerations, Ohlendorf had some further unkind words to say about his fellow Einsatzgruppen leaders, and Heydrich, Müller, and Bruno Streckenback in the RSHA. He claimed that all of these people exaggerated the numbers. Ohlendorf stated that the reports of other Einsatzgruppen were exaggerated by about twice the correct number.[57] Arthur Nebe, head of Einsatzgruppe B, was described as having been "not very exact with his zeros,"[58] and was singled out also by the leader of Sonderkommando 7a, Walter Blume, as having increased the figure "in order to improve his position in Berlin."[59] Paul Blobel, head of Sonderkommando 4a, also maintained that the number of Jews killed in Kiev (33,771) in September 1941 was too high. He said only half this number was shot.[60]

Not all the Einsatzgruppen personnel were quick to hide behind the exaggerated figures argument. Blume considered it "unworthy" to file a false report.[61] Seibert and Ohlendorf both stated that they tried to ensure that the numbers were as correct as possible, and deplored the changes carried out by others. (We see here the bizarre concept that it was quite acceptable to kill thousands of helpless people, but it was not acceptable to falsify the numbers in a report.) The defense submitted as evidence excerpts from Himmler's speech to the SS officers in Posen on 4 October 1943. In this speech, which Ohlendorf apparently heard,[62] the virtue of truthfulness in reporting was impressed upon the officers. While not specifically mentioning the Einsatzgruppen reports, Himmler complained bitterly that many reports sent by subordinates to their superiors in various German agencies were "plain lies or only half true or half correct."[63] If the Einsatzgruppen and Kommando leaders were distorting the true picture of their activities in the east, they were certainly doing it without Himmler's approval.

The argument that the numbers were distorted was part of the thesis that the reports were, in general, unreliable. The Kommandos had killed fewer people, and therefore, presumably the guilt of the defendants was not as great. The reports were filled with errors, thus their validity as proof of guilt was in doubt. Some defense counsel maintained that the specific reports used as evidence by the prosecution had not succeeded in establishing the guilt of their clients.[64]

Interestingly, the use of the reports as evidence was not limited to the prosecution. The defense had argued that the reports were untrustworthy; they also argued that the reports only appeared in excerpts as evidence, and that those parts of the reports not relevant to the prosecution's case had been omitted. This, the defense declared, gave a distorted, one-sided picture. By focusing on executions, the executions were "taken out of the context of the actual events and situations which were the reason behind them and magnified into the sole basis of the activity of the Einsatz-gruppen."[65] Yet in spite of their efforts to discredit the reports, the defense, was not above using them as evidence, and in excerpt form at that. Quite naturally, the defense was just as selective as the prosecution had been. Many of the Reports from the Occupied Eastern Territories appeared as evidence for the defense. The excerpts from these and other reports dealt with the antipartisan warfare that consumed more and more of the attention of the Kommandos. The Reports from the Occupied Eastern Territories offered almost no mention of anti-Jewish operations per se. The aim of the defense here was clear. The Einsatzgruppen were supposedly involved in a legitimate war against the partisan enemy. Much attention was given to reports that stressed the Einsatzgruppen's participation in this warfare.[66] With regard to the Jews and communists, reports were cited that described so-called retaliatory measures against them. Many reports were used as evidence to prove that at a given moment a particular Einsatzgruppe had not issued any reports on their activities, or were engaged in "legitimate" activities such as securing intelligence information, and so on. To this end, one defense exhibit stressed that reports about Estonia were over-whelmingly concerned with various spheres of life, and that only a small percentage of these reports dealt with Security Police activities.[67] Extracts from reports indicating that in certain areas many Jews had fled before the arrival of the Einsatzgruppen (Operational Situation Reports 123, 133, 146) attempted to convey the impression that killings could not have been done if the Jews were not there to be killed.

Also, reports were quoted where particular Kommandos were not specified as taking part in the operations. These measures, the attempt to offset the impression that the Einsatzgruppen were solely concerned with extermination, the "legitimizing" of at least some portion of the killings as having been reprisals for "illegal" partisan or sabotage actions against the occupying forces, the "distancing" of specific Kommandos and individuals from actions undertaken—all were combined with other defense documents and arguments in the hope of minimizing the culpability of the defendants.

One may ask how accurate was the defense assessment of the reports and how effective was the argument in the total presentation of the case for the defense? There does not seem to be any doubt that the reports, especially the Operational Situation Reports, were characterized to some degree by the faults put forward by the defense. In the earlier discussion of the methods used to describe the killing operations, it was clear that an inconsistency in the way this was done existed. Several methods were used to present this information, each with varying degrees of exactness. This lack of uniformity and the rather offhand way the facts were reported no doubt was a direct result of the attendant conditions in the RSHA, as described by Fumy and others. The claim that the numbers were exaggerated would also seem to have some basis in fact. Sources other than those used at the trial suggest that numbers were altered to produce a more favorable picture.[68] Some historians have quite readily accepted that exaggerations took place in order to prevent an impressive picture of the Kommandos' activities.[69] (This boastful aspect of the reports, of which the exaggerations of figures was only a part, will be examined in more detail in the next chapter.)

The reports, then, were not the paradigm of exactness hoped for by Himmler and Heydrich. The question is, did the errors in the reports have any bearing on the final judgment of the Tribunal? The answer to this is, very little, if one reads the Opinion and Judgment of the court.[70] Of course one should remember that the flawed quality of the reports was a minor element in the defense case, and that other arguments played a significant part in the deliberations of the judges. The defense counsel had, in fact, soon recognized that the reports were basically irrefutable evidence, and as a consequence, other lines of defense were necessary.[71] In the end none of the defense reasoning managed to persuade the judges. The errors in the reports, the other arguments and evidence had little impact. In fact the Opinion and Judgment of the court virtually repeated the evidence of the prosecution.[72] The various arguments put forward by the defense were considered and dismissed in turn. The court constantly cited reports as proof of the guilt of the individual leaders. Significantly, the court underlined that Jews were killed not because they were communists, but because they were Jews.[73] In this regard the court stated, "The Tribunal now declares that the record is absolutely bare of credible evidence that those listed in the column headed Jews fell into any category other than those who were shot merely because they were Jews. The whole documentation in this case is directly to the contrary."[74] Futhermore, the court pointed out the obvious—that even if all the Jews in the east *had been* Bolsheviks, killing them for this reason "would still be murder."[75] The reports, which formed the central core of the prosecution case, were thus largely responsible for the conviction of all but two of the twenty-two remaining defendants of crimes against humanity and war crimes.[76]

The court considered that the reports, errors and all, were more than sufficient proof of guilt. It is not difficult to see why. Ultimately, the objections to the reports were not really that substantive. (Nor were the various other arguments put forward by the defense.) While errors of time, place, etc., did appear, they did not disprove the guilt of the defendants. Every Kommando had carried out mass murder. Every defendant was to some degree responsible for his participation in these murders. The reports, combined with other evidence, proved this. The defense lawyers were grasping at straws, putting forth the "desperate nonsense" as the defense case was characterized in the closing brief for the prosecution.[77]

If one considers more closely the evidence of exaggerated numbers, for example, one notices that the Opinion of the court made no mention of this. The statistics of the reports were accepted as such. The only reference to the numbers in the Opinion of the court involved reference to defense counsel Hans Gawlik's skepticism concerning the totals. The court stated that Gawlik

claims the numbers are incredible. To say that these figures are incredible is an entirely credible and sane observation. This whole case is incredible. This is the case where the incredible has become the norm.[78]

While it is likely that exaggerations did occur, there is no way to determine to what extent this was true. Ohlendorf, in particular, was quite unconvincing in his presentation in this regard. He declared numbers were inflated but offered no real proof to support this claim. He simply stated, as others did, that the figures were altered. Ohlendorf, the alleged expert concerning numbers, was not even willing or able to give an estimate of the numbers of persons killed by Einsatzgruppe D in spite of repeated questioning.[79] We are perhaps correct in questioning also the general use of the argument of incorrect numbers as a way of lessening guilt, especially after the fact and in face of written evidence. Nor is it impossible that even those who denied changing the numbers, did so themselves and lied about it. The scope of these distortions will probably never be known and will continue to frustrate attempts at determining an exact overall total of persons killed in the east. It is ironical that it is common sense, and our knowledge of SS motivation and the desire for self-promotion, and not so much the testimony of the defendants, that lead us to believe that numbers were probably distorted, but this does not fundamentally change the situation. Mass murders *did* take place and were carried out by the defendants.

The counsel for the twenty-two leaders were defending their clients individually. They were under no obligation to present a uniform strategy in their cases, but the different approaches of the defense lawyers undermined the case of other defendants to a considerable degree. For example, a few defendants claimed that they either did not know of an order to kill the Jews or that their Kommandos did not take part in any shootings. The contention that numbers were exaggerated is based on the premise that killings did take place. This contradicts the defense argument just described, as does the idea that defendants were acting under the compulsion of superior orders. If some admitted they were ordered and had no choice but to carry out the killing, then the other defendants must have been aware of this order, too, and could not plead ignorance. Many of the defendants stated that the executions were justified on the basis that only partisans were executed in reprisal for attacks. This assertion was contradicted by both the specifics and scope of the evidence, and the fact that the destruction of Jews and communists had been planned before the Germans had invaded Russia. Therefore, the executions could in no sense he called reprisals.[80]

In presenting their closing statements, some of the defense lawyers made questionable remarks that did nothing to assist their case. We might note the following two examples:

> However, as was the case in the campaign against Russia, when a large number of the inhabitants of this land, whether young, old, men, women or child, contrary to all acts of humanity and against every provision of international law cowardly carries on a war from ambush against the occupying army, then certainly one cannot expect that the provisions of international law would be observed to the letter by the army.[81]

In response to this the court had this to say:

> No comment is here needed on the statement which characterizes the defense of one's country as "cowardly," and the other equally astounding remark that the invader has the right to ignore international law.[82]

An even more outrageous statement was made by Dr. Aschenauer, counsel for Ohlendorf. He complained that the presentation of excerpts from the reports by the prosecution gave the impression that executions were the only activity carried out by the Einsatzgruppen. He contended that this narrow use of the reports did not

> show the actual picture of the over-all activity of the Sonderkommandos which, predominantly directed toward an enlightened pacification of the Russian areas, included constructive and progressive measures for the benefit of the population.[83]

It is perhaps better not to dignify such a statement with any further comment.

Finally, in our consideration of the use of the reports as evidence, we might note that if, as was maintained by the defense, the RSHA officials selected only some of the material from the incoming reports, then it follows that what was in the reports was only a part of the story. If this were the case, the guilt of the Einsatzgruppen personnel was greater, not less, than was indicated by the prosecution. Ultimately, it is probable that the reports err on the side of incompleteness, rather than being an exaggerated version of what happened.[84]

14

The Einsatzgruppen Reports as Historical Source

While not underestimating the evidentiary value of the reports as emphasized at the Nuremberg Einsatzgruppen trial, we do recognize that along with the vast quantity of documents used at this and other trials, the reports are first and foremost of historical significance.[1] We must be thankful for the fact that the trials were held, not only for the obvious search for justice that was addressed by these trials, but because of the great amount of information that was made available as a result. Critics of the Nuremberg trials have raised valid questions about their jurisprudential shortcomings. Whatever the verdict of history may be concerning the trials, it is certain that without the trials it is unlikely that these documents would have been uncovered and scrutinized so quickly and to the same extent, if at all. This has contributed immeasurably to our present considerable knowledge of the National Socialist regime and its history as well as to our understanding of the Holocaust. These documents have undergone much analysis—an analysis that has increased our awareness beyond the immediate context of the documents. In a discussion of the Nuremberg documents, Brigadier General Telford Taylor, chief of Counsel of War Crimes, has commented on this historical value of the documents and their use at the trials. Taylor stated that:

> the use of these documents at the trials as evidence against defendants, most of whom took the stand and testified, meant that these documents were subjected to both explanation and scrutiny by those who were blamed for the crimes disclosed by the documents. Therefore, many of these documents, now have a gloss on them in the form of supplementary testimony by the men who wrote them or the men who were mentioned in them, thus creating an immense overlay of additional information and comment that in many settings is of great historical importance.[2]

We recognize the twofold historical significance of the Einsatzgruppen reports. First, their importance lies in what they tell us directly about specific events that happened in the eastern territories; second, they are important for what they tell us indirectly about the Nazis themselves. The first aspect, insofar as it concerns the killing operations, has to a large degree been discussed in the earlier chapters. The validity of the information in the reports describing the details of the mass killings and some of the major questions relating to this subject were debated at the Einsatzgruppen trial. In spite of occasional inaccuracies and instances of incompleteness in the reports, there can be no doubt about their general reliability as a record of the extermination of the Jews and others in the east.[3] We have also looked at the reports with respect to the attitudes of the eastern population and the examples of collaboration of some with the Einsatzgruppen. The involvement of German army units in the killings was also discussed. In this chapter we will look at the historical context in which the reports were written. This entails an overview of the complex framework of German institutions and their interrelationships. We will then examine the manner in which this context influenced the reporting process. We will also view details in the reports in relation to the current so-called intentionalist/functionalist debate and the particularly problematic question concerning the extermination order given to the Einsatzgruppen. These inquiries will give us a greater awareness of the special character of the reports as historical documents and will enable us to assess more accurately their reliability. We may then, in the final chapter, allow ourselves some general reflections concerning the nature of this murderous enterprise and the people who were involved in it.

In order to accomplish these objectives, we may begin by taking a closer look at the major organizations of the National Socialist regime, in particular those that affected and were a part of the Einsatzgruppen. For some time after the war the popular perception of Hitler's Reich was that of a monolithic, unified, and powerful state, where the institutions of the state were directed towards centralized goals, accepted by all. This perception was understandable. It was even logical to assume that it was correct. The German leaders had put forward this image, and the prosecution at the Nuremberg trials had presented this as the major thrust of its argument. The world was faced with the enormous success and control that Hitler and the National Socialist Party had achieved within Germany, and the awesome military power that had forced most of Europe and a good part of the Soviet Union to its knees. Moreover, it was evident that before being defeated in 1945, Germans had been responsible for the extermination of, among others, one-third of the Jewish population of the world. Looking at the events from 1933 to 1945 in these terms, it was quite natural to conclude that such power and destruction could be achieved only by a society that had all of its institutions focused and functioning as one. With the passage of time historians have presented a different, more complex view of the Hitler era. While admitting the fact of a tremendous centralized totalitarian power, historians have regarded the agencies of the German state as something other than a uniform machine constantly carrying out Hitler's personal will. The reality of the Third Reich belied the concept of absolute efficient rule. As one historian has put it, this reality refutes "the popular belief that a totalitarian dictatorship which sweeps away all political and moral controls, and as a result is able to operate quickly and spectacularly, guarantees a larger measure of order and stability than complex democratic systems."[4] The day-to-day workings of the organs of German rule have shown that there was by no means a consensus among their members as to policy and procedure. The relationships between and within these institutions were characterized by self-interest and conflict.

This grasping for power in order to advance their own positions in determining policy was a characteristic feature of various sectors of the German administration. That this was so was the inevitable consequence of Hitler's policy of establishing a decentralized system of regional authority where subordinates were given considerable freedom within their domain. This parcelling out of power, essentially a strategy of divide and conquer, encouraged competition among the lower ranks, and consolidated Hitler's own power as "feudal-like" arbitrator in matters where conflicts arose.[5] In fact this diffusion of authority, ostensibly "to encourage independence and aggressive problem-solving,"[6] was made even more complicated in that it almost invariably led to jurisdictional disputes in many sectors. Given leeway in running their own affairs, and encouraged to show initiative in performing assigned tasks, the members of the hierarchy generally tried both to do their jobs to the satisfaction of their immediate superiors and to acquire as much power as possible in the process. The resultant bureaucratic and personal rivalries and intrigues were often bitter and profound. In the jostling for power "before Hitler's throne," everyone was at some time or another against someone else.[7] The Einsatzgruppen were but one player in this complex drama. It is in this setting of rivalry and cross purposes that their operations must be seen. Their reports were to a considerable degree a reflection of this complicated environment of power-seeking.

In Chapter 1 we outlined the growth of the SS, the SA, the police organizations, the SD, and the RSHA. We will now return to these organizations in order to examine briefly the friction that existed between them and other agencies. Many of the conflicts materialized early in the rise of National Socialism. The SA and SS were virtual rivals, and Himmler's gradual development of the SS elitist ideology allowed the SS to distinguish itself from the SA.[8] The SA's desire for military power in competition with the Wehrmacht led to the crisis of the Röhm purge. This put an end to SA aspirations for further control within the Reich. No sooner was the SA eliminated as a rival when, to the displeasure of the Wehrmacht, the SS began to build up its own small army, the SS-Verfügungstruppe. Although suspicious of these developments, army leaders were tolerant since the SS units were viewed as having a political, rather than a military, function. They were also considered to be of insufficient numbers to constitute a threat. As well, the training and equipping of the SS units was under the control of the military.[9] Despite army objections, by the time of the Hitler order of 17 August 1938, events had shifted in favor of the SS. By the end of 1983 the SS had twenty-three thousand armed men within these units.[10] During the Polish campaign SS troops were deployed. The mutual distrust between the army and the Waffen SS (as it was now called) manifested itself when both apparently filed reports on atrocities carried out by the other.[11]

Another area of tension between the Wehrmacht and the SS centered around the struggle between Heydrich and Wilhelm Canaris's Abwehr over control of counterespionage and foreign intelligence gathering. An agreement reached on 17 January 1935 had given the Abwehr the control over foreign military and political intelligence as well as counterespionage at home as it affected military concerns. To the Gestapo was given the responsibility for executive matters concerning espionage and general political intelligence within Germany. On 21 December 1936 a further agreement had been reached outlining the areas of competence. The Abwehr was to deal with military espionage abroad as well as counter-espionage at home. The Gestapo was responsible for investigation and follow-up actions in matters relating to treason and was obligated to consult with the Abwehr in matters that were of concern to the latter, but the SD complicated matters greatly by its continued invasion of Canaris's territory.[12] In reality these agreements meant very little. They typified agreements between Nazi agencies where neither side really intended to adhere to its part of the bargain. The agreement was drawn up merely to preserve the "façade of common purpose among government agencies."[13]

Serious conflicts arose between other departments as well. Goebbels's Ministry of Propaganda was constantly critical of intrusions into its domain by Alfred Rosenberg's Ministry of the Eastern Territories, the Wehrmacht, and the Foreign Office. Goebbels complained that it wasn't Rosenberg's business to engage in propaganda, and that there were too many theoreticians and too few practical men in Rosenberg's Ministry. Goebbels further stated that every section chief in Rosenberg's Ministry built up his department simply "according to his personal taste." Resented too was the Wehrmacht's overstepping into the propaganda field in the occupied territories. The Wehrmacht had no right to engage in tasks that were "not germane to it." Goebbels also blamed Joachim von Ribbentrop for the bad political situation in the east and his attempt to sabotage the transfer of control of propaganda to Goebbels. It was characteristic of National Socialist practice that Goebbels sought Hitler's arbitration in his favor concerning these matters.[14]

Relations with the Foreign Office, just noted, were symptomatic of wider conflicts concerning that office. The need to defend their ministries against party encroachments was apparently the reason for the gradual involvement in the process of extermination of the Jews by officials in the Ministry of the Interior and the Foreign office.[15] Also, Goebbels's Ministry was not the only department with which Rosenberg had strong differences of opinion. An intense rivalry existed between Ribbentrop and Rosenberg, the latter having aspired to becoming Reich Foreign Minister, only to lose out to Ribbentrop in 1938. When Rosenberg was appointed leader of the newly formed Ministry of the Eastern Territories, he thereby added, along with his position as head of the Foreign Affairs Office of the party, a department that represented a further intrusion into the concerns of the Foreign Office.[16] Within Ribbentrop's office struggles for control took place. In 1943 one of the leading officials, Undersecretary of State Martin Luther, attempted to oust Ribbentrop by circulating a confidential report on the latter's mental capacity. For his trouble, Luther wound up in Sachsenhausen concentration camp.[17]

The relations between the SD and the Foreign Office could also hardly be described as friendly. Here, too, there existed a constant battle concerning SD agents in foreign missions and the right of the SD to work independently of the Foreign Office.[18]

The SS as a whole was not without internal tensions. Although very often depicted as such, the SS was not really a monolithic institution, but a conglomeration of different offices and branches, each concerned with different tasks. Within the ranks of the SS were men intent on as much empire building and power securing for themselves as possible.[19] As we discovered in Chapter 1, a constant feature of the SS was the gradual consolidation and expansion of its police and political power both within and without Germany.[20] Along the way the changes in the structure of the various police agencies penetrated by the SS had left many problems. Let us examine some of these problems in relation to those organizations that concern us the most, the SD, the Security Police (Gestapo and Criminal Police), and the RSHA.

The SD, from its modest beginning under Heydrich in 1931, had experienced an unsteady history, at times marked by crises of uncertainty. In times of internal or external peace (for instance 1934—38), the SD was on shaky ground in justifying its place in the scheme of things, whereas in times of aggression, with new enemies to deal with, the SD became indispensable.[21] The SD was always surrounded by controversy and was constantly at odds with other information gathering agencies, in particular those of the party and the Gestapo. Right from the start the SD had concerned itself with the dual function of monitoring internal Nazi affairs, including the party itself, and opponents of the regime, communists, churches, Freemasons, Jews, etc. Heydrich originally hoped to establish his intelligence network as the sole Security Police force in the Reich.[22] In spite of Heydrich's diligence, his dream of having the SD form the basis of a new type of police force failed to materialize. The old-school police officials were wary of the young intellectual upstarts that were attracted to the SD. Within the party itself the SD enjoyed a sinister reputation. The early SD practice of reporting on party matters was a source of resentment, and the intellectuals in the SD were also viewed with suspicion by many party members.[23]

Perhaps the most pressing problem of the SD was its relationship with the Gestapo.[24] With the passage of time the reporting operations of both agencies had come into conflict with each other. The fields of activity of the two had never been satisfactorily spelled out.[25] On 1 July 1937 Heydrich issued a decree that proposed to do just that. It was hoped that this would enable each group to compliment the other's work and to avoid duplication of activities and reporting. Marxism, treason, and emigration came under Gestapo control, while science, Germanism and folklore, art, education, party and state constitution and administration, foreign countries, Freemasonry and miscellaneous societies were to be the responsibility of the SD. Yet problems persisted since areas of common responsibility remained, that is, churches and religious groups, pacifism, Jews, hostile groups, economics, the press, etc. To deal with this, it was stated that in these areas the SD was to concern itself with general and basic questions, and the Gestapo was to be involved whenever executive Secret Police measures were concerned.[26]

The SD continued to stress its importance in relation to the Gestapo.[27] Despite these arguments, the upshot of all these strictures was the final relegation of the SD to the ideological field only. The SD thus had no power to arrest people and was basically assigned to a second-rate position within the SS.[28] The so-called "spheres of life" field (Lebensgebiete), which became an important area for the SD, later brought the SD into further conflict with the party and Himmler as a result of the critical nature of the SD reports.

The merger of the SD with the Security Police in the RSHA took place in September 1939. Shortly after, on 13 October 1939, all remaining SD functions that earlier had been concerned with executive actions were transferred to the Gestapo, theoretically ending the process of defining the areas of competence between the two groups.[29] The creation of the RSHA did not bring about a total resolution of the problems however. Heinrich Müller, chief of Office IV, had a dislike for the SD. This dislike he had held for years. Like many old police professionals, Müller considered the SD was made up of amateurs. His hatred for wit and intelligence (as exemplified by SD members) did not disappear in September 1939.[30] This antipathy for the SD, as already noted, was shared by party members as well as other civilian and military officials, both in the Reich and in the eastern territories. The very act of surrounding its activities in a cloak of secrecy and its constant watch on party and government officials for signs of corruption, had left the SD with many opponents.[31] The SD's product was information and opinion, and the "arrogant intellectuals" who comprised this "organization of informers" and "know-it-alls," as the SD members were called, were both feared and at the same time the object of derision by others outside the organization.[32]

As had been the case earlier, after the war began the SD faced competition within its own sphere from other information services in the east. These included Bormann's own reporting service, the Abwehr network, as well as other military and political channels of reporting.[33] Adding further to the isolation of the SD officials in the east was the fact that they were simply outnumbered by the more "dynamic" executive members of the Einsatzgruppen—the Gestapo, the Criminal Police, the Waffen SS, the Order Police, and the auxiliary police. Einsatzgruppe A, as of 15 October 1941, had 35 SD personnel, which amounted to only 3.5 percent of its total membership.[34] Within the SS as a whole the importance of the SD and the Security Police had to be made clear. It was sometimes necessary for Himmler to explain this situation to other groups within the SS. For example, in a speech to officers of the SS-Leibstandarte on 7 September 1940, Himmler declared that

> You must look upon the business of the SD or Security Police as an equally vital part of our overall activity as you are marching along with your weapons. You are in fact in an enviable position when you do something, when a unit covers itself with glory, that can be talked about openly and the unit can be suitably rewarded. It is much more difficult in many other positions—and with that I do not want to underestimate your achievements; I would be the last one to do that—but, believe me, in many places it is much more difficult, this silent activity, this standing guard over our ideology, this necessity of remaining steadfast, this necessity of not compromising is very much more difficult in places.[35]

Not only the SD had problems with the Gestapo. The union of the Criminal Police and the Gestapo in 1936, which established the Security Police, was also fraught with power struggles. As with the rivalry with the SD, these struggles never vanished completely. Unlike the Gestapo, the Criminal Police had experienced comparatively less penetration by the SS before 1936.[36] Many older men in the Criminal Police still retained more traditional notions of law.[37] The creation of the Security Police really merged the two forces only on higher levels. The lower chains of command remained intact under the Police Presidents of the Order Police, who remained outside the Security Police structure.[38] In order to undermine the power of the Police Presidents and bring about coordination between the Criminal Police and the Gestapo and the lower administrative ranks, Heydrich set up the office of Security Police Inspectors.[39] This manoeuvering was not completely successful in bridging the gap between the two agencies,[40] and the tension continued with further overlapping of interests as well as complaints by the Criminal Police of Gestapo spying.[41]

The RSHA provided the setting for the extension of long-existing antagonisms. Although Heydrich's directive establishing the RSHA[42] had insisted that there be cooperation between the offices, especially in matters of mutual interest, the reality was that personal and functional differences still prevailed. The separation of intelligence and execution aggravated the power struggles by the RSHA Offices involved in each of these areas. Müller, in particular, attempted to extend his personal influence beyond his own department. Heinz Jost, who in 1941 became the leader of Office VI (Foreign Intelligence),[43] resented Müller's intrusion. Jost felt that his office should be independent of other RSHA Offices, serving all the agencies of the Reich and all leadership offices. He felt that his department should not be dependent upon any one institution, especially the Gestapo.[44] Other evidence indicates also that Müller accused Office VI of defeatist tendencies and tried to use Office VI and other RSHA departments for his own purposes.[45] Furthermore, late in 1941 and early 1942, Müller extended his powers to nonoccupied countries without help from Office VI. He made contacts with police officials and agents abroad and exchanged information and sent orders without consulting correct channels.[46] The extent of the mistrust between Office IV and other departments is also illustrated by the fact that many reports were not even forwarded by Office III to Office IV. Office III officials apparently did not want to give Müller insight into some of their affairs.[47]

The complex rivalry that pervaded the leading institutions within Germany was, not surprisingly, also a dominant feature of the German presence in the Soviet territories. The situation in the east reflected the carry over of power struggles and bickering that already prevailed. These struggles were now to be intensified in the new setting of the conquered eastern regions. It is probably correct to say that nowhere else within the sphere of German influence did the overlapping of lines of authority exist to the same extent as in the east. Within this setting Alexander Dallin has distinguished eight major power structures,[48] most of which were in constant conflict with each other. Dallin describes these conflicts as being personal (animosity between individuals), power and prestige struggles (between individuals and institutions), functional (conflicts over jurisdiction), and political (decisions concerning the future of the east).[49]

The German army was the first to arrive on the scene and was thus the first to deal with administrative problems in the east. Following the takeover of an area the army assumed control, but according to Hitler's orders, this control was to be temporary. The civil adminstration that succeeded military control in approximately one-half the areas captured by the Germans was, at best, ineffectual. Led by the weak ideologist Rosenberg, the civil administration was engaged in a never-ending battle with a host of agencies within the Reich that were critical of its policies, with Göring's apparatus for economic authority, with Himmler's police for matters of security, and even with its own personnel in matters of policy and jurisdiction. Rosenberg's more "liberal" policies toward the population were in direct opposition to those of his subordinates Hinrich Lohse and Erich Koch,[50] of Heydrich and Himmler, and more importantly, of Hitler himself. In the end, as we shall see, the attempts to address the political and economic needs of the people were either mere deception without real substance, or when genuine, were simply applied too late.[51]

The Third Reich, then, was a backdrop of intrigue and personal and bureaucratic squabbling. We have sketched here only a few examples of this situation. Many more could be cited in other agencies and at all levels of the system. Heads of departments within the Nazi hierarchy were encouraged to seek all the power they could as long as their policies were in keeping with Hitler's wishes. They were therefore able to acquire much control over decision-making within their own preserve. Their ability to sustain power depended mainly on the strength of their own personality in dealing with other organizations and individuals.[52] In this way, the more forceful personalities and policies prevailed, especially if these policies were seen as being consonant with the political goals of the leadership. It must be realized, however, that the fractious rivalries that we have been describing did not prevent things from being done. Despite disagreements, leaders of the Reich still shared common beliefs and goals. They managed to work together.[53] In fact the reality of Hitler's regime was that it accomplished what it did *with such continuous competition as the norm.* The struggles for personal power carried out by men of similar overall views actually reinforced the system and pushed it forward.[54] As a result no single element in the mix was in itself able to obtain absolute and final control. The operations of the Einsatzgruppen were a part of this machinery and were greatly influenced by the situation just outlined. In any discussion of the Einsatzgruppen reports, this must be taken into consideration. Let us now investigate how this rivalry and antagonism affected the Einsatzgruppen and found expression in their reports.

As far as the Einsatzgruppen were concerned, the controversy centered mainly around the Security Police. One of the most salient aspects of the reports was the degree to which they continuously presented the activities of the Security Police in the best possible light. As we have seen, Müller had personal control over the structure and tone of the reports. He was able to decide what was appropriate for inclusion and which reports were to be emphasized or omitted.[55] It was, of course, the Security Police who were the "dynamic" element in the picture. They were the ones who were carrying out Hitler's extermination order. They were doing the dirty work.

It was natural during the course of the reporting of their operations that, given Müller's editorial clout, and given the antagonisms present vis-à-vis other participants in the east, the activities of the Security Police be treated in the most favorable way. Every attempt was made to remove anything that would appear to be critical of the Security Police. Mentioned earlier was the fact that Müller cautioned his editors to be "more diplomatic" and to realize that they could not always write exactly what they thought.[56] Also, whether incoming reports listed casualties suffered by the Kommandos on those occasions when they came under fire cannot be determined. It is certain that relatively few were included in the Operational Situation Reports.[57] It is possible that Müller believed that this might have detracted from the efficient, smooth-running image that the Security Police hoped to convey.

This "boasting" quality found throughout the reports left the impression that it was the members of the Security Police who were getting the all-important job of killing the Jews and others done properly. We frequently read, almost as a matter of course, statements such as "The execution of assignments during the time under report was carried on with unabated severity,"[58] or this boast by Einsatzgruppe B in a report dated 13 July 1941:

> The activities of all Kommandos developed in a satisfactory manner. Above all, liquidations were brought into smooth running order and are being carried out daily at an increasing rate. Anyway, the carrying out of the necessary liquidations is guaranteed under any circumstances.[59]

In one report Sonderkommando 4a declared that it had killed fifty-one thousand people. The report noted with self-satisfaction that except for the shootings carried out on 29 and 30 September 1941 in Kiev, these operations were performed without "outside help."[60] Another report bragged about the "clever organization" of the stages prior to the actual killing that prevented the Jews from realizing their fate until the last moment.[61] The leader of Sonderkommando 4b, Günther Herrmann, went into great detail in describing the "new methods" he had devised for capturing Jews. These involved announcing that local Jewish intellectuals were required to assemble for "registration work." When insufficient numbers of Jews showed up, they were sent home and ordered to bring more Jews the next day. This ploy was repeated until the entire Jewish intelligentsia was captured and then shot. Another method involved simply postponing any actions until the Jews who were in hiding returned unsuspectingly to their homes and then were captured.[62]

Even the descriptions of the difficulties confronting the Einsatzgruppen, the problems of bad weather, poor roads, great distances, and so on, may be seen as further examples of boasting on their part. The implication was that in spite of these problems the Kommandos were still performing their allotted tasks.[63] The "heavy mental burden" shouldered by Einsatz-kommando 5 for the killing of three hundred mental patients in Kiev, may also be viewed in this light.[64]

Jäger's report gives us a classic example of self-serving aggrandizement by detailing how the problems surrounding the killing actions could be overcome by careful organization. Jäger described the operations as follows:

> The implementation of such actions is in the first instance an organizational problem. The decision to free each district of Jews necessitated thorough preparation of each action as well as acquisition of information about local conditions. The Jews had to be collected in one or more towns and a ditch had to be dug at the right site for the right number. The marching distance from collecting points to the ditches averaged about three miles. The Jews were brought in groups of 500, separated by at least 1–2 miles, to the place of execution. The sort of difficulties and nerve-scraping work involved in all of this is shown by an arbitrarily chosen example:
>
> In Roskiskis 3208 people had to be transported 3 miles before they could be liquidated. To manage this job in a 24 hour period, more than 60 of the 80 available Lithuanian partisans had to be detailed to the cordon. The Lithuanians who were left were frequently being relieved while doing the work together with my men.
>
> Vehicles are seldom available. Escapes, which were attempted here and there, were frustrated solely by my men at the risk of their lives. For example, 3 men of the Kommando at Mariampole shot 38 escaping Jews and communist functionaries on a path in the woods, so that no one got away. Distances to and from actions were never less than 90–120 miles. Only careful planning enabled the Kommando to carry out up to 5 actions a week and at the same time to continue the work in Kovno without interruption.[65]

The "risk to the lives" of his men mentioned by Jäger raises the question of Jewish resistance to the onslaught of the Kommandos. It is imperative to remember that from the beginning the so-called "Jewish danger" formed the basis of Nazi rationalizations for destroying the Jews. Earlier we described how such descriptions of the Jewish danger were part of the Nazi language of self-justification. This practice had no basis in objective reality. In the Nazi mind Jews were a "danger" for a host of reasons: they were leaders of Bolshevism, they had planned to destroy Germany, they were the bearers of disease, and more fundamentally, they were simply Jews—

racially inferior beings. If, in addition to justification of this sort, Jews actually engaged in overt resistance, then such activity was but one more excuse, and a "legal" one at that, for destroying them. Because of the constant use of this fraudulent argument of "danger" it is impossible on the basis of the reports to state with certainty to what extent real overt physical resistance on the part of the Jews manifested itself. Understandably, in these reports, which attempted to emphasize the efficiency of the Kommandos, mention of genuine, successful resistance, which would detract from this positive picture, was rare.[66] It is noteworthy that Jäger mentioned that escapes occurred "here and there," and in the Mariampole incident he declared that it required only three of his men to kill all thirty-eight escapees. No further details were given. There is not the slightest suggestion that the escapes were due to incompetence on his part. Jäger's report also mentioned the Jewish rebellion during the action in Zagare on 2 October 1941. Jäger simply stated the rebellion was crushed, 150 Jews were killed on the spot, and that seven Lithuanian auxiliary police were wounded.[67] Jewish resistance, when it appears in the reports, therefore, is presented as a criminal act that is immediately put down by the Security Police. Naturally, there is no indication of the heroic nature that often characterized the resistance by the Jews. Given their perspective, the reports offer only a distorted picture, and they cannot be regarded as a trustworthy source concerning this subject. From other sources[68] we know that resistance did occur, and that Jews were able to escape execution, if at times only temporarily, by evasive action. Resistance was certainly far more pervasive than the reports indicated directly. It is probable that one has to read between the lines in the reports to see such phrases as "unrest among the Jews," etc., as possible signs of the disguising of physical resistance.

Among the units taking an active role in the killings, the Security Police was seen as the dominant one. We know, however, that it was often Müller's practice to omit reference to other groups such as the local auxiliary police. While they were included in the reports, the full extent of their participation was by no means made clear.[69] Even the role of the Higher SS and Police Leaders was underrepresented. Reports from other authorities were also part of the final reports, but this information from these outside sources was often not acknowledged.[70] One is left with the conclusion that the Security Police were solely responsible for the events described. Such omissions even applied to the SD itself. For example, the reports worked on by Knobloch, an inspector of the Criminal Police, were noteworthy for leaving the SD unmentioned.[71]

The Wehrmacht and the civil administration were the two major German organizations that the Security Police and the SD had to deal with in the east. We have alluded to the competition that existed between these organizations. Throughout the SD reports we encounter further evidence of this rivalry. From time to time the reports showed that the Einsatzgruppen were not above finding fault with the policies of the civil administration and the Wehrmacht, and in the case of the latter, of also pointing out the indispensable role the Security Police and the SD played in their operations. We saw earlier the problem over Jewish labor with the Wehrmacht and civil authorities.[72] Although Müller frequently removed criticism of other groups, differing opinions and criticisms did turn up to a surprising degree in the final SD reports. The SD reporters were used to viewing themselves as the barometer of political opinion and as the dispensers of general advice; they constantly put forward divergent views concerning events and policy.

Judging by the strong criticism in the Stahlecker and Jäger reports (which had not gone through the RSHA editorial process), it is likely that a good deal of the critical comments of the SD writers were censored from the final product. To deal with the remarks pertaining to the civil administration first, we may note the combination of boastfulness and criticism in the following passage from Stahlecker's report:

> In view of the constant changes in German troops and the fluctuation within the German authorities, which was caused by the transfer of the rear-area of the Wehrmacht to the rear-area of the Armies, and later to the civil administration and to the Commander of the Armed Forces, the personnel and thus the opinions of the German authorities changed far too often and far too quickly. In the Security Police this had to be avoided, which led us to adopt the policy of keeping the same commanders in the same locality as far as possible. Thereby the Security Police gained a considerable advantage over all comers, because it knew facts and people. As a matter of fact, they alone amongst all authorities may claim to have achieved a certain steadiness on the German side. The Lithuanians, Latvians, and the Estonians, who have a fine feeling for such matters, came soon to acknowledge this fact and acted accordingly. Under these circumstances the Security Police tried to guide political, economic, and cultural matters according to definite policies, and to advise the other German authorities on these subjects. In the political sphere particularly the several competent authorities followed different viewpoints. It was regrettable that the Ministry for Eastern Affairs had not given clear directions from the beginning, so that to date and in spite of our efforts the situation in the Baltic provinces is not clear.[73]

The passage is significant not only as a typical example of condescension and self-praise by the Security Police, but also for the fact that it indicates the Security Police felt free to influence political, economic, and cultural policies, areas certainly outside its prescribed security tasks.

Both Stahlecker's and Jäger's reports deplored the objections of the civil administration officials to the shooting of the Jews. While Stahlecker had accepted the necessity of letting some Jews live in order to exploit their labor, Jäger wanted to kill all the Jews. He complained strongly that the civil administration and the armed forces had "declared war" on him and had prohibited the liquidation of the working Jews and their families. One

190   **Messages of Murder**

can feel his irritation as he grudgingly states that the working Jews are urgently needed and that he imagines "that they will still be needed after the winter." He then quickly added that in his view the male Jews left alive should at least be sterilized immediately in order to prevent procreation, and that any Jewish women who became pregnant were to be liquidated.[74]

Jäger was not finished with his complaints. In his report he had further things to say, this time about the Lithuanian authorities. The Lithuanian partisans had arrested hundreds of non-Jews in each town on the flimsiest of charges. As a result, the prisons were filled, and no one had bothered to deal with them. Jäger declared the need for using "drastic measures to drum" sense into the Lithuanians. The members of Jäger's Einsatz-kommando 3 took the matter in hand, sorting out the various degrees of offenses committed, and separating the prisoners accordingly. Those who were set free were told the following: "Had we been Bolshevists we would have shot you dead, but as we are Germans we set you at liberty."

With this description of the reaction of the population to the release of these people, Jäger ended his report:

> It is well-nigh impossible to imagine the joy, gratitude and enthusiasm which this measure of ours caused each time among prisoners set free and the population at large. One had to use sharp words more often than not to drive off the grateful women, children and men who with tears in their eyes tried to kiss our hands and feet.[75]

Patronizing remarks coupled with self-congratulatory comments were also found in the reports concerning the Wehrmacht. Stahlecker was eager to show the usefulness of his men to the army. He pointed out that because of inadequate resources the army was usually unable to capture communist officials and documents. It was left to the Security Police to carry out this important job by organizing local volunteer units to assist. Stahlecker noted, with pride, that in those places where the volunteers were established the number of casualties suffered by the German soldiers was greatly reduced. The growing danger of the partisan operations necessitated that the Einsatzgruppen be called upon to help the army in this struggle. After all, Stahlecker commented, the fight against the partisans "was and still is a job for the Security Police." He then went on to claim that after "the failure of purely military activities" to fight the partisans (use of sentries and combing of areas with whole divisions), it was then that the Wehrmacht "adopted the experiences of the Security Police and their methods of combatting the partisans."[76]

Again these examples indicate the attempt to paint a positive picture, well-disposed to the Security Police. The criticism of the Wehrmacht, as seen in Stahlecker's report, could on occasion in other reports become quite vituperative. The "planless excesses" carried out by the Wehrmacht in Uman, which were "cleaned up" only after the arrival on the scene of Einsatzkommando 5,[77] were probably not unique. This manner of criticism was likely the object of the editors' censure more often than not. Yet as we remarked earlier, the finding of fault with allies and auxiliary forces was not uncommon.[78] There were further examples of mild criticism of the Wehrmacht, the involvement of Germans in the local black market, the carelessness of German soldiers in discussing shootings, and occasional subtle hints about the slow progress of the military campaign.[79]

More obviously, we also discovered in the examination of the army's collaboration with the Einsatzgruppen, that in spite of its criticism of the army the Security Police showed no reluctance to reap the praises of the army officials. Whether it was praise for their role in organizing the harvest of crops,[80] for providing valuable information of military use to the army,[81] for screening and shooting of undesirables in areas close to army headquarters,[82] or the Kommandos' help in the fight against the partisans,[83] the Kommandos were quite happy to include such approbation in their reports. Regarding the antipartisan struggle, we find a particularly glaring example of self-flattery in this excerpt from Operational Situation Report 92:

> Thus, the Einsatzgruppe and Kommandos by their constant intervention and preparedness have not only seized important material concerning the organization and tactics of the partisans, which will be of importance also to the Wehrmacht in their future fights against the partisans, but they have moreover gained an idea of the present import of the partisan combat and its effect.[84]

The fault-finding and self-praise present in the Operational Situation Reports carried over into the Reports from the Occupied Eastern Territories. In a report dated 26 June 1942, it was stated that

> Circles of the Wehrmacht and of the civil administration had generally supposed in the late fall of 1941 that the decrease in the aggressive activity of the partisans signified the ideological and material collapse of the partisan movement.

This report contrasted this mistaken assumption with the "correct" assessment of the situation by the Security Police and the SD. The latter maintained that the lull in the partisan operations was only the result of concentration and preparation for much larger operations.[85] Recent events had proven the Security Police and SD to have been correct.[86] One can well imagine that such an attitude on the part of the Security Police and SD was not appreciated by the Wehrmacht and civil authorities. Yet this type of criticism was perhaps tolerated in that the phrase "circles of the

Wehrmacht and civil administration'' was not too specific in pinpointing the source of this miscalculation. Wehrmacht and civil authorities reading this report could persuade themselves someone else within the system was to blame for such an error of judgment.

Even other Einsatzgruppen were criticized although this was done very seldom and in a subtle manner. For example, in Operational Situation Report 94, in a report on the Jewish Problem in the Ostland, Einsatzgruppe A presented a little jab at Einsatzgruppe B by pointing out the speed with which the ghettos were established within its territory. Only in Vilna, which had earlier been within Einsatzgruppe B's domain and which was later taken over by Einsatzgruppe A, was there a delay in the confinement of the Jews. The report then stated that Einsatzkommando 3 was taking firm action by suggesting to the civil administration that a ghetto be set up and by initiating "the necessary pacification actions against the political activity of the Jews."[87] According to the winter summary report of Einsatzgruppe A, forty-one thousand Jews had been killed in White Russia, not including those shot by Einsatzgruppe B.[88] No doubt there was competition between the Einsatzgruppen as each sought to outdo the other. We may recall as well Ohlendorf's criticism of other Einsatzgruppen leaders concerning the numbers of victims reported by their Einsatzgruppen and the methods used by others to kill the victims.[89]

The criticisms outlined above illustrate the fact that within the framework of their reports it was possible for the reporters to find fault with other German agencies in the eastern areas, and that criticism of these agencies, coupled with self-praise, could be made to serve the better interests of the Security Police and SD.

It is evident, therefore, that the SD officials were quite content to present things as they saw them. This was nothing new. As was observed earlier, before the war the SD had been the most reliable of the several information agencies and in general had issued reports that were objective and relatively unvarnished. Indeed, Ohlendorf's ideal of unhampered, insightful criticism of the regime and the presentation of impartial, trustworthy information would seem to speak strongly in favor of the dependability of the SD reports as an historical source. Ohlendorf had left his mark on the SD and, undoubtedly this impact continued to be felt in the east. Yet even these earlier SD reports were not without certain biases of their own. While factually impeccable, the Reports from the Reich (Meldungen aus dem Reich) for instance, had offered a means of putting forward Ohlendorf's views on a number of subjects.[90] Economic matters were always of primary concern to Ohlendorf, and in the pre-1939 SD reports as well as in the Reports from the Reich, this predilection was seen in the relatively constant and extensive place economic matters had in the reports.[91] Nor was it only a matter of frequency and quantity. The very notion of trying to change policy in various areas on the basis of intelligence furnished by the SD suggests some degree of manipulation in order to achieve these ends. Ohlendorf's own economic theories had found expression in the criticism leveled at big business.[92] Also the SD criticized the unmanageable government bureaucracy by including in the Reports from the Reich examples of the mountains of unnecessary paperwork often required to get even the simplest things done.[93]

In the same way other SD policies in a number of areas, such as law reform and propaganda, were advocated by including in the reports "objective" evidence to support these policies. The Reports from the Reich therefore, did put forward distortions and biases in favor of SD attitudes towards certain subjects, and concerning these specific subjects at any rate, they cannot be viewed as absolutely reliable source material for the study of public opinion in Germany.[94]

In addition, certain limitations were inherent in the methods used to prepare the Reports from the Reich. The anonymity of the reporting system, the random sampling of opinion, which had to be done discreetly, the use of unpaid amateurs at the grass roots level, the absence of quantitative analysis to evaluate the material, the lack of precision in distinguishing between various class, group, regional, and confessional categories in the reporting of the opinions—these factors also affected the dependability of the SD reports as a true measure of German public opinion.[95] The editorial process involved in preparing the Einsatzgruppen reports was already entrenched in the previous SD reports. The SD reports, while the most dependable of the categories of reports, had thus developed the practice of putting forth SD views as part of its methodology of reporting. This has to be kept in mind in any consideration of the SD reports found in the Einsatzgruppen reports. It can be assumed that in the east the SD reporters continued to perform their functions in much the same way as they had in the Reich. We cannot determine exactly just how much the very different circumstances in the east affected their work. In the chapter on the general attitude of the eastern population, we recognized the necessity for caution in accepting at face value some of the statements in the reports. These qualifications must be remembered in evaluating the reports, although it is impossible to quantify in any precise way the effect these biases held by the SD may have had on the reports. They must simply be recognized as being there.

We may now turn our attention to a subject already alluded to earlier in this chapter. This subject is the debate surrounding two differing interpretations of the nature of National Socialist rule and their effect on the process whereby the Jews were persecuted and finally exterminated. These two interpretative matrices are known as intentionalism and functionalism.[96] The intentionalist position sees the National Socialist regime as one where policies were carried out on the basis of clear and consistent direction from Hitler himself. From the intentionalist perspective the extermination of the Jews was a carefully planned, centralized program, stemming from Hitler's own anti-Semitism, which, in turn, formed a major part of the ideological foundation of National Socialism. In its extreme form, intentionalism accepts an intended and continuous link between Hitler's early anti-Semitism and the measures enacted against the Jews. This process culminated in a direct order from Hitler to physically destroy the Jews. The functionalist position regards National Socialism as a decentralized disorganized system, where policies were not necessarily formed on the basis of ideology, but were more often the result of improvisation and immediate pragmatic considerations. Functionalists see the extermination of the Jews as a process that evolved piece by piece by a series of decentralized decisions that were not the consequences of an overall uniform plan. In its extreme form, functionalism posits that no specific order was ever given by Hitler to kill all the Jews, but that the killings began as a series of locally initiated operations, and only gradually grew into a comprehensive program.

It is undoubtedly already apparent to the reader that the previous discussion of the German institutions suggests an essentially functionalist interpretation. In pointing out the competitive, almost anarchical and decentralized quality of the National Socialist system, with its rivalries, its ubiquitous personality politics, and the ever-present pursuit of power among its agencies, we have underscored a reality concerning Hitler's rule that functionalist historians have been describing for some time. Perhaps the greatest merit of the functionalist approach has been the extent to which it has delineated the chaotic character of the Third Reich and the often great complexity of factors involved in the decision-making process.[97] Yet, while functionalist thinking has stressed the polycratic quality of the Nazi state, it has not denied some of the tenets of the intentionalist view, for example, the importance of Hitler himself and his profound hatred of the Jews. Instead, functionalists interpret the latter as simply a "mobilizing and integrating agent," giving unity of purpose and direction to the Reich,[98] but not becoming "a direct source of action."[99] Intentionalists, in turn, do not deny the uncoordinated quality of the Nazi system, but point to this as being the deliberate and clever by-product of Hitler's own design, the better to achieve his long-term goals.[100] The undeniably chaotic characteristic of much of Nazi rule, we would suggest, does not rule out the possibility of an overall plan to kill the Jews.

An important aspect to this debate surrounds the question as to precisely when (before or after 22 June 1941?) the Einsatzgruppen leaders were given the order to kill the Jews in the Soviet territories.[101] It is this specific question, as well as the larger controversial debate described above, that we will now examine.

Before focusing on what insights the reports may offer concerning these matters, several observations are in order. It must be recognized that if the Germans had not yet decided by June 1941 to kill the Jews in the Soviet Union, as many claim, it was not because such an idea was a new one. As Christopher Browning has pointed out, by 1941 mass killing was already a fairly widespread state policy. The killing of opponents of the regime, communists, asocials, the murder of the SA leadership in 1934, the random killings of Jews in Poland as well as the methodical elimination of Polish intellectuals after the war started, and above all, the euthanasia program within Germany in which more than seventy thousand Germans considered "unworthy of life" were gassed—these events Browning rightly mentions as precedents for the concept of mass murder.[102] By May 1941, furthermore, a climate for wholesale death by starvation of millions of people in the soon to be conquered east was accepted by German bureaucrats. This was seen as the result of the anticipated plundering of food supplies for German use.[103] Hitler's statement in March 1941 that the upcoming war against the Soviets was to be a ruthless ideological war of extermination adds to this climate of calculated destruction. Some measure of the degree of brutality that characterized the Russian campaign from the beginning may be seen in an order issued on 25 June 1941 by General Lemelsen, the commander of the 48th German Panzer Corps. This order condemned the "senseless" shootings of both prisoners of war and civilians by German soldiers, and stated that a captured Russian soldier was entitled. to decent treatment. The order emphasized that this decent treatment did not apply to partisans and Bolshevik commissars.[104] That such an order was issued to soldiers only three days after the war started (and had to be repeated five days later) suggests that a very different attitude existed in the eastern theater of the war than existed in that of western Europe.

It is not unreasonable to conclude, therefore, that given the earlier examples of mass killing just mentioned, and the intended horrific nature of the war about to be launched, that the German leadership was predisposed for the destruction that was to ensue. Hitler now took the next step and made it known that the Soviet Jews were to be killed. The war offered the opportunity for carrying out this plan, which coupled squarely with Hitler's dreams of Lebensraum in the east that was free of Jews. Genocide could now be translated into a necessity of war.

What do the reports themselves indicate concerning German intentions? Like most documentary evidence that has survived, the Einsatzgruppen reports deal primarily with the *implementation* of the mass killings. In them one finds little indication of the larger *decision-making process* that led to the overall program. We are confronted with the results of a decision, not the decision itself. These results, however, point strongly to a program of murder. They suggest that if the four Einsatzgruppen did not have an overall plan, then they certainly acted as if they did.

On an immediate level the sheer bulk of the record left by the Kommando reports cannot but leave the impression of calculated genocide. The reports show that the Jews were constantly marked as a separate category, that they were the immediate victims of the Kommandos, and that they formed the overwhelming majority of those killed. The author has argued elsewhere that the instigation of pogroms by the local population and the setting up of ghettos must be seen as a temporary preliminary stage in the destruction process—they were not a substitute for the latter as some historians claim.[105] In Operational Situation Report 107, one finds this idea articulated. The report stated that the formation of ghettos and the exploitation of Jewish labor was "the first part of the Jewish question solved."[106] We also discovered the desperate need for Jewish labor. This was in contradiction to the policy to rid the east of all Jews and played a significant part in eventually enabling many Jews to survive.

Fundamental to the intentionalist position that holds that an order was given before June 22 are observations in the Stahlecker and Jäger reports as well as in several other reports. Stahlecker's October 15 report declared unequivocally that right from the beginning "according to basic orders the goal of the most complete removal possible of the Jews" was being undertaken "with all means and determination." Pursuant to this goal Stahlecker reported that his men had carried out extensive mass executions.[107] Evident here is a program of murder, previously decided upon and implemented to the greatest extent possible. Stahlecker mentioned two "restraining" factors affecting the operations: the requirements of Jewish labor and the necessity for secrecy. Stahlecker stated that "an annihilation of the Jews without leaving any traces could not be carried out, at least at the present moment."[108] Mass shootings had to be done as unobtrusively as possible, and because of the public nature of these executions, absolute secrecy was often not achieved although it was desired. Therefore, an immediate destruction of the entire Jewish population could not take place without causing attention.

Earlier Jäger's report, a mind-numbing inventory of murder, was analyzed. It is not simply the number of victims of the massacres cited in this report that points to an organized program of killing. The manner of presentation of the shootings also suggests such a program. In presenting the statistics, Jäger made no real qualitative distinction between the initial and later operations. Like Stahlecker's report, Jäger's report indicates that all the executions were perceived as part of one continuous process, a process in place from the beginning and undertaken to the greatest possible extent allowed by the circumstances in the east.[109]

Scattered throughout the early reports are many other details that allude to an intended plan of annihilation. Let us note several of those. Members of the Jewish intelligentsia were often included among the first victims. The removal of the intellectual elite of the Jewish community was a logical first step. By destroying the intellectual leaders first, the Einsatzgruppen hoped to make their task of total destruction easier. In Activity and Situation Report 1, for the period up to 31 July 1941, it was stated that "up to now actions have been directed at the Jewish leadership circles" without disturbing the economic situation in the interest of warfare.[110] One report remarked that it was simply the great number of Red army ambushes in the Kovno area that prevented "more severe measures" from being carried out.[111] Einsatzgruppe B reported that the liquidations were being brought into smooth running order and that the shootings were "carried out daily at an increasing rate." This report declared that five hundred Jews were being shot daily in Vilna by Einsatzkommando 9, and Nebe himself even complained that "only" ninety-six Jews had been shot in Grodno and Lida. The report also announced that in Minsk Einsatzgruppe B was now killing non-Jews. This suggests that the early priority of shooting Jews was already "routine," and that killing others was something "new."[112] Einsatzgruppe B further reported that an attack on the Security Police headquarters in Vilna forced a special action "above the normal daily liquidation quotas."[113] In the course of a report issued soon after the previous reference, Einsatzgruppe B declared that "large-scale executions would follow immediately."[114] Early on, Einsatzgruppe D voiced dissatisfaction about the slow pace and the manner in which the Rumanians were dealing with the Jews.[115] In Ohlendorf's mind no doubt, had matters been left exclusively up to his men, the operations would have been done correctly. In Operational Situation Report 45, Einsatzgruppe D indicated the efficient ruthlessness of its own methods by reporting that it had taken hostages upon arrival in each new area, and that these hostages were shot on the "slightest pretext."[116] That the Kommando leaders in a number of reports attributed an extermination plan to the Soviets themselves is further indication that this idea was not a novel one for them.[117]

In addition to the above references, one may take note of the scale of the operations. The mass shootings became routine very rapidly. Even in the first few weeks one encounters references to operations where large numbers of Jews were shot. Among many possible examples we mention the following: the 600 Jews shot by the Waffen SS in Zborow;[118] the 2,300 Jews killed in Riga by Einsatzkommando 2 with Latvian police help, and the 1,600 more Jews killed outside that city;[119] the 682 Jews shot by the

Rumanians and Sonderkommando 10b in Czernowitz;[120] the more than 7,000 Jews killed in pogroms and Einsatzgruppe C actions in Lvov in early July;[121] the 3,947 people killed between July 21 and 31 by Krakow based Security Police units;[122] the 11,084 people reported killed by Einsatzgruppe B alone, as of July 31;[123] and finally the total of *at least* 62,805 persons killed by all four Einsatzgruppen in the first five weeks of their operations.[124]

The details cited above lend credence to the argument that from the first days of the Soviet campaign the Einsatzgruppen were embarked on mass murder. However formless this undertaking may seem to some today (especially its early stages), it was nonetheless not simply a series of random retaliatory actions related to "policework."[125] Implied here was the presence of an order of some sort—intentionalist thinking demands the probability of such an order, yet the precise nature of this order to the Einsatzgruppen leaders is still undetermined. Therefore this aspect of the intentionalist approach still remains problematical. The reports, for the most part, suggest the likelihood that some direction was given to the Einsatzgruppen leaders, and indicate that, at the very least, the killing of the Soviet Jews was a recognized goal on 22 June 1941.[126] The predisposition for genocide, the unambiguous statements by Stahlecker about destroying the Jews, the scope of the killings, the careful recording of the numbers, and the many instances of towns and areas declared free of Jews, all point to a central purpose of extermination as having been conceived (as of 22 June 1941 at least) and then uniformly put into action. This places the Einsatzgruppen operations squarely within the intentionalist school of thought.

Yet if total extermination was the ultimate plan, the actual day-to-day working out of this plan depended upon circumstances beyond the simple will to do so. Certain unanticipated factors came to bear on policies practiced by the Germans in the east. It had been thought that the war against the Soviets would be won quickly, but this did not prove to be the case. As a result of the prolonged war, the Germans were faced with having to deal with the local populations in ways they had not foreseen. They had to deal with the problems of governing them, dealing with their national aspirations, with the problems of food supply, and so on—all the while still fighting the bitterest war in history. Above all it was recognized that not all the Jews could be killed as some were needed as labor for the war effort. These circumstances, combined with the lack of an overall coordinated positive political policy in the east,[127] plus the pervasive interdepartmental animosities mentioned earlier, led to a modification of the original notion of total extermination. These shiftings of policy depending on the local situation are seen by the advocates of the functionalist school as evidence supporting their position. As Hans-Heinrich Wilhelm has noted, it was possible that Hitler's orders were not always followed with the greatest enthusiasm, or they could be altered when necessary, and that even Hitler himself continued to speculate about differing courses of actions against the Jews.[128] Wilhelm points out that it was possible, in light of Hitler's at times ambiguous musings concerning the Jews, and the various alternative schemes that had received his endorsement at one time or another, for the SD reporters and other officials to put forward contradictory ideas.[129] Such a practice was entirely in keeping with the multilevelled nature of administrative procedures within the Third Reich.

What is the evidence of these differing views in the reports? In contrast to the Himmler—Heydrich position of complete extermination, in the reports of the very men who were carrying out this policy, we find at times a different position. It was mentioned earlier that even Stahlecker, whose Einsatzgruppe A was the most lethal in carrying out mass murder, recognized that it was not possible to carry out the complete annihilation of the Jews without leaving traces, "at least not at the present moment." He said this in the very same report where he announced that the "aim" was, in fact, complete annihilation.[130]

Stahlecker was not alone in his views concerning the difficulties of the Jewish question. In a report dated only one month after the attack on the Soviet Union, Arthur Nebe, head of Einsatzgruppe B, advanced the following opinion: "A solution to the Jewish problem while the war is going on is impractical in this region, since it can be attained only by resettlement, in view of the overwhelming number of Jews."[131] It is not absolutely certain what Nebe meant by "resettlement," whether he meant forced deportation or the euphemistic meaning of this term in Nazi parlance: extermination. It is probable that Nebe was referring to the forced deportation of the Jews. Owing to the overwhelming number of Jews to be killed, Nebe was declaring that deporting the Jews was a more practical solution. This statement is of great interest since it constitutes direct early evidence of an original intention to shoot all the Jews, even though Nebe did not believe this could be done. The report described the setting up of Jewish councils, the registration of the Jews, the organization of labor groups, etc. The main task was described as that of getting the Jews into ghettos.[132] (A report issued almost a year later still spoke of a later final solution of the Jewish question in White Russia, even though Security Police measures had "brought about a fundamental change" in the question already.)[133]

While Jews certainly continued to be handled with "unabated severity,"[134] many reports indicated that, of necessity, more and more of the attention of Einsatzgruppe B (and the other Einsatzgruppen) was centered on antipartisan operations. By March 1942 Einsatzgruppe B reported that it had shifted its activity to partisan detection, and that everything else dealing with security had been pushed into the background.[135]

Otto Rasch, head of Einsatzgruppe C, who was later described by a subordinate as having been particularly ruthless,[136] also expressed doubts about the extermination of the Jews. He advocated that the Jews be used for cultivating marshland, and in the process of this work the heavy labor would take its toll.[137] In a report by Einsatzkommando 5 as part of Operational Situation Report 81, we read that Rasch was content to suggest that his men had contributed to the solution of the Jewish question in Europe by having caused thousands of Jews to flee in terror.[138] This exodus of the Jews eastward was meant to impress Berlin as a viable alternative to their annihilation. A report issued a few days later presented even more divergent views. In a list of the three major sources of danger in the Ukraine, the Jews were placed third after Bolshevik agitation (partisans), and passive resistance by the peasants. The report stated that the total removal of Jewry would not remove the political source of the danger—others were also the source of Bolshevism. The report continued:

> In this situation the goal of a political police security would be missed, if the main task of the destruction of the communist machine were put back into second or third place in favor of the practically easier task of the exclusion of the Jews. Furthermore, concentrating on the Bolshevik official robs Jewry of its most able forces, so that the solution of the Jewish problem bcomes more and more a problem of organization. . . . If the Jewish labor force is entirely discarded, an economic reconstruction of the Ukrainian industry and the extension of the administration centers of the cities is almost impossible. There is only one possibility, which the German administration in the Generalgouvernement has neglected for a long time: Solution of the Jewish problem by extensive labor utilization of the Jews. This will result in a gradual liquidation of Jewry—a development which corresponds to the economic conditions of the country.[139]

In Operational Situation Report 94, Einsatzgruppe C further advocated the sparing of some Jews and their use as forced labor, noting that "Difficulties have arisen in so far as Jews are often the only skilled workers in certain trades."[140] The ideas put forth in these reports did not halt the overall extermination program in the area of Einsatzgruppe C. In fact, the publication of Operational Situation Report 94 preceded the massacres in Kiev by only a few days. Rather it was simply the strongest statement by an Einsatzgruppe leader for one side of a controversy that continued throughout the entire war in the east. A later Einsatzguppe C report, this time, issued when Rasch's successor, Dr. Thomas, was in charge, repeated the claim that liquidation "cannot be a possible solution of the Jewish problem." The problem of the sheer numbers continued to plague the Kommandos, especially in the larger cities where, after executions had taken place, the returning Kommandos involved usually found an even greater number of Jews still present.[141]

It is interesting to compare Rasch's comments on the Jews with those of Nebe. Nebe based his opinions on the enormity of the task—there were too many Jews to be killed by too few men. In contrast, Rasch described the elimination of the Jews as an "easier task" in comparison to the task of destroying Bolshevism. In our present context it is noteworthy that Rasch put forward two alternative solutions to the immediate annihilation of the Jews: forcing them to flee and forcing them to work. The latter alternative would lead eventually to the Jews' destruction, and in the meantime would force them to be of assistance to the local economy.

These examples of contrasting opinions may add fuel to both sides of the centralized-decentralized debate. On the one hand, we see the policy of planned extermination to be carried out unquestioningly, swiftly, and efficiently (intentionalist position). On the other hand, we see leading officials charged with implementing this task advocating arguments in opposition to this state policy (functionalist position). Yet as Wilhelm has remarked, opinions such as these could find acceptance among certain sectors, given the nature of the system.[142] Although the polarity of views as expressed in the intentional-functionalist approaches have thus far been seen as mutually exclusive, the reality of the unfolding of events may have been otherwise. The killing of the Jews can be viewed as containing elements found in both positions. The suggestion by, among others, Friedlander and Wilhelm,[143] that something of a synthesis of the two positions is possible, is probably a more accurate assessment of the situation.

In the context of the reporting process itself, the examples certainly indicate a tolerance for divergent opinions. It is evident that one cannot speak of a uniform, overall viewpoint that was adhered to slavishly by the reporters. Such viewpoints varied with individuals and particular areas depending on the local situation at any given moment.

The exterminations continued. Activity and Situation Report 9, covering the month of January 1942, still presented the major aim as ridding the Ostland of Jews "as completely as possible."[144] The pace of the killing varied at times, depending upon weather conditions, other priorities, the need for Jewish labor, or the inclinations of individuals. It is uncertain whether so fundamental a schism with the policy of extermination, as voiced by Stahlecker, Nebe, and Rasch, was what Ohlendorf had in mind when he hoped the SD would be able to provide alternative perspectives on government and party policy.[145] It is ironic that the strongest advocate for "objective" reporting did not offer the kind of criticism put forward by his confreres (at least on the Jewish question). To the end Ohlendorf followed the accepted thesis that the Jews were to be exterminated. The criticism that he did put forward was directed at the Rumanians for their sluggishness and disorganized methods in carrying out the anti-Jewish actions. The furthest modification of the extermination plan he permitted himself to express was found in an Einsatzgruppe D report of 25 August 1941. Here the Jewish question was called "one of the most important problems," which had been dealt with thus far "only in a hesitating manner."[146] It seems, therefore, that Ohlendorf did not want to leave himself open to attack. Right up to his death, Ohlendorf evidently believed that it was right to kill the Jews.[147]

The fact that the reports articulated these differing viewpoints on such a fundamental question concerning the Jews is a reflection of the extent to which divergent views were actually tolerated. Despite efforts by certain leaders and officials to curb criticism, the reports could be unsparing in their questioning of basic policies. In expressing these criticisms the reports have succeeded in mirroring the complexity that marked German rule in the east.

This complexity was embodied in the strange contradictions found in the reports, contradictions that resulted from the changing circumstances or that were inherent in the reporting itself. On the one hand, the reports put forward completely false or distorted statements concerning the "Jewish-Bolshevist" menace that simply dished out the party line,[148] and on the other, many genuinely perceptive and realistic evaluations of the situation were reported. Included among the latter were reports that recognized the serious negative impact on the people in the east of certain aspects of German policy—the harsh SS measures, unpopular labor recruitment, lack of adequate supplies of food, reluctance to respond to the political aspirations of the local population, inadequate German propaganda, and the uncertainty of the military situation.[149] One report even acknowledged that earlier perceptions concerning Ukrainian nationalism had been incorrect.[150] In the case of these insightful appraisals of the problems existing in the east, it was not so much a question of admitting the existence of these problems, but of acting upon them to ameliorate the situation. This was never done in any meaningful way.[151]

Other contradictions in the reports were the presence of strong complaints against, and the mention of good relations with, the Wehrmacht and the Rumanian soldiers.[152] In the case of the Wehrmacht, it was apparent that the Wehrmacht's acknowledgement of the Kommandos's assistance was viewed with great satisfaction by the Einsatzgruppen, in spite of the not infrequent antagonism between them. Jews were described as wielding controlling power and influence.[153] They were a "danger," yet the reports remain a profound testimony to their helplessness in the face of Nazi terror. Indications of the support of the local population for the partisans[154] were juxtaposed with reminders that the population feared or did not sympathize with them.[155] Finally we discovered the contradiction in the stated aim of the Einsatzgruppen concerning the Jews. Alongside the policy that all Jews in the east were to be destroyed, we found the added statement that this was not possible during the war and that the Jews capable of doing so were to be forced to work for the Germans.

In summary, given the often contradictory nature of the reports, the obvious self-promotion and self-serving criticisms that informed the reporting, and their incomplete, inconsistent, and at times, inaccurate quality, what weight may we attach to the reliability of the reports as historical evidence? In order to answer this question we have had to see that the initial purpose of the reports—to inform Heydrich, Himmler, and others of the events in the east—became transformed into something beyond this original function. We have seen that the providing of an up-to-date objective acount of the happenings in the east gradually came to be coupled with the self-serving machinations of the reporters themselves. In a very real way the reports were as much a reflection of these changes in emphasis as they were an account of events. The rivalry permeating the entire structure of the Nazi regime caused each agency within the structure to attempt to put forward its position at the expense of others. In the case of the Security Police and SD, it took the form in the reports of finding fault with the actions and policies of other organizations. At the same time the Security Police and SD were presented as the one agency that was performing its work properly. Indeed, the reports stressed this job was being done not just properly, but in a splendid fashion. The conflicts among the various groups were used and combined with the interests and self-image of the participants, and, in turn, affected the final makeup of the reports. This favorable self-image projected by the reports cannot be overlooked in evaluating their objectivity.

A further point of interest is the seeming lack of effect the reports had on broad policymaking. We cannot determine to what extent Hitler was kept informed of the details of the Einsatzgruppen operations or if he ever actually read any of the reports. Müller's instructions to the Einsatzgruppen leaders of 1 August 1941[156] suggest that at least Hitler was kept up to date to some degree at this time. Himmler himself reminded his men that reports formed the basis of policy decisions.[157] Yet the pragmatic criticisms of the idea of total destruction of the Jews and other policies affecting the situation throughout the eastern region seems in the end to have had little impact on decisions. The areas of foreign, military, and Jewish policy were ultimately in Hitler's hands, and his views in these areas were fixed and not subject to "outside" influence. The criticism of negative aspects of German rule in the east found in the Einsatzgruppen reports were not all that different from the opinions of other agencies in the east.[158] In spite of these "truthful" reports, little was done to change policy in a positive way. The increasingly negative quality of the domestic SD reports led Himmler

to refrain from passing these on to Hitler.[159] It is noteworthy that
Ohlendorf stated that he never actually met Hitler and that few of his
SD reports were ever read by the Führer.[160] In Hitler's case it is clear,
therefore, that the public opinion reports concerning important issues likely
had little (if any) impact on his thinking.[161] It is one of the ironies of the
National Socialist regime that, for all the emphasis on the alleged importance of the reports and the need for objectivity, aside from providing basic
information the reports seem ultimately not to have mattered all that
much.[162] It may very well be that the most important effect the Einsatzgruppen reports had was simply to reinforce the ideological beliefs of the
Nazi hierarchy and to advance the careers of the Einsatzgruppen personnel.

The contradictions found throughout the reports would seem to support
arguments for opposite sides of any consideration of their historical
validity. First, many of the contradictions would lead us to skepticism
concerning aspects of the reports. (It goes without saying that the reports
are a completely distorted source with regard to the Jews and their response
to the situation they were facing.) Second, the very presence of these contradictions and varied viewpoints would indicate the reliability of the
reports as a mirror of the complex vicissitudes and character of Nazi policy.

Therefore, it is imperative to keep in mind the considerations cited above.
Once the fact of their impact on the reports is recognized, we can then
regard the reports in a more objective manner. While recognizing the
presence of these qualifying factors in the reports, we still can state with
confidence that the reports are an extremely valuable historical source. They
did manage to reflect to a surprising degree the changing situation in the
east. As Wilhelm has pointed out, the reports are not the only source for
the study of events in the eastern territories.[163] From a wide variety of
other evidence, both German and non-German, we can cross-check and
verify most of the events and attitudes presented in the reports. Even the
SD reports, which were not always reliable, did manage to offer many solid
assessments of policy and circumstances in the east.[164] We may, in fact,
look upon the complaints against the critical tone of the reports, which had
long been put forward by Goebbels[165] and others, as an indication of their
value. The "defeatist" attitude, the lack of "political discernment" that
Himmler, Bormann, and Goebbels found lurking in the reports, suggests
the presence of a reasonably clear-sighted objectivity, that, because it was
frowned upon by the leaders of the regime, was all the more likely to be
truthful.

15

Concluding Remarks

This book has been concerned with an analysis of the reports and the context in which they were created. We may now put forward some concluding remarks about the perpetrators of this murderous enterprise and the process of which they were a part.

The mass murder of the European Jews continues to confound historians in their attempts to achieve a comprehensive understanding of this event. Historians apply the tools of objective and dispassionate analysis in their work, hoping to arrive at rational explanations for how and why the Jews were killed. The fact remains that the various methodological approaches employed by historians in many respects still seem to many to be inadequate.[1] Whatever necessary detachment historians may bring to their research, the gnawing horror of the firing squads and the gas chambers intrudes. There is a dimension of understanding here that eludes us. Despite what we know, on a fundamental level, what we know still does not make "sense." Yet demanding though the problem is, we cannot abandon our efforts to both learn of, and from, the Holocaust.[2]

The destruction of the Jews has been seen as an immense bureaucratic process that involved many institutions of German society, each one playing its part along a road that led inexorably to extermination.[3] It has long been a commonplace of sociological generalization to characterize Germans as being disciplined, efficient followers, in short, the epitome of the bureaucratic ideal. Whether this generalization is valid or not is a moot point, yet in light of the Holocaust one may perhaps be forgiven for accepting such a conclusion. Bureaucracy implies a complex administrative machinery where people are absorbed in their own particular tasks at hand. The bureaucrat is not overly concerned about the larger picture beyond the maintenance of his own power within the system. The world of the bureaucrat is a world of ordinances, letters, memos, meetings, administrative paperwork, day-to-day decisions, and—reports. The Einsatzgruppen reports were a good example of this process. The RSHA officials received the reports, read them, drafted summaries, submitted these for approval, made revisions, typed them up, made copies, filed these, and sent them on to others.

Bureaucracy is present in all modern societies. In an analysis of the role of bureaucracy in genocide,[4] Zygmunt Bauman explains that by its very structure, modern bureaucracy is characterized by both a "meticulous functional division of labour" and a substitution of a "technical for a moral responsibility."[5] The division of labor, including different levels of authority, creates a separation, a "distancing" between the bureaucrats and their particular task and the final outcome of the process. It is possible in this situation that the individual may not be aware of the ultimate consequences of his own activity in the scheme of things.[6] (In fact, in the case of National Socialists, this was desired by the leadership.) It is this fragmentation of the total process into several stages, each distinct from the other, each performed by people concerned with a specific task, that enables the system to operate smoothly.[7] The substitution of technical for moral responsibility, Bauman reminds us, is the consequence of people seeking the approval of their immediate superiors for their work, and allowing their work to become an end in itself.[8] Bauman warns, therefore, that bureaucracy contains the essential elements required to enact mass murder.[9]

The foregoing remarks are particularly pertinent to our subject since two levels of this bureaucratic destruction process that concern us here are represented: first, in the Einsatzgruppen bureaucracy itself, and second, in the RSHA personnel in Berlin. Members of the former actually did the shooting and therefore had to deal with it directly; the latter were removed from, but were still an integral part of, the total system. The RSHA was a prime example of bureaucracy in action. To the officials, the content of what they were dealing with did not matter too much. They were performing a clerical function. We have just noted the "distancing" mechanism found in modern bureaucracies. Unlike some situations where the individual bureaucrat may be unaware of the end result, the men and women involved in drawing up the reports in the RSHA could not but know what the end result was. Descriptions of the annihilation of whole villages were found side by side with discussions of education policy. Nor were the RSHA officials especially inventive when it came to structuring their reports. While the RSHA in 1941 became the center of a program of mass murder, the reports were written along the same lines as earlier reports. These officials continued the editorial and office work that had occupied them previously as if nothing had really changed, and like all bureaucrats, the men in the RSHA were understaffed and overworked. The great amount of material that came in from the east swamped the officials, and as time passed the quality of the editing suffered. The Kommandostab in the RSHA in May 1942 made life much easier for itself by publishing reports thereafter only once a week.

When studying National Socialist history, it is frequently in minor details that one inadvertently encounters larger truths. One such detail found in the reports is illustrative of the bureaucratic nature of the whole RSHA apparatus. If we examine the dates of the Operational Situation Reports, we discover that from 23 June until 26 October 1941 the reports were issued every single day, seven days a week.[10] Starting three days later on October 29 the reports were then issued regularly three times a week on Monday, Wednesday, and Friday. This pattern continued uninterrupted until Monday, 22 December 1941. The next report would normally have appeared two days later, on Wednesday, but this Wednesday was December 24, that is, Christmas Eve. Like any factory or ordinary business enterprise, the RSHA bureaucracy, which for six months, with clockwise regularity, had issued reports dealing with mass murder, closed up shop and took a break of a week and a half for the Christmas and New Year holiday. The reports were resumed on 2 January 1942.[11] This customary observation of the holiday by the RSHA officials tells us as much about the process of extermination and its perpetrators as any other evidence does. It underlines the way in which the recording of mass killing of human beings was brought down to the level of conventional office work, much like the preparation of a routine inventory of shoes or umbrellas.

Although the framework of functioning bureaucracy provides the necessary setting for the implementation of mass murder, the larger bureaucratic framework does not totally explain why mass murder can occur. The individual's immersion within the overriding momentum of the bureaucracy is an important factor. Other motivating elements, however, are worthy of mention as well. One such element relates to the nature of superior orders given to subordinates by the leaders of the Reich. The concept of Hitler's Reich as a dual state has long been recognized by historians.[12] Within the system two lines of authority existed side by side—the official state authority as constituted by regular legal institutions, and the authority of Hitler himself as Führer of the Reich. The dual authority that existed in Hitler's state created a deliberately ambiguous situation where the authority for duties carried out on the basis of official legal structures was deftly paired with those based on a Führer order. As Hans Buchheim has demonstrated, the killing of the Jews, which was done on the authority of a Führer order, had no legal foundation whatsoever. Hitler's order was grounded on ideology, and ideological assent formed the foundation of its acceptance by the SS and other participants. Yet there was clearly no legal backing for the ideological assent. Contrary to postwar claims by many leaders, including Einsatzgruppen members, the carrying out of this order founded on ideology was a crime. The system did offer its members certain ways of evading this order had they chosen to do so. Buchheim discusses the distinction that was made between military and political aims by citing Heydrich's Operational Order 8. (See Chapter 2.) Here "undesirables" among prisoners of war were ordered killed. The order stated that those carrying out the order must "be inhibited by no bureaucratic or administrative considerations." Earlier existing regulations concerning prisoners, the order continued, were based on *military* considerations, but now political considerations were to be taken into account—to protect the German people against Bolshevik rabble-rousers and to secure the occupied areas quickly. Therefore, ideological considerations took precedence, and were not based on normal rules. To obey such orders was to obey unofficial directives issued outside the normal code of existence, and thus outside accepted conceptions of legality and human conduct.[13] It is, of course, precisely because men gave their consent to such orders that the extermination of the Jews was realized.

The Einsatzgruppen and Kommando leaders were operating on orders from their superiors. Their statements to this effect after the war, although made as part of their defense against the charges of the court, were certainly correct. They hoped that the fact they were pursuing orders of their superiors would save them. It is beside the point that this tactic, because it was legally untenable, did not succeed. What is important is that by citing superior orders the Einsatzgruppen leaders tried to limit their reasons for executing the Jews to this one dimension. Little was said by these men at the trial about their personal acceptance of ideological hatred of the Jews as a motivating force. They could never make such an admission. The statements of most of the Einsatzgruppen leaders were simply desperate attempts to deny firmly held Nazi convictions. Yet events, and the reports of these men, speak for themselves. These secret reports can be considered a more dependable source than the self-serving testimony of men on trial for their lives. It almost goes without saying that the reports bear witness to the fanatic commitment of the leaders to their mission of extermination. The ever-present racial conceptions concerning Jews, communists, Gypsies, and other "inferior" or "asocial" elements show the degree to which these theories were held by the Einsatzgruppen leaders. One cannot hope to find a more persuasive confirmation of racial cruelty than these reports. The fierce hatred directed toward the Jews, the constant debasement of the victims in the descriptions, the often patronizing attitude, even to their allies—all indicate the leaders' belief that they were the superior race, engaged in bringing to the inferior populations of the east the benefits of the new Germanic order.[14] As a matter of course, it was maintained that this new order meant the total destruction of the Jews. We see, therefore, that ideology and racism were part of the thinking of these men.

Given the scope of the operations, it is also an understatement to say that the Einsatzgruppen leaders were killers of the first order. The ruthlessness and zeal with which they performed their mission is everywhere apparent throughout the hundreds of pages in the reports. These men worked with thoroughness and speed. The SS encouraged initiative on the part of its members,[15] who, in turn, would respond by performing their tasks well.[16] The desire to cover as much territory as possible to capture as many "unreliable elements" as they could, is seen in the great number of towns, cities, and areas visited by the Kommando subunits. One senses at times the impatience of the leaders at delays caused by the slow progress at the front. The boasting quality of the reports, whatever factors may have prompted its inclusion, was certainly not without foundation. The leaders were proud of the accomplishments of their men.

Another point must be kept in mind. In all societies the concept of the destruction of the so-called "criminal element" within the society is one that is firmly entrenched. The close association in the Nazi mind between crime, race, and the Jews, plus the harsh nature of the punishment of "criminals" in the Third Reich, laid the groundwork for the secret destruction of the Jews. In destroying the Jews, the police agencies of the Reich could see themselves as destroying a "criminal element"—something that would be accepted by any society.[17] We have already analyzed how this personification of the Jews as criminals was a feature of the reporting.

We must conclude from what the leaders did, therefore, that they shared the characteristics that have been attributed to the SS—the arrogant elitist mentality, the unwavering obedience to the leadership, the racial hatred, and so on. They could not admit to this, of course, after the war, but the evidence suggests that to a great extent this was the case. Yet this may not be the whole picture. To view the motives of these men solely in these terms runs the risk of being too simplistic. Evidence indicates that forces other than ideological conviction played a part in influencing the actions of these men (and SS members generally). If we are to reach an understanding of the destruction process, we must try to see it whole, with all its contributing factors.

It is apparent that personal ambition and the advancement of their careers played an important role in the behavior of these men. This was true for at least three of the first Einsatzgruppen leaders. Arthur Nebe volunteered to lead an Einsatzgruppe in order to acquire a military decoration and the good opinion of Heydrich. Similarly, Otto Rasch hoped that he would thereafter receive a senior SD position in Berlin; while Walter Stahlecker, who had been transferred to the Foreign Office, hoped that his performance in the east would land him a job back in the RSHA.[18] If this assessment of the initial motives of these men is correct, it suggests that they had every reason to pursue the radical policy of destruction to the best of their ability, regardless of the extent of their personal acceptance of this policy. The misgivings about the Jewish question that Nebe and Rasch may have entertained, which we have referred to earlier, did not prevent them from murdering, between the two of them, at least one hundred twenty-five thousand people, mostly Jews, during the four months they led their

respective units. We have discussed at some length the power-seeking nature
of German organizations and the self-serving quality found in the reports.
It comes as no surprise, then, that such crass motives should play a part in
the carrying out of their assignments. In the case of Ohlendorf, things were
evidently different, at least with respect to his becoming leader of
Einsatzgruppe D. Ohlendorf, who had earlier encountered differences of
opinion with Himmler,[19] had twice been ordered to serve in the east and
had twice refused. Finally, after being ordered a third time, Ohlendorf
could not evade his responsibility.[20] He, too, performed his job
efficiently.[21]

The presence of purely selfish motives, coupled with certain reservations
about the feasibility of destroying the Jews, indicates that it was possible
for people to participate directly in the murders without necessarily
subscribing completely to the ideological reasoning behind the program.[22]
This is not to suggest that the Einsatzgruppen leaders (and other officials
who were part of this killing machinery) were not anti-Semitic. They most
likely were, and as we indicated, their reports are vivid testimony to this
fact. Our point here is that mass murder can be implemented by people
whose immediate incentive for action might stem from somewaht more
mundane sources than the lofty heights of idealism.

Ohlendorf's acceptance of his position was done under pressure. He
accepted, apparently, to avoid being reproached for cowardice.[23] This
concept of community peer pressure was another factor in obtaining the
cooperation of men who were reluctant to perform their distressing
assignment. Buchheim has noted that many members of the Kommandos
obeyed orders not out of fear for their lives and not because they believed
that orders from above were always correct. They obeyed, in large part,
because the pressure of the social environment was too strong for them to
disobey. They lacked the courage to remove themselves from the SS, from
the ties and philosophy that they were a part of, and to which they had
sworn allegiance.[24] Closely akin to social pressure was the Nazi concept of
"Blutkitt," or blood cement. This was the practice of involving everyone
equally in the criminal acts—in this case the shootings—in order to
irrevocably bind everyone to the group by means of shared guilt.[25]
Evidence exists that indicates that it was the policy of some of the Einsatzgruppen and Kommando leaders to have all the members take part in the
shootings. For example, Erwin Schulz, head of Einsatzkommando 5, stated
that Rasch ordered that all the Kommando leaders were to participate
personally at the executions.[26] Walter Haensch, head of Sonderkommando
4b, stated that his Kommando did not employ the same men as a special
"shooting Kommando," but constantly changed the members of the
execution squads.[27]

Several factors played a part, therefore, in the participation of the

Einsatzgruppen personnel in mass murder. The degree to which these elements were present varied with the individual. As mentioned above, we must keep in mind that ideology alone was not the only ingredient at work. In addition, we must caution ourselves against another form of simplistic thinking—that of characterizing these men solely as barbarians. Mass killing is a barbaric act. No doubt there were those who were particularly sadistic in performing the killing, but we must not call these men barbarians and leave it at that. Such thinking produces little in the way of insight concerning the process of mass killing from which one can learn. As Robert Koehl has remarked, the attribution of "total perversion" to the SS, a common practice among many people, rather than being an accurate portrait, simply shows how much people must distance themselves from such behavior.[28]

Beyond their ideology and their career ambitions, it is probable that personal corruption played a part in the motives of these men. Obviously in the reports there is no direct reference to this, yet evidence to this effect does exist, in particular the testimony of survivors. The reports do offer hints, however. The boastful nature of the reporting and the tremendous arbitrary power over life and death possessed by these men, would suggest that the impulse for debauchery and immediate personal gain was too tempting to resist, SS "idealism" to the contrary.

The reports leave the impression that the rank and file members of the Kommandos carried out their security work with enthusiasm. The sheer number of murdered Jews and communists would seem to indicate this. The reports give us only the very occasional hint that there were any psychological problems on their part. Yet there is much proof that this was often a serious problem with these men and that this problem demanded constant attention. As far back as May 1940, Hans Frank, the governor general of Poland, had mentioned that the police had ordered that some account be taken of the physical state of those in charge of executions.[29] The shootings often did affect the men.[30] At the Eichmann trial one witness testified that some SS men got almost hysterical and were close to nervous breakdowns.[31] A witness to massacres in Uman and Winnitsa in September 1941 stated that some of the men did have complete nervous breakdowns because of the shootings.[32] One official testified that certain people "went to pieces" and that there were "individual catastrophes."[33] Arthur Nebe's chauffeur committed suicide.[34] Ohlendorf himself claimed that the Einsatzgruppen leaders "were inwardly opposed to the liquidation."[35] It was often necessary to use alcohol as both an incentive and stimulant for overcoming the inhibitions of the men. Consequently, many of the killers were often drunk during the shootings. Further proof that problems existed was the need for Himmler to constantly remind his men that he was aware of the painful difficulty of the great assignment they had been given. Himmler's speeches[36] reminded the men they had to be hard, that no one else was capable of doing this "most difficult duty." Himmler stated that his men knew what it meant to stand beside one hundred, or five hundred or one thousand corpses, and in spite of this, to have remained "decent fellows."[37] Of course, one efficient way of getting someone to do something distasteful is to impress upon him the unique importance and awesome burden of the task. Himmler stated that most men of the SS had been able to do their job, with some exceptions "caused by human weakness"—possibly a reference to sadism on the part of some men. Himmler also indicated that personal corruption among "a number" of SS men had existed.[38] It is likely, however, that Himmler deliberately downplayed the real extent of such conduct. Finally, we know that several major SS leaders, including Jäger, Blobel, and Higher SS and Police Leader Bach-Zelewski suffered from mental problems brought on by the killings.[39]

The act of mass killing was seen by its executors as an extremely onerous task that had to be done, however unpleasant this was for Germans, who, as Himmler pointed out, were really a decent people. In his Posen speech Himmler mentioned that Germans possessed an "inoffensive soul and spirit" and a "good nature." Germans, he reminded his audience, were the "only people in the world to assume a decent attitude toward animals."[40] To follow routine orders, which anyone could easily obey, represented little challenge to the SS men. It was the enormity of the undertaking that gave the killing of the Jews so much meaning and set the SS apart from others. It was the ability to be harsh toward oneself, to suppress one's own conscience, that was seen as a moral achievement, that is, the greatest good.[41] In the same vein, at Nuremberg Ohlendorf stated that there was "nothing worse for people spiritually" than to have to shoot defenseless people.[42] Did it not occur to Ohlendorf and others who made observations of this kind that they had simply to cease shooting innocent people to relieve themselves of this "spiritual" burden? If shooting defenseless people *was* the most difficult burden, as they claimed, then the burden of social ostracism and accusations of disloyalty, which supposedly would have followed disobeying the orders to kill, would have been less difficult by comparison. By Ohlendorf's own reasoning, then, it would have been easier to disobey and not kill than to continue killing. *But nothing was done.* The ideological war against the Jews remained paramount and continued to be realized as an absolute necessity, regardless of any psychological doubts. The Jews were killed as part of the securing of the captured territories and the removing of unwanted members of the population—a grim job, but one that was done in a "correct" manner. Ohlendorf even testified that anyone who "enjoyed" the executions was removed from his Einsatzgruppe.[43] This distortion of morality, which characterized SS ethos, enabled men to accept Himmler's comparison of the justice of mass murder with the injustice of a stolen cigarette. Side by side with the brutality toward the Jews there existed a strict code of decent behavior, which was to be scrupulously followed.[44]

Moral distortions were also noticeably present in the rationalizations of SD members in the Einsatzgruppen. As George Browder has demonstrated, the SD men denied "they were total men," and pretended there was a distinction between their SD investigative functions and the criminal actions of which they were a part.[45] This denial forced the split personality that was so common among adherents to Nazism.[46] Our analysis of the reports has revealed this split personality phenomenon. Although couched in mundane style, the reports suggest a strange world (strange to the normal mind) where the most disparate conceptions existed side by side. Thus we find that the officials could express horror at the "awful atrocities" of the retreating Soviets,[47] and at the same time carry out mass murder on a scale unprecedented in history, while at times referring to the implementation of such operations as being simply an "organizational" problem.[48] It was a world where one might read well-considered appraisals of German social or economic policy, and at the same time read that the "Jews constitute the most evil disintegration factor."[49] One could come across sober advice about taking into account the interests of the indigenous population[50] or be confronted with such statements as the following typical example of Nazi logic:

Since the Jewish population, despite severe punishment continually disturbed the desired pacification of the occupied regions, the severest measures will have to be continued against them.[51]

These ideas were part of the same world. Each was thought to be significant. They existed side by side. The Einsatzgruppen leaders were capable men, especially when it came to killing. They took care to record details, and while they were not always consistent in this regard, what they did report mattered to them. It mattered to these men, for instance, that on 4 February 1942, of the twenty-five "criminals" arrested in Dnjepropetrowsk by Einsatzkommando 6, it was reported that two were mass murderers and another was a forger.[52] These details were deemed significant. It was not enough that all twenty-five men would be shot; the descriptive categories had to be recorded. We find in these ardently held racist theories, the cold-blooded inventories of murdered victims, the rational conclusions of the SD reports, and the many preposterous political generalizations, a clear mirror of the contradictions that informed the thinking of the Einsatzgruppen personnel and other leaders.

While the reports may be the primary evidence of the ruthlessness of the leaders, we have seen that some of these men were not completely convinced that the goal of total extermination was possible or desirable. We can only speculate as to the extent other leaders may have held the same beliefs and what factors may have influenced their thinking.[53] The reports alone seem to show that doubts in this regard were motivated by practical, not moral, considerations. It would appear that Nebe very soon became sure that a German victory was unattainable.[54] It may be that others also believed this, but were less vocal about it. The many references to the reluctance of the local population to cooperate for fear of the imminent return of the Soviets may have been an indication that this fear was shared by Einsatzgruppen staff members. The men of the Einsatzgruppen were killers, but they were not stupid. It is not unreasonable to suggest that the absence of further mention of actions against the Jews as such in the Reports from the Occupied Eastern Territories was due, in part, to a loss in the confidence that the war was going to be won. The men in the RSHA were perhaps casting an eye to the future when they might be held accountable for their deeds. Short of the "stronger" positions of Nebe or Rasch, and in the hope that the operations might be stopped, any doubts concerning the mass shooting might be expressed circuitously in the repeated claims of the need for Jewish labor, in the mounting importance of the Kommandos in the antipartisan war, in statements of concern regarding many other very real problems facing Germany on the eastern front—problems that required careful attention. But all this is speculation. We must repeat that many postwar statements by these men cannot be accepted at face value, so we may never be sure as to what they really felt at the time regarding the idea of extermination.[55] We do know the killings continued. The direct record of the reports weighs heavily in support of the idea that, despite any reservations the Einsatzgruppen leaders may have had, they managed to carry out their terrible responsibilities with frightening thoroughness.

The strange juxtapositions of contradictory conceptions found in the reports are paralleled in the strange psychological dynamics of the Einsatzgruppen-RSHA bureaucracy. On the one hand, we have the Einsatzgruppen personnel, for the most part convinced of the legality and the historic necessity of their dreadful mission, diligently massacring the Jews. On the other hand, the Berlin officials, quite removed from, but very much aware of what was taking place, were matter-of-factly drawing up reports describing this destruction in such a way as to reduce the whole operation to mundane administrative busy work, which could easily be put aside at Christmas in order to enjoy the holiday with their families. The RSHA officials could take comfort in the fact that they did not have to participate directly in the unpleasant duty of shooting people, however "important" this work was for Germany.[56] They could be grateful indeed not to be among those people Himmler had said knew what it was like to stand beside hundreds of bloodied corpses. If, on occasion, some officials may have had misgivings about the activities of the Security Police, it was not too troublesome to "accept" and "understand" the fundamental importance of the ideological war that was being waged in the east. One could remind oneself of the special nature of this war and of the need for absolute ruthlessness. Far from the reality of the antitank ditches and the shootings, the men in Berlin could also close their minds to what was happening. If their consciences continued to trouble them, they only had to read their own reports and assure themselves that the actions were "countermeasures" against "seditious and agitative" Jewish-Bolshevik "gangs" who were "terrorizing" the German representatives and indigenous peoples in the territories. The Einsatzgruppen members and the RSHA personnel, more than most, could take advantage of the moral evasions that were so fundamental to National Socialist thinking in general, and its reporting methods in particular.

In these ways a range of options lay open for these men to make everything acceptable, from a firm belief in the legality and rightness of the killing to various methods of self-exoneration via linguistic subterfuge, from simply not thinking about the matter to burying oneself in the daily routine of one's duties within the bureaucracy. One can understand how, with the help of these mental gymnastics, the Berlin officials could celebrate Christmas relatively untroubled by feelings of personal culpability. Yet one wonders if any of these bureaucrats ever really pondered deeply over their own work. Did they ever consider that, in drawing up these reports day after day, they, too, were actually a part of the process of murder? Are we perhaps right in agreeing with Raul Hilberg, who views such bureaucrats not as cogs in the wheel who simply turn whenever the wheel turns, but as the very force that drives the wheel, that, in fact, without these bureaucrats the wheel would not turn?[57]

In summary, the Nazi genocide was possible largely because it allowed existing German bureaucratic structures to function as usual, and at the same time it gave to those entrusted with this enterprise the motivation, distancing mechanisms, and "legal" armature necessary for carrying it out. By 1941 relatively little that was new, administratively or conceptually, had to be found to realize this murderous plan.[58] The criminal nature of the murder of millions was ignored or rationalized. The act of mass murder was performed as a function of police work and was perceived by its perpetrators as having been accomplished humanely. Within the historical framework of modern nation-states, the mass murder by the Nazis may be perceived as evidence of the "fragility" of the structures of modern civilization, or as evidence of the awesome potential for wielding power that these structures can achieve.[59]

The filing of secret reports was an important part of the overall mechanics of this murderous bureaucratic system. The Einsatzgruppen reports, though limited in the ways that have been described earlier, remain a major, fertile source for historians of German rule and the Holocaust. Time, and more recent examples of mass murder, have not diminished the staggering impact of these reports. To date, no events have unfolded quite comparable to Hitler's destruction program. Nor has there yet been uncovered anything quite equivalent, in kind and quantity, to these reports. The systematic annihilation of the European Jews was unparalleled in the intention and method by which it was accomplished. The operations of the Einsatzgruppen were the first stage in this horrific undertaking. Both the events themselves and their recording have remained unique.

In the end the Einsatzgruppen reports embody the profound sense of despair that is the legacy of the Holocaust. The destruction of the Jews is an event that humankind cannot ignore. We are unable to escape from the numbing realization that nothing is the same in light of this event. He who would seek to truly understand himself and his time must take this message to his heart.

Appendix A

Operational Situation Reports

Number	Date	Nuremberg Number	Number of Pages	Einsatzgruppen Included
1.	23-06-1941		6	
2.	23-06-1941	NO-4494	2	
3.	24-06-1941	NO-4495	4	
4.	25-06-1941	NO-4496	5	
5.	26-06-1941	NO-4530	4	
6.	27-06-1941	NO-4528	6	
7.	28-06-1941	NO-4531	3	A
8.	30-06-1941	NO-4543	6	A B C
9.	01-07-1941	NO-4536	6	A B
10.	02-07-1941	NO-4534	6	B C
11.	03-07-1941	NO-4537	9	A B C D
12.	04-07-1941	NO-4529	8	A B D
13.	05-07-1941	NO-4532	6	A B C D
14.	06-07-1941	NO-2940	8	A B
15.	07-07-1941	NO-2935	6	A C
16.	08-07-1941		6	A B
17.	09-07-1941	NO-2933	16	C
18.	10-07-1941	NO-4527	3	No Reports
19.	11-07-1941	NO-2934	7	A C D
20.	12-07-1941	NO-2936	7	B C
21.	13-07-1941	NO-2937	15	B
22.	14-07-1941	NO-4135	4	A C D
23.	15-07-1941	NO-4526	21	B C
24.	16-07-1941	NO-2938	17	A B C
25.	17-07-1941	NO-2939	9	D
26.	18-07-1941	NO-2941	10	A C
27.	19-07-1941	NO-2942	10	B C
28.	20-07-1941	NO-2943	15	A C
29.	21-07-1941	NO-4525	19	B
30.	22-07-1941	NO-2944	4	C
31.	23-07-1941	NO-2956	14	A B
32.	24-07-1941	NO-2955	20	B C
33.	25-07-1941	NO-4428	9	B
34.	26-07-1941	NO-2954	18	A B
35.	27-07-1941	NO-4421	7	A

Number	Date	Nuremberg Number	Number of Pages	Einsatzgruppen Included
36.	28-07-1941	NO-2953	11	B
37.	29-07-1941	NO-2952	13	C D
38.	30-07-1941	NO-2951	13	C
39.	31-07-1941	NO-4484	6	D
40.	01-08-1941	NO-2950	28	A C D
41.	02-08-1941	NO-4490	5	No Reports
42.	03-08-1941	NO-4491	3	C
43.	05-08-1941	NO-2949	33	B D
44.	06-08-1941	NO-4492	10	B C
45.	07-08-1941	NO-2948	14	B C D
46.	08-08-1941	NO-4499	7	No Reports
47.	09-08-1941	NO-2947	24	A C
48.	10-08-1941	NO-2946	6	A
49.	11-08-1941	NO-4485	6	A
50.	12-08-1941	NO-2945	12	B
51.	13-08-1941	NO-2850	8	A
52.	14-08-1941	NO-4540	18	A C
53.	15-08-1941	NO-4539	20	A
54.	16-08-1941	NO-2849	21	A C
55.	17-08-1941	NO-4523	5	C
56.	18-08-1941	NO-2848	6	No Reports
57.	19-08-1941	NO-4522	13	A
58.	20-08-1941	NO-2846	15? Incomplete	A C
59.	21-08-1941	NO-2847	22	A C
60.	22-08-1941	NO-2842	30	A C
61.	23-08-1941	NO-2841	6	A C D
62.	24-08-1941	NO-4521	6	D
63.	25-08-1941	NO-4538	9	C D
64.	26-08-1941	NO-2840	13	D
65.	27-08-1941	NO-4520	14	A B
66.	28-08-1941	NO-2839	6	No Reports
67.	29-08-1941	NO-2837	32	A B D
68.	30-08-1941	NO-2838	6	A
69.	31-08-1941	NO-4519	4	A
70.	01-09-1941	NO-4518	7	B
71.	02-09-1941	NO-2843	11	A
72.	03-09-1941	NO-4517	4	No Reports
73.	04-09-1941	NO-2844	37	A B
74.	05-09-1941	NO-2845	14	C
75.	06-09-1941	NO-4516	8	C
76.	07-09-1941	NO-2852	6	No Reports
77.	08-09-1941	NO-4524	6	A B
78.	09-09-1941	NO-2851	22	B
79.	10-09-1941	NO-4420	14	No Reports
80.	11-09-1941	NO-3154	16	C
81.	12-09-1941	NO-3153	24	C

Number	Date	Nuremberg Number	Number of Pages	Einsatzgruppen Included
82.	13-09-1941	NO-4419	7	No Reports
83.	14-09-1941	NO-4414	4	No Reports
84.	15-09-1941	NO-4416	5	No Reports
85.	16-09-1941	NO-3152	24	B C
86.	17-09-1941	NO-3151	37	A C
87.	18-09-1941	NO-3150	18	C
88.	19-09-1941	NO-3149	30	A C D
89.	20-09-1941	NO-3148	20	C D
90.	21-09-1941	NO-4415	27	B
91.	22-09-1941	NO-3142	17	B
92.	23-09-1941	NO-3143	46	B
93.	24-09-1941	NO-4417	6	C
94.	25-09-1941	NO-3146	35	A C
95.	26-09-1941	NO-3147	45	A D
96.	27-09-1941	NO-3144	27	A
97.	28-09-1941	NO-3145	26	B C
98.	29-09-1941	NO-4418	5	C
99.	30-09-1941	NO-4413	16	A
100.	01-10-1941	NO-4777	12	C D
101.	02-10-1941	NO-3137	7	C D
102.	03-10-1941	NO-4779	9	No Reports
103.	04-10-1941	NO-4489	12	D
104.	05-10-1941	NO-4488	10	D
105.	06-10-1941	NO-3138	11	D
106.	07-10-1941	NO-3140	25	B C D
107.	08-10-1941	NO-3139	25	B C D
108.	09-10-1941	NO-3156	27	B D
109.	10-10-1941	NO-4487	7	No Reports
110.	11-10-1941	NO-3141	4	No Reports
111.	12-10-1941	NO-3155	11	A C
112.	13-10-1941	NO-4486	10	C
113.	14-10-1941	NO-4544	17	D
114.	15-10-1941	NO-4422	5	No Reports
115.	16-10-1941	NO-4786	5	No Reports
116.	17-10-1941	NO-3407	8	A
117.	18-10-1941	NO-3406	16	C D
118.	19-10-1941	NO-4423	12	C
119.	20-10-1941	NO-3404	14	C
120.	21-10-1941	NO-3402	14	C
121.	22-10-1941	NO-4424	15	B
122.	23-10-1941	NO-4783	7	B D
123.	24-10-1941	NO-3239	14	A B
124.	25-10-1941	NO-3160	7	B
125.	26-10-1941	NO-3403	9	B C D
126.	29-10-1941	NO-4134	13	No Reports
127.	31-10-1941	NO-4136	9	C
128.	03-11-1941	NO-3157	10	C

Number	Date	Nuremberg Number	Number of Pages	Einsatzgruppen Included
129.	05-11-1941	NO-3159	15	C D
130.	07-11-1941	NO-2823	20	A C
131.	10-11-1941	NO-2829	12	A
132.	12-11-1941	NO-2830	21	A C D
133.	14-11-1941	NO-2825	39	A B C D
134.	17-11-1941	NO-4426	31	D
135.	19-11-1941	NO-2832	30	A C D
136.	21-11-1941	NO-2822	13	A D
137.	24-11-1941	NO-2826	22	A B
138.	26-11-1941	NO-4515	13	A D
139.	28-11-1941	NO-2836	7	D
140.	01-12-1941	NO-2831	8	A D
141.	03-12-1941	NO-4425	15	D
142.	05-12-1941	NO-4787	9	C D
143.	08-12-1941	NO-2827	11	A B C D
144.	10-12-1941	NO-4776	17	A B
145.	12-12-1941	NO-2828	13	B D
146.	15-12-1941	NO-2835	25	A B D
147.	17-12-1941	NO-2821	7	B
148.	19-12-1941	NO-2824	10	B
149.	22-12-1941	NO-2833	16	A B C D
150.	02-01-1942	NO-2834	24	A D
151.	05-01-1942	NO-3257	18	A
152.	07-01-1942	NO-4541	30	A D
153.	09-01-1942	NO-3258	16	A D
154.	12-01-1942	NO-3278	38	A
155.	14-01-1942	NO-3279	38	A D
156.	16-01-1942	NO-3405	58	A C D
157.	19-01-1942	NO-3338	13	A D
158.	Missing			
159.	23-01-1942	NO-4427	9	A D
160.	26-01-1942	NO-4778	10	A
161.	28-01-1942	NO-4782	8	A D
162.	30-01-1942	NO-4784	30	A
163.	02-02-1942	NO-3400	12	A C
164.	04-02-1942	NO-3399	10	A C
165.	06-02-1942	NO-3401	16	A D
166.	09-02-1942	NO-4785	13	A
167.	11-02-1942	NO-4542	12	A D
168.	13-02-1942	NO-4533	10	A
169.	16-02-1942	NO-4545	14	A B
170.	18-02-1942	NO-3339	22	A D
171.	20-02-1942	NO-4412	14	A
172.	23-02-1942	NO-3341	14	A
173.	25-02-1942	NO-3340	7	A C
174.	27-02-1942		21	A B D
175.	02-03-1942		10	A B

Number	Date	Nuremberg Number	Number of Pages	Einsatzgruppen Included
176.	04-03-1942		5	A
177.	06-03-1942	NO-3240	7	C
178.	09-03-1942	NO-3241	18	A B D
179.	11-03-1942		12	A B
180.	13-03-1942	NO-3232	11	A B
181.	16-03-1942		7	A
182.	18-03-1942	NO-3233	12	A
183.	20-03-1942	NO-3234	12	A B C
184.	23-03-1942	NO-3235	11	A D
185.	25-03-1942		12	A C
186.	27-03-1942	NO-3236	28	A B D
187.	30-03-1942	NO-3237	21	A C D
188.	01-04-1942	NO-5941	15	A B
189.	03-04-1942	NO-3238	24	A B C
190.	08-04-1942	NO-3359	35	A C D
191.	10-04-1942	NO-3256	48	A C
192.	14-04-1942		22	A
193.	17-04-1942	NO-3281	18	A B C D
194.	21-04-1942	NO-3276	19	A B
195.	24-04-1942	NO-3277	26	A B C D

This list of the Operational Situation Reports indicates that all but a few of the 194 surviving reports bear a Nuremberg document number. The complete set was found in seven folders, which were given file numbers by American investigators that resulted in the following distribution: Folder One (E328) Reports 1–30; Folder Two (E 330) Reports 31–78; Folder Three (E 329) Reports 79–100; Folder Four (E 327) Reports 101–129; Folder Five (E 325) Reports 130–150; Folder Six (E 326) Reports 151–173; and Folder Seven (E 331) Reports 174–195. The number of pages listed includes all pages grouped together with each report as found on the microfilm copy of the originals consulted by the author. (See below Appendix E.) Each number includes all such pages, including appendices, location lists, and duplicates of single pages. For example, Operational Situation Report 24 has two copies of page 14, while Operational Situation Report 52 contains two copies of the title page in the folder. No doubt the position of these pages corresponds to their arrangement as they existed upon discovery, and it is likely they were filmed in this manner. As a result there appear to be some loose ends here and there. It is not always absolutely clear where some of the pages belong. Operational Situation Report 94 includes two pages of military reports that are different from the military reports contained within the report itself.

The column on the right lists the Einsatzgruppen whose reports are included in the reports, even when such inclusion is limited to descriptions of locations in the text (but not the locations list itself), as was the case particularly in the earlier reports. Operational Situation Reports 1–6 describe events without specifying individual Einsatzgruppen.

Appendix B

Summary of Operational Situation Reports

Einsatzgruppe A

Subject	Report
Shootings	OSR 8, 9, 12, 14, 15, 19, 24, 26, 54, 88, 94, 96, 111, 116, 131, 136, 150, 154–156, 163–165, 168, 169, 172, 175, 178, 180–182, 184, 186, 191, 195
General Mood, Activity, and Situation Reports	OSR 14, 24, 26, 34, 40, 53, 54, 57, 88, 94–96, 99, 123, 130, 131, 135–137, 140, 144, 146, 150–156, 159–162, 166–195
Partisans/Communists	OSR 48–49, 57, 59, 60, 67, 71, 86, 88, 94–95, 133, 135, 137–138, 149, 153–155, 179, 189
Agents	OSR 130, 137, 138, 149, 156
Propaganda	OSR 137, 150, 155, 156, 162
Economy	OSR 40, 53, 54, 57, 95, 96, 99, 131, 156, 195
Churches	OSR 54, 69, 95, 96, 99, 132, 156, 162, 163, 165, 195
Education, Culture, Science	OSR 53, 54, 95, 131, 156, 195
Press	OSR 130, 131, 156, 160
Agriculture/Food	OSR 170, 191, 195
Jews/Jewish Question	OSR 94, 95, 111, 155
HSSPL	OSR 12, 19, 48, 151, 155, 156
Ethnic Groups	OSR 40, 51, 53, 54, 95, 96, 130, 135, 151, 153, 162

Einsatzgruppe B

Subject	Report
Shootings	OSR 9, 14, 21, 24, 31, 32, 36, 43, 50, 67, 73, 92, 108, 123–125, 133, 146–149, 194

Subject	Report
General Mood, Activity, and Situation Reports	OSR 20, 21, 23, 24, 29, 31, 32, 34, 36, 43, 65, 67, 70, 73, 90, 92, 106, 108, 121, 123, 125, 133, 144, 175, 178–180, 182, 188, 193–195
Partisans/Communists	OSR 23, 50, 65, 67, 70, 85, 92, 97, 108, 123, 133, 143, 146, 169, 186
Agents	OSR 137, 143
Propaganda	OSR 73, 107, 121, 133, 144, 145, 169, 179, 189, 194
Economy	OSR 33, 43, 67, 73, 91, 107, 122, 133, 145
Churches	OSR 32, 36, 73, 107, 122, 145, 180, 194
Education, Culture, Science	OSR 78, 145
Agriculture/Food	OSR 21, 180, 189, 194
Jews/Jewish Question	OSR 31, 32, 33, 78, 146
HSSPL	OSR 27, 32, 50
Ethnic Groups	OSR 31, 32, 43, 67, 73, 97, 107, 133, 145, 195

Einsatzgruppe C

Subject	Report
Shootings	OSR 13, 17, 19, 20, 24, 27, 30, 37, 38, 47, 58, 59, 80, 86, 88, 94, 101, 106, 111, 119, 128, 132, 135, 143, 156, 164, 173, 177, 189, 190
General Mood, Activity, and Situation Reports	OSR 17, 20, 24, 26, 28, 30, 37, 38, 40, 42, 45, 47, 59, 60, 81, 85–87, 89, 106, 112, 125, 127, 132, 133, 135, 142, 143, 149, 156, 163, 164, 177, 185
Partisans/Communists	OSR 27, 52, 60, 74, 80, 133, 156, 185, 187
Agents	OSR 47, 88, 164
Propaganda	OSR 40, 80, 88, 90
Economy	OSR 40, 47, 59, 60, 81, 88, 94, 107, 118, 125, 132, 133, 187
Churches	OSR 52, 81, 90, 112, 117, 120, 128, 133, 142
Education, Culture, Science	OSR 45, 60, 81, 87, 88, 112

Subject	Report
Agriculture/Food	OSR 45, 47, 59, 60, 74, 85, 87, 107, 112, 128, 132, 156, 187, 191
Jews/Jewish Question	OSR 31, 37, 81, 86, 112, 128, 129, 156, 191
HSSPL	OSR 59, 80, 86, 88, 97, 101
Ethnic Groups	OSR 20, 23, 24, 26, 30, 32, 38, 44, 47, 52, 75, 81, 86, 87, 89, 90, 100, 121, 133, 142, 143, 156, 164, 183, 185, 187, 191

Einsatzgruppe D

Subject	Report
Shootings	OSR 19, 22, 25, 37, 40, 45, 61, 67, 89, 95, 101, 117, 129, 136, 139, 145, 150, 153, 156, 157, 165, 167, 170, 178, 184, 190, 193
General Mood, Activity, and Situation Reports	OSR 25, 37, 40, 43, 63, 64, 67, 88, 100, 106, 107, 108, 134, 135, 136, 145, 150, 153, 157, 161, 165, 167, 170, 178, 184, 186
Partisans/Communists	OSR 62, 104, 107, 113, 122, 129, 134–136, 138–143, 145, 146, 149, 150, 152, 153, 156, 159, 165, 170, 174, 178
Agents	OSR 113
Propaganda	OSR 37, 43, 100, 134, 187
Economy	OSR 37, 43, 64, 88, 100, 108, 134
Churches	OSR 43, 64, 100, 113, 134, 141, 145
Education, Culture, Science	OSR 64, 100, 105, 108, 134, 141
Agriculture/Food	OSR 43, 61, 67, 88, 134, 167, 170, 184, 190
Jews/Jewish Question	OSR 63, 64, 107, 117, 145, 149
Ethnic Groups	OSR 25, 40, 43, 67, 100, 103, 104, 107, 108, 113, 132, 134, 141, 142, 149, 155

Appendix B summarizes under several headings for each Einsatzgruppe the main themes that recur throughout the Operational Situation Reports. Beside each heading are the numbers of the reports dealing with the subjects in question. The various categories listed certainly do not exhaust the material in the reports. We have tried to present the major themes treated by all four Einsatzgruppen. The topics cited were not limited only to the reports given above. There was considerable overlapping in the reports, even within the categories themselves. In particular, the general mood and political situation reports often dealt with a range of material that is difficult to classify. Consequently, within one of the latter reports alone, one might encounter discussion of some of the subjects that we have presented separately. Our list for the most part cites those reports where the subject is either a distinct report on its own, or forms the main part of a larger report. The Higher SS and Police Leader category (HSSPL) includes the chief (and infrequent) references to these men. The heading called Shootings refers to the killings that have formed the principal subject of this book.

Appendix C

Reports from the Occupied Eastern Territories

Number	Date	Nuremberg Number	Number of Pages
1.	01-05-1942	PS-3943	13
2.	08-05-1942	NO-5191	18
3.	15-05-1942	NO-5190	28
4.	22-05-1942	NO-5189 (PS-3943)	9
5.	29-05-1942	NO-5188	20
6.	05-06-1942	NO-5187	31
7.	12-06-1942		19
8.	19-06-1942		18
9.	26-06-1942	PS-3943	27
10.	03-07-1942		22
11.	10-07-1942		16
12.	17-07-1942		18
13.	24-07-1942		61
14.	31-07-1942		22
15.	07-08-1942		34
16.	14-08-1942	NO-5175	27
17.	20-08-1942		23
18.	28-08-1942		29
19.	04-09-1942		37
20.	11-09-1942		27
21.	18-09-1942		32
22.	25-09-1942		24
23.	02-10-1942		27
24.	09-10-1942		25
25.	16-10-1942		46
26.	23-10-1942	NO-5174	31
27.	30-10-1942		44
28.	06-11-1942		32
29.	13-11-1942		29
30.	20-11-1942		21
31.	27-11-1942		29
32.	04-12-1942		30
33.	11-12-1942	NO-5172	32
34.	18-12-1942		40
35.	23-12-1942	NO-5171	23
36.	08-01-1943	NO-5170	49

Number	Date	Nuremberg Number	Number of Pages
37.	15-01-1943		30
38.	21-01-1943	NO-5169 (PS-3943)	32
39.	29-01-1943	NO-5168	40
40.	05-02-1943		47
41.	12-02-1943	NO-5167	31
42.	19-02-1943		28
43.	26-02-1943	NO-5166	33
44.	05-03-1943		23
45.	12-03-1943	NO-5165	37
46.	19-03-1943	NO-5164 (PS-3943)	32
47.	26-03-1943	NO-5162	37
48.	02-04-1943	NO-5163	40
49.	09-04-1943	NO-5161	22
50.	16-04-1943		28
51.	23-04-1943		24
52.	30-04-1943		21
53.	07-05-1943		31
54.	14-05-1943		35
55.	21-05-1943		41

Not all the Reports from the Occupied Eastern Territories bear Nuremberg document numbers, as seen in the above list. The number of pages presented includes every page as grouped together on the microfilmed copy of the originals consulted by the author. These numbers therefore include the table of contents of the reports, any Locations and Communications list and any other appendices, as well as the report proper.

Appendix D

Distribution List for Operational Situation Report 128

Reichsführer-SS u. Chef der Deutschen Polizei	1. AUSF. (copy)
Chef der Sicherheitspolizei u. SD.	2.
Hauptampt d. Ordnungspolizei	3.
Amtschef I	4.
Amtschef II	5.
Amtschef V	6.
Amtschef VI	7.
Amtschef VII	8.
Gruppe II D	9.
Gruppe II A	10.
II A 1	11.
Gruppe II B	12.
IIB 2	13.
Gruppe II D 3a	14.
Gruppe IVc	15.
Gruppe VIc	16.
IV A 3	17.
IV A 4	18. u. 19
IV E	20.
IV E 5	21.
Pol. Rat Pommerening	22.
IV D	23.
IV D 1	24.
IV D 2	25.
IV D 3	26.
IV D 4	27.
Amtschef III	28.
Gruppe III A	29.
Gruppe III B	30.
Gruppe III C	31.
Gruppe III D	32.
IV B 4	33.
IV E 2	34.
Gruppe IV B	35.
Höh-SS-U. Pol. Führer Russland Nord	36.
Höh-SS-U. Pol. Führer Russland Mitte	37.
Höh-SS-U. Pol. Führer Russland Sud	38.
Höh-SS-U. Pol. Führer z.b.v.	39.

Appendix E

Document Sources

The complete original surviving set of the Operational Situation Reports (Ereignismeldungen UdSSR) and the Reports from the Occupied Eastern Territories (Meldungen aus den besetzten Ostgebieten) is today found in the Bundesarchiv in Koblenz, under Bestand R58, Reichssicherheitshauptamt, Numbers 214–221, and Numbers 697, 698, 222, 223, and 224. A complete set of the Operational Situation Reports is found in the National Archives in Washington, on microfilm as part of the National Archives and Records Service (NARS) Microfilm Publication T175, Records of the Reich Leader of the SS and Chief of the German Police, rolls 233–235. A complete set of the Reports from the Occupied Eastern Territories is found on Microfilm Publication T175, rolls 235–236. Copies of the reports are found in other archives, including the Institut für Zeitgeschichte in Munich.

The originals of all the Activity and Situation Reports (Tätigkeits- und Lageberichte der Einsatzgruppen der Sicherheitspolizei und des SD in der UdSSR) with the exception of Report 9, are found in the Political Archives of the Foreign Office in Bonn under the reference: Inland IIg, 431 Russland: SD–Einsatzgruppen, Berichte 1941–1942. See Helmut Krausnick and Hans-Heinrich Wilhelm, Die Truppe des Weltanschauungskrieges, Stuttgart, 1981, pp. 649–54, for a list and discussion of these documents.

Further documentary materials used in preparation of this study were the records of the Einsatzgruppen trial, Case 9, *United States of America v. Otto Ohlendorf, et al.*, in particular the complete prosecution and defense exhibits and document books (found in English on NARS Microfilm Publication M895, rolls 11, 12, 26, 27, and 28). In the notes during the course of this study, the Nuremberg document number or defense exhibit number only has been given. Also consulted were the prosecution briefs (English) M895, roll 29, and complete daily transcript of the trial proceedings (English) M895, rolls 2–7.

An extremely helpful guide to the above material was also used. This is Special List NARS: no. 42, compiled by John Mendelsohn.

Other publications containing documents referred to in this study included the following:

Trial of the Major War Criminals before the International Military Tribunal, 42 volumes. Nuremberg: 1947–48.

Nazi Conspiracy and Aggression. 8 volumes and 2 supplemental volumes. Washington D.C.: United States Government Printing Office, 1946–48.

John Mendelsohn, ed. *The Holocaust—Selected Documents in Eighteen Volumes*. New York: Garland Publishing, 1982. Volumes 10, 17, and 18 in this series deal with material related to the Einsatzgruppen.

Notes

Introduction

1. For an overall study of the history of the Einsatzgruppen and a detailed case study of Einsatzgruppe A, see Helmut Krausnick and Hans-Heinrich Wilhelm, *Die Truppe des Weltanschauungskrieges: Die Einsatzgruppen der Sicherheitspolizei und des SD 1938–1942* (Stuttgart: Deutsche Verlags-Anstalt, 1981). (Hereafter cited variously as Krausnick and/or Wilhelm, *Die Truppe.*)

2. Affidavit by Otto Ohlendorf, 24 April 1947, NO–2890. Affidavit by Otto Ohlendorf (Affidavit B) 20 November 1945, in *Nazi Conspiracy and Aggression* (Washington, D.C.: United States Government Printing Office, 1946–48), vol. 8, 596.

3. See NOKW–256 and NOKW–2302. See also Walter Schellenberg affidavit, 26 November 1945, PS–3710. Otto Ohlendorf affidavit, 24 April 1947, NO–2890.

4. See Raul Hilberg, *The Destruction of the European Jews, 3 Vols.*, revised and definitive edition (New York: Holmes & Meier, 1985), vol. 1, 273. See Chapter 14 for a discussion of the differences of opinion among historians concerning the decision to kill the Jews.

5. A more exact translation of Ereignismeldungen is Reports of Events, as pointed out by the defense in Case 9, *United States v. Otto Ohlendorf et al.*, Preliminary Remarks to Excerpts from Ereignismeldungen UdSSR 8–73, Blume Defense Exhibit 6. All Defense Exhibits cited below are from Case 9. Operational Situation Report is the usual English translation and is the one used in this study. See Appendix A for a list of the Operational Situation Reports.

6. L–180 and PS–2273. Franz Walter Stahlecker was the head of Einsatzgruppe A until March 1942.

7. Report by Karl Jäger, leader of Einsatzkommando 3, a part of Einsatzgruppe A, on the operations of this Kommando as of 1 December 1941.

8. See Wilhelm, *Die Truppe*, 333.

9. Excerpts from Reports from the Occupied Eastern Territories 1, 4, 6, 7, 9, 38, 41, 46, and 49 did surface as evidence at this trial. They bore the Nuremberg document reference PS–3943.

10. Trial of the Major War Criminals before the International Military Tribunal, Nuremberg, 1947–48, vol. 4, 338. (Hereafter *IMT.*) In an affidavit Ohlendorf acknowledged that regular courier and radio communications with Berlin had existed, but did not offer any further specifics. Affidavit of Otto Ohlendorf, 24 November 1945, PS–2620.

11. Letter to the author from Daniel P. Simon, director of the Berlin Document Center, 9 February 1987; subsequent letter, dated 6 April 1987, and copies of documents from the files of the Berlin Document Center. The author is grateful to Mr. Simon and the Berlin Document Center for providing this information pertaining to the discovery of the reports. The author is also grateful to Benjamin B, Ferencz and Barbara Bitter for providing additional details concerning the discovery and analysis of the reports.

12. The reports would certainly have been welcome evidence for the prosecution at the first Nuremberg trial.

13. Seymour J. Pomrenze, "Policies and Procedures for the Protection, Use, and Return of Captured German Records," in Robert Wolfe, ed. *Captured German and Related Records* (Athens, Ohio: Ohio University Press 1974), 20.

14. Letters to the author from Benjamin B. Ferencz, 11 June 1986 and 26 December 1986. See also Benjamin B. Ferencz, *Less Than Slaves: Jewish Forced Labor and the Quest for Compensation* (Cambridge, Mass.: Harvard University Press, 1979), Preface, xv, xvi. A letter, dated 15 January 1947, by Rolf Wartenberg, who interrogated the Einsatzgruppen

leaders, was sent to OCCWS analysts asking them to look for reports of the Einsatzgruppen. See John Mendelsohn, "Trial by Document: The Use of Seized Records in the United States Proceedings at Nuremberg," unpublished doctoral dissertation, University of Maryland, 1974, 59, 60.

15. One analyst on the OCCWC staff who worked on the documents was Barbara Bitter. The work was carried out on the site of the present Berlin Document Center, which before 1945 had been a telephone exchange incorporating vast underground areas. Bitter recalled the massive amount of documents that were examined and the tremendous excitement of the staff members as they discovered in the reports the precise kind of evidence they were looking for. Letter from Barbara Bitter to author, 26 January 1987, and telephone conversation with author, 13 April 1987. See Chapter 13 for a brief discussion of the preparation of documents for use as prosecution evidence.

16. The book as a whole follows a roughly chronological sequence—the outline of the Nazi agencies before the war, the events of the war itself as reflected in the reports, and the post-war "life" of these documents as legal and historical documentation, and their meaning for us today. (Appendix B contains a listing of the major subject categories of the reports.)

Chapter 1. SS Power and the RSHA

1. Martin Broszat, *The Hitler State: The Foundation and Development of the Internal Structure of the Third Reich* (London and New York: Longman, 1981), 37; Hans Buchheim, and others, *Anatomy of the SS State* (New York: Walker and Company, 1968), 140–41; Heinz Höhne, *The Order of the Death's Head. The Story of Hitler's SS*, (London: Secker & Warburg, 1972), 19–24; Robert Lewis Koehl, *The Black Corps. The Structure and Power Struggles of the Nazi SS* (Madison, Wisc.: University of Wisconsin Press, 1983), 11–12, 21–24. The germ of the strong-arm guard concept can, in fact, be traced earlier to the use of guards at the founding meeting of the National Socialist Party on 24 February 1920, or even earlier to the party guards used in October 1919. Koehl, *Black Corps*, 6–7.

2. Buchheim, *Anatomy*, 141.

3. Ibid.

4. Broszat, *Hitler State*, 38; Höhne, *Order of the Death's Head*, 23–28.

5. Höhne, *Order of the Death's Head*, 57.

6. Buchheim, *Anatomy*, 142. Koehl states that by May 1933 the SS doubled its membership to one hundred thousand. Koehl, *Black Corps*, 79.

7. Werner T. Angress and Bradley F. Smith, "Diaries of Heinrich Himmler's Early Years," *Journal of Modern History* 31 (1959): 207.

8. Joachim C. Fest, *The Face of the Third Reich. Portraits of the Nazi Leadership* (New York: Pantheon Books, 1970), 112–13.

9. Höhne, *Order of the Death's Head*, 32.

10. Bradley F. Smith, *Heinrich Himmler: A Nazi in the Making 1900–1926* (Stanford, Calif.: Hoover Institution Press. Stanford University, 1971), 8–94.

11. Höhne, *Order of the Death's Head*, 33.

12. Ibid., 33–34. Koehl, *Black Corps*, 29; Smith, *Heinrich Himmler*, 77–129.

13. Höhne, *Order of the Death's Head*, 38.

14. Ibid., 28.

15. SS membership was to be a community of men of pure Nordic race. Koehl sees this attitude as the values of the old officer class translated into Nazi racism. Koehl, *Black Corps*, 48. In 1931 Himmler set up a Racial Office that was to oversee the marriages of SS men. In 1933 this office expanded and became the Race and Resettlement Office (Rasse-und Siedlungsamt), which dealt with the screening of SS members along racially acceptable lines. It was Richard Walter Darré who provided the SS with the supposedly rational underpinnings for its racial theories. These ideas were well in tune with Himmler's own "blood and soil" concepts and formed the basis of the elitist character of the SS. Koehl, *Black Corps*, 51, 81–84; Höhne, *Order of the Death's Head*, 47–48, 145–48, 156.

16. Höhne, *Order of the Death's Head*, 57–58.

17. Shlomo Aronson, *Reinhard Heydrich und die Frühgeschicte von Gestapo und SD* (Stuttgart: Deutsche Verlags–Anstalt, 1971), 55; Höhne, *Order of the Death's Head*, 170.
18. Aronson, *Heydrich*, 11.
19. Ibid., 34–35; Höhne, *Order of the Death's Head*, 168–69.
20. Fest, *Face of the Third Reich*, 100–2.
21. Ibid., 98.
22. Aronson, *Heydrich*, 311; Höhne, *Order of the Death's Head*, 171. A ban on the SS and SA in April 1932 forced Heydrich to change the name of this agency to Presse-und Informationsdienst (Press and Information Service–PID). Höhne, *Order of the Death's Head*, 170.
23. Koehl, *Black Corps*, 123.
24. Lawrence Duncan Stokes, "The Sicherheitsdienst (SD) of the Reichsfuehrer SS and German Public Opinion, September 1939–June 1941," unpublished doctoral dissertation, John Hopkins University, 1972, 37–41; Koehl, *Black Corps*, 126–27.
25. Koehl, *Black Corps*, 80. This combination of paid and unpaid personnel was to remain characteristic of the SD.
26. Koehl, *Black Corps*, 80–81, 83, 92–93, 95, 127, 150.
27. Ibid., 83, 92–93.
28. Aronson, *Heydrich*, 195–96; Buchheim, *Anatomy*, 170.
29. Aronson, *Heydrich*, 196.
30. George C. Browder, "SIPO and SD, 1931–1940. Formation of an Instrument of Power," unpublished doctoral dissertation, University of Wisconsin, 1968, 99–100.
31. Buchheim, *Anatomy*, 171.
32. Stokes, "Sicherheitsdienst," 74. For a discussion of the gradual occupation of the buildings in the Prinz-Albrecht-Strasse-Wilhelmstrasse area, see Rainer Kölmel, "A Holocaust Memorial in Berlin?" in Remembering for the Future. (A paper presented at the international conference held in Oxford in 1988), 1755–58. See also Johannes Tuchel and Reinhold Schattenfroh, *Zentrale des Terrors, Prinz-Albrecht-Strasse 8: Das Hauptquartier der Gestapo* (Berlin: Siedler Verlag, 1987); Reinhard Rürup and others, ed., *Topographie des Terrors: Gestapo, SS, und Reichssicherheitshauptamt auf dem "Prinz-Albrecht-Gelände," Eine Dokumentation* (Berlin: Verlag Willmuth Arenhövel, 1987).
33. Koehl, *Black Corps*, 95; Aronson, *Heydrich*, 191–94; Stokes, "Sicherheitsdienst," 62–63.
34. Höhne gives a figure of eighty-three as the numbe of persons killed. Höhne, *Order of the Death's Head*, 128. The number may have been in the hundreds. See Broszat, *Hitler State*, 213.
35. Broszat, *Hitler State*, 213. For the importance of the June 30 date in the rise of the SS, see Fest, *Face of the Third Reich*, 117, 340, note 24.
36. Koehl, *Black Corps*, 87. On 3 January 1935 Hitler declared that the Reichswehr was the sole bearer of arms. Ibid., 102.
37. This term emerged during the 1933–34 period. Koehl, *Black Corps*, 135, 335, note 68.
38. Koehl, *Black Corps*, 135.
39. George H. Stein, *The Waffen SS: Hitler's Elite Guard at War 1939–1945* (Ithaca, N.Y.: Cornell University Press, 1966), 9.
40. See Koehl, *Black Corps*, 64–65.
41. Stein, *Waffen SS*, 285; Koehl, *Black Corps*, 196. The Waffen SS membership on 22 June 1941 was 160, 405, with a combat force of 95,868. Koehl, *Black Corps*, 200.
42. PS–647. See Stein, *Waffen SS*, 20–26.
43. See Yehoshua Büchler, "Kommandostab Reichsführer-SS: Himmler's Personal Murder Brigades in 1941," *Holocaust and Genocide Studies*, Vol. 1, no. 1 (1986): 11–25. Stein estimates that about one thousand five hundred Waffen SS members served with the Einsatzgruppen. Stein, *Waffen SS*, 264.
44. Buchheim, *Anatomy*, 144–45.
45. Ibid., 134.
46. It was apparently with Diels that the idea of objectively monitoring the full range of the areas of German life originated. Aronson, *Heydrich*, 176–77.

47. The key law here was that of 26 April 1933, which established the Geheimes Staatspolizeiamt (Gestapa) at No. 8 Prinz-Albrecht-Strasse. Its purpose was to deal with political police tasks along with, or in place of, the normal police authorities. Buchheim, *Anatomy*, 145–46; Höhne, *Order of the Death's Head*, 84, 85.
48. Buchheim, *Anatomy*, 147; Höhne, *Order of the Death's Head*, 173.
49. Buchheim, *Anatomy*, 148; Höhne, *Order of the Death's Head*, 173.
50. Buchheim, *Anatomy*, 148–51; Koehl, *Black Corps*, 88.
51. Buchheim, *Anatomy*, 151; Höhne, *Order of the Death's Head*, 176.
52. Broszat, *Hitler State*, 211; Buchheim, *Anatomy*, 151; Koehl, *Black Corps*, 230.
53. Broszat, *Hitler State*, 270; Koehl, *Black Corps*, 88; Fest, *Face of the Third Reich*, 117.
54. Koehl, *Black Corps*, 109–211; Buchheim, *Anatomy*, 291–301.
55. Buchheim, *Anatomy*, 153–56.
56. PS–2073. Koehl, *Black Corps*, 112; Buchheim, *Anatomy*, 157.
57. On the day of his appointment Himmler indicated that he intended to incorporate the police into the SS. See Buchheim, *Anatomy*, 203–4.
58. Buchheim, *Anatomy*, 157–66; Koehl, *Black Corps*, 112.
59. Buchheim, *Anatomy*, 144, 203.
60. Buchheim, *Anatomy*, 163; Koehl, *Black Corps*, 121–26; Höhne, Order of the Death's Head, 198–99. For a study of the Ordnungspolizei, see Hans-Joachim Neufeldt and others, *Zur Geschichte der Ordnungspolizei 1936–1945* (Koblenz: Bundesarchivs, 1957). See p. 107 for biographical details of Daluege.
61. Höhne, *Order of the Death's Head*, 63, 76–77, 193–95; Koehl, *Black Corps*, 56, 69–70, 94, 121–23.
62. Koehl, *Black Corps*, 123–24.
63. Ibid., 123, 126, 129; Buchheim, *Anatomy*, 203–13, contains a discussion of the conditions for police entry into the SS.
64. Koehl, *Black Corps*, 113, 159–60, 174.
65. Stein, *Waffen SS*, xxix, xxx. Einsatzgruppe A, for example, reported that it had 133 Ordnungspolizei members within its ranks. See L–180.
66. Koehl, *Black Corps*, 161. In the summer of 1938 Heydrich had ordered the submission of proposals for the amalgamation of the Security Police and the SD. Browder, "SIPO and SD." 245. See also pp. 273–309 for a summary of the subsequent proposals and problems encountered.
67. Koehl, *Black Corps*, 162–63.
68. L–361. Internal correspondence would use "Reichssicherheitshauptamt" as the heading, while other circumstances might entail the use of the headings "Reichsführer SS and Chief of the German Police," or "The Reich Minister of the Interior." Offices IV and V would use "Geheimes Staatspolizeiamt" or "Reichskriminalpolizeiamt", respectively. The incorrect use of these titles required periodic clarification. Browder, "SIPO and SD," 348.
69. L–361.
70. See L–361; Buchheim, *Anatomy*, 175–76.
71. Koehl, *Black Corps*, 161. It is likely that the SD was retained as a party rather than a state organization after the formation of the RSHA since this allowed Himmler to maintain his power base within the National Socialist movement. See Buchheim, *Anatomy*, 169.
72. Buchheim, *Anatomy*, 175–76.
73. See L–361 and organizational charts of the RSHA as of 1 January 1941 and 1 October 1943, respectively. L–185 and L–219. During the transition period from the beginning of September until the decree of September 27, there was a lot of confusion in Berlin as the changeover to the new offices stabilized. See Browder, "SIPO and SD," 342–43.
74. In 1940 Office I was divided in two: the new Office I, headed by Bruno Streckenbach, was concerned with personnel matters; Office II, under Werner Best, dealt with organization, administration, and legal matters. The former Office II under Franz Six became Office VII, which was responsible for ideological research and evaluation. Included in this shuffle was the departure of Werner Best from the RSHA due to differences of opinion with Heydrich. See Buchheim, *Anatomy*, 173–74; L–185, L–219; Höhne, *Order of the Death's Head*, 257–58; Koehl, *Black Corps*, 128, 162. An eighth Office, dealing with military intelligence, previously

the domain of the Abwehr, was created in 1944 when the RSHA took over the functions of the Abwehr. See David Kahn, *Hitler's Spies: German Military Intelligence in World War II*, (New York: Macmillan, 1978), 268–71. PS–2346. By the time Ernst Kaltenbrunner took over as Heydrich's replacement as head of the RSHA on 30 January 1943, the labyrinthine organization occupied thirty-eight buildings throughout Berlin. Jacques Delarue, *The Gestapo: A History of Horror* (New York: Morrow, 1964), 262. For Kaltenbrunner's takeover, see Peter R. Black, *Ernst Kaltenbrunner: Ideological Soldier of the Third Reich* (Princeton N.J.: Princeton Universtity Press, 1984), 127–33.

    75. See L–185, L–219.

    76. L–185.

    77. L–185. As of 1 October 1943 another Group (IVF) had been added. This had five subsections. L–219.

    78. Kahn, *Hitler's Spies*, 10, 266. By January 1945 Office VI had twelve Groups and forty-eight subsections. Ibid., 262.

    79. Buchheim, *Anatomy*, 180; (Case 9) affidavit by Walter Blume, 22 October 1947, Defense Exhibit Blume 4; English transcript of the trial of the Einsatzgruppen leaders at Nuremberg (Case 9), hereafter Tr. Tr. 2797.

    80. The RSHA and Einsatzgruppen positions held by these men were as follows: Otto Ohlendorf: head of Office III, leader of Einsatzgruppe D, returned as head of Office III; Arthur Nebe: head of Office V, leader of Einsatzgruppe B, returned as head of Office V; Heinz Jost: head of Office VI, leader (after Franz Walter Stahlecker) of Einsatzgruppe A; Martin Sandberger; head of Group I B 3, leader of Einsatzkommando 1a, returned as head of Group VI 6; Willy Seibert: head of Group III D, deputy chief of Einsatzgruppe D; Erwin Weinmann: head of Group IV D, leader of Sonderkommando 4a; Alfred Filbert: head of Group VI A, leader of Einsatzkommando 9; Erwin Schulz: head of Group I B, leader of Einsatzkommando 5, returned as head of Office I; Albert Rapp: leader of Sonderkommando 7a, head of Group VI C; Karl Tschierschky: leader of Einsatzkommando 1, head of Group VI C; Friedrich Panzinger: head of Group IV A, leader (after Humbert Achamer-Pifrader) of Einsatzgruppe A; Franz Six: head of Office II, head of Office VII, leader of Vorkommando Moskau, returned as head of Office VII; Eugen Steimle: leader of Sonderkommando 7a, leader of Sonderkommando 4a, head of Group VI B; Werner Braune: head of Sonderkommando 11 B, liaison officer of the RSHA to the Reichstudentenführer Dr. Scheel; Paul Schulz: officer in Group I A 5, head of Sonderkommando 11B; Emil Haussmann: officer of Einsatzkommando 12, officer in Group I F; Erich Müller: deputy chief, Group III B, leader of Einsatzkommando 12; Heinz Schubert: officer in Einsatzgruppe D, officer in Group I A 4; Walter Haensch: deputy in Group I D, leader of Sonderkommando 4 B, returned to Office I; Erich Ehlinger: served first as leader of Sonderkommando 1b, KdS Kiev, leader of Einsatzgruppe B, then as head of Office I. See L–185, L–219, NO–5111; Kahn, *Hitler's Spies*, 262, 263; see the biographical sketches and the tables listing the leaders of the Einsatzgruppen and the Kommandos with the time periods when they served, in Krausnick and Wilhelm, *Die Truppe*, 639–46.

    81. Marlis G. Steinert, *Hitler's War and the Germans: Public Mood and Attitude during the Second World War* (Athens, Ohio: Ohio State University Press, 1977), 16.

    82. The SS operations in Poland and those carried out earlier in Czechoslovakia and Austria do not fall within the scope of this study. See Krausnick, *Die Truppe*, 19–106.

Chapter 2. Reporting in the Third Reich

    1. Wilhelm, *Die Truppe*, 341.

    2. Hans Buchheim, *Totalitarian Rule: Its Nature and Characteristics* (Middletown, Conn.: Wesleyan University Press, 1968), 16.

    3. Ibid., 19.

    4. See Otto Dov Kulka, " 'Public Opinion' in Nazi Germany and the 'Jewish Question,' " *The Jerusalem Quarterly* 25, (1982): 122; Aryeh L. Unger, "The Public Opinion Reports of the Nazi Party," *The Public Opinion Quarterly* 29, (1965): 565.

5. Unger, "Public Opinion Reports," 565. One of the successes of Goebbels's Propaganda Ministry (at least at the beginning) was its ability to respond to the varying moods of the population. See Fest, *Face of the Third Reich*, 83.

6. Steinert, *Hitler's War*, 2.

7. PS-2284.

8. Unger, "Public Opinion Reports," 566.

9. Ibid.

10. Ibid., 567, 573; Steinert, *Hitler's War*, 14. Steinert (22–23, notes 74 and 75) cites sources of guidelines issued to party and SD reporters.

11. Unger, "Public Opinion Reports," 566–69.

12. Steinert, *Hitler's War*, 5.

13. Ibid., 16.

14. Stokes, "Sicherheitsdienst," 13–14; Steinert, *Hitler's War*, 11.

15. See Ernest K. Bramsted, *Goebbels and National Socialist Propaganda 1925–1945*, (London: Cresset Press, 1965).

16. Steinert, *Hitler's War*, 23, note 87.

17. Stokes, "Sicherheitsdienst," 213–20.

18. Ibid., 13.

19. Steinert, *Hitler's War*, 15–17.

20. Ibid., 11–14. Towards the end of the war each military district in the Reich tried to strengthen the will to continue fighting and reported to Berlin on public response to the unfolding events. Stokes, "Sicherheitsdienst," 14.

21. See Michael Burleigh, *Germany Turns Eastwards: A Study of Ostforschung in the Third Reich* (Cambridge: Cambridge University Press, 1988). The invasion of the Soviet Union extended the scope of the Publikationsstelle. Burleigh (218) provides a list of research report titles for 1941, typical of the SD reports in the Einsatzgruppen reports. For example, these included the following titles: (May) The Distribution of the Germans in Lithuania; (August) The Formation of States by Germanic Peoples in the East; (September) The Bolshevisation of Schools in Latvia; (October) The Impoverishment of Estonia During a Year of Bolshevik Rule. Reports on Jews were written. See pp. 243, 266–74, 281–82.

22. Burleigh, *Germany Turns Eastwards*, 9. Within this framework of reporting on the east, the Institut für deutsche Ostarbeit was created in Krakow on 20 April 1940. Ibid., 257.

23. Ibid., 244–46.

24. Ibid., 268.

25. Aronson, *Heydrich*, 176–77. See Bernhard Vollmer, ed. *Volksopposition im Polizeistaat. Gestapo und Regierungsberichte 1934–1936* (Stuttgart: Deutsche Verlags-Anstalt, 1957), for a collection of Gestapo and government reports from Aachen dating from March 1934 to 1936. Of particular interest are the reports written by Heinz Seetzen. See Vollmer, *Volksopposition*, 196–385, passim. Seetzen was an example of a Gestapo officer who later served in the Einsatzgruppen, first as leader of Sonderkommando 10a and later as leader of Einsatzgruppe B. Seetzen committed suicide on 28 September 1945 in Hamburg. See Krausnick and Wilhelm, *Die Truppe*, 642, 646. Although employing somewhat different headings and subheadings, the monthly government reports to the Reich minister of the Interior generally dealt with a similar range of topics: the mood of the population, church and state matters, the political cultural situation, hostile activities, and Jews. See Vollmer, *Volksopposition*, passim. (See the guidelines for Gestapo reports mentioned in the text.) For reports concerning Jews, see Kulka (note 4, including that author's continuation of the same article in *The Jerusalem Quarterly* 26 (1983): 34–45.)

26. For an extensive collection of SD and Gestapo reports concerning the churches in Germany over a ten year period, see Heinz Boberach, ed., *Berichte des SD und der Gestapo über Kirchen und Kirchenvolk in Deutschland 1934–1944* (Mainz: Matthias-Grünewald, 1971).

27. See Boberach, *Berichte*, xxxii–xxxiii. For excerpts from these reports, see 552 ff.

28. Wilhelm, *Die Truppe*, 341.

29. Höhne, *Order of the Death's Head*, 69–70.

30. Koehl, *Black Corps*, 30; Aronson, *Heydrich*, 48.

31. Stokes, "Sicherheitsdienst," 24–25; Höhne, *Order of the Death's Head*, 69.

32. Stokes, "Sicherheitsdienst," 27–28; Aronson, *Heydrich*, 55.

33. Aronson, *Heydrich*, 56 ff.

34. Browder, "SIPO and SD," 194, 196; Steinert, *Hitler's War*, 14.

35. Wolfgang H. Kraus and Gabriel A. Almond, "Resistance and Repression under the Nazis," in *The Struggle for Democracy in Germany*, ed. Gabriel A. Almond (Chapel Hill, N.C.: University of North Carolina Press, 1949), 39.

36. See for example, the Sonderberichte concerning church related matters in Boberach, *Berichte*, passim.

37. Höhne, *Order of the Death's Head*, 226–27.

38. See Buchheim, *Anatomy*, 167–69; Höhne, *Order of the Death's Head*, 226–27; Heinz Boberach, ed. *Meldungen aus dem Reich: Auswahl aus den Geheimen Lageberichten des Sicherheitsdienstes der SS 1939–1944.* (Neuwied and Berlin: Hermann Luchterhand, 1965), xiii, xiv.

39. Another section, "Folkdom and Public Health," was added to the Meldungen aus dem Reich in April 1940. Boberach, *Meldungen*, xv–xvi.

40. Ibid., xvii.

41. Ibid.

42. See Steinert, *Hitler's War*, 23, note 77. At Nuremberg Ohlendorf testified that the reports were sent to "all Reich departments and authorities." Tr. 505. Earlier situation reports on the domestic scene had been praised by Göring at a ministerial conference on 18 September 1939. Göring ordered that the reports were to be sent to all the ministers and that the problems revealed in the reports be corrected immediately. Browder, "SIPO and SD," 337.

43. See Boberach, *Berichte*, passim. In the east the overlapping of responsibilities was a frequent occurrence within the Einsatzgruppen. Concerning economic matters, especially those relating to agriculture, the Security Police themselves were often directly concerned with this subject in addition to the SD reporters.

44. See the process as it relates to SD reports, in Stokes, "Sicherheitsdienst," 78–80, 144.

45. The Reports from the Reich contained relatively little discussion of the Jews. See Boberach, *Meldungen*, xxi; Steinert, *Hitler's War*, 134; Stokes, "Sicherheitsdienst," 200–4.

46. I am grateful to Otto Dov Kulka for bringing these documents to my attention and for providing me with copies. The two documents cited appeared in Kulka's article, " 'Public Opinion' in National Socialist Germany and the 'Jewish Question.'" (In Hebrew.) *Zion, Jewish Quarterly for Research in Jewish History* XL (1975): 193, 204.

47. PS–3363.

48. PS–078.

49. PS–502.

50. Ibid.

51. PS–078.

52. The final reports were by no means completely uniform with respect to each Einsatzgruppe's presentation of its operations. See Chapter 9.

53. Koehl, *Black Corps*, 30–31.

54. Unger, "Public Opinion Reports," 571.

55. Kahn, *Hitler's Spies*, 253; Browder, "SIPO and SD," 338.

56. Wilhelm, *Die Truppe*, 336.

Chapter 3. How the Einsatzgruppen Reports Were Compiled

1. The problems of inaccuracy and incompleteness that resulted from the way the original reports were processed will not be dealt with for the moment. This will be discussed in later chapters.

2. Koehl, *Black Corps*, 160.

3. Heinrich Müller had been a pilot during the war. Shlomo Aronson, *Beginnings of the Gestapo System: The Bavarian Model in 1933* (Jerusalem: Israel Universities Press, 1969), 2.

4. Browder, "SIPO and SD," 418. Browder questions Gerald Reitlinger's assessment of the leaders as having been failures. Ibid., 416–18.

5. For the background of the leaders of Einsatzgruppe A, see Wilhelm, *Die Truppe*, 281–85.

6. Krausnick, *Die Truppe*, 145. Einsatzgruppe B was originally called Einsatzgruppe C, and Einsatzgruppe C was called Einsatzgruppe B. As of 11 July 1941, "for reasons of organization" the designation of these two Einsatzgruppen was reversed. The Kommando numbers remained unchanged, resulting in the interruption of the numerical order of the Kommandos from north to south. See Operational Situation Report 19. (Hereafter in the notes the Operational Situation Reports will be cited as OSR.)

7. See Krausnick and Wilhelm, *Die Truppe*, 145–50, 287. According to one estimate, Einsatzgruppe D had a total strength of about six hundred men, including a company of Ordnungspolizei. Affidavit by Heinz Schubert, 7 December 1945, NO–5111. Otto Ohlendorf estimated that Einsatzgruppe D had between four hundred to five hundred men and had at its disposal approximately 170 vehicles. Affidavit of Otto Ohlendorf, 24 November 1945, PS–2620. As of October 1941 Einsatzgruppe A reported a total strength of 990 people. L–180.

8. L–180.

9. Affidavit of Walter Blume, 22 October 1947, Defense Exhibit Blume 4. The size of the Einsatzkommandos of Einsatzgruppe B was estimated as being between 130 and 150 men, while the Sonderkommandos included between sixty and seventy men. Tr. 810.

10. Einsatzgruppe A alone had 172 motorcycle drivers. L–180.

11. Tr. 2794.

12. Blume Defense Exhibit 4. In Sonderkommando 4a, for example, the man in charge of all vehicles was Walter Ostermann. See affidavit of Walter Ostermann, 23 November 1947, Blobel Defense Exhibit 11.

13. Tr. 1514.

14. Tr. 1103, 2490, 2560, 4575, 5813.

15. See the example of Einsatzkommando 6. Tr. 2797.

16. For example, Sonderkommando 4a apparently did not have an independent radio installation. Tr. 1513–1514.

17. Affidavit and supplement by Karl Hennicke, 2 October 1947 and 28 November 1947, Defense Exhibits Radetzky 13 and 14. Affidavit by Walter Blume, 22 October 1947, Defense Exhibit Blume 4. Tr. 1670–1671.

18. See the list of leaders and staff officers and their positions for Einsatzgruppe A as well as those for Einsatzkommando 2 in Wilhelm, *Die Truppe*, 290–93. For a description of the staff of Einsatzgruppe D, see affidavit by Heinz Schubert, 7 December 1945, NO–5111. The headquarters staff of Einsatzgruppe B numbered about sixty men, including the commanding officer, an adjutant, a department chief, administrative assistants, the signal corps, guard personnel, and drivers. Tr 810.

19. Affidavit by Heinz Schubert, 7 December 1945, NO–4816.

20. Affidavit by Karl Hennicke, 2 October 1947, Defense Exhibit Radetzky 13; Affidavit by Walter Blume, 22 October 1947, Defense Exhibit Blume 4; Affidavit by Kurt Lindow, 21 July 1947, NO–4327; Affidavit by Heinz Schubert, 4 February 1947, NO–2716; Tr. 1545–1546, 2490, 2493, 2557–2559; Wilhelm, *Die Truppe*, 291.

21. Testimony of Paul Blobel. Tr. 1671.

22. British Intelligence was able to intercept many of the wireless messages sent from the east to Berlin. On 13 September 1941 ORPO Chief Kurt Daluege warned that top secret reports might be deciphered by the enemy. Daluege ordered that reports on executions henceforth be sent by courier and not by radio. The British deciphered many reports that gave details on the mass shootings. The ban imposed by Daluege was apparently not strictly observed. See F. H. Hinsley and others, *British Intelligence in the Second World War: Its Influence on Strategy and Operations*, Vol. 2 (London: Her Majesty's Stationery Office, 1981), 669–73.

23. Affidavit by Erich Naumann, 27 June 1947, NO–4150; Affidavit by Rudolf Fumy, 23 October 1947, Defense Exhibit Ohlendorf 53.

24. Affidavit by Heinz Schubert, 4 February 1947, NO–2716; Affidavit by Otto Ohlendorf, 24 April 1947, NO–2890. Einsatzgruppe B sent written reports about every three weeks. See

letter from Erich Naumann, leader of Einsatzgruppe B to Waldemar Klingelhoefer, commander of Vorkommando Moskau, No–5450. Concerning the reporting of the numbers of persons executed by Einsatzgruppe D, Willy Seibert testified that the reports sent to Berlin "contained at the end always the same sentence: during the time of the report so and so many people were executed. The number had been omitted in the report, and in this report which the signal man Fritsch made out, of course as a result of a dictation by me, or by Ohlendorf, in this report he went into the signal room and from the reports of the Einsatzkommandos during the period that the report was covering, he took out the numbers and he added them for this period of the report, and this figure then was coded by him personally in the signal room, and did not appear in the written reports for reasons of secrecy; this had been ordered by Ohlendorf." Tr. 2591–2592.

25. Affidavit by Heinz Schubert, 4 February 1947, NO–2716.

26. See interrogation of Günther Knobloch by the Zentrale Stelle Ludwigsburg, 30 January 1959, in Wilhelm, *Die Truppe*, 337. See also testimony of Kurt Lindow in LKA-Baden-Württemberg, 3 December 1956, in Wilhelm, *Die Truppe*, 340, 341. Office III of the RSHA, for example, apparently requested SD reports from Einsatzgruppe D. Affidavit by Hans Ehlich, 8 December 1947, Defense Exhibit Seibert 2.

27. Affidavit by Hans Ehlich, 10 December 1947, Defense Exhibit Jost 28.

28. See NOKW–256.

29. Affidavit by Otto Ohlendorf, 24 April 1947, NO–2890; Affidavit B by Otto Ohlendorf, 20 November 1945, in *Nazi Conspiracy and Aggression*, Vol. 8, 598–602. In this statement Ohlendorf claimed that Himmler stated that Hitler had informed army leaders of the tasks of the Einsatzgruppen. Affidavit by Walter Blume, 22 October 1947, Defense Exhibit Blume 4. See also Tr. 1511, 1513–1514, 1520, 2563.

30. Examples of reports to the army are included in the following Nuremberg documents: NOKW–586, NOKW–628, NOKW–631, NOKW–635, NOKW–636, NOKW–641, NOKW–1165, NOKW–3234, NO–3453, NO–2066, NO–2073, PS–3012.

31. Tr. 1548, 1556.

32. Affidavit by Kurt Lindow, 21 July 1947, NO–4327. Interrogation of Günther Knobloch in Wilhelm, *Die Truppe*, 337–38.

33. Aronson, *Beginnings of the Gestapo*, 2; Höhne, *Order of the Death's Head*, 142, 177, 178. For details of Müller's early career, see Aronson, *Beginnings of the Gestapo*, 2–5, 26–30.

34. Aronson, *Beginnings of the Gestapo*, 26.

35. Affidavit by Rudolf Fumy, 23 October 1947, Defense Exhibit Ohlendorf 51. Müller's influence on the reports continued to be felt.

36. Affidavit of Kurt Lindow, 21 July 1947, NO–4327. Affidavit of Kurt Lindow, 20 September 1945, PS–2542.

37. Affidavit by Kurt Lindow, 21 July 1947, NO–4327. In this statement, Lindow, after being shown examples of the reports, said that he recognized the initials written on the various reports as those of RSHA officials as well as handwritten notes by Günther Knobloch. In his statement of 3 December 1956 (LKA Baden–Württemberg) Lindow stated he did not summarize the Operational Situation Reports, nor did Vogt. Lindow stated he did compile the Activity and Situation Reports. See Wilhelm, *Die Truppe*, 340. See also interrogation of Knobloch, ibid., 337, 338; affidavit by Rudolf Fumy, 23 October 1947, Defense Exhibit Ohlendorf 51; affidavit by Willy Litzenberg, 8 November 1945, PS–2752. See also Tr. 3495.

38. Statement by Kurt Lindow, 3 December 1956, in Wilhelm, *Die Truppe*, 340.

39. Cited in an internal letter to the Offices of the RSHA dated 21 October 1941. This two-page letter, written on Müller's behalf, was included in Operational Situation Report (OSR) 126. In the report dated the next day (4 July 1941) the title page included in the left-hand margin for the first time the name of this signal officer, Theodor Paeffgen. OSR 12. For Paeffgen, see the next chapter.

40. See OSR 125.

41. Previously cited Müller letter of 21 October 1941 (note 39) in OSR 126.

42. Affidavit of Hans Ehlich, 16 January 1948, Defense Exhibit Nosske 5. Ehlich was born on 1 July 1901 in Leipzig. From 1 February 1937 until the end of the war he was a full-time SD

employee. Ehlich, a medical doctor, at first became a specialist for questions of race and public health in the Main Office II 2 of the SS Main Office and held the same position in Office III after the formation of the RSHA. At the end of October 1939 Ehlich worked as an SD Officer on matters concerning immigration and resettlement, and at the beginning of March 1940 he became chief of Group III B (Folkdum and Public Health) in the RSHA. Affidavit by Hans Ehlich, 10 December 1947, Defense Exhibit Jost 28. Friedrich Rang confirmed that Ehlich worked on the reports for his section in the Kommandostab and that Gustav Nosske (leader of Einsatzkommando 12 and head of Group IV D 5) acted as Heinrich Müller's deputy in the Kommandostab conferences. Affidavit of Friedrich Rang, 24 September 1947. NO–5153. See also Affidavit by Otto Ohlendorf, 24 February 1947, NO–2890.

43. Affidavit by Otto Ohlendorf, 24 February 1947, NO–2890.

44. Affidavit of Hans Ehlich, 16 January 1948, Defense Exhibit Nosske 5. The manager (Geschäftsführer) of the Kommandostab was appointed by the Gestapo.

45. Affidavit by Friedrich Rang, 24 September 1947, NO–5153. Rang was born in Grottau on 9 April 1899. His earliest jobs involved military service and teaching agriculture. From January 1935 to spring of 1941 Rang was press referent with the SD and the Gestapo as well as referent with the chief of the Civilian Administration of AOK III. From January to July 1943 he was chief of Group IV C, and in July 1943 he became leader of Group IV D where he remained until March 1944 (NO–5153). For a further description of the Kommandostab, see Tr. 3490. That alterations by the Kommandostab had to be confirmed would indicate that Müller (as well as other Office chiefs) retained some measure of control over the reports.

Chapter 4. General Features of the Operational Situation Reports

1. The first seven reports were either signed by or on behalf of Müller.

2. It is interesting to note the strictness with which this title was adhered to among many German officials. When examining a document during a police interrogation in Jerusalem, Adolf Eichmann noted that the sender of the document wrote the "Chief of the Security Police and the Sicherheitsdienst." Eichmann immediately corrected this by saying, "That's wrong, of course, it has to be "Chief of the Security Police and the SD." See Jochen von Lang and Claus Sibyll, ed., *Eichmann Interrogated: Transcripts from the Archives of the Israeli Police* (Toronto: Lester & Orpen Dennys, 1983), 144.

3. See Chapter 1, note 68.

4. The number of copies first appeared in the sixth report.

5. Reich top secret.

6. OSR 101, 103, 104, 112, 114, 118, 123, 124, and 125 did not contain this section. Some reports had this heading but did not include any reports under it.

7. As these reports in this section were not reports of the four Einsatzgruppen, they lie outside the scope of this study (with one or two exceptions).

8. The heading is missing in OSR 20 and 23.

9. OSR 21, 22, 24, 25, 30, 42, 48, 83.

10. Interrogation of Günther Knobloch by the Zentrale Stelle Ludwigsburg, 30 January 1959 in Wilhelm, *Die Truppe*, 338. Knobloch stated that the distribution list for the Activity and Situation Reports was the same as for the Operational Situation Reports. Wilhelm points out that while Canaris's name was not included in the distribution lists, it is probable that Canaris became aware of the reports via internal OKW distribution lists. Wilhelm, *Die Truppe*, 338.

11. For example, at least twenty-two different officials in the Foreign Office read copies of the Activity and Situation Reports. See Christopher R. Browning, *The Final Solution and the German Foreign Office. A Study of Referat D III of Abteilung Deutschland, 1940–43* (New York: Holmes & Meier, 1978), 72–79. It is also known that Hitler was kept up to date on the Einsatzgruppen operations. On 1 August 1941 Heinrich Müller sent coded messages to the Einsatzgruppen leaders stating that "the Führer is to be kept informed continually from here

about the work of the Einsatzgruppen in the East." Mention was made also of sending photographs, etc., illustrating the operations. See Gerald Fleming, *Hitler and the Final Solution* (Berkeley, Calif.: University of California Press, 1984), 45, 109–10. During the period after April 1942 compilations of reports about partisans were sent back to the east in order to inform the authorities there how the enemy operated. See the testimony of Gustav Nosske, Tr. 3490–3493.

12. OSR 126 was the last report to include the Political Overview heading. It did so immediately after the Locations and Lines of Communication list. In that the previous three reports (123–125) had not included this heading, the Political Overview section had already been phased out.

13. Affidavit by Theodor Paeffgen, 6 August 1947, NO–4761. Paeffgen was born 12 June 1910 in Cologne. He studied law in Geneva, Bordeaux, Edinburgh, and in Bonn, where he graduated from the university in Bonn in 1933. After further studies and a number of assignments in Cologne, Paeffgen was recruited in 1938 for work in the SD. He was later transferred to the RSHA. On 1 November 1941, after his section within Group II D was discontinued, Paeffgen was appointed to the State Police in Tilsit. An assignment in Allenstein from May to August 1942 was followed by Paeffgen's return to the RSHA as leader of Group VI D. He remained there until the end of the war. Ibid. Paeffgen's statement makes no mention of an assignment with a Kommando in the east. Paeffgen was characterized by his superiors as being of the correct "Nordic" racial type, unexcitable, undynamic, a good methodical worker whose political philosophy was in order. He was not considered suitable as a Kommando leader in antipartisan operations in Russia. See Kahn, *Hitler's Spies*, 7, 262, 264, 266.

14. Reports that contained a complete Locations and Communications list were OSR 126, 129, 132, 135, 138, 139, 141, 144, 146, 148, 149, 150, 151, 152, 154, 155, 156, 160, 161, 162, 165, 166, 168, 171, 172, 179, 186, 188, 190, and 191.

15. Affidavit of Willy Litzenberg, 8 November 1945, PS–2752. The Locations list was not always complete and did not include every area where Teilkommandos operated.

16. Himmler order determining the functions of the Higher SS and Police Leaders, 21 May 1941, NOKW–2079. In the occupied eastern territories there were four Higher SS and Police Leaders. They were: HSSPL (North) Hans Adolf Prützmann, replaced by HSSPL Friedrich Jeckeln; HSSPL (Center) Erich von dem Bach-Zelewski; HSSPL (South) Jeckeln, replaced by Prützmann; HSSPL Gerret Korsemann was installed in the Caucasus in the summer of 1942. Earlier Korsemann had been on special assignment, with his headquarters in Rovno. See OSR 126. Jeckeln was appointed HSSPL for northern Russia on 31 October 1941 and for Ostland on 11 December 1941. See Fleming, *Hitler and the Final Solution*, 98. Jeckeln served in this capacity until 18 January 1945. See Ruth Bettina Birn, *Die Höheren SS-und Polizeiführer*: Himmlers Vertreter im Reich und in den besetzten Gebieten (Düsseldorf: Droste Verlag, 1986), 331, 337, 339, 342. For further analysis of the powers of the Higher SS and Police Leaders, see Buchheim, *Anatomy*, 213–24.

17. Some reports did include the names of these leaders in the area of Einsatzgruppe B as well. See OSR 166 and 168.

18. These leaders were known as Befehlshaber der Sicherheitspolizei und des SD (BdS). Under each BdS were several Kommandeure der Sicherheitspolizei und des SD (KdS). Operational Situation Report 149 (22 December 1941) was the first report to include the KdS ranks. As of this date in the Locations list, the Kommandos of Einsatzgruppe A were no longer designated as such, although within the reports proper they continued to be called Sonderkommandos and Einsatzkommandos. For a discussion of these police forces see Buchheim, *Anatomy*, 180–87; and Hilberg, *Destruction of the European Jews*, Vol. 1, 368–72.

19. OSR 19, 31, 67, 94, 116.

20. OSR 19, 31, 34, 43.

21. OSR 19, 37, 60, 101.

22. OSR 19, 63, 101, 132.

23. Affidavit of Walter Schellenberg, 26 November 1945, PS–3710.

24. This heading was not included in OSR 153, 161, 164, 165, 168, 169, 174, 176, 178, 181–185, 187, 193–195. OSR 141 and 160 had only the heading Occupied Territories.

25. OSR 18. See also affidavit by Theodor Paeffgen, 6 August 1947, NO–4761.

26. See Robert Wolfe, introductory notes (1961) to the National Archives and Records Service (NARS) Microfilm Publication T 175, roll 233. (See Appendix E.) See also Krausnick and Wilhelm, *Die Truppe*, 649. On 16 February 1945 all files dealing with anti-Jewish measures were ordered destroyed to prevent them from being captured by the enemy. Saul Friedlander, "From Anti-Semitism to Extermination: A Historiographical Study of Nazi Policies Toward the Jews and an Essay in Interpretation," *Yad Vashem Studies* XVI (1984): 15, note 36.

Chapter 5. The Killing Operations: Methods of Presentation

1. See Hilberg, *Destruction of the European Jews*, Vol. 3, 863–989; Yitzhak Arad, *Belzec, Sobibor, Treblinka: The Operation Reinhard Death Camps* (Bloomington and Indianapolis: Indiana University Press, 1987).

2. See George L. Mosse, *The Crisis of German Ideology: Intellectual Origins of the Third Reich* (London: Weidenfeld and Nicolson, 1966); idem, *Toward the Final Solution: A History of European Racism*, (New York: Howard Fertig, 1978).

3. This subject will be discussed in Chapter 14.

4. See Eberhard Jäckel, *Hitler's Weltanschauung: A Blue-print for Power* (Middletown, Conn.: Wesleyan University Press, 1972).

5. Yehuda Bauer, "Genocide: Was it the Nazis' Original Plan?" *The Annals of the American Academy of Political and Social Science* 450 (July 1980): 39.

6. See Philip Friedman, "The Lublin Reservation and the Madagascar Plan: Two Aspects of Nazi Jewish Policy during the Second World War," *Yivo Annual of Jewish Social Studies* VII, (1953): 151–77; Jonny Moser, "Nisko: The First Experiment in Deportation," in *Simon Wiesenthal Center Annual* 2, Henry Friedlander and Sybil Milton, eds. (White Plains, N.Y.: Kraus International Publications, 1985), 1–30.

7. See Chapter 14.

8. See Appendix A for the representation of the four Einsatzgruppen within each report.

9. OSR 143. For other examples of approximate totals, see OSR 24, 88, 94, 125, 128, 135, 156, and 170.

10. See OSR 11, 20, 21, 45, 67, 73, 85, 86, 88, 89, 92, 94, 101, 108, 111, 119, 124, 136, 145, 148, 150, 159, 177, 184, 187, 190.

11. OSR 184. See also OSR 19, 21, 60, 86, 88, 101, 124, 132, 135, 165.

12. OSR 190. See also OSR 131, 132, 135, 143, 153, 170, 173, 177, 178, 184, 189, 193, 194, 195.

13. OSR 130. See also OSR 19, 31, 43, 67, 73, 116, 130, 136, 178, 186, 193.

14. Almost every report.

15. OSR 43, 67, 73.

16. OSR 73, 92.

17. OSR 86.

18. OSR 124.

19. Almost any report. In order to further lower the status of partisans, after August 1942 they were referred to as "bandits." See Timothy P. Mulligan, "Reckoning the Cost of People's War: The German Experience in the Central USSR," *Russian History* 9 (1982): 38.

20. See examples cited in the following chapter.

21. Almost any report.

22. OSR 108, 111, 193.

23. OSR 132, 184.

24. OSR 21, 43, 92, 124, 165, 178, 184, 193.

25. OSR 21, 47, 73, 92, 133.

26. See examples cited in the the following chapter.

27. OSR 73.

28. OSR 21, 47, 86, 92, 108.

29. See examples cited in the following chapter.

30. See examples cited in the following chapter.

31. OSR 43, 47, 73, 86, 92, 94, 111, 124, 129, 132, 135, 143, 156, 170, 173, 177, 178, 183, 184, 187, 189, 190.
32. OSR 124, 177.
33. OSR 183.
34. OSR 111.
35. OSR 157, 170.
36. OSR 67, 73, 124, 133.
37. OSR 43.
38. OSR 86, 94, 111, 170, 178, 184, 190.
39. OSR 47.
40. OSR 111.
41. OSR 21, 24, 43, 173, 191.
42. OSR 86.
43. OSR 80, 86, 92, 108, 191.
44. OSR 81.
45. OSR 173.
46. OSR 14, 47, 67, 73, 80.
47. OSR 24, 43, 47, 73, 86, 92, 94, 108, 111, 132, 135, 153, 156, 170, 173, 177, 189, 190, 193, 194.
48. See examples in discussion of "whispering propaganda" in the following chapter.
49. OSR 86, 94, 108, 124, 135, 143, 184.
50. OSR 24, 47, 124, 165, 187, 191, 193.
51. OSR 47, 67, 94, 111.
52. OSR 47.
53. OSR 47.
54. OSR 173, 187, 193.
55. OSR 73.
56. OSR 80.
57. OSR 92.
58. OSR 43, 124.
59. See Chapter 7 for an examination of the rationalization of the killings by the Einsatzgruppen reporters. Mention of national groups among the victims, Latvians, Ukrainians, and so on, tend to be coupled with reasons for their execution.
60. See Chapter 13, table 7, for a breakdown of the main reports listing the killing operations of each Einsatzgruppe and Kommando. See also Appendix B.
61. For example, see the operations of Sonderkommando 4a in Operational Situation Report 119.
62. OSR 11.
63. OSR 19, dated 11 July 1941. This report mentioned killings on July 2 and 3, as well as pogroms in Kovno (June 25 and 26).
64. Willy Seibert, the deputy chief of Einsatzgruppe D, testified to the fact that as the Einsatzgruppen got further into Soviet territory communications with Berlin became increasingly difficult. Tr. 2599.
65. OSR 154.
66. OSR 156.
67. OSR 157.
68. OSR 176.
69. OSR 190. This report lists 1,315 people killed by Einsatzgruppe C between 1 March and 3 April 1942.
70. OSR 155. This report includes events from 22 October 1941 to 2 January 1942.
71. For example, see report of Einsatzgruppe D in OSR 45.
72. OSR 154.
73. See Chapter 9.
74. Cited in Wilhelm, *Die Truppe*, 571–74, 638. The action mentioned in this document, carried out from 15 to 18 December 1941 (*Die Truppe*, 572), is the action depicted in the photographs reproduced in Plates 5a and b in Fleming, *Hitler and The Final Solution*.
75. See OSR 24 and 135.

76. See draft report of Einsatzgruppe A, PS–2273.

77. OSR 132. Activity and Situation Report 1 reported the "extreme psychic tension induced by the great number of liquidations." Otto Ohlendorf spoke of the strain involved in the use of gas vans. Tr. 701. See affidavit B by Otto Ohlendorf, 20 November 1945, in *Nazi Conspiracy and Aggression*, Vol. 8, 602. Ohlendorf, Paul Blobel, and Walter Haensch also employed mass firing at executions to avoid the problem of "personal responsibility" that shooting individuals in the neck entailed. See affidavit by Otto Ohlendorf, 5 November 1945, PS–2620. Affidavit by Paul Blobel, 6 June 1947, NO–3824. Statement by Walter Haensch, 21 July 1947, NO–4567. Werner Braune considered shooting more "honourable" than using gas vans. Affidavit by Werner Braune, 8 July 1947, NO–4234.

78. See affidavit by Paul Blobel, 18 June 1947, NO–3947.

79. OSR 133, 165, 168, and 178 included the names of Jews who were executed. It is probable that the Kommando reports sent to Kommando headquarters and to Berlin included more details concerning executions, including names of victims. These reports were destroyed. Heydrich's Operational Order 8 (cited in Chapter 2), dealing with the screening of prisoners in military camps, had demanded that a record be kept of all executions, including the names of the people killed. PS–502.

80. OSR 108. Other reports mentioned the use of hanging. See OSR 47, 107, 183, 184, 187, 193.

81. Mathias Beer, "Die Entwicklung der Gaswagen Beim Mord an den Juden" *Vierteljahrshelfte für Zeitgeschichte*, 35 (1987): 412.

82. Christopher R. Browning, "The Development and Production of the Nazi Gas Van" in *Fateful Months: Essays on the Emergence of the Final Solution* (New York: Holmes & Meier, 1985) 63. See Beer, "Die Entwicklung der Gaswagen," 412–13.

83. Willy Seibert testified that the word "shot" was used in reports when victims had been killed by gas vans. Seibert stated that reports he received from the Kommandos never mentioned the use of the vans. Tr. 2602.

84. Affidavit by Otto Ohlendorf, 5 November, 1945, PS–2620; Affidavit by Ernst Biberstein, 2 July 1947, NO–4314; Affidavit by Werner Braune, 8 July 1947, NO–4234; Affidavit by Paul Blobel, 6 June 1947, NO–3824. In this affidavit Blobel mentioned using a gas van in September or October 1941. Beer concludes that this date was incorrect. See Beer, "Die Entwicklung der Gaswagen," 412.

85. Browning, *Fateful Months*, 65, 102, note 38.

86. Affidavit by Erich Naumann, 27 June 1947, NO–4150.

87. See testimony of Otto Ohlendorf on the use of gas vans by Einsatzgruppe D, Tr. 694, 695, 697, 698. Gas vans were used in Serbia. For a discussion of their use there see Christopher R. Browning, "The Final Solution in Serbia: The Semlin Judenlager—A Case Study," *Yad Vashem Studies* XV (1983): 55–90. Ernst Biberstein, head of Einsatzkommando 6, testified that the use of gas vans was "easier for both the victim and the executioner." He further claimed, "Like the electric chair, the procedure had been invented for humanitarian reasons." Tr. 2785.

Chapter 6. Examples of Killing Operations

1. Cited in Kulka, "Public Opinion," 129.

2. See report by Walter Stahlecker up to 15 October 1941 (hereafter L–180). The Germans photographed and filmed these actions as evidence that the Lithuanians and Latvians had carried out "spontaneous executions."

3. OSR 8 and L–180.

4. OSR 15, 24.

5. OSR 11, 14. The latter report mentioned that in Tarnopol seventy Jews, rounded up by Ukrainians after the discovery of mutilated German corpses, were killed with dynamite.

6. OSR 9.

7. OSR 47.

8. OSR 20.

9. OSR 28.

10. OSR 24.

11. Activity and Situation Report 2, NO–2652.

12. See OSR 19, 31, 43, 47, 111, Activity and Situation Reports 2 and 6, L–180, and PS–2273.

13. OSR 81.

14. OSR 14. For the order disarming the partisan detachments, see B. Baranauskas and K. Ruksenas, comps. *Documents Accuse* (Vilnius: Gintaras, 1970), 83.

15. See OSR 111, 128, 150, 153, 155, 190.

16. OSR 155.

17. Ibid. See also PS–2273. For a discussion of the number of Estonians believed to have been deported to the Soviet Union during 1940–41, see J. H. Jackson, *Estonia* (London: Allen & Unwin, 1948), 241. For a discussion of the number of Estonian Jews who escaped or were deported, see Dov Levin, "Estonian Jews in the USSR (1941–1945): Research Based on Survivors' Testimony," *Yad Vashem Studies* XI (1976): 273–97. The Germans were not sure of the exact number of Jews who had been deported by the Soviets. They estimated that about half the Estonian Jews had escaped (about 2,000–2,500). See OSR 111.

18. See Hilberg, *Destruction of the European Jews*, Vol. 1, 273–390, for a survey of the killing operations of the Einsatzgruppen. Hilberg divides these operations into two sweeps, the first of which was completed by the fall of 1941 in the Baltic States. At this time the first sweep was still continuing in the southern areas.

19. OSR 170. Some areas had been combed more than once. OSR 95 mentioned that areas that "had already been worked on" were being cleared of Jews, partisans, and communists.

20. OSR 190.

21. OSR 101, 106.

22. OSR 125. For a discussion of the mass killings in Odessa, see Dora Litani, "The Destruction of the Jews of Odessa in the Light of Rumanian Documents," *Yad Vashem Studies* VI (1967): 135–54.

23. OSR 80.

24. OSR 151. By this time Jeckeln had become HSSPL North. The 30 November 1941 massacre was supposed to have been carried out by HSSPL forces alone, but after a while twenty men from Einsatzkommando 2 were called in to help. See OSR 156, which gave a total of 10,600 Jews shot in this operation. OSR 155 stated that the Jewish population of Riga had been reduced from 29,500 to 2,600 as a consequence of the actions of HSSPL Jeckeln. For a detailed description of the November 30 killings, see Fleming, *Hitler and the Final Solution*, 78–79.

25. OSR 135.

26. OSR 94. In Rovno, on 6 and 7 November 1941, Jeckeln directed the killing of fifteen thousand Jews. OSR 143.

27. OSR 60.

28. OSR 92.

29. Ibid.

30. OSR 124.

31. OSR 154, 155, and 163. See also Activity and Situation Report 9.

32. OSR 181.

33. OSR 190.

34. OSR 88. See the report by Karl Jäger for details of the shootings carried out in these districts.

35. OSR 150.

36. OSR 111.

37. For other examples, see OSR 89, 92, 94, 101, 108, 119, 136, 148, 150, 159, 177, 187.

38. For a survey of the literature concerning the destruction of European Gypsies, see Gabrielle Tyrnauer, *Gypsies and the Holocaust: A Bibliography and Introductory Essay* (Montreal: Interuniversity Centre for European Studies and Montreal Institute for Genocide Studies, 1989).

39. Tr. 515.

40. Letter from Karl Jäger, head of Einsatzkommando 3, to his subordinate KdS leader in

Ukmerge, in Baranauskas and Ruksenas, *Documents Accuse*, 264–65. See also letter from the RSHA to police officials, 5 November 1942, L–179.

41. OSR 150.

42. OSR 153.

43. See OSR 157, 178, 184, 190. Activity and Situation Report 11, covering the month of March 1942, mentioned that one thousand Jews and Gypsies had been executed in the Crimea. Examples of killings of Gypsies by other Einsatzgruppen were found in other reports, including OSR 94, 108, 119, 165, 181, 194, and 195. Some "nonmigrating Gypsies" were spared death. See Hilberg, *Destruction of the European Jews*, Vol. 1, 367, note 107. According to a member of Sonderkommando 10b, Gypsies and Krimtchaks were also killed with gas vans. Affidavit by Robert Barth, 8 October 1943, NO–3663.

44. Rudolf Loewenthal, "The Extinction of the Krimchaks in World War II," *The American Slavic and East European Review* 10 (1951): 132.

45. Ibid., 131, 132.

46. Joseph Tenenbaum, *Race and Reich: The Story of an Epoch* (New York: Twayne Publishers, 1956), 495. In Report from the Occupied Eastern Territories 4, the total figure of Krimtchaks was given as six thousand. See Tr. 616–618, 626–628.

47. OSR 153.

48. OSR 190.

49. OSR 150.

50. OSR 157.

51. See Hilberg, *Destruction of the European Jews*, Vol. 1, 367; Tenenbaum, *Race and Reich*, 495; Loewenthal, *The Extinction of the Krimchaks in World War II*, 131, 132. In the Caucasus another group of mountain Jews known as the Tati were killed by Einsatzgruppe D. Many of them had been killed by the local population before the arrival of Germans in the area in October 1942. Some Tati were later saved from liquidation because they were able to give proof that they differed in blood from the Jews and that this difference had enabled them to enjoy equality under the Czarist regime. Tenenbaum, *Race and Reich*, 495. Hilberg, *Destruction of the European Jews*, Vol. 1, 367, note 107. Killings of Tati are not mentioned in the Operational Situation Reports.

52. See Philip Friedman, "The Karaites under Nazi Rule," in *On the Track of Tyranny*, Max Beloff, ed., (Freeport, N.Y.: Books for Libraries Press, 1971), 106–11. See also Burleigh, *Germany Turns Eastwards*, 219–220, for further discussion of the Karaites and excerpts from reports dealing with their treatment.

53. See Arno J. Mayer, *Why Did the Heavens Not Darken? The "Final Solution" in History* (New York: Pantheon Books, 1988), 381–88.

54. OSR 132.

55. OSR 88. Other German documents were found giving evidence of extensive killing of mental patients. These include a reference to the just cited killings in Aglona on 22 August 1941. This source mentioned that about seven hundred adults and fifty children were killed in this action, including twenty healthy children who had been temporarily transferred there. See Document USSR41.

56. OSR 108. This same report mentioned the killing of 632 mental patients in Minsk and 836 in Mogilev. In both cases the patients were given "special treatment."

57. OSR 94.

58. OSR 86.

59. For example, see OSR 135, 156, 173, and 184.

60. OSR 135, 143.

61. OSR 135, 156, and 173. At Mariupol, a Kommando of Einsatzgruppe D gassed all the syphilitic patients in a hospital. This caused an entire group of TB patients to escape to the woods in fear. Gerald Reitlinger, *The House Built on Sand: The Conflicts of German Policy in Russia, 1939–1945.* (London: Weidenfeld and Nicolson, 1960), 201.

62. Wehrmacht policy toward the shooting of hostages was based on the premise that this practice was an acceptable form of conduct. See Richard Cavell Fattig, "Reprisal: The German Army and the Execution of Hostages during the Second World War," unpublished doctoral dissertation, University of California, San Diego, 1980, 22. Even earlier in Poland in

1939 mass shootings by the SS were often viewed as "hostage executions" in response to anti-German activities. Ibid., 26.

63. PS–829.

64. OSR 136.

65. OSR 37, 149, and 183.

66. OSR 45.

67. OSR 143.

68. OSR 135.

69. OSR 92.

70. OSR 19, 24, 107, 108, 119, and 184.

71. OSR 73.

72. OSR 108.

73. OSR 88.

74. For example, see OSR 163. In Audrini eighty-eight women and fifty-one children were listed as victims. See also OSR 88 and 131.

75. OSR 193.

76. OSR 119. At Nuremberg Ohlendorf stated that the Kommando reports he received usually did not specify women and children among the victims, although they were certainly included. Tr. 694, 695.

77. OSR 47.

78. See OSR 73. This report mentioned that in the camp in Minsk 733 civilians were killed as they were found to have "Asiatic blood." See also OSR 21, 36, 133.

79. OSR 92. See also OSR 21.

80. See Robert Koehl, *RKFDV: German Resettlement and Population Policy, 1939–1945: A History of the Reich Commission for the Strengthening of Germandom*, (Cambridge, Mass.: Harvard University Press, 1957).

81. See OSR 156, 178. Prisoner-of-war camp commanders even gave preference to ethnic German prisoners for administrative work. See OSR 47.

82. For example, see OSR 86.

83. See Chapter 10. References to victims designated as "Russians" were found throughout the reports. See OSR 73, 81, 178. Of course, communist officials, etc., were mostly Russians and thus the numbers of Russians killed were greater than those called "Russians" in the reports. The same is true for other groups. In OSR 131 there is a reference to the killing of two Latvians: in Libau, Einsatzgruppe A killed these two for robbing Jewish apartments. They had identified themselves as German security policmen. Both were shot, and the incident was mentioned in the local newspaper as a warning to combat looting.

84. OSR 183.

85. Ibid.

86. Ibid. Other anti-Bandera operations were described in a number of reports, including OSR 177 and OSR 129, which mentioned the considerable influence Bandera propaganda was having on the population.

87. OSR 183. Other actions against Ukrainians were included in OSR 20, 37, 42, 47, 58, 59, 73, and 119.

88. OSR 81.

89. Ibid.

90. For a discussion of the Einsatzgruppen and the killing of prisoners of war, see Krausnick, *Die Truppe*, 251–54. See also Christian Streit, "The German Army and the Policies of Genocide," in Gerhard Hirschfeld, ed., *The Policies of Genocide: Jews and Soviet Prisoners of War in Nazi Germany* (London: Allen & Unwin, 1986), 1–14; and in the same volume, see Jürgen Förster, "The German Army and the Ideological War against the Soviet Union," 15–29. Three major studies of the subject are: Alfred Streim, *Sowjetische Gefangene in Hitlers Vernichtungskrieg: Berichte und Dokumente, 1941–1945* (Heidelberg: C.F. Müller Juristischer Verlag, 1982); Christian Streit, *Keine Kameraden: Die Wehrmacht und die sowjetischen Kriegsgefangenen 1941–1945* (Stuttgart: Deutsche Verlags-Anstalt, 1978); Szyman Datner, *Crimes Against POWs: Responsibility of the Wehrmacht* (Warsaw: Zachodnia Agencja Prasowa, 1964).

91. PS–078. Full agreement with the army had not been achieved as of 28 June 1941.

92. Affidavit of Hadrian Ried, Prisoner-of-War Camp Commander, Brest-Litovsk, 22 October 1947, NO–5523.

93. Operational Order 8, 17 July 1941, PS–502 (NO–3414). See also two letters dated 13 and 25 October 1941, signed by Heinrich Müller, describing procedures for executing prisoners of war and the gathering of intelligence in the prisoner-of-war camps. NO–3421.

94. Affidavit by Kurt Lindow, 30 September 1945, PS–2542. The testimony of Lindow has been called into question. See Gerald Reitlinger, *The Final Solution: The Attempt to Exterminate the Jews of Europe, 1939–1945* (South Brunswick, N.J.: T. Yoseloff, 1968), 200.

95. Datner, *Crimes Against POWs: Responsibility of the Wehrmacht,* 91.

96. For a discussion of the details of this meeting and further relations between the RSHA and the army concerning prisoners, see Hilberg, *Destruction of the European Jews,* Vol. 1, 334–41.

97. Heydrich directive to various Security Police leaders, 12 September 1941, NO–3416.

98. OSR 128. This report was issued almost a month after Reichenau had issued his order of 10 October 1941 to his troops, telling them to be harsh with the "Jewish-Bolshevists," and to have "full understanding for the necessity of a severe but just revenge on subhuman Jewry." It is interesting to notice in this order that Reichenau actually complains that "gruesome partisans and unnatural women" are treated as prisoners of war, that is, they are not shot, but are instead sent to the prisoner-of-war camps. NOKW–309.

99. OSR 132. See also OSR 47, which mentioned screening operations in prisoner-of-war camps; OSR 111, which reported the killing by Sonderkommando 4a of fifteen commissars, four Jews, and fourteen partisans in camps; and OSR 116, which mentioned the request by the Wehrmacht that Security Police investigations be undertaken in the transit camps.

100. OSR 143.

101. OSR 149.

Chapter 7. Reasons and Justifications for the Killings

1. The term "Final Solution" was in itself a euphemism.

2. For an analysis of the use of disguised language and related matters on the part of the Nazis, see Hilberg, *Destruction of the European Jews,* Vol. 1, 328–34, and Vol. 3, 1007–29.

3. For a discussion of the laws of war as they relate to hostages, see J. A. Appleman, *Military Tribunals and International Crimes* (Westport, Conn.: Greenwood Press, 1971), 29–39; H. W. William Caming, "Nuremberg Trials: Partisans, Hostages and Reprisals," *The Judge Advocate Journal* 4 (1950): 16–22; Lord Wright, "The Killing of Hostages as a War Crime," *The British Year Book of International Law* 25 (1948): 296–310. In case 7, *United States v. Wilhelm List, et al.* (The Hostage Case, sometimes referred to as the Southeast Case) the shooting of hostages under strictly limited conditions was allowed. The same court also found that Greek and Yugoslav partisans could not be classified as lawful belligerents as proscribed by the Hague Regulations. They were, therefore, not entitled to the same privilege of protection as regular soldiers. Appleman, *Military Tribunals,* 192; Caming, "Nuremberg Trials," 17–20. In Case 12, *United States v. Wilhelm von Leeb, et al.* (The High Command Case), the Tribunal ruled that in this instance no attempt had been made to comply with the pre-conditions concerning hostages as outlined in the Hostage Case. Caming, "Nuremberg Trials," 21; Wright, "The Killing of Hostages," 308.

4. For example, see Tr. 544, 545, and 5731.

5. The Tribunal in the Einsatzgruppen trial stated in its Judgment that the "reports have spoken for themselves as to the extent to which they respected the limitations laid down by International Law on reprisals in warfare." Tr. 6761.

6. Summary of conference held on 16 July 1941. L–221.

7. OSR 21. In OSR 34 Einsatzgruppe B simply stated that "Large-scale executions of Jews will follow immediately." In OSR 31 Nebe directly acknowledged the desire to kill all the Jews, although he stated this was not possible during the war.

8. See Krausnick, *Die Truppe,* 165–66; idem, "Hitler und die Befehle an die Einsatzgrup- pen im Sommer 1941," in *Der Mord an den Juden im zweiten Weltkrieg: Entschlussbildung*

und Verwirklichung, Eberhard Jäckel and Jürgen Rohwer, eds. (Stuttgart: Deutsche Verlags-Anstalt, 1985), 97–98.

9. PS–3363.

10. OSR 128 contained what is perhaps the most flagrant use of the reprisal argument. Einsatzgruppe C reported that it had killed eighty thousand people. About seventy-five thousand of these were "killed as a retaliatory measure."

11. For a discussion of Nazi use of language, see Nachman Blumenthal, "On the Nazi Vocabulary," *Yad Vashem Studies* 1 (1957): 49–66. See also Henry Friedlander, "The Manipulation of Language," in *The Holocaust: Ideology, Bureaucracy and Genocide,* Henry Friedlander and Sybil Milton, eds. (Millwood, N.Y.: Kraus International Publications, 1980), 103–13.

12. Hilberg, *Destruction of the European Jews,* Vol. 3, 1012.

13. For example, see OSR 9, 20, 24, 29, 47, 51, 113.

14. In a discussion of the language of the reports, Yaacov Lozowick has noted that the euphemisms and beliefs of the Nazis prevented the Einsatzgruppen from comparing their activities with those of the Soviets. See Yaacov Lozowick, "Rollbahn Mord: The Early Activities of Einsatzgruppe C, *Holocaust and Genocide Studies,* Vol. 2, no. 2, (1987): 232.

15. See almost every report. For a discussion of the word "action," including its meanings both before and during the war, see Nachman Blumenthal, "Action," *Yad Vashem Studies* IV (1960): 57–96.

16. OSR 37.

17. OSR 73, 92, 94.

18. OSR 97.

19. OSR 48, 86, 94, 108, 125.

20. OSR 60, 92, 149.

21. OSR 88, 89, 92, 94, 95, 101, 111, 117, 119, 129, 136, 148, 150, 153, 155, 177, 187.

22. OSR 92, 108, 124, 189, 194.

23. OSR 37, 73, 101, 106.

24. Almost every other report.

25. OSR 89, 108, 155, 178, 184, 190.

26. OSR 63, 89, 95, 107, 136, 153.

27. OSR 92, 108.

28. OSR 92.

29. OSR 170.

30. OSR 19, 85, 146, 148.

31. OSR 153.

32. OSR 157.

33. OSR 86.

34. OSR 108.

35. Hilberg, *Destruction of the European Jews,* Vol. 1, 329.

36. See previous list in Chapter 5.

37. NOKW–1962.

38. Tr. 3754–3756.

39. Cited in Büchler, "Kommandostab Reichsführer–SS," 15.

40. Cited in Yury Boshyk, ed., *Ukraine during World War II: History and Its Aftermath* (Edmonton: Canadian Institute of Ukrainian Studies. University of Alberta, 1986), 175.

41. It is interesting to note that it was felt necessary to present an "explanation" to the German population of the events in the east to counter the "distorted" rumors of the treatment of the Jews, which had been passed on by soldiers on leave who had witnessed the shootings. See PS–3244.

42. See, for example OSR 38, 40, 88, 96, 106, 108, 125, 131, 150.

43. See, for example OSR 73, 92, 108, 124, 133, 147. These same reports also included killings under the equally formulaic heading, Measures against Criminals and Plunderers.

44. In the second to last report, OSR 194, the Kommandos of Einsatzgruppe B reported that between 6 and 30 March 1942 they had "specially treated" 3,733 people. Of these 3,258 were Jews.

45. OSR 94.

46. Lozowick, "Rollbahn Mord," 232.

47. NO–5196. This order was issued in the context of the statistical report on the "Final Solution" prepared by Richard Korherr.

48. OSR 19.

49. OSR 14.

50. OSR 24.

51. OSR 97, 106.

52. OSR 73.

53. OSR 92.

54. OSR 108. See OSR 124 for another example of rumor spreading that had a bad effect on the population.

55. OSR 73. See also OSR 124, 179, and 183.

56. OSR 184.

57. OSR 124.

58. OSR 92. This report pointed out that 176 Jews were shot by Einsatzgruppe B for "opposing the establishment of the ghetto." See also OSR 108, 133.

59. OSR 108, 124, 136, 154.

60. OSR 92, 107, 108, 124, 148.

61. OSR 34, 92, 136.

62. OSR 178.

63. OSR 111.

64. OSR 124, 133, 148.

65. OSR 119. See also OSR 94.

66. OSR 86.

67. OSR 73.

68. OSR 14, 45, 86.

69. Almost every other report gives examples of reprisals for suspected sabotage.

70. OSR 24.

71. See Hilberg, *Destruction of the European Jews*, Vol. 3, 1023.

72. For other examples, see OSR 88, 92, 94, 124, 149, 155 and report of Einsatzgruppe A, PS–2273.

73. OSR 195.

74. OSR 148.

Chapter 8. Factors Affecting the Rate and Extent of the Killings

1. Estimates of losses on Soviet and German sides are as follows: Soviets: total dead, 20 million soldiers and civilians; Germans: 1,001,000 dead; 3,966,000 wounded; 1,288,000 missing. Albert Seaton, *The Russo-German War 1941–1945* (London: Arthur Barker Limited, 1971), 586.

2. Hitler made this statement at a speech before Wehrmacht leaders.

3. Activity and Situation Report 1.

4. L–180.

5. Ibid.

6. This number included the original Jewish population of the country plus the Jews of the Vilna area incorporated into Lithuania in September 1939, plus the additional numbers of refugees who had escaped from German occupied Poland. About fifteen thousand Jews managed to escape before the arrival of the Germans. For details concerning these figures, see Yitzhak Arad, "The 'Final Solution' in Lithuania in the Light of German Documentation," *Yad Vashem Studies* XI (1976): 234.

7. Solomon Schwarz, *The Jews in the Soviet Union* (Syracuse, N.Y.: Syracuse University Press, 1972), 220.

8. Hilberg, *The Destruction of the European Jews*, Vol. 1, 291.

9. Schwarz, *The Jews in the Soviet Union*, 220.

10. Hilberg, *Destruction of the European Jews*, Vol. 1, 291.

11. Ibid.

12. See John Erickson, *The Road to Stalingrad*, (London: Weidenfeld and Nicolson, 1975), 101–35.

13. Seaton, *Russo-German War*, 98. Alexander Werth, *Russia at War 1941–1945* (New York: Dutton, 1964), 153 and 164.

14. Hans-Adolf Jacobsen, ed. *Generaloberst Halder Kriegstagebuch: Tägliche Aufzeichnungen des Chefs des Generalstabes des Heeres 1939–1942* Vol. 3. (Stuttgart: W. Kohlhammer Verlag, 1963), 38.

15. OSR 106. This report also complained that many Jews were able to escape from Shitomir to the western Ukraine.

16. See L–180, and Jäger report. See Arad, "The 'Final Solution' in Lithuania," 234.

17. Arad, "The 'Final Solution' in Lithuania," 246, 247.

18. Seaton, *Russo-German War*, 103.

19. Mendel Bobe, ed. *The Jews in Latvia* (Tel Aviv: Association of Latvian and Estonian Jews In Israel, 1971), 352.

20. Joseph Tenenbaum, *Underground: The Story of a People* (New York: Philosophical Library, 1952), 366. Ten days later one thousand two hundred Jews were killed in the nearby woods.

21. Werth, *Russia at War*, 153.

22. Seaton, *Russo-German War*, 137.

23. Arnold Toynbee and Veronica Toynbee, eds., *Hitler's Europe. Survey of International Affairs, 1939–1946*, Vol. 4 (London: Royal Institute of International Affairs. Oxford Univerity Press, 1954), 632. Charkov was occupied on 24 October 1941 by the Germans, who found about twenty thousand Jews left in the city. See Reitlinger, *The Final Solution*, 237, 238.

24. OSR 34.

25. Werth, *Russia at War*, 193, 194. Seaton, *Russo-German War*, 175. See mention of the delay in the advance in OSR 34.

26. See Krausnick, *Die Truppe*, 195.

27. OSR 13.

28. OSR 25.

29. OSR 92. See also OSR 88. Einsatzgruppe C, after the front in its area had stabilized, reported that the long stay of Einsatzkommando 5 led to an accumulation of "cases." OSR 177.

30. See L–180.

31. OSR 19, 26. On 19 July Einsatzgruppe B reported that the lack of troops beyond the former border between Russia and Poland had led to a security vacuum. OSR 27.

32. OSR 43, 56, 58, 66, 67, 78.

33. OSR 156.

34. OSR 164.

35. OSR 19. Feodossija was also recaptured during the winter of 1941–42. During this period the Soviets executed collaborators. See report from Seibert of Einsatzgruppe D to 11th Army Ic, 16 April 1942, NOKW–628.

36. OSR 60. This report declared that in the interim the advance Kommandos of Sonderkommando 4a would remain in Wassilkow to "clean up" that area.

37. L–180.

38. See Levin, "Estonian Jews in the USSR (1941–1945)," 273–97. See also PS–2273.

39. For example, see OSR 10, 13, 37, 95, 135, 145. See also L–180.

40. OSR 89.

41. OSR 101.

42. OSR 145.

43. Concerning this subject in Schwarz, *The Jews in the Soviet Union*, we read as follows: "The great majority of the Jewish population of the German-occupied areas were neither encouraged nor given an opportunity by the Soviet authorities to flee." Schwarz states that there was a schedule of priorities for evacuation operations based on administrative and economic considerations. He concludes that "several hundred thousand Jews" were

evacuated, including about half the Jewish farm population in the Crimea. See Schwarz, pp. 197, 198, 220–32. Another source indicates that in Lithuania many Jews were included among the government and party officials, leftist intellectuals, and writers who were evacuated. The Jews who tried to escape on their own consisted mainly of men of army age and included youth groups. Many Jews were forced back from the borders and perished under German bombs, or at the hands of Lithuanian fascists and the Einsatzgruppen. Only an estimated fifteen thousand Jews were able to cross the Soviet border or the front-line. Dov Levin, *Fighting Back: Lithuanian Jewry's Armed Resistance to the Nazis, 1941–1945* (New York: Holmes & Meier, 1985), 27–28. Einsatzgruppe A estimated that seventy thousand out of the approximately ninety-five thousand Jews in Latvia remained in Latvia when the Germans marched in. PS–2273. Hilberg concludes that about 1.5 million Jews in the entire Soviet territories managed to escape. See Hilberg, *Destruction of the European Jews*, Vol. 1, 291. See also Wilhelm, *Die Truppe*, 621, 622.

44. OSR 40.
45. OSR 90.
46. OSR 123.
47. OSR 133. Compare this report with the description of the evacuation of people and factories in Erickson, *The Road to Stalingrad*, 232–37.
48. OSR 146.
49. OSR 135. Other reports mentioning the flight of Jews include OSR 47, 63, 94, 136.
50. OSR 81. For rumors of executions of Jews, see also OSR 90 and 150.
51. OSR 108.
52. OSR 47. See also OSR 135.
53. OSR 86.
54. OSR 94.
55. Ibid.
56. For a discussion of the long term goals and policies of German rule in the Soviet territories, see Alexander Dallin, *German Rule in Russia 1941–1945: A Study of Occupation Policies.* Second revised edition. (Boulder, Colo.: Westview Press, 1981). See also Reitlinger, *The House Built on Sand*; and Norman Rich, *Hitler's War Aims: The Establishment of the New Order* (New York: Norton & Company, 1974), 326–93. For a study of Rumanian rule in the Odessa region (Transnistria), see Alexander Dallin, *Odessa, 1941–1944: A Case Study of Soviet Territory under Foreign Rule* (Santa Monica, Calif.: The Rand Corporation, 1957).
57. See OSR 21, 31, 34, 73, 94. In OSR 43, a report by the leader of the Security Police and SD in Krakow referred to the ghettos as "separate dwelling areas," a euphemism if there ever was one. The ghettos were invariably located in the worst districts (a fact acknowledged by Stahlecker concerning the Riga Ghetto in his first summary report). Hilberg points out that the initial ghettoizations, which were carried out by the Kommandos themselves, were done for two reasons. First, certain communities had so many Jews it was not possible to kill them at once, and second, the Jews were needed as skilled laborers. See Hilberg, *Destruction of the European Jews*, Vol. 1, 343. See also L–180 concerning these two points.
58. OSR 11.
59. OSR 111.
60. OSR 151.
61. See Dallin, *German Rule in Russia*, 18, 19.
62. OSR 92.
63. OSR 94. Einsatzgruppe A complained about the attitude of members of the civil administration who "offered resistance, at times even a strong one, against the carrying out of larger executions. This resistance was answered by calling attention to the fact that it was a matter of carrying out basic orders." L–180.
64. OSR 94. See also PS–2273.
65. OSR 86.
66. Letter by Armament Inspector Ukraine, enclosing a report drafted by Oberkriegsverwaltungsrat Prof. Peter-Heinz Seraphim to General Thomas, Chief of the Industrial Armament Office in the OKW, 2 December 1941, PS–3257. Seraphim's report complained mainly about the "manner" of the executions and the brutalizing effect on those carrying out the shootings. His concern for the negative economic effects of the killing of the

Jews was also stressed, with little actual concern for the Jews. Seraphim was one of many scholars recruited to gather research on the east. For a discussion of Seraphim's career and his research on the Jews, see Burleigh, *Germany Turns Eastwards*, 116–17, 143–45, 220–22, 243, 247, 271, 281–82, 309, 314.

67. Bernd Wegner, "The 'Aristocracy of National Socialism:' The Role of the SS in National Socialist Germany," in Michael Marrus, ed., *The Nazi Holocaust: Historical Articles on the Destruction of European Jews*, Vol. 1, part 2 (Westport and London: Meckler Corporation, 1989), 402.

68. PS–3664.

69. PS–579. See also OSR 194.

70. OSR 193.

71. See Arad, "The 'Final Solution' in Lithuania," 263–72.

Chapter 9. Comparison of Methods of Reporting and Statistics of the Four Einsatzgruppen

1. It is probable that routine information, locations, dates, and numbers were not altered by the RSHA, although we cannot be certain about this.

2. Nebe was leader of Einsatzgruppe B until the end of October 1941. See Krausnick and Wilhelm, *Die Truppe*, 644. The material concerning Einsatzgruppe B in Operational Situation Report 133 dealt with events during October.

3. OSR 148, 149, 194.

4. OSR 194.

5. See Appendix A.

6. See interrogation of Günther Knobloch, 30 January 1959, in Wilhelm, *Die Truppe*, 337.

7. Affidavit by Heinz Schubert, 4 February 1947, NO–2716. This statement would appear to be contradicted by certain facts. Ohlendorf testified that he was in Berlin from the beginning of March to the end of April 1942. Tr. 554. Yet Einsatzgruppe D was certainly represented in the Operational Situation Reports during this period.

8. After Nikolajew became the headquarters, Einsatzgruppe D reports appeared more frequently.

9. OSR 18, 41, 46, 56, 66, 72, 76, 79, 82, 83, 84, 102, 109, 110, 114, 115, 126.

10. Exact totals for Kommandos and Einsatzgruppen after the last overall totals given in the reports are difficult to calculate. Even when the subsequent reports may contain statistics, we often encounter in the same reports places where no figures are included in the description of an operation. For example, the figure of 23,732 (table 1, Einsatzgruppe A chart) derived from OSR 165 to 195 is certainly incomplete, since OSR 181 mentions no numbers for the killings in Ussaditsche. The report states only that the village was burned down, and all the inhabitants were killed. Another example from OSR 183 may be cited. After mentioning that two men were hanged for sabotage at Selidowka, Sonderkommando 4a reported that it was planning on arresting and shooting communists as hostages. No further details were provided. Such examples of incompleteness are found throughout the entire series of reports.

11. This number was probably credited to the totals of Einsatzgruppe A. See Hilberg, *Destruction of the European Jews*, Vol. 3, 1215.

12. See, for example, the shootings in Balti (Belzy) as reported by Sonderkommando 10a in OSR 37. See also Activity and Situation Report 2. For the Odessa killings, see Litani, "The Destruction of the Jews of Odessa in the Light of Rumanian Documents," 135–54.

13. See Wilhelm, *Die Truppe*, 618.

14. See Hilberg, *Destruction of the European Jews*, Vol. 3, 1201–20, for a discussion of the problems involved in determining the number of Jews killed. Other tabulations of Jews killed in the Russian territories are found in Wila Orbach, "The Destruction of the Jews in the Nazi-Occupied Territories of the USSR", *Soviet Jewish Affairs*, Vol. 6, no. 2 (1976): 14–51. For another examination of the totals of the Einsatzgruppen figures, see Wilhelm, *Die Truppe*, 605–9, 618–22.

15. This will be dealt with in Chapter 13, which concerns the use of the reports as evidence at the Einsatzgruppen trial.

16. See, for example, the figures in OSR 80, 135, 143.

17. These causes of death, while not quantified, are occasionally alluded to in the reports. See, for example, the description of the conditions in the Riga ghetto found in PS–2273. See Tr. 6677, 6678.

18. There also is the possibility that killings were carried out by Kommandos that were not reported, although this is unlikely.

19. It must be kept in mind that this total includes all categories of victims.

20. It is assumed that the seventy-five thousand persons killed by Einsatzkommando 3 (OSR 94) are included in the numbers given for Einsatzgruppe A as a whole.

21. See Arad, "The 'Final Solution' in Lithuania," 245–46.

22. Actually, if one takes into account the further killings by detachments of Einsatzkommando 3 in various locations cited separately in Jäger's report, the number is greater.

23. The breakdown by Kommando, which began in Operational Situation Report 73, is as follows:

OSR 73: VK Moscow 144. SK7a 996. SK7b 886. EK8 6842. EK9 8096. Total: 16,964.

OSR 92: VK Moscow 312. SK7a 1,011. SK7b 1,153. EK8 11,354. EK9 9,974. Total: 23,804.

OSR 108: VK Moscow 2029. SK7a 1,252. SK7b 1,544. EK8 15,000. EK9 10,269. Total: 30,094.

OSR 125: VK Moscow 2,457. SK7a 1,344. SK7b 1,822. EK8 20,108. EK9 11,449. Total: 37,180.

OSR 133: VK Moscow 2,457. SK7a 1,517. SK7b 1,822. EK8 28,219. EK9 11,452. Total: 45,467.

The only other breakdown by Kommando occurred in Operational Situation Report 194 as follows: VK Moscow 52. SK7a 1,657. SK7b 82. EK8 1,609. EK9 273. Trupp Smolensk 60. Total: 3,733. The care with which Einsatzgruppe B seemed to record its statistics is seen by comparing Reports 125 and 133. The latter report mentioned that complete reports of VK Moscow, SK7b and EK9 had not yet arrived—hence the repetition of the totals for the Kommandos in both reports. Report 133, on the other hand, stated that SK7a shot 173 people during the time of the report. This tallies with that Kommando's total in Report 125, an example where such addition does work out.

24. See Wilhelm, *Die Truppe*, 620, note 4. Another document dealing with killings after May 1942 is the report by Kommandant Sauer that gave a figure of 26,200 Jews killed in Pinsk between 29 October and 1 November 1942. Document USSR 119a. The one hundred thirty-four thousand total cited in Krausnick and Wilhelm is the final total for Einsatzgruppe B used in our calculations.

25. See Arad, "The 'Final Solution' in Lithuania," 241, 242. This total amounts to at least five thousand. See also OSR 21 and 67.

26. Report No. 51 to Hitler, 29 December 1942. These killings were directed by HSSPL Prützmann. See Hilberg, *Destruction of the European Jews*, Vol. 3, 1212, note 32.

27. See OSR 19, 22, 37, 40, 45, 67.

28. For the complete text of the Korherr reports and related documents, see George Wellers, "The Number of Victims and the Korherr Report", *The Holocaust and the Neo-Nazi Mythomania*, Serge Klarsfeld, ed. (New York: The Beate Klarsfeld Foundation, 1978), 163–211. The same volume includes analysis of the reports. See 145–61. See also Hilberg, *Destruction of the European Jews*, Vol. 3, 1204–6, 1208–16. In January 1943 Himmler informed Kaltenbrunner, the head of the RSHA, of Korherr's assignment to prepare this report. Himmler was obviously not satisfied with the statistical reports of the RSHA. He informed Kaltenbrunner as follows: "The (RSHA) is hereby relieved of its statistical responsibilities in this area, since the statistical material submitted to date has consistently fallen short of professional standards of precision." According to Eichmann, Korherr worked on the report at Eichmann's office for "eight to fourteen days." See Fleming, *Hitler and the Final Solution*, 136.

29. The three numbers for Einsatzgruppe A require clarification. The 274,605 total is for the entire Einsatzgruppe up to February 1942. The 23,732 figure follows after this period, that is, from Operational Situation Reports 165 to 195. In turn, the sixty-five thousand total mentioned in Kube's letter to Lohse follows after the Operational Situation Reports.

30. The Higher SS and Police Leaders were in charge of other SS units that, along with, and independently from, the Einsatzgruppen, carried out mass killings. In addition to Waffen SS and Ordnungspolizei forces, these units included SS Brigades One and Two, as well as the SS Cavalry Brigade. In a study of these latter forces, Yehoshua Büchler has estimated that they killed at least one hundred thousand Jews. Büchler mentions some of the problems we have encountered in our study of the totals for the Einsatzgruppen, and he suggests that it is possible that much more documentary evidence has been hidden than has been revealed to date. Büchler also points out that the same group of Jews cited in some sources may well have been reported killed by other groups. See Büchler, "Kommandostab Reichsführer–SS," 20. For reports by the just cited SS groups operating in tandem with the Einsatzgruppen, see *Unsere Ehre Heisst Treue: Kriegstagebuch des Kommandostabes Reichsführer SS Tätigkeitsberichte der 1. und 2. SS-Inf.-Brigade, der 1. SS-Kav.-Brigade und von Sonderkommandos der SS*, ed. Fritz Baade and others (Wien, Frankfurt, Zurich: Europa Verlag, 1965.) These reports have much in common with the Einsatzgruppen reports.

31. Hilberg, *Destruction of the European Jews*, Vol. 3, 1219.

Chapter 10. Attitude and Collaboration of the Eastern Populations

1. A number of studies have dealt with the relationship between Jews and non-Jews in Eastern Europe. The subject of collaboration with the Germans still awaits comprehensive scholarly examination, although some of the works cited here are important initial steps in this direction. For studies of Jews in Eastern Europe, see Ezra Mendelsohn, *The Jews of East Central Europe Between the World Wars* (Bloomington, Ind.: Indiana University Press, 1983); Bela Vago and George L. Mosse, ed., *Jews and Non-Jews in Eastern Europe 1918–1945* (Jerusalem: Israel Universities Press, 1974); Wilhelm, *Die Truppe*, 294–321; Mayer, *Why Did The Heavens Not Darken?* [already cited] 39–89; Celia S. Heller, *On the Edge of Destruction: Jews of Poland Between the Two World Wars* (New York: Columbia University Press, 1977); Bobe, *The Jews in Latvia*; [already cited] Salo W. Baron, *The Russian Jew under Tsars and Soviets* (New York: Macmillan, 1976); Schwarz, *The Jews in the Soviet Union*. [already cited] For works dealing with Ukrainians and Jews, see Philip Friedman, "Ukrainian-Jewish Relations during the Nazi Occupation," in Philip Friedman, *Roads to Extinction: Essays on the Holocaust* (New York: Jewish Publication Society, 1980), 176–208; Stefan T. Possony, "The Ukrainian-Jewish Problem," *The Ukrainian Quarterly*, Vol. XL, no. 4, (1984): 369–81; John A. Armstrong, *Ukrainian Nationalism 1939–1945* (New York: Columbia University Press, 1955); Idem., "Collaborationism in World War II: The Integral Nationalist Variant in Eastern Europe," *Journal of Modern History* 40 (1968): 396–410; Boshyk, *Ukraine during World War II*; Peter J. Potichnyj and Howard Aster, eds., *Ukrainian-Jewish Relations in Historical Perspective* (Edmonton: Canadian Institute of Ukrainian Studies. University of Alberta, 1988).

2. Jackson, *Estonia*, 25.

3. Arthur E. Adams, *Bolsheviks in the Ukraine: The Second Campaign, 1918–1919* (New Haven, Conn.: Yale University Press, 1963), 142, 235, 236.

4. In Vilna alone, 102 factories owned by Jews were nationalized. Out of 370 businesses and stores that were nationalized, 265 belonged to Jews. Yitzhak Arad, *Ghetto in Flames: The Struggle and Destruction of the Jews in Vilna in the Holocaust* (Jerusalem: Yad Vashem, 1980), 22.

5. See Azriel Shochat, "Jews, Lithuanians and Russians 1939–1941," in Vago and Mosse, *Jews and Non-Jews in Eastern Europe 1918–1945*, 308. See Levin, *Fighting Back*, 21–25.

6. Shochat, "Jews, Lithuanians and Russians," 309. Arad, *Ghetto in Flames*, 10. Levin, *Fighting Back*, 24.

7. For Estonia, see Jackson, *Estonia*, 249. For Latvia, see Bobe, *The Jews in Latvia*, 352.

8. Shochat, "Jews, Lithuanians and Russians," 309. Levin, *Fighting Back*, 23.

9. Arad, *Ghetto in Flames*, 35–38.

10. Shochat, "Jews, Lithuanians and Russians," 309, 310. See also Levin, *Fighting Back*, 17–25.

11. Aharon Weiss, "Jewish-Ukrainian Relations in Western Ukraine during the Holocaust," in Potichnyj and Aster, *Ukrainian-Jewish Relations in Historical Perspective*, [already cited] 409–10.

12. Ibid., 411.

13. Ibid., 411–12.

14. Orest Subtelny, "The Soviet Occupation of Western Ukraine, 1939–41: An Overview," in Boshyk, *Ukraine during World War II*, [already cited] 12–13.

15. See Myroslav Prokop, "Ukraine in Germany's World War II Plans," *Ukrainian Quarterly* 11 (1955): 134–44.

16. The reports of the Nazi Party were marred by distortions, omissions, and even misrepresentations as the result of the covering up of shortcomings within its sphere of activity. See Unger, "Public Opinion Reports," 570–78.

17. See Kulka, "Public Opinion," 122.

18. Stokes, "Sicherheitsdienst," 126–28. See also Supplement, 28 November 1947, to affidavit of 2 October 1947, by Karl Hennicke, Defense Exhibit Radetzky 14.

19. Tr. 2489, 2490, 2558.

20. See Unger, "Public Opinion Reports," 565.

21. C–50.

22. See Wilhelm, *Die Truppe*, 335, concerning the SD reporting of the attitude of the population toward the Jews. The difficulty in gauging accurately the general political attitudes of the population in the Soviet territories under both German and Rumanian control resulted from the frequent existence of a large gap between attitude and behavior on the part of the Russian population. The attitude was generally pragmatic. The aim was to "stay out of trouble" and to keep tabs on the course of the war. This fact must be taken into account when trying to determine the response of the local population. See Dallin, *Odessa, 1941–1944*, 250–51.

23. Michael R. Marrus, *The Holocaust in History* (Toronto: Lester & Orpen Dennys, 1987), 95.

24. In a study of collaboration in Eastern Europe during World War II (dealing mainly with the Ukraine, Slovakia, and Croatia) it has been observed that the basic motivation for collaboration was the ethnic conflict among the population. Nationalist thinking in the Ukraine, for example, shared many of the tenets of the Nazi Party, above all, the placing of absolute value, to the detriment of all others, on the importance of the nation. This ethnic-centered collaboration is contrasted with collaboration motivated more by social antagonisms, as in the case of France. See Armstrong, "Collaborationism in World War II: The Integral Nationalist Variant in Eastern Europe," 396–410.

25. OSR 8.

26. OSR 23. No source for this message was included in the report.

27. OSR 19.

28. OSR 14.

29. OSR 17.

30. OSR 19, 31.

31. Activity and Situation Report 1.

32. OSR 10.

33. OSR 11.

34. OSR 17. Poles were the chief rivals of the Lithuanians in Vilna. Lithuanian police investigated Polish organizations, which were included in OSR 10. See Arad, *Ghetto in Flames*, 43–46.

35. OSR 19. OSR 24 reported the establishment of a Ukrainian Government that welcomed the Germans.

36. Reitlinger, *The House Built on Sand*, 145–47.
37. See Baranauskas and Ruksenas, *Documents Accuse*, 56, 57.
38. OSR 15.
39. OSR 22. Karl Ulmanis had been the leader of the Latvian government during most of Lativa's existence as an independent state (1918–40).
40. See, for example, the objections given by the Security Police to the presence of Valdmanis in the Latvian self-government in OSR 195.
41. OSR 81.
42. Ibid. OSR 31 also mentioned the greater "receptiveness" for German policies in the eastern regions. For examples of reports from non-Einsatzgruppen sources that showed a generally favorable reaction to the killings in the Ukraine, see Burleigh, *Germany Turns Eastwards*, 270.
43. OSR 125.
44. OSR 126. The policy of the Bandera wing of the OUN toward the Jews had changed as of August 1943. See Yaroslav Bilinsky, "Methodological Problems and Philosophical Issues in the Study of Jewish-Ukrainian Relations during the Second World War," in Potichnyj and Aster, *Ukrainian-Jewish Relations in Historical Perspective*, [already cited] 375.
45. OSR 34.
46. OSR 86.
47. OSR 133.
48. OSR 153.
49. OSR 190.
50. OSR 61.
51. OSR 47.
52. OSR 177.
53. OSR 178. This report combines the outright fabrication that the Jews had lots of food with the calculated avoidance of mentioning why their apartments had "become empty."
54. OSR 129.
55. OSR 92.
56. OSR 155.
57. OSR 106. In this case it is unlikely that they held this belief for long as the clothing of these Jews was given soon after to the people in Kiev. See Reitlinger, *The Final Solution*, 234. For Ukrainian awareness of Babi Yar, see also Bilinsky, "Methodological Problems and Philosophical Issues in the Study of Jewish-Ukrainian Relations during the Second World War," 379.
58. OSR 31.
59. OSR 43. Difficulties in inciting pogroms in the Ukraine and in Estonia were also encountered. See OSR 47 and 111. In OSR 27 Einsatzgruppe B reported that the population had to be asked to cooperate in seizing communists and Jews. Similarly Einsatzgruppe C reported that the inhabitants did not betray the Jews who were hiding. See OSR 127.
60. OSR 31.
61. OSR 165.
62. See Dallin, *German Rule in Russia*, 73, 74, 214, 215. Many other documents provide evidence that German officials were very aware of the negative effect the slaughter of women and children was having on the population in occupied areas. See for example, NOKW–469, NOKW–893, and NOKW–1487.
63. OSR 186.
64. See Hilberg, *Destruction of the European Jews*, Vol. 1, 322.
65. OSR 181.
66. OSR 125. See also OSR 179, 181.
67. OSR 181.
68. OSR 183.
69. OSR 179.
70. Bread was used as currency. See OSR 31.
71. OSR 179.
72. OSR 194.
73. OSR 179. This report, in spite of negative comments about the military, food, and fuel

situation, noted a more positive, calmer mood had settled in Brjansk and Kursk. (It should be noted that a report issued three weeks later stated that further reports on the morale in Brjansk, Kursk, and Orel had not been able to get through because of major snow drifts.) OSR 188.

74. OSR 183.

75. OSR 187.

76. OSR 32.

77. OSR 125. For the use of adolescents as agents, see OSR 130.

78. L–180. Einsatzgruppe D exhumed twenty-six corpses of persons shot in Mariupol by the NKWD. A public inquest was held, and the corpses were publicly buried. See OSR 136. When Einsatzgruppe C was confronted with the fact that Jews were numbered among those murdered by the retreating Soviets, this was dismissed with the explanation that these Jews knew too much about Soviet activities. OSR 24. OSR 150 declared that as the result of a propaganda campaign against the partisans a "temporary decline of mood" had set in.

79. Activity and Situation Report 10.

80. Ibid. See also OSR 195. By 1942 Joseph Goebbels also noted in his diary the changed feeling of the Ukrainians. He recognized that the Germans had hit the Russians, and especially the Ukrainians "too hard on the head." Goebbels further acknowledged that the Germans had been "much too thorough" and were always installing "a bureaucracy instead of building up a mere supervisory apparatus." See Louis P. Lochner, ed., *The Goebbels Diaries 1942–1943* (Garden City, N.Y.: Doubleday, 1948), 185, 246.

81. OSR 178.

82. See L–180, PS–2273. Sarah Neshamit has distinguished three categories among the Lithuanians who participated in the killing of Jews: 1) political activists, who hoped for Lithuanian independence, and who showed their loyalty to the Nazis by killing Jews and communists; 2) Lithuanian intellectuals, military, and government officials, who had lost their positions under the Soviets, or who had relatives deported or killed by the Soviets; and 3) opportunists who hoped to seize Jewish property. See Sarah Neshamit, "Rescue in Lithuania during the Nazi Occupation June 1941–August 1944," in *Rescue Attempts During The Holocaust. Proceedings of the Second Yad Vashem International Historical Conference*, April 1974. (Jerusalem: Yad Vashem, 1977), 295–96.

83. See OSR 8, 9.

84. L–180. The support of fascist elements in Lithuania and the desire to have them instigate pogroms in Lithuania preceded the war. There is evidence of the help Germany gave to the leaders of a secret National Socialist Party. It was originally intended that they stage pogroms against the Jews in Lithuania. The Germans agreed to offer financial assistance, but declined to offer weapons. See letter from Heydrich to Ribbentrop with enclosure concerning pogroms in Lithuania, 29 June 1939, PS–2953. See also Arad, *Ghetto in Flames*, 35–36.

85. OSR 14.

86. OSR 19.

87. Ibid.

88. OSR 21.

89. Ibid.

90. OSR 15. This force numbered about four hundred men. It was reported that so far four men had been killed by snipers.

91. Ibid.

92. OSR 9.

93. OSR 25. A survivor, a German Jew, who worked as a member of a burial team in Latvia, stated that the "Latvian SS wore Latvian military uniforms which were identified by a yellow armband and black death's head and numbers." Later in the summer of 1942, the Latvians wore German uniforms. Affidavit by Alfred Winter, 15 October 1947, NO–5448.

94. OSR 111. L–180. There seems to be a discrepancy in the reports as to the participation of the Estonian units in the killings. The two reports just cited both stated that the Self-Protection forces carried out executions. In the Einsatzgruppe A draft in the section under Estonia, we read as follows: "Only by the Security Police and the SD were the Jews gradually executed as they became no longer required for work." PS–2273. (This difference may be explained in that this quote probably does not refer to the initial killing of male Jews,

which were carried out by the Estonian units, but the subsequent weeding out of unfit laborers, who may not have been killed by the Estonians. At Nuremberg, Martin Sandberger stated that the Estonians participated in the executions. Tr. 2383.)

95. See also the Jäger report, discussed in Chapter 12.

96. PS–2273.

97. Ibid.

98. See OSR 48, 88, 131.

99. OSR 88. For other evidence of Latvian involvement in killing operations from other sources, see the killing of Jews at Rositten, in Reitlinger, *The Final Solution*, 196; and Secret Report of HSSPL describing operations involving the 15th Latvian Police Battalion, Riga, 6 November 1942, PS–1113.

100. PS–2273.

101. See Activity and Situation Report 1. Estimates of the numbers of Ukrainians killed by the Soviets vary. See Bilinsky, "Methodological Problems and Philosophical Issues in the Study of Jewish-Ukrainian Relations during the Second World War," 376. What is certain is that Ukrainians *were* murdered by the retreating Soviets. See Alfred M. de Zayas, *The Wehrmacht War Crimes Bureau, 1939–1945* (Lincoln, Neb.: University of Nebraska Press, 1989), 210–27, 240–44. De Zayas (214) distinguishes the three stages of murders carried out in Lvov: 1) the killing of Ukrainian and Polish political prisoners by the NKVD in June 1941; 2) the pogroms by Ukrainian and Polish civilians against Jews; and 3) the murder of Polish intellectuals and approximately seven thousand Jews by the Germans. De Zayas (223) presents evidence that German military authorities issued orders to prevent violence against the Jewish population.

102. OSR 9.

103. OSR 11. According to OSR 24, at Zloczow, before they withdrew, the Soviets murdered seven hundred Ukrainians, mainly the intelligentsia. It was claimed that Jews had played a leading part in these killings.

104. OSR 14. See also OSR 19.

105. OSR 20, 24.

106. OSR 24. This report included a recommendation by "reliable Ukrainian circles" that a propaganda campaign be started to convince Ukrainians in the Russian Army to desert. The Russians had warned them that the Germans would kill them on the spot. The Russians were said to have ordered the destruction of all crops and asked the farmers to retreat as well or else they, too, would be shot by the Germans. The report regretted that this propaganda campaign was not started.

107. OSR 80. Paul Blobel, head of Sonderkommando 4a, admitted at Nuremberg that he directed executions in Korosten in August or September 1941. He confirmed that the Jews were seized by the Ukrainian militia, the local population, and members of Sonderkommando 4a. The Ukrainian militia as well as the police took part with his Kommando in the shootings. Affidavit of Paul Blobel, 6 June 1947, No–3824. OSR 47 reported that Ukrainian militia Kommandos shot people who did not "please" them. For charts of the organization and subordination of Sonderkommando 4a for June and August 1941, including the Ukrainian militia units, see Blobel Defense Exhibits 1 and 2.

108. OSR 88. This report also stated that as a consequence of the military standstill the Kommandos intensified their activities and received the help of both ethnic Germans and reliable Ukrainians.

109. OSR 119.

110. See OSR 106, 119, 132, 156, 173.

111. OSR 106. In light of the evidence linking Ukrainians with Sonderkommando 4a, it is probable that Ukrainian militia assisted at these killing operations in Kiev, although they are not specifically named in this report. One non-Jewish witness at Babi Yar, the watchman of the Lukianow Cemetery, stated that Ukrainian police formed a corridor through which Jews were herded to the execution site. See Martin Gilbert, *The Holocaust: The Jewish Tragedy* (London: Collins, 1986), 202, 203. The clothing of the Jews killed at Babi Yar and Shitomir was made available to the National Socialist People's Welfare Agency. Over one hundred trucks were required to transport this clothing. OSR 132.

112. OSR 135. One cannot but question the statement that "almost everyone" denounced

their relatives and friends, given the consequences of this action. We see here, also, another example of the incredible irony found often in the reports: a Kommando engaged in systematic murder complaining of the "low level of the moral character" of the local population.

113. OSR 132.

114. OSR 86.

115. OSR 19.

116. OSR 37.

117. OSR 40. See also report by Major Hans-Wolf Riesen concerning the arrest and executions by Rumanian units and Sonderkommando 10b in Czernowitz, 9 July 1941, NOKW-587.

118. OSR 63.

119. OSR 125. See OSR 156 for details of Rumanian participation in antipartisan operations.

120. OSR 145. See OSR 190, where the "active cooperation" of the Crimean population is mentioned. See also OSR 157 for the use of Tartars in the work of Einsatzgruppe D.

121. OSR 178.

122. OSR 194.

123. OSR 108.

124. Directive issued on 11 November 1942. NO-2673.

125. OSR 21, 34, 47, 95, 129, and Activity and Situation Report 1. There were also occasions when NKWD files were seized intact. See OSR 10, 13, 15, 20, 24, 31, 37, 44, 45, 67, 132, 149, 156; Activity and Situation Reports 1, 2, and 3.

126. We noted earlier that agents were used in the prisoner-of-war camps.

127. Activity and Situation Reports 1 and 3. See also OSR 88, 170.

128. L-180.

129. OSR 92. This report also pointed out the still generally hostile attitude of the country population to the partisans and acknowledged the "valuable information" that was received from them.

130. OSR 86. Other examples of informers assisting the Kommandos in antipartisan warfare are found in OSR 81, 116, 125, 150, 194.

131. OSR 21.

132. OSR 22. The sparing of Estonian Jewish doctors was mentioned in OSR 111, and in OSR 32 Einsatzgruppe B reported that in Minsk doctors were spared. See also Tr. 6690.

133. OSR 47.

134. OSR 67.

135. OSR 132, 143.

136. OSR 80. Other references to the use of agents appeared in the reports. See, for example, their use in the area of Einsatzgruppe D, in OSR 157, 165. See also OSR 31, 151.

137. OSR 17, 21, 43, 133.

138. See OSR 103, 106, and Activity and Situation Report 2. For a discussion of the seizure of Jewish property, see Hilberg, *Destruction of the European Jews*, Vol. 1, 360–66.

139. See OSR 47, 88, 127. Some ethnic Germans were employed as members of the shooting squads. Ernst Biberstein, head of Einsatzkommando 6, stated that he was "really frightened by their eagerness to kill." Interrogation of Ernst Biberstein, 29 June 1947, NO-4997. Ethnic Germans were also recruited for service in Waffen SS units. For example, in the late summer of 1941, the SS Kavallerie Brigade, later the 8th Kavalleriedivision "Florian Geyer," which was engaged in "pacification" operations in the Pripet Marshes, was 40 percent ethnic German. Stein, *Waffen SS*, 193, note 65, and 275. Ironically, in November 1941, Theodor Eicke, leader of the SS Death's Head Division, complained about the poor qualities exemplified by the ethnic Germans sent as replacements for his units. Eicke considered them to be cowardly, lazy, weak, and inexperienced. Charles W. Sydnor, *Soldiers of Destruction: The SS Death's Head Division, 1933–1945* (Princeton, N.J.: Princeton University Press, 1977), 205. According to one study, a good percentage of the approximately seventy-six thousand ethnic Germans in Estonia and Latvia had been Nazified by the spring of 1939. Most of these ethnic Germans were resettled in Germany as a consequence of the pact with the Soviets. Therefore, in this instance, the opportunity for exploiting the support of

these people did not materialize to the extent as might have been the case had this resettlement not taken place. See C. Leonard Lundin, "Nazification of Baltic German Minorities: A Contribution to the Study of the Diplomacy of 1939," *Journal of Central European Affairs*, Vol. 7, no. 1 (1947): 1–28.

140. See OSR 80, 132, 156, 178. In the prisoner-of-war camps, camp commanders would often give preference to ethnic German prisoners for administrative work. See OSR 47.

141. OSR 81.

142. At a conference on 16 July 1941, Hitler had cautioned that while relations with Rumania at the moment were good, it was not possible to predict what they would be like in the future. L–221.

143. Activity and Situation Report 1.

144. Cited in Krausnick, *Die Truppe*, 195.

145. OSR 19. This report complained that Rumanian soldiers were looting the houses in Czernowitz. See also the report by Sonderkommando 10a in OSR 25.

146. Activity and Situation Report 2. Ohlendorf later complained about the performance of the Rumanians in his testimony at Nuremberg. Tr. 724.

147. Activity and Situation Report 2. Further complaints of looting were found in OSR 47.

148. The area of north Bukovina had apparently been claimed by the Ukrainians. See Krausnick, *Die Truppe*, 196.

149. OSR 22.

150. OSR 47.

151. OSR 67 and Activity and Situation Report 3. See Martin Gilbert, *Atlas of the Holocaust* (New York: Macmillan, 1982), 70–73.

152. OSR 21.

153. OSR 31.

154. See also Activity and Situation Report 11.

155. Directive of Oberkommando der Wehrmacht, Abteilung Kriegsgefangere, 16 June 1941, PS–888.

156. OSR 47.

157. OSR 187. In Borisov, the "Russian" (Ukrainian?) Security Police who took part in the shooting of Jews there were said to have been former communists. Report received by Erwin Lahousen, signed Soennecken, 24 October 1941, PS–3047. Occasionally in the reports we read of the arrest of auxiliary police members. See, for example, the arrest of three auxiliary policemen for helping prisoners to escape in OSR 165.

158. Randolph L. Braham, "The Kamenets Podolsk and Délvidék Massacres: Prelude to the Holocaust in Hungary," *Yad Vashem Studies* IX (1973): 134.

159. OSR 23. The pro-Jewish attitude of the Hungarians was repeated in Activity and Situation Report 1. There were even complaints that the Hungarians were sending reports and photographic evidence of massacres of Jews by the Rumanians to the U.S. State Department. See Browning, *The Final Solution and the German Foreign Office*, 73.

160. OSR 67. Hungarian soldiers in the Ukraine were upset by the Einsatzgruppen killings and reported the shootings in letters home. Braham, "The Kamenets Podolsk and Délvidék Massacres," 141.

161. OSR 135.

162. L–180.

163. OSR 181.

164. Ibid.

165. See Dallin, *German Rule in Russia*, 73.

Chapter 11. Army Cooperation with the Einsatzgruppen

1. Koehl, *Black Corps*, 196.

2. For examples of negative army reaction to SS atrocities in Poland, see Jeremy Noakes and Geoffrey Pridham, eds. *Documents on Nazism 1919–1945* (London: Jonathan Cape, 1974), 611–13.

3. For example, see Krausnick, *Die Truppe*, 173–278, passim; Datner, *Crimes Against*

POWs: Responsibility of the Wehrmacht; [already cited] Hilberg, *Destruction of the European Jews*, Vol. 1, 273–390, passim. Other studies of Wehrmacht involvement in mass killings include: Streit, *Keine Kameraden*; [already cited] Omer Bartov, *The Eastern Front 1941–45: German Troops and the Barbarisation of Warfare* (London: Macmillan, 1985); Gerhard Hirschfeld, ed., *The Policies of Genocide: Jews and Soviet Prisoners of War in Nazi Germany*, (London: Allen & Unwin, 1986); Alfred Streim, *Die Behandlung sowjetischer Kriegsgefangener im "Fall Barbarossa:" eine Dokumentation* (Heidelberg and Karlsruhe: Müller Juristischer Verlag, 1981); Jürgen Förster, "The Wehrmacht and the War of Extermination Against the Soviet Union," *Yad Vashem Studies* XIV (1981): 7–34.

    4. PS–647. Similar arrangements in 1939 affected the Death's Head Regiments.

    5. Directive by OKW/L signed by Wilhelm Keitel, 13 March 1941, NOKW–2302 (PS–447).

    6. NOKW–256.

    7. The areas under civil administration were ruled by the Ministry for the Occupied Eastern Territories, headed by Alfred Rosenberg, whose headquarters remained in Berlin. These areas consisted of two administrative divisions: The Reichskommissariat Ostland, which embraced Estonia, Latvia, Lithuania, and parts of White Russia; The Reichskommissariat Ukraine, which included most of the north, central, and southern parts of the Ukraine, as well as part of the northern Crimea. See Dallin, *German Rule in Russia*, 84–95.

    8. Ibid., 95–98.

    9. Walter Schellenberg, *The Schellenberg Memoirs* (London: André Deutsch, 1956), 210.

    10. Affidavit of Walter Schellenberg, 26 November 1945, PS–3710. See also the just cited memoirs for a more detailed discussion of the negotiations with Wagner, 209–14. See also affidavit of Generalrichter Mantel, *IMT*, Vol. 21, 17. See also affidavit by Otto Ohlendorf, 24 April 1947, NO–2890.

    11. PS–3710. Ohlendorf testified that during the negotiations no mention was made of the extermination of the Jews. As the result of conversations with Himmler, Ohlendorf concluded that the Wehrmacht generals were informed before 22 June 1941. See *IMT*, Vol. 4, 346–47.

    12. Buchheim, *Anatomy*, 213–16. Koehl, *Black Corps*, 64–65, 129–30, 160–61.

    13. Koehl, *Black Corps*, 180–81.

    14. NOKW–2079.

    15. Buchheim, *Anatomy*, 221–22.

    16. Himmler's powers for carrying out police security were extended to areas under civil administration by a decree of 17 July 1941. This decree stated that Himmler had the power to give directives on security matters to members of the civil administration. PS–1997. See Dallin, *German Rule in Russia*, 85, note 1.

    17. NOKW–1076. For a discussion of the Commissar Order and its implementation, see Hans-Adolf Jacobsen, and others, *Anatomy of the SS State* (New York: Walker and Company, 1968), 505–34. See also Streit, *Keine Kameraden*, 44–49, 83–89. Streit (88–89) gives an incomplete total of approximately eight hundred documented killings of commissars. Even before June 22 the horrific nature of the orders to the troops was apparent. In his diary entry for 5 May 1941 Ulrich von Hassell stated that Wehrmacht Commander in Chief Walther von Brauchitsch had "sacrificed the honour of the German Army in submitting to these orders of Hitler." See Ulrich von Hassell, *The Von Hassell Diaries, 1938–1944* (Garden City, N.Y.: Doubleday and Company, 1947), 189.

    18. Koehl, *Black Corps*, 182. See also the praise of the Einsatzgruppen by Halder to army commanders in Orscha in December 1941, in Höhne, *Order of the Death's Head*, 369. It is essential to note that Hitler justified the killing of commissars by saying that the Soviets had not signed the 1929 Geneva Convention and would therefore react in a murderous fashion against captured German soldiers. In spite of clear indications to the contrary, both from a diplomatic note sent to Berlin by the Soviets as well as from captured Soviet documents, and in spite of representations to Keitel from certain German military leaders to act in accordance with accepted customary law, these attempts at ensuring the proper conduct of warfare were ignored by the Germans, and the criminal orders were sent out to the troops. Streim, *Die Behandlung sowjetischer Kriegsgefangener*, 33–34. Streit, *Keine Kameraden*, 231–32. Streim has underlined that while captured German soldiers were often killed by the Soviets, this was

not done in response to a fundamental policy of the Soviet government but by individual commanders after they had learned of the Commissar Order. Streim includes specific evidence that Soviet killing of German soldiers was prohibited and points out that the Wehrmacht's own statistics concerning Soviet criminal acts indicated that they in no way compared to the acts of the Germans. Streim, *Die Behandlung sowjetischer Kriegsgefangener* vii–viii.

19. OSR 8, 9, 10, 31.
20. OSR 19.
21. OSR 22. Ohlendorf later presented a much less positive image of this meeting with Generaloberst von Schobert. See Krausnick, *Die Truppe*, 196, 197.
22. See L–180.
23. OSR 9, 17.
24. See, for example, OSR 17, 94 and L–180.
25. OSR 150.
26. OSR 128.
27. OSR 132. Other reports dealt with the planning and carrying out of joint operations. See OSR 10, 28, 38, 58.
28. L–180. Höppner's 4th Panzer army was doing its share of killing. In the first four weeks it had liquidated 172 political commissars. See Streit, *Keine Kameraden*, 88.
29. Sonderkommando 4b reported that the "Armed forces surprisingly welcome hostility against Jews." OSR 14.
30. OSR 21.
31. OSR 24.
32. OSR 73.
33. OSR 132. Stahlecker reported also that "understanding" had been shown by army authorities. See L–180. Other reports also indicated an attitude of understanding and satisfaction with the killings. See OSR 14, 58, 119.
34. See OSR 47, 67, 73, 92, 130, 132, 135, 150.
35. NOKW–256.
36. OSR 128.
37. OSR 80. For the horrific character of the Secret Field Police operations, see affidavit by Robert Barth, 8 October 1943, NO–3663.
38. OSR 92. See also OSR 21 and 73.
39. OSR 38.
40. OSR 133.
41. OSR 130.
42. OSR 106.
43. OSR 108.
44. OSR 135.
45. OSR 184. See also OSR 193.
46. Activity and Situation Report 2.
47. We will not concern ourselves here with the deaths of Soviet prisoners of war who simply perished in German captivity. Two estimates of the total number of Soviet prisoners who died are: at least 2,530,000 (Streim, *Die Behandlung sowjetischer Kriegsgefangener*, 224); and 3,300,000 (Streit, *Keine Kameraden*, 244).
48. Affidavit by Erwin Lahousen, 13 November 1945, PS–2846.
49. See Hilberg, *Destruction of the European Jews*, Vol. 1, 326.
50. Halder diary entry for 19 May 1941, in Jacobsen, *Generaloberst Halder Kriegstagebuch*, Vol. 2, 419.
51. PS–2273.
52. OSR 34, 43, 60, 128, 148, 150.
53. OSR 48. It has been pointed out that Einsatzgruppe A reports exaggerated the role of the Security Police in the war against the partisans. See Alfred Streim, "The Tasks of the SS Einsatzgruppen," in *Simon Wiesenthal Center Annual* 4, Henry Friedlander and Sybil Milton, eds. (White Plains, N.Y.: Kraus International Publications, 1987), 318. A detailed discussion of the war against partisans in the area of Einsatzgruppe A is found in Wilhelm, *Die Truppe*, 505–32.

54. OSR 92.

55. OSR 186. For other examples of army gratitude, see OSR 47 and 94. The exchange of intelligence worked both ways. An Einsatzgruppe D report noted as follows: "Several actions are also being planned for the Eastern Sector on the basis of data made available by the Wehrmacht." OSR 170.

56. See OSR 92, 94.

57. Other sources do give us an indication of the problems that surfaced between the Einsatzgruppen and the army. A great part of the complaining came from army leaders upset at the very negative reaction of the population caused by the work of the Kommandos. (OSR 186 reported the "insecurity and anxiety" of the local White Russian populace.) One former chief of staff recalled the "great disturbance among the local population" brought about by the SD in the area of Army Group Center. The commanding officer in the area asked General Fieldmarshal Günther von Kluge to order the SD units out of the front-line areas. This was done. Statement of Hans Roettiger, 28 November 1945, PS–3714. For other army reactions to the shootings, see Hilberg, *Destruction of the European Jews*, Vol. 1, 322–27.

58. OSR 119.

59. OSR 150.

60. Tr. 5748–5750, 6132.

Chapter 12. Other Reports

1. The first Activity and Situation Report concerned the events that occurred during the month of July 1941.

2. See interrogation of Günther Knobloch, in Wilhelm, *Die Truppe*, 338.

3. During the period covered by Activity and Situation Report 6, that is, the month of October 1941, reports of Einsatzgruppe D appeared only twelve times in the Operational Situation Reports. See Appendix A.

4. See the distribution list of Activity and Situation Reports 9 and 11, PS–3876. Günther Knobloch stated that the distribution list was the same as the Operational Situation Reports. This does not appear to be the case if one examines the lists for the two reports just mentioned. (Of course we are limited in our knowledge of the recipients of the Operational Situation Reports to the last surviving list, that of Operational Situation Report 128. See Appendix D.) Knobloch also stated that it was possible that the sequence of events described in the daily reports was reversed in the Activity and Situation Reports. See Wilhelm, *Die Truppe*, 338.

5. See Browning, *The Final Solution and the German Foreign Office*, 72–76.

6. See Reitlinger, *The Final Solution*, 200.

7. Affidavit by Rudolf Fumy, 12 January 1948, Defense Exhibit Sandberger 28.

8. Folder 1 contained reports 1–15; folder 2, reports 6–28; folder 3, reports 29–37; folder 4, reports 38–55.

9. In the first folder, filed separately, were enclosures that included one complete Locations and Communications list (dated by hand, 22 May 1942, the date of the fourth report in the series), another such list for Report 9, and three enclosures with revisions for Reports 7, 10, and 13. Reports 18 and 12 included corrections applying to the Kommandos of Einsatzgruppe D and C, respectively.

10. The pages of the Locations and Communications list were numbered separately from the rest of each report. Reports 2, 3, 4, 5, 6, 26, 31, 38, 40, 47, and 54 had such lists. Report 1 obviously contained a list, but it is missing. In Reports 31 and 47 the information is missing for Einsatzgruppe D.

11. Reports 1, 15, 31, 47, 48.

12. Reports 14, 22, 34. This last report contains two copies of the title page. They are not simply the same copy duplicated since the Geheim stamp is placed differently in each copy.

13. For example, see Reports 1, 3, 4, 5, 7, 12, 46.

14. See especially Reports 3, 5, 15, 26, 35, 38, 39, 41, 43, 45, 46, 49.

15. See Reports 18, 41.

16. Tr. 3490, 3496.

17. Tr. 3491.

18. Tr. 3500.
19. Affidavit by Hans Ehlich, 16 January 1948, Defense Exhibit Nosske 5.
20. Reitlinger, *The Final Solution*, 200. The final result of this is that the statistics of shootings for 1942 and 1943 are less complete than those for 1941. Hilberg, *Destruction of the European Jews*, Vol. 3, 1203.
21. See Wilhelm, *Die Truppe*, 346. Party and Propaganda Ministry offices, as well as other agencies, were also reprimanded for the negative quality of their reports. Steinert, *Hitler's War*, 15–16.
22. The reports that followed the Reports from the Reich were the "SD-Berichte zu Inlandsfragen," Reports on Domestic Affairs, the first of which was issued on 10 June 1943. The Reports from the Occupied Eastern Territories had no successors. See Stokes, "Sicherheitsdienst," 195. From 1944 on, the number of recipients of reports was reduced, along with the number of reporting agents. The SD was restricted in the range of subjects reported on, and was instructed not to get involved in details and to evaluate events from a National Socialist perspective. By June 1944 only scattered reports appeared, although SD reporting did continue until the end of the war. Steinert, *Hitler's War*, 15.
23. Krausnick and Wilhelm, *Die Truppe*, 22, 642.
24. L–180. For a discussion and presentation of details from this report, see Wilhelm, *Die Truppe*, especially 476–83, and 605–8.
25. Enclosure 4 of the report. See the details of this enclosure in Wilhelm, *Die Truppe*, 478.
26. Ibid., 477. Also included (476) are details of enclosure 11, a statistical report on the work of the Latvian criminal police.
27. PS–2273. This report was apparently captured in Riga by the Russians and was issued as Document USSR 357a as evidence at the first Nuremberg trial. The report contains no date or heading. Reitlinger, *The Final Solution*, 560. The original of this report is found in the Central Archives in Moscow. A more extensive portion than that used at Nuremberg may be found in the Zentrale Stelle Ludwigsburg, binder 402, picture 530–73. See exhibit no. 60, *Federal Republic of Germany vs. Helmut Rauca*, Supreme Court of Ontario, 12 October 1982, "A Study of the Einsatzgruppen," an unpublished study by Wolfgang Scheffler, 33.
28. Wilhelm, *Die Truppe*, 606.
29. For example, compare the descriptions of operations in the Ostland in the two Stahlecker reports with corresponding sections in Operational Situation Report 111, Activity and Situation Report 6, and Reports from the Occupied Eastern Territories 6 and 7. Another example of duplication is the word for word repetition of the partisan report found in Stahlecker's first report contained in Operational Situation Report 60.
30. See the discussion of the totals in Wilhelm, *Die Truppe*, 606–9.
31. L–180.
32. PS–2273.
33. Ibid. The report then mentioned the use of Jewish doctors to combat the epidemics that were frequent in the crowded ghettos. It is interesting to note the description of the devious method used to deceive the Jews as to their fate. Sick Jews with contagious diseases were told they were to be sent to a hospital or a home for the aged. They were then shot.
34. Krausnick and Wilhelm, *Die Truppe*, 536, 641, 644. Operational Situation Report 149 was the first report to include the KdS ranks of the Kommando leaders.
35. Hilberg, *Destruction of the European Jews*, Vol. 3, 1097.
36. The Jäger report contains three errors: the total for August 13 should be 718, not 719; the total for August 19 should be 643, not 645; and the total for September 12 (Vilna) should be 3,434, not 3,334. The correct overall total is therefore 137,443, which includes the approximately four thousand Jews killed by Lithuanian partisans.
37. A complete copy of the report in English is found in Baranauskas and Ruksenas, *Documents Accuse*, 230–41. Other English copies are found in *Documents of Destruction*, Raul Hilberg, ed. (Chicago: Quadrangle Books, 1971), 46–57 (complete except for a portion of the last part of the text); and in William W. Mishell, *Kaddish for Kovno: Life and Death in a Lithuanian Ghetto 1941–1945*, (Chicago: Chicago Review Press, 1988), 381–89.
38. For a discussion of the report's authenticity, see Scheffler, "A Study of the Einsatzgruppen," 30–35.
39. Earlier Operational Situation Reports mentioned specific actions by Einsatzkommando

3 that were later confirmed by the Jäger report. For example, OSR 19 mentioned that small units of the Kommando had been working at Mariampole and (Paseinial?). OSR 24 noted that detachments had been concentrating in Dwinsk. OSR 31 noted the impending taking over of the Vilna area by Einsatzgruppe A. Vilna had been serviced by Einsatzkommando 9 previously. It is noteworthy that the listing of executions carried out by Einsatzkommando 3 in Operational Situation Report 54 is done with the same degree of precision as found in Jäger's report. OSR 88 mentioned actions carried out in Raseiniai, Rokiskis, Sarasai, Prienai, and Perzai, and that these districts were "cleared of Jews." Other executions, for example, in Aglona and Dwinsk also were included in this report.

40. Other victims included Poles, Armenians, Gypsies, NKWD agents, prisoners-of-war, mental patients, partisans, "murderers," and "criminals."

41. Yitzhak Arad has concluded that at least one Einsatzkommando 3 operation in Vilna during October was not included in Jäger's report. This was the action on Yom Kippur (October 1 and 2). Arad speculates that the reason for this omission may have been the fact that some German agencies had complained against the seizure of workers, and that German Army units had even secured the release of some of the arrested Jews. See Arad, *Ghetto in Flames*, 136–39.

42. This was the only instance in the report that specified that all the Jews in a particular town were killed. That this was true of other places is certain. For example, see note 39.

43. Note that when the period of time for entries of executions spans two months the total has been added to that of the second month due to the impossibility of knowing how many people were killed during each month. These monthly totals incorporate the corrections discussed earlier. (See note 36.)

44. This number includes the Kommando-directed pogroms of 4 and 6 July 1941.

45. See Hilberg, *Destruction of the European Jews*, Vol. 3, 1211. See also Arad, "The 'Final Solution' in Lithuania," 247. Arad observes that the ghetto in Swenciany was not included in Jäger's report, possibly due to the fact that it was very small, or because it was left untouched by the local officials without Jäger's knowledge. Arad, *Ghetto in Flames*, 171, note 8.

46. Wilhelm, *Die Truppe*, 605, 606. The total number of Jews killed (136, 421) was included in the Einsatzgruppe A draft report. PS–2273.

Chapter 13.   The Einsatzgruppen Reports as Legal Evidence

1. Special List no. 42, Nuernberg War Crimes Trials. Records of Case 9. *United States of America v. Otto Ohlendorf, et al.*, compiled by John Mendelsohn, National Archives and Records Service, Washington, 1978, 1–2. Immediately after the war the reconstituted German courts were permitted to deal only with ordinary crimes. Until 1950 only Allied courts could deal with war crimes. See Henry Friedlander, "The Judiciary and Nazi Crimes in Postwar Germany," in *Simon Wiesenthal Center Annual* 1, Henry Friedlander and Sybil Milton, eds. (Chappaqua, N.Y.: Rossel Books, 1984), 30–33. See also Adalbert Rückerl, *The Investigation of Nazi Crimes 1945–1978: A Documentation* (Hamden, Conn.: Archon Books, 1980), 32–33. The Einsatzgruppen trial lasted until 10 April 1948.

2. See Robert E. Conot, *Justice at Nuremberg* (New York: Harper & Row, 1983), 89, 90, 150, 151. See Whitney R. Harris, *Tyranny on Trial: The Evidence at Nuremberg* (Dallas: Southern Methodist University Press, 1954), xxxv. See Telford Taylor, "The Use of Captured German and Related Records in the Nürnberg War Crimes Trials" in Wolfe, ed., *Captured German and Related Records*, 96 [already cited]. This article describes the chaotic system of the gathering of documents at Nuremberg. The book as a whole is a good summary of the scope, use, and processing of captured German documents and their evolution since the war. See also Klaus Oldenhage, "International Joint Ventures for Exchange of Archival Materials through Reprography," a paper presented at the Tenth International Congress on Archives, Bonn, 1984. Another detailed source, which focuses on the documents in the NP, NG, NOKW, and NM series, is Mendelsohn, "Trial by Document." (See Chapter 1, note 14.)

3. For a list of the various symbols used to catalog Nuremberg documents, see Jacob

Robinson and Henry Sachs, *The Holocaust: The Nuremberg Evidence, Part One: The Documents* (Jerusalem and New York: Yad Vashem and Yivo, 1976), 11.

4. At the Einsatzgruppen trial one defense counsel demanded to see the original reports, not the copies. See note 18.

5. This description of the processing of the reports is found in the affidavit by William Coogan, 19 November 1945, *IMT* Vol. 2, 157–60. A similar process prevailed for the twelve later Nuremberg trials. See affidavit by Fred Niebergall, 22 August 1947. An even more detailed description is found in Mendelsohn, "Trial by Document," 66–109.

6. Benjamin B. Ferencz, "Nürnberg Trial Procedure and the Rights of the Accused," *Journal of Criminal Law and Criminology* 39 (1948–49): 149. For a discussion of the frequent problems of the defense to secure documents to support their case, see John Mendelsohn, "Trial by Document: The Problem of Due Process for War Criminals at Nuernberg," *Prologue*, 7, no. 4 (1975): 227–34.

7. Mendelsohn, "Special List no. 42," 4.

8. Tr. 3–16.

9. Tr. 67.

10. The determining of the guilt of defendants in war crimes trials during the 1950s onward, when such trials came under the control of German courts, involved different and more complex legalistic interpretations than was the case in Nuremberg. Later trials were founded on the application of German Penal and Military codes. Pertinent in these cases were the legal problems concerned with defining the distinction between murder and manslaughter, the distinction between perpetration and participation, as well as criteria for dealing with the concept of acting under superior orders. For a discussion of these legal problems, see Helge Grabitz, "Problems of Nazi Trials in the Federal Republic of Germany," *Holocaust and Genocide Studies*, Vol. 3, no. 2 (1988): 209–22; Friedlander, "The Judiciary and Nazi Crimes in Postwar Germany," 32–38; Rückerl, *The Investigation of Nazi Crimes*, 39–101.

11. For a complete list of the Einsatzgruppen and Kommando leaders, including the time periods when they served as leaders, see Krausnick and Wilhelm, *Die Truppe*, 644–46. For a list of the sentences and fate of these leaders as of 1978, see Rückerl, *The Investigation of Nazi Crimes*, 129–32.

12. In many cases it is not difficult to connect a particular Kommando with specific operations even if this Kommando is not listed in the report. This can be done by consulting the current Locations and Lines of Communications list.

13. Mendelsohn, "Special List no. 42," 5.

14. For an examination of the main lines of defense used at the trial, including the concept of superior orders, the argument of "tu quoque," the so-called putative threat to national security, and the challenge against the validity of the court's jurisdiction, see Robert Wolfe, "Putative Threat to National Security as a Nuremberg Defense for Genocide," *The Annals of the American Academy of Political and Social Science* 450 (1980): 46–67.

15. This was also true of later trials. See Wilhelm, *Die Truppe*, 335.

16. See affidavit of Otto Ohlendorf, 24 April 1947, NO–2890; affidavit of Kurt Lindow, 21 July 1947, NO–4327; affidavit B of Otto Ohlendorf, 20 November 1945, in *Nazi Conspiracy and Aggression*, Vol. 8, 596; affidavit D of Walter Schellenberg, 23 January 1946, in *Nazi Conspiracy and Aggression*, Vol. 8, 622; affidavit of Heinz Schubert, 4 February 1947, NO–2716; affidavit of Rudolf Fumy, 12 January 1948, Defense Exhibit Sandberger 28; affidavit of Rudolf Fumy, 23 October 1947, Defense Exhibit Ohlendorf 53; affidavit of Friedrich Rang, 9 September 1947, NO–5153; affidavit of Theodor Paeffgen, 25 June, 1947, NO–4142; affidavit of Theodor Paeffgen, 6 August 1947, NO–4761; affidavit of Gustav Nosske, 29 June 1947, NO–4146. For post-Nuremberg testimony authenticating the reports, see the interrogation of Günther Knobloch and extract of evidence from Kurt Lindow cited in Wilhelm, *Die Truppe*, 337–41.

17. Tr. 79.

18. Tr. 79–81.

19. Tr. 88, 89, 5822.

20. Tr. 90.

21. Tr. 71, 5762, 5768. In reply the prosecution stated that some of the documents

concerned many defendants and that several concerned all of them. Each defendant's connection with particular documents would be clarified when the prosecution issued separate briefs for each defendant. Tr. 73.

22. Tr. 363, 364, 5762, 5763, 6225.

23. Tr. 57, 6283.

24. Tr. 5762–5768.

25. See Chapter 3.

26. Tr. 2560, 2561.

27. Tr. 2583, 2584. See also Tr. 5765, 5766.

28. Tr. 2493, 2559.

29. Affidavits of Rudolf Fumy, 23 October 1947, and 12 January 1948. Fumy's statements were part of the Defense Exhibits for Ohlendorf and Sandberger. (See note 16.)

30. Affidavit of Rudolf Fumy, 23 October 1947.

31. Ibid. Weather conditions sometimes delayed arrival at Einsatzgruppe headquarters of reports from the Kommandos. See OSR 133 and 188.

32. In his interrogation in Ludwigsburg on 30 January 1959, Günther Knobloch tended to downplay the possibility of mistakes having taken place, although he did not rule this out. He maintained that the actual contents of the incoming reports were rarely altered since the final reports were made up largely with sections considered important from the original reports that had been bracketed in red. Knobloch did point out that while Müller sometimes made changes in the reports because of political considerations, he considered it out of the question that Müller ever altered dates, locations, or descriptions of events concerning the Einsatzgruppen and the Kommandos. See Wilhelm, *Die Truppe*, 337, 338.

33. Tr. 363, 364.

34. Tr. 5822.

35. Tr. 5823.

36. Tr. 5763. See also Tr. 537.

37. Tr. 431, 537.

38. Tr. 5766, 5767.

39. For example, see OSR 138, 139, 145, 162, 172, 190. In OSR 146 (15 December 1941) HSSPL Prützmann and Jeckeln's names were crossed out, and their names were reversed. This switch in the areas of their leadership had occurred before this date, but had not yet been reflected in the reports. In the same report the heading Sonderkommando 1a was crossed out and replaced with the KdS Estland heading. This referred to the change in status of Martin Sandberger, whose name was also now prefaced with a "Dr." Similar corrections were made concerning Einsatzkommandos 2 and 3. The next report to include the list was OSR 148. Some, but not all, of these corrections appeared in this new list. The fact that the corrections dealing with Strauch, Sandberger, and Jäger found in OSR 146 had not yet been incorporated into OSR 148 would indicate that these handwritten changes may have been added sometime later, not immediately. It was not until the next report, OSR 149, that the KdS ranks of these leaders were included. Some corrections testify to the zeal for accuracy of these officials. Even typing errors were corrected. For example, see OSR 168, where the word "Generalbezirk" was corrected.

40. Tr. 5812, 5813. OSR 148 and 149 are dated December 19 and 22, respectively. These reports are not specific as to the exact dates of the killings carried out by Einsatzgruppe B. Allowing for the usual gap of two to three weeks between events and their appearance in the reports, it is clear that most, if not all, of these actions took place in November 1941. As further evidence of this it is true that reports of other Kommandos found in OSR 149 contain dates within the month of November. The evidence proving Naumann had taken over the leadership of Einsatzgruppe B on 1 November 1941 was quite convincing. See Tr. 6793.

41. Tr. 5815, 5817.

42. Tr. 362. Other defendants attempted to prove their absence during certain periods. For example, see affidavit by Paul Blobel, 6 June 1947, NO–3824.

43. OSR 80, 86.

44. OSR 92.

45. Tr. 536, 537.

46. The error was reversed in Operational Situation Report 62. Here, above a report (by

Einsatzgruppe D) on Russian partisans in Kischinew, the headquarters of Einsatzgruppe A was listed as Ananjew.

47. OSR 89.
48. OSR 95. Further examples of mistakes were discussed. See, for instance, Tr. 538–540, 808, 1583, 1584. The incorrect spelling of names of places was a constant feature of the reports.
49. Tr. 2561, 2573, 2583, 2584.
50. Tr. 2573.
51. Affidavit of Otto Ohlendorf, 2 April 1947, NO–2856.
52. *IMT*, Vol. 4, 319.
53. Tr. 534.
54. Tr. 621, 622.
55. Tr. 534, 535, 2591, 2593, 4577, 4582.
56. At the trial these men would not even give an estimate of the cumulative numbers killed by the Kommandos. This claim to ignorance was questionable, since they had only to add up the figures given periodically to Fritsch to arrive at such a figure. Furthermore, Ohlendorf's estimate of ninety thousand people killed, given at the IMT trial, was remarkably close to the 91,678 total given for Einsatzgruppe D in OSR 190. (See table 6.) It will be recalled that when Ohlendorf testified at the IMT trial, the details of the Einsatzgruppen reports were not yet known.
57. Tr. 535.
58. Tr. 5766.
59. Affidavit by Walter Blume, 22 October 1947, Defense Exhibit Blume 4.
60. Affidavit by Paul Blobel, 6 June 1947, NO–3824. See also Tr. 375.
61. Tr. 1789.
62. Tr. 621. It was later clarified that Ohlendorf "heard about" the Himmler speech at Nuremberg, not when the speech was originally given. Tr. 675–676.
63. PS–1919. This speech took place after the Reports from the Occupied Eastern Territories had been discontinued.
64. Tr. 5762, 5824, 6283.
65. Tr. 5763, 5764.
66. See, for example, the description of these reports in the affidavit of 19 November 1947 by Rudolf Meyer, defense witness for Adolf Ott, the leader of Sonderkommando 7b. Defense Exhibit Ott 6.
67. Sworn certificate by Kurt Otmar Mintzel of 7 January 1948. Defense Exhibit Sandberger 53. Mintzel pointed out that the Operational Situation Reports contained 155 pages that pertained to Estonia. Of these, approximately nineteen pages related to Security Police work. Similarly in the Reports from the Occupied Eastern Territories only nine out of 115 pages concerned Security Police work in Estonia.
68. For example, see a letter dated 19 July 1943, from Police General Herf to Obergruppenführer von Herff, cited in Buchheim, *Anatomy*, 346, 347. In this letter the writer Herf complained that German casualty figures were lowered and that six thousand partisans had been shot to augment the figure of enemy losses. It is interesting to note that Herf states that the "increase in guerilla warfare is simply and solely due to the way the Russians have been treated." See also interview with Alfred Filbert, in Henry Dicks, *Licensed Mass Murder* (London: Chatto, Heinemann. Sussex University Press, 1972), 204–29. Filbert was leader of Einsatzkommando 9, and he also claimed he inflated the numbers executed. For evidence of Kommando leaders boasting about the number of Jews they killed, see affidavit by Günther Otto, July 1947, NO–4434, and affidavit by Robert Barth, 8 October 1943, NO–3663.
69. Reitlinger, *The Final Solution*, 200–1.
70. Tr. 6646–6889.
71. See Wolfe, "Putative Threat to National Security as a Nuremberg Defense for Genocide," 46–67.
72. See section titled Authenticity of Reports in Opinion of the court. Tr. 6656–6670.
73. Tr. 6720.
74. Tr. 6801.
75. Tr. 6724.

76. The following defendants were sentenced to death: Ohlendorf, Biberstein, Blobel, Blume, Braune, Haensch, Klingelhoefer, Naumann, Ott, Sandberger, Schubert, Seibert, Steimle, Strauch. Sentences of life imprisonment were given to Jost and Nosske. Sentences of twenty years imprisonment were given to Schulz, Six, and von Radetzky. Sentences of ten years were given to Fendler and Ruehl. Graf was found guilty on Count III (membership in a criminal organization). He was sentenced for time already served and was released. Tr. 6785–6895. Of the defendants sentenced to death, only Blobel, Braune, Naumann, and Ohlendorf were eventually executed. They were hanged at Landsberg Prison on 7 June 1951. All other sentences were reduced to terms of imprisonment, and by 1958 all surviving defendants had been freed. Rückerl, *The Investigation of Nazi Crimes*, 47; Mendelsohn, "Special List no. 42," 3–4.

77. Tr. 6577.

78. Tr. 6795.

79. Tr. 620, 6675.

80. These and other shortcomings of the defense case were pointed out by the prosecution in its closing statement, 13 February 1948. See Tr. 6577–6595. For other contradictions, see Tr. 6725.

81. Tr. 6147.

82. Tr. 6722.

83. Tr. 5764.

84. Alfred Streim has pointed out that not all operations were included in the reports. Sonderkommando 4a carried out approximately 115 separate mass shootings, but the reports cite only a few of these. Streim, "The Tasks of the SS Einsatzgruppen," 320.

Chapter 14. The Einsatzgruppen Reports as Historical Source

1. The reports have provided essential source material for many historians. They have figured prominently in major works by, among others, Reitlinger, Hilberg, Arad, Streit, Streim, and Krausnick and Wilhelm. (See bibliography.) In particular, Krausnick's and Wilhelm's detailed study offers extensive excerpts from the reports. In addition, Wilhelm's perceptive appraisal of the reports and the "critical consciousness" of the reporters (*Die Truppe*, 333–47) includes valuable insights, many of which have come to bear on the present discussion.

2. Taylor, "The Use of Captured German and Related Records in the Nürnberg War Crimes Trials," [already cited] 100.

3. As was mentioned earlier, this study does not deal with the reports concerned with the social and economic situation existing in the occupied areas. These subjects will be considered only in broad terms in the discussion. These reports are an important source for historians concerned with these aspects of German rule in the east.

4. See Karl Dietrich Bracher, *The German Dictatorship: The Origins, Structure, and Effects of National Socialism* (New York: Praeger, 1970), 465.

5. Robert Koehl, "Feudal Aspects of National Socialism," *American Political Science Review* 54 (1960): 921–33. See also Michael H. Kater, *The Nazi Party. A Social Profile of Members and Leaders, 1919–1945* (Cambridge, Mass.: Harvard University Press, 1983), 171–72.

6. Koehl, "Feudal Aspects of National Socialism," 111.

7. Fest, *Face of the Third Reich*, 302–3.

8. Koehl, *Black Corps*, 51.

9. Wegner, "The 'Aristocracy of National Socialism,'" 394; idem, "'My Honour is Loyalty.' The SS as a Military Factor in Hitler's Germany," in *The German Military in the Age of Total War*, Wilhelm Deist, ed. (Warwickshire: Berg Publishers Ltd., 1985), 224.

10. Ibid., 225–28.

11. Eugen Kogon, *The Theory and Practice of Hell: The German Concentration Camps and the System Behind Them* (New York: Octagon Books, 1973), 261. Hilberg, *Destruction of the European Jews*, Vol. 1, 189–91.

12. Black, *Kaltenbrunner*, 189–90; Höhne, *Order of the Death's Head*, 229–33; Gerald Reitlinger, *The SS: Alibi of a Nation, 1922–1945* (New York: Viking, 1957), 34, 35; Delarue, *The Gestapo*, 184; Fest, *Face of the Third Reich*, 105.

13. Browder, "SIPO and SD," 121. For an examination of the continued rivalry between the SD and the Abwehr during Kaltenbrunner's leadership of the RSHA, see Black, *Kaltenbrunner*, 189–99.

14. See Lochner, *The Goebbels Diaries*, 202, 302, 366, 476, 508, 546, 547. Goebbels's criticism of the Wehrmacht did not prevent his ministry from working with the Wehrmacht in the propaganda field. See Robert Edwin Herzstein, "Anti-Jewish Propaganda in the Orel Region of Great Russia, 1942–1943: The German Army and Its Russian Collaborators," in *Simon Wiesenthal Center Annual* 6, Henry Friedlander and Sybil Milton, eds. (New York: Philosophical Library, 1989), 33–55.

15. Christopher R. Browning, "The Government Experts," in Friedlander and Milton, *The Holocaust: Ideology, Bureaucracy and Genocide*, 195, 196.

16. Eugene Davidson, *The Trial of the Germans* (New York: Collier Books, 1972), 132–33.

17. Browning, "Government Experts," 192. See also Richard Grunberger, *Hitler's SS* (New York: Delacorte Press, 1970), 97. Davidson, *The Trial of the Germans*, 161–62.

18. Black, *Kaltenbrunner*, 177–89.

19. Koehl, *Black Corps*, 225; Grunberger, *Hitler's SS*, 95; Buchheim, *Anatomy*, 186. See in particular Browder's summary of the various power struggles between the major German institutions. Browder, "SIPO and SD," especially 268–71, 366–433.

20. Not discussed in Chapter 1 was the not insignificant economic power that the SS managed to build up, especially after the war began. For an examination of this subject, in particular with respect to SS encroachments into the field of armaments, see Albert Speer, *Infiltration: How Heinrich Himmler Schemed to Build an SS Industrial Empire* (New York: Macmillan, 1981).

21. Browder, "SIPO and SD," 181–85.

22. Höhne, *Order of the Death's Head*, 171.

23. Ibid., 233–34; Buchheim, *Anatomy*, 171; Browder, "SIPO and SD," 32, 174, 197, 382. Similar suspicions were often directed at Goebbels, whose intellectualism and physical deformity were not viewed as ideal qualities by many party members. Fest, *Face of the Third Reich*, 87. For an analysis of SD rivalry with Bormann's party chancellery, see Black, *Kaltenbrunner*, 199–217. Much resentment was directed at the party reporters themselves. For a discussion of the unenviable spying tasks of the party Blockleiters, see Kater, *The Nazi Party*, 192–93.

24. The party itself had also long been suspicious of the "police civil service mentality." The police had been the "enemy" during the party's years of struggle. Browder, "SIPO and SD," 174.

25. Höhne, *Order of the Death's Head*, 226. The SD reports in many respects resembled those of the Gestapo. They were distinguished from the Gestapo reports, however, in their more "scientific" approach to investigating enemies and in the generally greater freedom from higher authorities possessed by Heydrich in carrying out his duties. Stokes, "Sicherheitsdienst," 177; Koehl, *Black Corps*, 83, 92.

26. Browder, "SIPO and SD," 186–89; Höhne, *Order of the Death's Head*, 226; Wilhelm, *Die Truppe*, 342. An earlier directive issued by Himmler on 4 July 1934 had defined the basic investigative and executive roles of the SD and the police but had apparently not been completely successful in regulating the areas of competence of each agency. Stokes, "Sicherheitsdienst," 67, 68. In a speech given in January 1937, Himmler stated that the SD was basically concerned with ideological questions, not "detailed executive problems." See Buchheim, *Anatomy*, 167, 168. The separation of reporting that followed these directives was in fact later abandoned in the Operational Situation Reports to the extent that little difference could be found between the manner of the Gestapo and SD reports. Wilhelm, *Die Truppe*, 342.

27. Höhne, *Order of the Death's Head*, 227.

28. Koehl, *Black Corps*, 162. It has been pointed out that the SD did retain some

executive powers and that the SD and the Gestapo, in spite of their continued rivalry, were able to work in close collaboration with each other. See Stokes, "Sicherheitsdienst," 45, 52, 66–70, 86.

29. Browder, "SIPO and SD," 349.

30. Delarue, *The Gestapo*, 144, 217. Stokes, "Sicherheitsdienst," 65.

31. For what is perhaps typical of other organizations' reactions to negative SD reports, see Speer's views on reports critical of the armament industry. Speer, *Infiltration*, 94–108.

32. Wilhelm, *Die Truppe*, 344, 345. In spite of the tensions that existed between the SD and the Gestapo, their relationship was also marked by the necessity for practical, mutual cooperation. Stokes, "Sicherheitsdienst," 66. Even before the decree of 1 July 1937 attempts had been made to achieve a good working arrangement between the SD and Gestapo. For example, see the letter from Office II calling for weekly or fortnightly meetings with Gestapo officials in order to achieve a "close, confidential" rapport between the two organizations. Report dated 16 June 1937, NO–5877.

33. Wilhelm, *Die Truppe*, 344. Bormann kept secret card files on important party and government officials. These were never found after the war, although his file on Heydrich's genealogy did survive. See Fest, *Face of the Third Reich*, 100. Heydrich's genealogical table is reproduced in Aronson, *Heydrich*, 310.

34. L–180, enclosure 1a. See enclosure 1b for a numerical breakdown of the Kommandos of Einsatzgruppe A.

35. Himmler speech, 7 September 1940, PS–1918.

36. Browder, "SIPO and SD," 150.

37. Kraus and Almond, "Resistance and Repression," 41.

38. Höhne, *Order of the Death's Head*, 206.

39. Ibid., 206–7. Browder, "SIPO and SD," 161.

40. Höhne, *Order of the Death's Head*, 207–8. The Criminal Police retained certain officials who managed to resist Gestapo influence. Ibid., 207. Browder, "SIPO and SD," 151.

41. Browder, "SIPO and SD," 156.

42. L–361.

43. Affidavit by Heinz Jost, 27 June 1947, NO–4151.

44. Tr. 1138, 1140.

45. See affidavit by Wilhelm Waneck, 17 September 1947, Defense Exhibit Fendler 19; affidavit by Wilhelm Waneck, 17 November 1947, Defense Exhibit Jost 21; affidavit by Friedrich Vollheim, 4 November 1947, Defense Exhibit Jost 17; affidavit by Theodor Paeffgen, 15 January 1948, Defense Exhibit Sandberger 35.

46. Delarue, *The Gestapo*, 183.

47. Affidavit by Rudolf Fumy, 12 January 1948, Defense Exhibit Sandberger 28.

48. These power structures were: 1) Hitler; 2) Martin Bormann and the Nazi party machine; 3) Rosenberg and the Ministry for the Occupied Eastern Territories and the Reichskommissars Hinrich Lohse and Erich Koch; 4) Goebbels and the Propaganda Ministry; 5) Ribbentrop and the Foreign Office; 6) Göring and the economic agencies of the Four Year Plan; 7) Himmler and the SS; 8) the Wehrmacht. Dallin, *German Rule in Russia*, 20.

49. Ibid., 20–22.

50. Koch, in particular, stubbornly refused to follow Rosenberg's orders. Interestingly, at the conference on 16 July 1941 when the Reichskommissars were selected, Rosenberg had predicted this would happen. L–221.

51. For a summary of the personalities and power struggles in the east, see Dallin, *German Rule in Russia*, 20–43, 84–103, and Rich, *Hitler's War Aims*, 326–93. For examples (among many) of SS rivalry with Rosenberg, see Buchheim, *Anatomy*, 190–92.

52. See Broszat, *Hitler State*, 44; Buchheim, *Totalitarian Rule*, 107–8.

53. See Black, *Kaltenbrunner*, 215–17; Sydnor, *Soldiers of Destruction*, 346. Koehl underlines this point in connection with the takeover of Austria, where rival German groups functioned smoothly in the situation of a "real emergency." Koehl, *Black Corps*, 143.

54. Black, *Kaltenbrunner*, 216.

55. See affidavit by Rudolf Fumy, 12 January 1948, Defense Exhibit Sandberger 28.

56. See statement by Günther Knobloch in Wilhelm, *Die Truppe*, 337.

57. There is somewhat greater mention of German casualties in the descriptions of antipartisan warfare in the Reports from the Occupied Eastern Territories.
58. OSR 73.
59. OSR 21. Unlike Einsatzgruppe B's boast, HSSPL Prützmann, operating in the area of Einsatzgruppe A, stated that "severe measures" had been delayed due to isolated Red Army ambushes. OSR 19.
60. OSR 111.
61. OSR 128.
62. OSR 47.
63. See OSR 67, 92, 155, 177, 178, 180; PS–2273; Report from the Occupied Eastern Territories 35.
64. OSR 132. At his trial, Walter Blume, leader of Sonderkommando 7a, boasted that his men had thanked him for sparing them the mental anguish of shooting women and children. Defense Exhibit Blume 8, 29 June 1947.
65. Jäger report.
66. See L–180, PS–2273, OSR 92, 155, 168, Activity and Situation Report 9.
67. This incident is included in OSR 155. According to one eyewitness, it was a man called Alter Zhagorsky who incited this rebellion. Zhagorsky is believed to have stabbed a Lithuanian guard to death. Levin, *Fighting Back*, 264.
68. For example, see *Jewish Resistance during the Holocaust. Proceedings of the Conference on Manifestations of Jewish Resistance*, Jerusalem, April 1968 (Jerusalem: Yad Vashem, 1971); Reuben Ainsztein, *Jewish Resistance in Nazi-Occupied Eastern Europe* (London: Paul Elek 1974).
69. Affidavit by Rudolf Fumy, 12 January 1948, Defense Exhibit Sandberger 28.
70. Ibid. In this affidavit Rudolf Fumy gives specific examples of reports where this occurred.
71. See Wilhelm, *Die Truppe*, 342.
72. See Chapter 8.
73. L–180.
74. Jäger report. Jäger's problems with the civil administration did not only center on the question of killing Jews. There were also problems concerning his confiscation of Jewish property. See letter by Regional Kommissar Hans Gewecke complaining of Jäger's meddling in matters that were outside his concern, 8 September 1941, PS–3661.
75. Jäger report.
76. L–180. In this report Stahlecker bragged that the leaders of the Waffen SS and the regular uniformed police who were reserve members of his Einsatzgruppe expressed a desire to "stay on with the Security Police and SD." Alfred Streim has noted the exaggerated role of the Einsatzgruppen in the partisan war as presented in the reports. See Streim, "The Tasks of the SS Einsatzgruppen," 318.
77. OSR 119.
78. See OSR 19, 22, 64, 135, 181, Activity and Situation Reports 1, 2, 3.
79. See OSR 47, 86, 90, 108, 145, 150, 151, 168, 169, 183. Concerning black market activities, this practice had become so widespread that in April 1943 Göring ordered that all such operations were strictly forbidden in occupied countries. See Buchheim, *Anatomy*, 347.
80. OSR 47, 128.
81. OSR 116.
82. OSR 94.
83. OSR 48, 92, 108, 150, 186.
84. OSR 92. Franz Halder, assembled army commanders in Orscha in December 1941. They were unanimous in their praise of the Einsatzgruppen. See Höhne, *Order of the Death's Head*, 369.
85. Report from the Occupied Eastern Territories 9. In a report dated 1 December 1941, Einsatzgruppe A itself had reported that in the rear zone partisan activity had lessened. OSR 140.
86. In a later report Einsatzgruppe B made the same mistake of underestimating the morale of the partisans. See Report from the Occupied Eastern Territories 26.

87. OSR 94.

88. PS–2273.

89. Tr. 535. Affidavit of Otto Ohlendorf, 5 November 1945, PS–2620.

90. Stokes, "Sicherheitsdienst," 238. Speer, *Infiltration*, 94–95.

91. Stokes, "Sicherheitsdienst," 195.

92. Ibid., 210. See also the discussion of Ohlendorf's economic theories in Felix Kersten, *The Kersten Memoirs 1940–1945* (New York: Macmillan, 1957), 206–10, and in Speer, *Infiltration*, 76–84.

93. Stokes, "Sicherheitsdienst," 205.

94. The SD reports distorted in particular the claim of popular support for judicial terror, the extent of church opposition to Nazism, and the difficulties experienced by small business. See Stokes, "Sicherheitsdienst," 239–40.

95. Ibid., 242–46.

96. For a discussion of these terms, see Tim Mason, "Intention and Explanation: A Current Controversy about the Interpretation of National Socialism," in *The Führer State": Myth and Reality. Studies on the Structure and Politics of the Third Reich*, Gerhard Hirschfeld and Lothar Kettenacker, eds. (London: German Historical Institute, 1981), 23–40.

97. Friedlander, "From Anti-Semitism to Extermination," 28–29.

98. Browning, *Fateful Months*, [already cited] 9.

99. Friedlander, "From Anti-Semitism to Extermination," 22.

100. Browning, *Fateful Months*, 9.

101. No written order to kill the Jews has ever been found, hence the difficulty in determining with certainty when and in what form the order was given. For the role of the Einsatzgruppen and the Final Solution, see Krausnick and Wilhelm, *Die Truppe*, 150–72, 622–37; Mayer, *Why Did the Heavens Not Darken?*, 200–75. For views concerning the timing of the order to the Einsatzgruppen, see Helmut Krausnick and others, *Anatomy of the SS State* (New York: Walker and Company, 1968), 69–75; idem, "Hitler und die Befehle an die Einsatzgruppen im Sommer 1941," in Eberhard Jäckel and Jürgen Rohwer, eds., *Der Mord an den Juden im zweiten Weltkrieg: Entschlussbildung und Verwirklichung* (Stuttgart: Deutsche Verlags-Anstalt, 1985), 88–106; Alfred Streim, ibid., "Zur Eröffnung des allgemein Judenvernichtungsbefehls gegenüber den Einsatzgruppen," 107–19; idem, *Die Behandlung sowjetischer Kriegsgefangener*, 74–93; idem, "The Tasks of the SS Einsatzgruppen," 309–28; Lozowick, "Rollbahn Mord," 221–41; Ronald Headland, "The Einsatzgruppen: The Question of Their Initial Operations," *Holocaust and Genocide Studies*, Vol. 4, no. 4 (1989): 401–12. See also the correspondence by Helmut Krausnick (311–29) and reply by Alfred Streim (331–47), in *Simon Wiesenthal Center Annual* 6 (New York: Philosophical Library, 1989).

102. Browning, *Fateful Months*, 4–5. Browning also cites the often quoted Hitler statement of January 1939 that if war were to come to Europe the Jews would be destroyed.

103. EC–126; PS–2718.

104. Bartov, *The Eastern Front*, 116–17.

105. Headland, "The Einsatzgruppen," 403. Stahlecker's report maintained that pogroms had the dual purpose of putting blame on the local population and disguising German participation in the killings. L–180. Pogroms were still considered a useful tactic by Himmler even months later when the extermination program had long been well entrenched. See Krausnick, letter in *Simon Wiesenthal Center Annual* 6, 315–16. For ghettos, see OSR 45, 54, 63, 89, 92, 106, 107, 124.

106. OSR 107.

107. L–180. The later summary report of Einsatzgruppe A also stated: "The systematic mopping up of the eastern territories embraced in accordance with the basic orders the complete removal, if possible, of Jewry." PS–2273.

108. L–180.

109. For Alfred Streim's interpretation of the Stahlecker and Jäger reports, see his reply to Helmut Krausnick's letter in *Simon Wiesenthal Center Annual* 6, 336.

110. Activity and Situation Report 1. Other early references to Jewish intelligentsia appeared in OSR 17, 22, 47.

111. OSR 19.

112. OSR 21. The killing of "Asiatics" mentioned in this early report and in OSR 47 already indicates a racial dimension to the killings.

113. OSR 24.

114. OSR 34.

115. OSR 20, 22, 25.

116. OSR 45.

117. OSR 24, 29, 51.

118. OSR 19.

119. OSR 24.

120. OSR 40.

121. OSR 24.

122. OSR 43.

123. Ibid.

124. For a discussion of this total, which is derived from the reports, and which includes all categories of victims, and which is almost certainly incomplete, see Headland, "The Einsatzgruppen," 406. For other examples of massacres carried out immediately by the Einsatzgruppen, see Krausnick, letter (Note 101), 311–29. Krausnick (326) concludes the number of *Jews* killed by the end of July 1941 was about forty-four thousand.

125. See Headland, "The Einsatzgruppen," 404–6.

126. This is the conclusion of, among others, Krausnick and Wilhelm, *Die Truppe*, 150–72, 634; Browning, *Fateful Months*, 8–38; and Hilberg, *Destruction of the European Jews*, Vol. 1, 273.

127. Dallin, *German Rule in Russia*, 18–20.

128. Wilhelm, *Die Truppe*, 630.

129. Ibid.

130. L–108. Some evidence indicates that Stahlecker actually disapproved of the killing operations. See Wilhelm, *Die Truppe*, 628.

131. OSR 31. This idea is repeated in OSR 32.

132. OSR 31.

133. Report from the Occupied Eastern Territories 9.

134. OSR 73.

135. OSR 180, 194. See also OSR 123, Reports from the Occupied Eastern Territories 2, 3, 5, 9, 35, 43, and Activity and Situation Report 3.

136. Affidavit by Erwin Schulz, 20 December 1945, NO–3841.

137. OSR 52.

138. OSR 81.

139. OSR 86. An Einsatzgruppe C report, dated 6 March 1942, reiterated the idea that it was not only the Jews who were causing the "unrest." OSR 177.

140. OSR 94.

141. OSR 128.

142. Wilhelm, *Die Truppe*, 630, 633.

143. Friedlander, "From Anti-Semitism to Extermination," 1–50. Wilhelm, *Die Truppe*, 622–36. Wilhelm underlines the guiding role of Hitler, yet stresses that the "centralized" goal of extermination was carried out with the encouragement of initiative on the part of subordinates as to the manner of its implementation.

144. Activity and Situation Report 9.

145. Stokes, "Sicherheitsdienst," 90–192.

146. OSR 63.

147. Wilhelm, *Die Truppe*, 629. On this point see also Ferencz, *Less Than Slaves*, 192. In one Einsatzgruppe D report, dated 8 October 1941, we discover that the "first part" of the Jewish question was considered solved. (Jews were registered, confined to ghettos, made to work.) OSR 107. OSR 157 stated that Einsatzgruppe D intensified its security work, the intention being to remove completely all "unreliable elements."

148. See OSR 34, 60, 61, 73, 80, 81, 125, 129, 148, Activity and Situation Report 9, Reports from the Occupied Eastern Territories 4, 6, 9.

149. See OSR 22, 31, 32, 43, 47, 86, 90, 108, 168, 169, 179, 181, 183, 186, 194, 195, Activity and Situation Report 10, Reports from the Occupied Eastern Territories 1, 6, 9, 15, 16, 26, 35, 49, 55.
150. OSR 52.
151. See Dallin, *German Rule in Russia*, and Rich, *Hitler's War Aims* (Note 51).
152. See previous examples concerning the Wehrmacht. For praise of, and complaints against, the Rumanians, see OSR 19, 37 and OSR 19, 22, 47, 61, 67 and Activity and Situation Reports 1, 2, 3.
153. OSR 47, 81, 129.
154. OSR 34, 181. Report from the Occupied Eastern Territories 43.
155. OSR 90, 92, 123, 179.
156. Fleming, *Hitler and the Final Solution*, 45.
157. PS–1919.
158. For example, see the memorandum, dated 25 October 1942, by Otto Bräutigam. PS–294.
159. Kersten, *Kersten Memoirs*, 214–19.
160. Tr. 506.
161. Steinert, *Hitler's War*, 3, 341.
162. Wilhelm, *Die Truppe*, 346.
163. Wilhelm, *Die Truppe*, 333–35.
164. Responding to SD criticism of Erich Koch's policies in the Ukraine, Ernst Kaltenbrunner asked Ohlendorf "at least to camouflage the reports as reports of the adversary or sabotage reports." Tr. 505–6.
165. See Lochner, *The Goebbels Diaries*, 333, 334, 373, 400. See other entries concerning various reports from the east, 114–16, 126, 185, 195, 201, 202, 219, 246, 298, 309, 364, 366, 507, 508.

Chapter 15. Concluding Remarks

1. See Friedlander, "From Anti-Semitism to Extermination," 48–50; George Kren and Leon Rappoport, "Failures of Thought in Holocaust Interpretation," Michael N. Dobrowski and Isidor Wallimann, eds., *Towards the Holocaust. The Social and Economic Collapse of the Weimer Republic* (Westport, Conn.: Greenwood Press, 1983), 377–401.
2. See Marrus, *The Holocaust in History*, 199–202.
3. This bureaucratic machinery of destruction has been traced in detail by Raul Hilberg in his work that has been cited throughout this study, *The Destruction of the European Jews*. Hilberg has maintained that there was little difference between German institutions and the machinery of destruction. See Vol. 3, 994.
4. Zygmunt Bauman, *Modernity and the Holocaust* (Oxford: Polity Press, 1989), 86–116.
5. Ibid., 98.
6. Ibid., 98–99.
7. Hilberg, *Destruction of the European Jews*, Vol. 3, 993–99.
8. Bauman, *Modernity and the Holocaust*, 100–1.
9. Ibid., 104. Obedience to orders is, of course, not unique to the Third Reich. All bureaucracies have people who wish to profit by their actions within the system, but the setting of the totalitarian system is different. Here the moral stakes are higher as the crimes are so much greater when participation in mass murder is a means of rising in the hierarchy.
10. There were only two gaps in this regular daily pattern. On 29 June and 4 August 1941 no reports were issued. See Appendix A.
11. Between 2 January and 3 April 1942 the Monday-Wednesday-Friday pattern was repeated. The last six reports in the series were issued somewhat irregularly on April 8, 10, 14, 17, 21, and 24. The break was also observed at Christmas in December 1942 and January 1943 with the Reports from the Occupied Eastern Territories. The latter reports were issued every Friday starting on 1 May 1942. Reports from the Occupied Territories 17 and 35 were issued on other days.
12. See Ernst Fraenkel, *The Dual State* (New York: Oxford University Press, 1941).
13. See Buchheim, *Anatomy*, 303–96.

14. At his trial, Ernst Biberstein, head of Einsatzkommando 6, because he had been a member of the clergy, was asked if he had tried to give spiritual comfort to those about to be killed. He replied that he had not done this, saying it would have been throwing "pearls to swine." Tr. 2789. Biberstein further betrayed the twisted arrogance typical of so many leaders by stating "how little value human life" had for a Soviet citizen. Tr. 2853. Arrogant confidence in the ultimate success of their work may explain why the RSHA officials made so many copies of the reports and distributed them. It was one thing to report to Heydrich and Himmler what was being accomplished by the Kommandos; it was something else again to inform seventy to one hundred other agencies. Recipients of these reports would be informed of the effective and orderly manner in which the Security Police were performing their operations. The decision to send out so many copies was probably Heydrich's.

15. According to one Einsatzgruppe member, Kommando leaders had the opportunity to execute orders in ways that were felt to be appropriate for the particular circumstances in their area. Tr. 2600. See also Fred E. Katz "Implementation of the Holocaust: The Behavior of Nazi Officials," *Comparative Studies in Society and History* 24 (1982): 510–29. Katz emphasizes the autonomy given to Nazi leaders. See 522–27.

16. Kommando leaders often earned the praise of their superiors. For instance, Eugen Steimle, in 1941 head of Sonderkommando 7a, and in 1942 head of Sonderkommando 4a, was said to have shown "outstanding qualities in leading and handling the men assigned to him." Kahn, *Hitler's Spies*, 265.

17. See Browder, "SIPO and SD," 152–55. The general antiliberal attitude present throughout much of Europe served to isolate the Jews, which in the long run helped in their destruction. Yehuda Bauer and Nathan Rotenstreich, eds., *The Holocaust as Historical Experience* (New York: Holmes & Meier, 1981), 10.

18. Höhne, *Order of the Death's Head*, 356–57.

19. See Tr. 492, 498–501.

20. Tr. 513.

21. At Nuremberg, Albert Hartl, an SD official, testified that Max Thomas, Rasch's successor as leader of Einsatzgruppe C, had "great antipathy" for Ohlendorf's "bureaucratic correctness." Tr. 2882.

22. See Katz, "Implementation of the Holocaust," 516–20.

23. See Höhne, *Order of the Death's Head*, 357, citing a conversation with Frau Kathe Ohlendorf.

24. Buchheim, *Anatomy*, 386–87; Leo Alexander, "War Crimes and Their Motivation: The Socio-Psychological Structure of the SS and the Criminalization of a Society," *Journal of Criminal Law and Criminology* 39 (1949): 306. For example, Werner Braune, head of Einsatzkommando 11b, stated that Ohlendorf would have considered him a "shirker" if he had demanded to be relieved of his post. Tr. 3062.

25. Alexander, "War Crimes and Their Motivation," 299–300.

26. Affidavit by Erwin Schulz, 20 December 1945, NO–3841. Schulz's statement was confirmed by an affidavit by Karl Hennicke, an SD officer with Einsatzgruppe C. Hennicke said Rasch ordered that all officers and noncommissioned officers "as a matter of principle" were to attend executions. Affidavit by Karl Hennicke, 4 September 1947, NO–4999.

27. Affidavit by Walter Haensch, 21 July 1947, NO–4567.

28. Koehl, *Black Corps*, 245.

29. Buchheim, *Anatomy*, 317. One of the responsibilities of a Kommando leader was to prevent his men from being brutalized. Ibid., 372.

30. See Hilberg, *Destruction of the European Jews*, Vol. 3, 1007–9.

31. Gilbert, *The Holocaust: The Jewish Tragedy*, [already cited] 188.

32. Ibid., 198.

33. Tr. 2890.

34. Höhne, *Order of the Death's Head*, 363.

35. *IMT*, Vol. 4, 348.

36. For perhaps the most famous of these, see PS–1918 and PS–1919.

37. PS–1919.

38. Ibid., for additional evidence of problems among Himmler's men, see Fleming, *Hitler and the Final Solution*, 146–52.

39. For Jäger, see Fleming, *Hitler and the Final Solution*, 98; Wilhelm, *Die Truppe*, 536.

For Blobel, see Tr. 1524. For Bach-Zelewski, see Hilberg, *Destruction of the European Jews*, Vol. 1, 328.

40. PS–1919. Himmler was likely echoing Göring's sentiments toward animals. See Davidson, *The Trial of the Germans*, 63.

41. Fest, *Face of the Third Reich*, 119; Buchheim, *Anatomy*, 334, 336, 338, 362.

42. Tr. 633. The prosecuting attorney countered by saying that there was nothing worse than being shot when you are defenseless.

43. Tr. 2603.

44. Fest, *Face of the Third Reich*, 119, 302. In his Operational Order 8 of 17 July 1941, Heydrich demanded from his men "excellent behavior during and after duty." PS–502.

45. Browder, "SIPO and SD," 424–25.

46. Ibid., 426.

47. OSR 9, 19.

48. Jäger report. In OSR 86 Rasch called the solution to the Jewish problem an "organizational" problem. He had forced labor, not shooting, in mind.

49. OSR 80.

50. OSR 47, 81, 92.

51. OSR 146.

52. OSR 173.

53. At Nuremberg, Albert Hartl testified as a defense witness. Hartl stated that there were three attitudes among the Einsatzgruppen leaders: 1) those who accepted as valid the authority for the orders and carried them out; 2) those who were considered "soft" and suffered from pangs of conscience over the orders; and 3) those with conflicts about the killings who tried to evade the orders. Tr. 2890.

54. Wilhelm, *Die Truppe*, 629.

55. A postwar study of approximately three hundred former SS members included interviews with former Einsatzgruppen personnel. Unlike members of the Waffen SS interviewed in this study, who expressed no regrets about their wartime experiences and who stated they would do it all over again, the Einsatzgruppen members consulted *did* express regrets for what they did and admitted they would not want to have to play their role again. See John M. Steiner, "The SS Yesterday and Today: A Sociopsychological View," in Joel E. Dimsdale, ed. *Survivors, Victims and Perpetrators: Essays on the Nazi Holocaust* (Washington, D.C.: Hemisphere Publishing Corporation, 1980), 442.

56. Koehl has noted that many Germans throughout many agencies looked away and were thankful that they were not "called upon." Koehl, *Black Corps*, 204. Another historian had pointed out the great irony in the fact that in spite of their trampling on the fundamental moral values of western civilization, the Einsatzgruppen leaders at their trial put forward witness after witness who called attention to the presence of these same values in the defendants. See Leon Poliakov, *Harvest of Hate: The Nazi Program for the Destruction of the Jews of Europe* (Westport, Conn.: Greenwood Press, 1971), 132.

57. Raul Hilberg, "The Significance of the Holocaust," in *The Holocaust: Ideology, Bureaucracy and Genocide*, ed. Henry Friedlander and Sybil Milton. (Millwood, N.Y.: Kraus International Publications, 1980), 101.

58. Hilberg, *Destruction of the European Jews*, Vol. 1, 5–28, 273.

59. Bauman, *Modernity and the Holocaust*, 95.

Bibliography

Adam, Uwe Dietrich. *Judenpolitik im Dritten Reich*. Düsseldorf: Droste, 1972.

———. "An Overall Plan for Anti-Jewish Legislation in the Third Reich?" *Yad Vashem Studies* XI (1976): 33–55.

Adams, Arthur E. *Bolsheviks in the Ukraine: The Second Campaign, 1918–1919*. New Haven, Conn.: Yale University Press, 1963.

Ainsztein, Reuben. *Jewish Resistance in Nazi-Occupied Eastern Europe*. London: Paul Elek, 1974.

Alexander, Leo. "War Crimes and Their Motivation. The Socio-Psychological Structure of the SS and the Criminalization of a Society." *Journal of Criminal Law and Criminology* 39 (1949): 298–326.

Almond, Gabriel A., ed. *The Struggle for Democracy in Germany*. Chapel Hill, N.C.: University of North Carolina Press, 1949.

Angress, Werner T., and Bradley F. Smith. "Diaries of Heinrich Himmler's Early Years." *Journal of Modern History* 31 (1959): 206–24.

Apenslak, Jacob, ed. *The Black Book of Polish Jewry. An Account of the Martyrdom of Polish Jewry under the Nazi Occupation*. New York: Roy Publishers, 1943.

Appleman, J. A. *Military Tribunals and International Crimes*. Westport, Conn.: Greenwood Press, 1971.

Arad, Yitzhak. "The 'Final Solution' in Lithuania in the Light of German Documentation." *Yad Vashem Studies* XI (1976): 234–72.

———. "Alfred Rosenberg and the 'Final Solution' in the Occupied Soviet Territories." *Yad Vashem Studies* XIII (1979): 263–86.

———. *Ghetto in Flames: The Struggle and Destruction of the Jews in Vilna in the Holocaust*. Jerusalem: Yad Vashem, 1980.

———. *Belzec, Sobibor, Treblinka: The Operation Reinhard Death Camps*. Bloomington and Indianapolis: Indiana University Press, 1987.

Arad, Yitzhak, Yisrael Gutman, and Abraham Margaliot, eds. *Documents on the Holocaust: Selected Sources on the Destruction of the Jews of Germany and Austria, Poland and the Soviet Union*. Jerusalem: Yad Vashem, 1981.

Arendt, Hannah. *Eichmann in Jerusalem. A Report on the Banality of Evil*, rev. and enl. London: Penguin Books, 1976.

Armstrong, John A. *Ukrainian Nationalism 1939–1945*. New York: Columbia University Press, 1955.

———. "Collaborationism in World War II: The Integral Nationalist Variant in Eastern Europe." *Journal of Modern History* 40 (1968): 396–410.

———, ed. *Soviet Partisans in World War II*. Madison, Wisc.: University of Wisconsin Press, 1964.

Aronsfeld, C. C. *The Text of the Holocaust. A Study of the Nazis' Extermination Propaganda 1919–1945*. Marblehead, Mass.: Micah Publications, 1985.

Aronson, Shlomo. *Beginnings of the Gestapo System. The Bavarian Model in 1933*. Jerusalem: Israel Universities Press, 1969.

———. *Reinhard Heydrich und die Frühgeschichte von Gestapo und SD*. Stuttgart: Deutsche Verlags-Anstalt, 1971.

Aschheim, Steven E. *Brothers and Strangers. The East European Jew in German and German Jewish Consciousness 1800–1923*. Madison, Wisc.: University of Wisconsin Press, 1982.

Baranauskas, B., and K. Ruksenas, comps. *Documents Accuse*. Vilnius: Gintaras, 1970.

Baron, Salo W. *The Russian Jew under Tsars and Soviets*. 2nd ed. New York: Macmillan, 1976.

Bartov, Omer. *The Eastern Front 1941–45: German Troops and the Barbarization of Warfare*. London: Macmillan, 1985.

Bauer, Yehuda. "Genocide: Was it the Nazis' Original Plan?" *The Annals of the American Academy of Political and Social Science* 450 (1980): 35–45.

———. *A History of the Holocaust*. New York: Franklin Watts, 1982.

Bauer, Yehuda, and Nathan Rotenstreich, eds. *The Holocaust as Historical Experience*. New York: Holmes & Meier, 1981.

Bauman, Zygmunt. *Modernity and the Holocaust*. Oxford: Polity Press, 1989.

Beer, Mathias. "Die Entwicklung der Gaswagen Beim Mord an den Juden." *Vierteljahrshefte für Zeitgeschichte* 35 (1987): 403–17.

Beloff, Max, ed. *On the Track of Tyranny*. Freeport, N.Y.: Books for Libraries Press, 1971.

Bilinsky, Yaroslav. "Methodological Problems and Philosophical Issues in the Study of Jewish-Ukrainian Relations during the Second World War." In *Ukrainian-Jewish Relations in Historical Perspective*, edited by Peter J. Potichnyj and Howard Aster, pp. 373–407. Edmonton: Canadian Institute of Ukrainian Studies. University of Alberta, 1988.

Birn, Ruth Bettina. *Die Höheren SS-und Polizeiführer: Himmlers Vertreter im Reich und in den besetzten Gebieten*. Düsseldorf: Droste Verlag, 1986.

Black, Peter R. *Ernst Kaltenbrunner: Ideological Soldier of the Third Reich*. Princeton, N.J. Princeton University Press, 1984.

Blumenthal, Nachman. "On the Nazi Vocabulary." *Yad Vashem Studies* I (1957): 49–66.

———. "Action." *Yad Vashem Studies* IV (1960): 57–96.

Bobe, Mendel, ed. *The Jews in Latvia*. Tel Aviv: Association of Latvian and Estonian Jews In Israel, 1971.

Boberach, Heinz, ed. *Meldungen aus dem Reich: Auswahl aus den Geheimen Lageberichten des Sicherheitsdienstes der SS 1939–1944*. Neuwied and Berlin: Hermann Luchterhand, 1965.

———, ed. *Berichte des SD und der Gestapo über Kirchen und Kirchenvolk in Deutschland 1934–1944*. Mainz: Matthias-Grünewald, 1971.

Boog, Horst, and others, eds. *Der Angriff auf die Sowjetunion*. Stuttgart: Deutsche Verlags– Anstalt, 1983.

Boshyk, Yury, ed. *Ukraine during World War II: History and Its Aftermath*. Edmonton: Canadian Institute of Ukrainian Studies. University of Alberta, 1986.

Bracher, Karl Dietrich. *The German Dictatorship: The Origins, Structure, and Effects of National Socialism*. New York: Praeger, 1970.

Brady, Robert A. *The Spirit and Structure of German Fascism*. New York: Howard Fertig, 1969.

Braham, Randolph L. "The Kamenets Podolsk and Délvidék Massacres: Prelude to the Holocaust in Hungary." *Yad Vashem Studies* IX (1973): 133–56.

Bramsted, Ernest K. *Goebbels and National Socialist Propaganda 1925–1945*. London: Cresset Press, 1965.

Brissaud, André. *The Nazi Secret Service*. London: The Bodley Head, 1974.

Broszat, Martin. *The Hitler State: The Foundation and Development of the Internal Structure of the Third Reich*. London and New York: Longman, 1981.

Browder, George Clark. "SIPO and SD, 1931–1940. Formation of an Instrument of Power." Ph.D. diss., University of Wisconsin, 1976.

Brown, MacAlister. "The Third Reich's Mobilization of the German Fifth Column in Eastern Europe." *Journal of Central European Affairs* 19 no. 2 (1959): 128–48.

Browning, Christopher R. *The Final Solution and the German Foreign Office. A Study of Referat D III of Abteilung Deutschland, 1940–43.* New York: Holmes & Meier, 1978.

———. "The Government Experts." In *The Holocaust: Ideology, Bureaucracy and Genocide,* edited by Henry Friedlander and Sybil Milton, pp. 183–97. Millwood, N.Y.: Kraus International Publications. 1980.

———. "The Final Solution in Serbia: The Semlin Judenlager—A Case Study." *Yad Vashem Studies* XV (1983): 55–90.

———. "A Reply to Martin Broszat Regarding the Origins of the Final Solution." In *Simon Wiesenthal Center Annual* I, edited by Henry Friedlander and Sybil Milton, pp. 113–32. Chappaqua, N.Y.: Rossel Books, 1984.

———. *Fateful Months: Essays on the Emergence of the Final Solution.* New York: Holmes & Meier, 1985.

———. "Nazi Ghettoization Policy in Poland: 1939–41." *Central European History* 19, no. 4 (1986): 343–68.

———. "Nazi Resettlement Policy and the Search for a Solution to the Jewish Question, 1939–1941." *German Studies Review* 9 (1986): 497–519.

Buchheim, Hans, and others. *Anatomy of the SS State.* New York: Walker and Company, 1968.

———. *Totalitarian Rule: Its Nature and Characteristics.* Middletown, Conn.: Wesleyan University Press, 1968.

Büchler, Yehoshua. "Kommandostab Reichsführer–SS: Himmler's Personal Murder Brigades in 1941." *Holocaust and Genocide Studies* I, no. 1 (1986): 11–25.

Burdick, Charles B. "Tradition and Murder in the Wehrmacht." In *Simon Wiesenthal Center Annual* 4, edited by Henry Friedlander and Sybil Milton, pp. 329–36. White Plains, N.Y.: Kraus International Publications, 1987.

Burleigh, Michael. *Germany Turns Eastwards: A Study of Ostforschung in the Third Reich.* Cambridge: Cambridge University Press, 1988.

Calic, Edouard. *Reinhard Heydrich: Schlüsselfigur des Dritten Reiches.* Düsseldorf: Droste Verlag, 1982.

Caming, H. W. William. "Nuremberg Trials: Partisans, Hostages and Reprisals." *The Judge Advocate Journal* 4 (1950): 16–22.

Chalk, Frank, and Kurt Jonassohn. *The History and Sociology of Genocide. Analyses and Case Studies.* New Haven and London: Yale University Press, 1990.

Conot, Robert E. *Justice at Nuremberg.* New York: Harper & Row, 1983.

Conway, John S. "The Holocaust and the Historians." *The Annals of the American Academy of Political and Social Science* 450 (1980): 153–64.

Crankshaw, Edward. *The Gestapo: Instrument of Tyranny.* New York: Viking Press, 1956.

Creel, George. *War Criminals and Punishment.* London: Hutchinson, 1944.

Dallin, Alexander. *Odessa, 1941–1944: A Case Study of Soviet Territory under Foreign Rule.* Santa Monica, Calif.: The Rand Corporation, 1957.

———. *German Rule in Russia 1941–1945: A Study of Occupation Policies.* Second revised edition. Boulder, Colo.: Westview Press, 1981.

Datner, Szyman. *Crimes Against POWs: Responsibility of the Wehrmacht.* Warsaw: Zachodnia Agencja Prasowa, 1964.

Davidson, Eugene. *The Trial of the Germans.* New York: Collier Books, 1972.

Dawidowicz, Lucy S. *The War Against the Jews 1933–1945.* New York: Holt, Rinehart & Winston, 1975.

Deist, Wilhelm, ed. *The German Military in the Age of Total War.* Warwickshire: Berg Publishers Ltd., 1985.

Delarue, Jacques. *The Gestapo: A History of Horror.* New York: Morrow, 1964.

Deschner, Gunther. *Reinhard Heydrich: A Biography.* New York: Stein and Day, 1981.

De Zayas, Alfred M. *The Wehrmacht War Crimes Bureau, 1939–1945.* Lincoln and London: University of Nebraska Press, 1989.

Dicks, Henry. *Licensed Mass Murder.* London: Chatto, Heinemann. Sussex University Press, 1972.

Dimsdale, Joel E., ed. *Survivors, Victims, and Perpetrators. Essays on the Nazi Holocaust.* Washington, D.C.: Hemisphere Publishing Corporation, 1980.

Dmytryshyn, Basil. "The Nazis and The SS Volunteer Division 'Galicia.'" *The American Slavic and East European Review* 15 (1956): 3–10.

Dobroszycki, Lucjan, ed. *The Chronicle of the Lodz Ghetto 1941–1944.* New Haven: Yale University Press, 1984.

Drozdznski, Alexander, and Jan Zaborowski. *Oberlander: A Study in German East Policies.* Poznan: Wydawnictwo Zachodnie, 1960.

Eckhardt, Alice L., and Roy A. Eckhardt. "The Holocaust and the Enigma of Uniqueness: A Philosophical Effort at Practical Clarification." *The Annals of the American Academy of Political and Social Science* 450 (1980): 165–78.

Ehrenburg, Ilya, and Vasily Grossman, eds. *The Black Book.* New York: Holocaust Library, 1981.

Erickson, John. *The Road to Stalingrad: Stalin's War with Germany.* London: Weidenfeld and Nicolson, 1975.

Ettinger, S. "Jews and Non-Jews in Eastern and Central Europe Between the Wars: An Outline." In *Jews and Non-Jews in Eastern Europe 1918–1945*, edited by B. Vago and George L. Mosse, pp. 1–19. Jerusalem: Israel Universities Press, 1974.

Facius, Friedrich, Hans Booms, and Heinz Boberach, eds. *Das Bundesarchiv und seine Bestände.* Boppard am Rhein: Harald Boldt Verlag, 1968.

Fattig, Richard Cavell. "Reprisal: The German Army and the Execution of Hostages during the Second World War." Ph.D. diss., University of California, 1980.

Ferencz, Benjamin B. "Nürnberg Trial Procedure and the Rights of the Accused." *Journal of Criminal Law and Criminology* 39 (1948): 144–51.

———. *Less than Slaves: Jewish Forced Labor and the Quest for Compensation.* Cambridge, Mass. and London: Harvard University Press, 1979.

Fest, Joachim C. *The Face of the Third Reich. Portraits of the Nazi Leadership.* New York: Pantheon Books, 1970.

Fishman, Jack. *Long Knives and Short Memories: The Spandau Prison Story.* St. John's, Newfoundland: Breakwater Books, 1986.

Fleming, Gerald. *Hitler and the Final Solution.* Berkeley, Calif.: University of California Press, 1984.

Förster, Jürgen. "The Wehrmacht and the War of Extermination Against the Soviet Union." *Yad Vashem Studies* XIV (1981): 7–34.

———. "New Wine in Old Skins? The Wehrmacht and the War of 'Weltanschauungen', 1941." In *The German Military in the Age of Total War*, edited by Wilhelm Deist, pp. 304–22. Warwickshire: Berg Publishers Ltd., 1985.

———. "The German Army and the Ideological War against the Soviet Union." In *The Policies of Genocide: Jews and Soviet Prisoners of War in Nazi Germany*, edited by Gerhard Hirschfeld, pp. 15–29. London: Allen & Unwin, 1986.

Fox, John P. "The Final Solution: Intended or Contingent?" *Patterns of Prejudice* 18 no. 3 (1984): 27–39.

Fraenkel, Ernst. *The Dual State.* New York: Oxford University Press, 1941.

Friedlander, Henry. "The Manipulation of Language." In *The Holocaust: Ideology, Bureaucracy, and Genocide*, edited by Henry Friedlander and Sybil Milton, pp. 103–13. Millwood, N.Y.: Kraus International Publications, 1980.

————. "The Judiciary and Nazi Crimes in Postwar Germany." In *Simon Wiesenthal Center Annual* 1, edited by Henry Friedlander and Sybil Milton, pp. 27–44, Chappaqua, N.Y.: Rossel Books, 1984.

Friedlander, Saul. "From Anti-Semitism to Extermination: A Historiographical Study of Nazi Policies Toward the Jews and an Essay in Interpretation." *Yad Vashem Studies* XVI (1984): 1–50.

Friedman, Philip. "The Lublin Reservation and the Madagascar Plan: Two Aspects of Nazi Jewish Policy during the Second World War." *Yivo Annual of Jewish Social Studies* VII (1953): 151–77.

————. "The Karaites under Nazi Rule." In *On the Track of Tyranny*, edited by Max Beloff, pp. 97–123. Freeport, N.Y.: Books for Libraries Press, 1971.

————. *Roads to Extinction: Essays on the Holocaust.* New York: Jewish Publication Society, 1980.

————. "Ukrainian-Jewish Relations during the Nazi Occupation." In Philip Friedman, *Roads to Extinction: Essays on the Holocaust*, 176–208. New York: Jewish Publication Society, 1980.

Gefen, Aba. *Unholy Alliance.* New York: Yuval Tal Ltd., 1973.

Gilbert, Martin. *Atlas of the Holocaust.* New York: Macmillan, 1982.

————. *The Holocaust: The Jewish Tragedy.* London: Collins, 1986.

Gilboa, Yehoshua A. *The Black Years of Soviet Jewry 1939–1953.* Boston: Little Brown, 1971.

Gisevius, Hans Bernd. *To the Bitter End.* Boston, Mass.: Houghton Mifflin Company, 1947.

Glicksman, William. "Violence and Terror: The Nazi-German Conception of Killing and Murder." In *Internationl Terrorism in the Contemporary World*, edited by Marius H. Livingston, Lee Bruce Kress, and Marie G. Wanek, pp. 423–29. Westport, Conn.: Greenwood Press, 1978.

Grabitz, Helge. "Problems of Nazi Trials in the Federal Republic of Germany." *Holocaust and Genocide Studies* 3 no. 2 (1988): 209–22.

Grunberger, Richard. *Hitler's SS.* New York: Delacorte Press, 1970.

Harris, Whitney R. *Tyranny on Trial: The Evidence at Nuremberg.* Dallas: Southern Methodist University Press, 1954.

Hassell, Ulrich von. *The Von Hassell Diaries, 1938–1944.* Garden City, N.Y.: Doubleday and Company, 1947.

Headland, Ronald. "The Einsatzgruppen: The Question of Their Initial Operations." *Holocaust and Genocide Studies* 4 no. 4 (1989): 401–12.

Heller, Celia S. *On the Edge of Destruction: Jews of Poland Between the Two World Wars.* New York: Columbia University Press, 1977.

Henkys, Reinhard. *Die Nationalsozialistischen Gewaltverbrechen: Geschichte and Gericht.* Stuttgart and Berlin: Kreuz–Verlag, 1964.

Herzstein, Robert Edwin. "Anti-Jewish Propaganda in the Orel Region of Great Russia, 1942–1943: The German Army and Its Russian Collaborators. "In *Simon Wiesenthal Center Annual* 6, edited by Henry Friedlander and Sybil Milton, pp. 33–55. New York: Philosophical Library, 1989.

Hilberg, Raul. "The Significance of the Holocaust." In *The Holocaust: Ideology, Bureaucracy and Genocide*, edited by Henry Friedlander and Sybil Milton, pp. 95–102. Millwood, N.Y.: Kraus International Publications, 1980.

————. *The Destruction of the European Jews.* Revised edition in 3 vols. New York: Holmes & Meier, 1985.

————, ed. *Documents of Destruction.* Chicago: Quadrangle Books, 1971.

Hillgruber, Andreas. "The Extermination of the European Jews in Its Historical Context—A Recapitulation." *Yad Vashem Studies* XVII (1986): 1–15.

————. "War in the East and the Extermination of the Jews." In *The Nazi Holocaust:*

Historical Articles on the Destruction of European Jews, edited by Michael R. Marrus, vol. 3 no. 2, pp. 85–114. Westport and London: Meckler Corporation, 1989.

Hinsley, F. H., and others. *British Intelligence in the Second World War: Its Influence on Strategy and Operations.* 2 vols. London: Her Majesty's Stationery Office, 1981.

Hirschfeld, Gerhard, ed. *The Policies of Genocide: Jews and Soviet Prisoners of War in Nazi Germany.* London: Allen & Unwin, 1986.

Hirschfeld, Gerhard, and Lothar Kettenacker, eds. *"The Führer State": Myth and Reality. Studies on the Structure and Politics of the Third Reich.* London: German Historical Institute, 1981.

Höhne, Heinz. *The Order of the Death's Head: The Story of Hitler's SS.* London: Secker & Warburg, 1970.

Huberband, Shimon. *Kiddush Hashem: Jewish Religious and Cultural Life in Poland during the Holocaust.* Hoboken, N.J.: KTAV Publishing House Inc., 1987.

Huneke, Douglas K. *The Moses of Rovno.* New York: Dodd, Mead & Company, 1985.

International Military Tribunal. *Trial of the Major War Criminals before the International Military Tribunal.* 42 vols. Nuremberg: 1947–48.

Jäckel, Eberhard. *Hitler's Weltanschauung: A Blueprint for Power.* Middletown, Conn.: Wesleyan University Press, 1972.

———. *Hitler in History.* Hanover and London: University Press of New England, 1984.

Jäckel, Eberhard, and Jürgen Rohwer, eds. *Der Mord an den Juden im zweiten Weltkrieg: Entschlussbildung und Verwirklichung.* Stuttgart: Deutsche Verlags-Anstalt, 1985.

Jackson, J. Hampden. *Estonia.* London: Allen & Unwin, 1948.

Jacobsen, Hans-Adolf, ed. *Generaloberst Halder Kriegstagebuch: Tägliche Aufzeichnungen des Chefs des Generalstabes des Heeres 1939–1942.* 3 vols. Stuttgart: W. Kohlhammer Verlag, 1963.

———, and others. *Anatomy of the SS State.* New York: Walker and Company, 1968.

Jewish Resistance during the Holocaust. Proceedings of the Conference on Manifestations of Jewish Resistance, Jerusalem, April 1968. Jerusalem: Yad Vashem, 1971.

Kahn, David. *Hitler's Spies: German Military Intelligence in World War II.* New York: Macmillan, 1978.

Kamentsky, Ihor. *Secret Nazi Plans for Eastern Europe: A Study of Lebensraum Policies.* New York: Bookman Associates, 1961.

Kater, Michael H. *The Nazi Party: A Social Profile of Members and Leaders, 1919–1945.* Cambridge, Mass.: Harvard University Press, 1983.

Katz, Fred E. "Implementation of the Holocaust: The Behavior of Nazi Officials." *Comparative Studies in Society and History* 24 (1982): 510–29.

Kaufmann, Max. *Die Vernichtung der Juden Lettlands.* Munich: Churbn Lettland, 1947.

Kempner, Robert M. W. "Nuremberg Trials as Sources of Recent German Political and Historical Materials." *American Political Science Review* 44 (1950): 447–59.

———. *SS im Kreuzverhör.* Munich: Rutten & Leoning Verlag, 1964.

Kershaw, Ian. *The Nazi Dictatorship: Problems and Perspectives of Interpretation.* London: Edward Arnold, 1985.

Kersten, Felix. *The Kersten Memoirs 1940–1945.* New York: Macmillan, 1957.

Klarsfeld, Serge, ed. *The Holocaust and the Neo-Nazi Mythomania.* New York: The Beate Klarsfeld Foundation, 1978.

Kleinfeld, Gerald R., and Lewis A. Tambs. *Hitler's Spanish Legion: The Blue Division in Russia.* Carbondale: Southern Illinois University Press, 1979.

Knoebel, Edgar Erwin. "Racial Illusion and Military Necessity: A Study of SS Political and Manpower Objectives in Occupied Belgium." Ph.D. diss., University of Colorado, 1965.

Kochan, Lionel, ed. *The Jews in the Soviet Union Since 1917.* Third edition. Oxford and New York: Published for the Institute of Jewish Affairs by Oxford University Press, 1978.

Koehl, Robert. *RKFDV: German Resettlement and Population Policy, 1939–1945: A History of the Reich Commission for the Strengthening of Germandom.* Cambridge, Mass.: Harvard University Press, 1957.

———. "Feudal Aspects of National Socialism." *American Political Science Review* 54 (1960): 921–33.

———. "The Character of the Nazi SS." *Journal of Modern History* 34 (1962): 275–83.

Koehl, Robert Lewis. *The Black Corps: The Structure and Power Struggles of the Nazi SS.* Madison Wisc.: University of Wisconsin Press, 1983.

Kogon, Eugen. *The Theory and Practice of Hell: The German Concentration Camps and the System Behind Them.* New York: Octagon Books, 1973.

Kölmel, Rainer. "A Holocaust Memorial in Berlin?" A paper presented at the international conference, *Remembering for the Future*, held in Oxford, 1988.

Kraus, René. *Europe in Revolt.* New York: Macmillan, 1942.

Kraus, Wolfgang H., and Gabriel A. Almond. "Resistance and Repression under the Nazis." In *The Struggle for Democracy in Germany*, edited by Gabriel A. Almond, pp. 33–63. Chapel Hill N.C.: University of North Carolina Press, 1949.

Krausnick, Helmut, and others. *Anatomy of the SS State.* New York: Walker and Company, 1968.

Krausnick, Helmut, and Hans-Heinrich Wilhelm. *Die Truppe des Weltanschauungskrieges: Die Einsatzgruppen der Sicherheitspolizei und des SD, 1938–1942.* Stuttgart: Deutsche Verlags-Anstalt, 1981.

———. "Hitler und die Befehle an die Einsatzgruppen im Sommer 1941." In *Der Mord an den Juden im zweiten Weltkrieg: Entschlussbildung und Verwirklichung*, edited by Eberhard Jäckel, and Jürgen Rohwer, pp. 88–106. Stuttgart: Deutsche Verlags-Anstalt, 1985.

———. Letter to the Editors. In *Simon Wiesenthal Center Annual* 6, edited by Henry Friedlander and Sybil Milton, pp. 311–29. New York: Philosophical Library, 1989.

Kren, George M. "The SS: A Social and Psychohistorical Analysis." In *International Terrorism in the Contemporary World*, edited by Marius H. Livingston, Lee Bruce Kress, and Marie G. Wanek, pp. 436–43. Westport, Conn.: Greenwood Press, 1978.

Kren, George M., and Leon Rappoport. *The Holocaust and the Crisis of Human Behaviour.* New York: Holmes & Meier, 1980.

———. "Failures of Thought in Holocaust Interpretation." In *Towards the Holocaust: The Social and Economic Collapse of the Weimar Republic*, edited by Michael N. Dobkowski, and Isidor Wallimann, pp. 377–401. Westport Conn.: Greenwood Press, 1983.

Kriegstagebuch des Oberkommandos der Wehrmacht, Band I: 1 August 1940–31 Dezember 1941. Edited by Hans-Adolf Jacobsen. Frankfurt am Main: Bernard & Graefe Verlag für Wehrwesen, 1965.

Kulka, Otto Dov. "'Public Opinion' in Nazi Germany and the 'Jewish Question.'" *The Jerusalem Quarterly* 25 (1982): 121–44; 26 (1983): 34–55.

Kulka, Otto Dov, and Aron Rodrigue. "The German Population and the Jews in the Third Reich: Recent Publications and Trends in Research on German Society and the 'Jewish Question.'" *Yad Vashem Studies* XVI (1984): 421–35.

———. "Singularity and Its Relativization: Changing Views in German Historiography on National Socialism and the 'Final Solution.'" A paper presented at the international conference, *Remembering for the Future*, held in Oxford, 1988.

Kuznetsov, Anatoli. *Babi Yar: A Document in the Form of a Novel.* London: Jonathan Cape, 1970.

Lang, Jochen von, and Claus Sibyll, eds. *Eichmann Interrogated: Transcripts from the Archives of the Israeli Police.* Toronto: Lester & Orpen Dennys, 1983.

Laqueur, Walter. *The Terrible Secret: Suppression of the Truth about Hitler's "Final Solution."* London: Penguin Books, 1982.

Lazar, Chaim. *Destruction and Resistance: A History of the Partisan Movement in Vilna*. New York: Shengold Publishers, Inc., 1985.

Lerner, Daniel, with Ithiel de Sola Pool, and George K. Schueller. *The Nazi Elite*. Stanford, Conn.: Hoover Institute Studies, Stanford University Press, 1951.

Leverkuehn, Paul. *German Military Intelligence*. New York: Praeger, 1954.

Levin, Dov. "Estonian Jews in the USSR (1941–1945): Research Based on Survivors' Testimony." *Yad Vashem Studies* XI (1976): 273–97.

———. "July 1944 — The Crucial Month for the Remnants of Lithuanian Jewry." *Yad Vashem Studies* XVI (1984): 333–61.

———. *Fighting Back: Lithuanian Jewry's Armed Resistance to the Nazis, 1941–1945*. New York: Holmes & Meier, 1985.

Levin, Nora. *The Holocaust: The Destruction of European Jewry 1933–1945*. New York: Crowell, 1968.

Litani, Dora. "The Destruction of the Jews of Odessa in the Light of Rumanian Documents." *Yad Vashem Studies* VI (1967): 135–54.

Littman, Sol. *The Rauca Case: War Criminal on Trial*. Markham, Ontario: PaperJacks, 1984.

Littlejohn, David. *The Patriotic Traitors: A History of Collaboration in German-Occupied Europe, 1940–45*. London: Heinemann, 1972.

Lochner, Louis P., ed. *The Goebbels Diaries, 1942–1943*. Garden City, N.Y.: Doubleday, 1948.

Lowenthal, Rudolf. "The Extinction of the Krimchaks in World War II." *The American Slavic and East European Review* 90 (1951): 130–36.

Lozowick, Yaacov. "Rollbahn Mord: The Early Activities of Einsatzgruppe C." *Holocaust and Genocide Studies* 2 no. 2 (1987): 221–41.

Lundin, C. Leonard. "Nazification of Baltic German Minorities: A Contribution to the Study of the Diplomacy of 1939." *Journal of Central European Affairs* 7 (1947): 1–28.

Manvell, Roger, and Heinrich Fraenkel. *The Incomparable Crime. Mass Extermination in the Twentieth Century: The Legacy of Guilt*. New York: G. P. Putnam's Sons, 1967.

Marrus, Michael R. *The Holocaust in History*. Toronto: Lester & Orpen Dennys, 1987.

———, ed. *The Nazi Holocaust: Historical Articles on the Destruction of the European Jews*, 9 vols. Westport and London: Meckler Corporation, 1989.

Marsh, Norman S. "Some Aspects of the German Legal System under National Socialism." *Law Quarterly Review* 62 (1946): 366–74.

Maser, Werner. *Nuremberg: A Nation on Trial*. London: Allen Lane, 1979.

Mason, Tim. "Intention and Explanation: A Current Controversy about the Interpretation of National Socialism." In *"The Führer State:" Myth and Reality, Studies on the Structure and Politics of the Third Reich*, edited by Gerhard Hirschfeld and Lothar Kettenacker, pp. 23–40. London: German Historical Institute, 1981.

Mayer, Arno J. *Why Did the Heavens Not Darken? The "Final Solution" in History*. New York: Pantheon Books, 1988.

Mendelsohn, Ezra. *The Jews of East Central Europe Between the World Wars*. Bloomington: Indiana University Press, 1983.

Mendelsohn, John. "Trial by Document: The Use of Seized Records in the United States Proceedings at Nuernberg." Ph.D. diss., University of Maryland, 1974.

———. "Trial by Document: The Problem of Due Process for War Criminals at Nuernberg." *Prologue* 7 no. 4 (1975): 227–34.

———, comp. *Special List—NARS no. 42. Nuernberg War Crime Trials. Records of Case 9. United States of America v. Otto Ohlendorf, et al*. Washington, D.C.: National Archives and Records Service, 1978.

———, ed. *The Holocaust: Selected Documents in Eighteen Volumes*. New York: Garland Publishing, 1982.

Merkl, Peter H. *Political Violence under the Swastika: 581 Early Nazis*. Princeton, N.J.: Princeton University Press, 1975.

Messenger, Charles. *Hitler's Gladiator: The Life and Times of Oberstgruppenführer and Panzergeneral—Oberst der Waffen–SS Sepp Dietrich*. London: Brassey's Defense Publishers, 1988.

Messerschmidt, Manfred. "The Wehrmacht and the Volksgemeinschaft." *Journal of Contemporary History* 18 (1983): 719–44.

Mishell, William W. *Kaddish for Kovno: Life and Death in a Lithuanian Ghetto 1941–1945*. Chicago: Chicago Review Press, 1988.

Moritz, Erhard, ed. *Fall Barbarossa: Dokumente zur Vorbereitung der Faschistischen Wehrmacht auf die Aggression gegen die Sowjetunion (1940/41)*. Berlin: Deutscher Militarverlag, 1970.

Moser, Jonny. "Nisko: The First Experiment in Deportation." *In Simon Wiesenthal Center Annual* 2, edited by Henry. Friedlander and Sybil Milton, pp. 1–30. White Plains, N.Y.: Kraus International Publications, 1985.

Mosse, George L. *The Crisis of German Ideology: Intellectual Origins of the Third Reich*. London: Weidenfeld and Nicolson, 1966.

———. *Toward the Final Solution: A History of European Racism*. New York: Howard Fertig, 1978.

Mulligan, Timothy P. "Reckoning the Cost of People's War: The German Experience in the Central USSR." *Russian History* 9 (1982): 27–48.

Musmanno, Michael. *The Eichmann Kommandos*. Philadelphia: Macrae Smith Co., 1961.

(The) Nazi Concentration Camps. Structure and Aims. The Image of the Prisoner. The Jews in the Camps. Proceedings of the Fourth Yad Vashem International Historical Conference. January 1980. Jerusalem: Yad Vashem, 1984.

Nazi Conspiracy and Aggression. 8 vols. and 2 supplemental vols. Washington D.C.: United States Government Printing Office, 1946–1948.

Neshamit, Sarah. "Rescue in Lithuania during the Nazi Occupation June 1941–August 1944." In *Rescue Attempts during the Holocaust. Proceedings of the Second Yad Vashem International Historical Conference*. Jerusalem, April 1974, 289–331. Jerusalem: Yad Vashem, 1977.

Neufeldt, Hans-Joachim, Jürgen Huck, and Georg Tessin. *Zur Geschichte der Ordnungspolizei 1936–1945*. Koblenz: Bundesarchivs, 1957.

Niebergall, Fred. "Brief Survey Concerning the Records of the War Crime Trials Held in Nürnberg, Germany." *Law Library Journal* 42 (1949): 87–90.

Noakes, Jeremy, and Geoffrey Pridham, eds. *Documents on Nazism, 1919–1945*. London: Jonathan Cape, 1974.

Oldenhage, Klaus. "International Joint Ventures for Exchange of Archival Materials through Reprography." Paper presented at Special Plenary Session: The Fate of German Contemporary Records After World War II. Tenth International Congress on Archives, Bonn. 1984.

Orbach, Wila. "The Destruction of the Jews in the Nazi-Occupied Territories of the USSR." *Soviet Jewish Affairs* 6 no. 2 (1976): 14–51.

Paucker, Arnold, ed. *Die Juden im Nationalsozialistischen Deutschland*. Tübingen: J. C. B. Mohr, 1986.

Peterson, E. N. "The Bureaucracy and the Nazi Party." *The Review of Politics* 28 no. 2 (1966): 172–92.

Poliakov, Leon. *Harvest of Hate: The Nazi Program for the Destruction of the Jews of Europe*. Westport, Conn.: Greenwood Press, 1971.

Pomrenze, Seymour J. "Policies and Procedures for the Protection, Use, and Return of Captured German Records." In *Captured German and Related Records*, edited by Robert Wolfe, pp. 5–30. Athens, Ohio: Ohio University Press, 1974.

Possony, Stefan T. "The Ukrainian-Jewish Problem." *The Ukrainian Quarterly* XL no. 4 (1984): 369–81.

Potichnyj, Peter J., and Howard Aster, eds. *Ukrainian-Jewish Relations in Historical Perspective*. Edmonton: Canadian Institute of Ukrainian Studies. University of Alberta, 1988.

Prokop, Myroslav. "Ukraine in Germany's World War II Plans." *Ukrainian Quarterly* II (1955): 134–44.

Redlich, Shimon. "The Jews in Soviet Annexed Territories, 1939–1941." *Soviet Jewish Affairs* 1 (1971): 81–90.

Reitlinger, Gerald. *The SS: Alibi of a Nation, 1922–1945*. New York: Viking, 1957.

———. *The House Built on Sand: The Conflicts of German Policy in Russia, 1939–1945*. London: Weidenfeld and Nicolson, 1960.

———. *The Final Solution: The Attempt to Exterminate the Jews of Europe, 1939–1945*. Second revised and augmented edition. South Brunswick, N.J.: T. Yoseloff, 1968.

Rich, Norman. *Hitler's War Aims: The Establishment of the New Order*. New York: Norton & Company, 1974.

Robinson, Jacob. *And the Crooked Shall Be Made Straight: The Eichmann Trial, the Jewish Catastrophe, and Hannah Arendt's Narrative*. New York: Macmillan, 1965.

Robinson, Jacob, and Henry Sachs. *The Holocaust; The Nuremberg Evidence, Part One: The Documents*. Jerusalem and New York: Yad Vashem and Yivo, 1976.

Rückerl, Adalbert. *The Investigation of Nazi Crimes 1945–1978: A Documentation*. Hamden, Conn. Archon Books, 1980.

———, ed. *NS-Prozesse. Nach 25 Jahren Strafverfolgung: Mölichkeiten-Grenzen-Ergebnisse*. Karlsruhe: C. F. Müller, 1971.

Rudashevski, Yitskhak. *The Diary of the Vilna Ghetto, June 1941–April 1943*. Tel Aviv: Ghetto Fighters' House, 1973.

Rürup, Reinhard, and others, eds. *Topographie des Terrors: Gestapo, SS, und Reichssicherheitshauptampt auf dem "Prinz-Albrecht-Gelände," Eine Dokumentation*. Berlin: Verlag Willmuth Arenhövel, 1987.

Sabini, John P., and Maury Silver. "Destroying the Innocent with a Clear Conscience: A Sociopsychology of the Holocaust." In *Survivors, Victims, and Perpetrators: Essays on the Nazi Holocaust*, edited by Joel E. Dimsdale, pp. 329–58. Washington, D.C.: Hemisphere Publishing Corporation, 1980.

Scheffler, Wolfgang. "A Study of the Einsatzgruppen." An unpublished study. Exhibit no. 60, *Federal Republic of Germany v. Helmut Rauca*. Supreme Court of Ontario, 12 October 1982.

Schellenberg, Walter. *The Schellenberg Memoirs*. London: André Deutsch, 1956.

Schleunes, Karl A. *The Twisted Road to Auschwitz: Nazi Policy toward German Jews 1933–1939*. Urbana: University of Illinois Press, 1970.

Schnabel, Reimund. *Macht Ohne Moral: Eine Dokumentation über die SS*. Frankfurt am Main: Roderbergverlag, 1957.

Schneider, Gertrude. *Journey into Terror: Story of the Riga Ghetto*. New York: Ark House, 1979.

———, ed. *Muted Voices: Jewish Survivors of Latvia Remember*. New York: Philosophical Library, 1987.

Schoenberner, Gerhard. *The Holocaust: The Nazi Destruction of Europe's Jews*. Edmonton: Hurtig Publishers, 1985.

Schwarz, Solomon. *The Jews in the Soviet Union*. Syracuse, N.Y.: Syracuse University Press, 1972.

Seaton, Albert. *The Russo-German War 1941–45*. London: Arthur Barker Limited, 1971.

———. *The German Army 1933–45*. London: Sphere Books, 1983.

Shechtman, Joseph B. "The Transnistria Reservation." *Yivo Annual of Jewish Social Science* 8 (1953): 178–96.

Shils, Edward A., and Morris Janowitz. "Cohesion and Disintegration in the Wehrmacht in World War II." *Public Opinion Quarterly* 12 (1948): 280–315.

Shochat, Azriel. "The Beginnings of Anti-Semitism in Independent Lithuania." *Yad Vashem Studies* II (1958): 7–48.

———. "Jews, Lithuanians and Russians 1939–1941." In *Jews and Non-Jews in Eastern Europe 1918–1945*, edited by Bela Vago, and George L. Mosse, pp. 301–14. Jerusalem: Israel Universities Press, 1974.

Smith, Arthur L. "Life in Wartime Germany: Colonel Ohlendorf's Opinion Service." *Public Opinion Quarterly* 36 (1972): 1–7.

Smith, Bradley F. *The Road to Nuremberg.* New York: Basic Books, 1981.

———. *Heinrich Himmler: A Nazi in the Making, 1900–1926.* Stanford: Hoover Institution Press. Stanford University, 1971.

Speer, Albert. *Infiltration: How Heinrich Himmler Schemed to Build an SS Industrial Empire.* New York: Macmillan, 1981.

Stein, George H. *The Waffen SS: Hitler's Elite Guard at War 1939–1945.* Ithaca, N.Y.: Cornell University Press, 1966.

Steiner, John M. "The SS Yesterday and Today: A Sociopsychological View." In *Survivors, Victims and Perpetrators: Essays on the Nazi Holocaust*, edited by Joel E. Dimsdale, pp. 405–456. Washington, D.C.: Hemisphere Publishing Corporation, 1980.

Steinert, Marlis G. *Hitler's War and the Germans: Public Mood and Attitude during the Second World War.* Athens, Ohio: Ohio State University Press, 1977.

Stokes, Lawrence Duncan. "'The Sicherheitsdienst' (SD) of the 'Reichsfuehrer' SS and German Public Opinion, September 1939–June 1941." Ph.D. diss., John Hopkins University, 1972.

———. "The German People and the Destruction of the European Jews." *Central European History* VI (1973): 167–91.

Stolfi, Russel H. S. "Barbarossa Revisited: A Critical Reappraisal of the Opening Stages of the Russo-German Campaign." *Journal of Modern History* 54 (1982): 27–46.

Streim, Alfred. "Zum Beispiel: Die Verbrechen der Einsatzgruppen in der Sowjetunion." In *NS-Prozesse. Nach 25 Jahren Strafverfolgung: Möglichkeiten-Grenzen-Ergebnisse*, edited by Adalbert Rückerl, pp. 65–106. Karlsruhe: C. F. Müller, 1971.

———. *Die Behandlung sowjetischer Kriegsgefangener im "Fall Barbarossa": eine Dokumentation.* Heidelberg and Karlsruhe: Müller Juristischer Verlag, 1981.

———. *Sowjetische Gefangene in Hitlers Vernichtungskrieg: Berichte und Dokumente, 1941–1945.* Heidelberg: C. F. Müller Juristischer Verlag, 1982.

———. "Zur Eröffnung des allgemeinen Judenvernichtungsbefehls gegenüber den Einsatzgruppen." In *Der Mord an den Juden im zweiten Weltkrieg: Entschlussbildung und Verwirklichung*, edited by Eberhard Jäckel and Jürgen Rohwer, pp. 107–19. Stuttgart: Deutsche Verlags-Anstalt, 1985.

———. "The Tasks of the SS Einsatzgruppen." In *Simon Wiesenthal Center Annual 4*, edited by Henry Friedlander and Sybil Milton, pp. 309–28. White Plains, N.Y.: Kraus International Publications, 1987.

———. Letter to the Editors. In *Simon Wiesenthal Center Annual 6*, edited by Henry Friedlander and Sybil Milton, pp. 331–47. New York: Philosophical Library, 1989.

Streit, Christian. *Keine Kameraden: Die Wehrmacht und die sowjetischen Kriegsgefangenen, 1941–1945.* Stuttgart: Deutsche Verlags-Anstalt, 1978.

———. "The German Army and the Policies of Genocide." In *The Policies of Genocide: Jews and Soviet Prisoners of War in Nazi Germany*, edited by Gerhard Hirschfeld, pp. 1–14. London: Allen & Unwin, 1986.

Subtelny, Orest. "The Soviet Occupation of Western Ukraine, 1939–41: An Overview." In

Ukraine during World War II: History and its Aftermath, edited by Yury Boshyk, pp. 5–14. Edmonton: Canadian Institute of Ukrainian Studies. University of Alberta, 1986.

Suhl, Yuri, ed. *They Fought Back: The Story of the Jewish Resistance in Nazi Europe*. New York: Schocken Books, 1975.

Sydnor, Charles W. *Soldiers of Destruction: The SS Death's Head Division, 1933–1945*. Princeton, N.J.: Princeton University Press, 1977.

Taylor, Telford. "An Outline of the Research and Publication Possibilities of the War Crimes Trials." *Louisiana Law Review* 9 (1949): 496–508.

———. "The Use of Captured German and Related Records in the Nürnberg War Crimes Trials." In *Captured German and Related Records*, edited by Robert Wolfe, pp. 92–100. Athens, Ohio: Ohio University Press, 1974.

Tenenbaum, Joseph. *Underground: The Story of a People*. New York: Philosophical Library, 1952.

———. "The Einsatzgruppen." *Jewish Social Studies* 17 (1955): 43–64.

———. *Race and Reich: The Story of an Epoch*. New York: Twayne Publishers, 1956.

Toynbee, Arnold, and Veronica Toynbee, eds. *Hitler's Europe. Survey of International Affairs, 1939–1946*, Vol. 4. London: Royal Institute of International Affairs. Oxford University Press, 1954.

Trevor-Roper. H. R., ed. *Hitler's War Directives 1939–1945*. London: Pan Books, 1966.

Trials of War Criminals before the Nürnberg Military Tribunals under Control Council Law no. 10. 15 Vols. Washington, D.C.: United States Government Printing Office, 1949–1953.

Tuchel, Johannes, and Reinhold Schattenfroh. *Zentrale des Terrors, Prinz-Albrecht-Strasse 8: Das Hauptquartier der Gestapo*. Berlin: Siedler Verlag, 1987.

Tyrnauer, Gabrielle. *Gypsies and the Holocaust: A Bibliography and Introductory Essay*. Montreal: Interuniversity Centre for European Studies and Montreal Institute for Genocide Studies, 1989.

Unger, Aryeh. "The Public Opinion Reports of the Nazi Party." *The Public Opinion Quarterly* 29 (1965): 556–82.

Unsere Ehre Heisst Treue: Kriegstagebuch des Kommandostabes Reichsführer SS. Tätigkeitsberichte der 1. und 2. SS-Inf.-Brigade, der 1.SS-Kav.-Brigade und von Sonderkommandos der SS. Edited by Fritz Baade and others. Wien, Frankfurt, Zurich: Europa Verlag, 1965.

Vago, Bela, and George L. Mosse, eds. *Jews and Non-Jews in Eastern Europe, 1918–1945*. Jerusalem: Israel Universities Press, 1974.

Vollmer, Bernhard, ed. *Volksopposition im Polizeistaat: Gestapo–und Regierungsberichte 1934–1936*. Stuttgart: Deutsche Verlags-Anstalt, 1957.

Warlimont, Walter. *Inside Hitler's Headquarters, 1939–1945*. London: Weidenfeld & Nicolson, 1964.

Wegner, Bernd. "'My Honour is Loyalty.' The SS as a Military Factor in Hitler's Germany." In *The German Military in the Age of Total War*, edited by Wilhelm Deist, pp. 220–39. Warwickshire: Berg Publishers Ltd., 1985.

———. "The 'Aristocracy of National Socialism': The Role of the SS in National Socialist Germany." In *The Nazi Holocaust: Historical Articles on the Destruction of European Jews*, 3. Vol. 1., edited by Michael R. Marrus, pp. 387–411. Westport and London: Meckler Corporation, 1989.

Weiss, Aharon. "Jewish-Ukrainian Relations in Western Ukraine during the Holocaust." In *Ukrainian-Jewish Relations in Historical Perspective*, edited by Peter J. Potichnyj and Howard Aster, pp. 409–420. Edmonton: Canadian Institute of Ukrainian Studies. University of Alberta, 1988.

Wellers, George. "The Number of Victims and the Korherr Report." In *The Holocaust and the Neo-Nazi Mythomania*, edited by Serge Klarsfeld, pp. 163–211. New York: The Beate Klarsfeld Foundation, 1978.

Wellers, George, ed. *Mémoire du Génocide.* Paris: Centre de Documentation Juive Contemporaine and L'Association "Les Fils et Filles des Déportés Juifs de France," 1987.

Werth, Alexander. *Russia at War, 1941–1945.* New York: Dutton, 1964.

We Shall Not Forgive: The Horrors of the German Invasion in Documents and Photographs. Moscow: Foreign Languages Publishing House, 1942.

Wiener, Jan. G. *The Assassination of Heydrich.* New York: Grossman Publishers, 1969.

Wolfe, Robert. "Putative Threat to National Security as a Nuremberg Defense for Genocide." *The Annals of the American Academy of Political and Social Science* 450 (1980): 46–67.

———, ed. *Captured German and Related Records.* Athens, Ohio: Ohio University Press, 1974.

Wolfson, Manfred. "Constraint and Choice in the SS Leadership." *Western Political Quarterly* XVIII (1965): 551–68.

Wright, Gordon. *The Ordeal of Total War, 1939–1945.* New York: Harper & Row, 1968.

Wright, R. A. "The Killing of Hostages as a War Crime." *The British Year Book of International Law* 25 (1948): 296–310.

Wytwycky, Bohdan. *The Other Holocaust: Many Circles of Hell.* Washington, D.C.: The Novak Report on the New Ethnicity, 1980.

Zeck, William Allen. "Nuremberg: Proceedings Subsequent to Goering et al." *North Carolina Law Review* 26 (1948): 350–89.

Zeiger, Henry A., ed. *The Case against Adolf Eichmann.* New York: The New American Library, 1960.

Zeman, Z. A. B. *Nazi Propaganda.* London: Oxford University Press, 1973.

Zipfel, Friedrich. *Gestapo und Sicherheitsdienst.* Berlin-Grünewald: Arani, 1960.

Index

294